# THE SEARCH FOR SECURITY
# IN THE PACIFIC, 1901–1914

**THE FIGHT OF THE SHEPHERDS**
*(Being an Australian view of the European situation.)*
**THE VULTURE: "I think my chance is coming shortly."**

By Norman Lindsay, from *the Bulletin*, 5 December 1912

A HISTORY OF AUSTRALIAN DEFENCE AND
FOREIGN POLICY 1901–23: VOLUME 1

# THE SEARCH FOR SECURITY
# IN THE PACIFIC,
# 1901–1914

Neville Meaney

SYDNEY UNIVERSITY PRESS

Published 2009 by Sydney University Press
SYDNEY UNIVERSITY PRESS
University of Sydney Library
www.sup.usyd.edu.au
© Neville Meaney 2009
© Sydney University Press 2009

First published 1976 by Sydney University Press
This book was originally funded by money from THE ELEANOR SOPHIA WOOD BEQUEST

National Library of Australia Cataloguing-in-Publication data
Author:          Meaney, N. K. (Neville Kingsley)
Title:           A history of Australian defence and foreign policy 1901-23.
                 Volume I. The search for security in the Pacific, 1901–14./ Neville Meaney.
ISBN:            9781920899189 (pbk.)
Notes:           Includes index.
                 Bibliography.
Subjects:        Australia — Foreign relations — Pacific area.
                 Pacific area — Foreign relations — Australia.
                 Australia — Military policy. 4. Australia — Defences.
Dewey Number:    327.9409

# Contents

# Tables

# Preface

In dedicating this book to my fellow-countrymen during a spuriously dubbed period of 'new nationalism' I do not wish to give further aid and comfort to that spirit of chauvinism which is summed up in the adoption of 'Advance Australia Fair' as our national song. The efforts of our 'ministers for nationalism' and our city aldermen in this direction, including their attempts to create a cardboard history festival in honour of our founding fathers, do not speak to an Australian experience and have so far failed to evoke any widespread support. Australians quite properly turn their back on such frippery and spend Australia Day at the beach. As a new country, a country of immigrants and the descendants of immigrants, Australia has not, after the pattern of most European countries, been able to lay claim to a separate national identity based on a self-validating, self-perpetuating and self-sufficient cultural heritage. Moreover, unlike the United States, Australia has not rebelled against the old world, against the sources from which it has derived its values and traditions and so has never been forced to define its own nature in contradistinction to its land of origin. For Australia there has been no single decisive act of creation. Like the continental plate on which it sits it has simply drifted apart from its old moorings.

Yet some Australian writers, historians and politicians, in slavish imitation of European and American national religions and rites, have endeavoured to invent local equivalents. The Eureka Stockade incident, dressed up in borrowed robes, has often been given a ludicrously inflated importance and even presented as a Declaration of Independence. And the Bush Legend of the 1890s, a noble savage frontier-thesis idyll, has often been cited by this small band of literary nationalists as the source of a distinctive Australian character. It has been a foolish and futile enterprise. Australians, except in moments of libidinous camaraderie, have been little affected by such posturing.

In so far as Australians have sought a cultural identity and authority it has been by aspiring to hold fast, even if in a fragmentary and peripheral way, to the predominant British traditions of their forebears. During the first half of the twentieth century this commitment to British race patriotism was reinforced not only by a continuing stream of immigrants from 'Home' but also by the institutionalizing of society, most notably in education, where formal values taken from the British Isles were set above those learnt in the common life. The Australian expression of the British attachment has had at times a passion and a fervour which only the exile and expatriate can bring to the celebration of the Mother Country. The visit of Queen Elizabeth to Australia in 1954 was the most popular public event in the history of the nation. However, since World War II these concepts of loyalty and allegiance have been undergoing a substantial and decisive transformation, and the last stage of this journey to nationalism is no less perplexing and paradoxical than the first. With the dissolution of the British Empire-Commonwealth, the retreat of Britain into Europe, the arrival of large numbers of non-British migrants and even perhaps a growing maturity of Australian society, this overwhelming sense of Britishness has slowly eroded and the vestigial symbols of the British connection have become historical shells largely empty of meaning and significance. Similarly the Bush Legend, despite the fact that it is exclusively Australian in its origin and appeal, has, under the impact of urbanization and civilization, also disappeared, even as a minority alternative to the British race ethos. A new generation considers both patterns of cultural identity to be anachronistic, and our most eminent contemporary novelists, dramatists, poets and painters, where they touch upon it, treat the question with a wry irony. Indeed even the nationalism of the battle-field, which has united elements from both traditions, is fading away with Anzac Day. What then remains of the nationalism of sentiment and symbol is nothing but a brittle chrysalis, and it is not altogether to be deplored that very few seem either to be aware or to care.

Nevertheless, despite this ambiguity and uncertainty with respect to its perception of nationalism, Australia has, since the founding of the Commonwealth, clearly acted as a separate nation state. This national behaviour, though, has been based not on a distinctive culture or ideology but rather on an instinctive sense of shared interests and experience, and it has expressed itself not in songs and symbols but in politics and policies. Nationalism is a jealous master exacting an exclusive obedience from its devotees, and Australians in determining their political community and in developing their policies, especially towards the external world, have revealed that they are subject to such a discipline. Australians have shared sufficient common ground to enable them to unite together in one political community, and despite their affection for Britain and their dependence on a British cultural tradition they have rejected all suggestions for a wider imperial union and have guarded closely their own political sovereignty. It is only by an examination of the policies fashioned by successive Commonwealth governments in defence of the national interest that the enigma of Australian nationalism can be unravelled. It is in the study of trade, immigration and most especially defence and foreign policy that the true character of Australian nationalism can be discerned.

This book is presented as the first of two projected volumes dealing with the history of Australian defence and foreign policy, 1901–23. Though in these years Australia was still constitutionally a dependent part of the British Empire and lacked all the forms and frills of a fully developed foreign policy, nevertheless it evolved a distinctive view of its own position in the world, a view based on its peculiar geographical position. Working out the logic of its strategic analysis the Commonwealth government attempted to gain British sympathy and support for its peculiar anxieties and, failing in this, it undertook diplomatic initiatives and defence programmes aimed at safeguarding the security of the nation in the Asian-Pacific region. In short, it came to possess the substance of a foreign policy. The people, property and power of the Commonwealth were in policy-making mobilized first and foremost for the protection of Australia.

The story I have to tell is not altogether new. A number of historians such as Donald C. Gordon, C. Grimshaw, J. A. La Nauze and Richard Preston have in pursuing somewhat different purposes or against rather different contexts already opened up the subject. Gordon and Grimshaw have hinted at a partial or particular relationship between the rise of Japan in Asia and the development of Australian defence policy. More often than not, however, such suggestions have been overshadowed by assertions that Australia's defence concerns were inspired by a status-conscious nationalism or by a desire to make a contribution to the general protection of the empire at a time when Britain was being challenged by German power in Europe. Only D. C. S.

Sissons in his MA study of 'Australian attitudes to Japan, 1895–1923' has urged the key importance of Japan's victory over Russia in 1905 in shaping Australian strategic thinking and in stimulating defence preparations from 1907 to 1910, and all students undertaking research in this field owe a considerable debt to his pioneering work. Nevertheless, scholars have had to wait upon the opening to public scrutiny of the Australian and British archives and the private papers of the leading statesmen in order to understand the full scope and significance of Australia's first foreign policy.

For its own reasons Australia's defence and foreign policy in these early years of the Commonwealth was articulated in an indirect, almost clandestine, manner. Though vital clues can be found in the public record, they frequently appear in a disguised form and the historian needs the evidence from inside the structure of policy-making to interpret and connect the surface sources. Because Australia occupied a subservient position in the Empire's constitutional structure, because Australians felt emotionally dependent on the relationship with the Mother Country, because the authority of the Admiralty and the other policy planning bodies at the centre of empire could not be easily flouted and finally because Japan was an ally of the empire, the Commonwealth leaders as a rule felt obliged to mute and muddle their public explanations for seeking a strong defence force in the Pacific and their public discussions of differences with the Mother Country. Taking this into account I have attempted to bring together the published and unpublished, the official and non-official, the Australian and British records in order to gain a more complete picture of policy-making and a better appreciation of the factors and forces shaping that process. The evidence now available adds a new dimension to the understanding of the subject.

In this regard I have been centrally concerned with the way in which Australia's Pacific context has determined its strategic perspective, with the influence of racial ideas and images in identifying external threats, the impact of domestic politics and pragmatic circumstances on government attitudes, and the importance of advice emanating from British authorities and local experts in bringing the Australian ministers to make up their minds and take their decisions. This study by no means exhausts the possibilities of the topic. Many aspects are only touched upon; some are ignored. In external affairs I would direct the attention of future students to trade policy and to the details of Pacific-island policy and in defence to the relationship between social structure and the military system, to the institutional and administrative ethos of the naval and military forces, and to the rate and nature of the armed forces' adaptation to the new technology of the industrial, communication and transport revolutions.

Australians, then, though sometimes pressing their interests too aggressively, have emerged into independence with a quiet nationalism. Or to put it in another way they have found themselves possessed of a nationality without a nationalism. With the waning of the British connection Australians are now faced directly with this question of national identity and unfortunately one of the legacies of a tradition of cultural deference is that many feel only the assumption of a European or American style nationalism will give the new Australia respect at home and respectability abroad. Such people are seduced by the hope of acquiring a 'Land of Hope and Glory' or an 'America the Beautiful'. It is hard for them to contemplate the novel idea that Australian nationalism is different, and to see that this difference is not only something to which they must adapt but also something which they should value.

Gough Whitlam and John Gorton, two independent-minded Australian leaders in the Deakin-Fisher mould, have, in an appropriately restrained manner, shown some appreciation of this difference. They have favoured 'Waltzing Matilda' as our national song, not because they have seen in it a radical social message nor because they have accepted it as a parable out of the Bush legend. The argument for it is simpler and more straightforward. A national song we must have; the forms of international intercourse require it. The virtues of 'Waltzing Matilda' are to be found in the very criticisms of its detractors, namely in that it is a ballad and not a hymn, in that it is well liked but not deeply moving. It does not praise Australia's greatness, assert a special monopoly over liberty or claim a special divine sanction or blessing. Indeed, even the class conflict portrayed in the story belongs to a past which is lost; and all that is left is the whimsical flavour of something peculiarly Australian. Australia is already known throughout the world by 'Waltzing Matilda' and why should it be otherwise?

This study has evolved over a number of years and in the course of time I have accumulated a great number of debts both to individuals and institutions. I must above all acknowledge the continuing support of the University of Sydney. Its generous grant of sabbatical leave and research assistance has enabled me to plan and carry through my study programme. I must also thank the National Library of Australia, especially Mr. G. Powell of the Manuscripts Division, and the Australian Archives Office, especially Mr. L. Cleland, the Senior Archivist, Reference and Access, for their painstaking attention to a multitude of requests and inquiries. These two institutions contain the richest collections of unpublished materials relating to the history of Australian defence and foreign policy. For the opportunity to spend a summer as a Visiting Scholar in Canberra examining these materials I am grateful to Professor J. A. La Nauze and the History Department of the Institute of Advanced Studies, Australian National University.

In London I enjoyed the hospitality of the Institute of Commonwealth Studies and made free use of its substantial library. In my research in Great Britain I drew most heavily upon the collections of private papers in the British Museum and the official despatches and papers in the Public Record Office, and in both cases I was very well served. Indeed my acquaintance with the Public Record Office has brought home to me in the most striking way the defects of our own archives system. It is perfectly explicable why historians should be tempted to rely on British rather than Australian sources for their work on the making of Australian defence and foreign policy. The historian in the PRO finds well-ordered indexes, a comprehensive coverage of unpublished official records and for the most part ready access to all materials in the 'open' period. Due to causes outside the control of the Australian Archives Office archivists—the long neglect of archives, the caution and possessiveness of departments, the lack of a historical sense, the poverty and maltreatment of early records—the position in Australia is very different and the processes of discovery, acquisition, indexing and clearing of materials have tended to make a farce of the 'open' policy covering the years to 1945. Only by enormous patience and at the cost of valuable time have a small doughty band of students and scholars been able to gain any return for their labours in the Australian government's records. In these circumstances I endorse wholeheartedly the recommendation of Dr. W. Kaye Lamb, the former Canadian Archivist, who in his recent report on Commonwealth Archives urged the government to make all records to 1922 in such areas as defence and foreign policy available to researchers without further check or scrutiny. No lesser decision can break the log-jam of access to knowledge and place the Australian record on something approaching parity with the British.

Among other institutions, the Australian War Memorial, the Melbourne University Archives, the New South Wales Archives, the Birmingham University Library, the Beaverbrook Library, the Canadian National Archives, the Library of Congress and the United States National Archives have each in their own specific way made a significant contribution to my research. Mr. R. C. Cook very kindly allowed me to use the notebooks and diaries of his father, Sir Joseph Cook.

All products of scholarly endeavour are the work of many hands, and though it would be impossible to try and meet all my obligations in this respect by listing them singly here, nevertheless I feel bound to recognize the care and devotion of Miss Marguerite Nicholson and Miss S. A. Oglesby in the typing of the manuscript and also to mention the intelligent interest and critical acumen shown by many of my fourth year honours students over a number of years.

Finally, I think it incumbent upon me, while extending thanks for help received, to exculpate all others from any responsibility for the book's short-comings. The responsibility for these is mine and mine alone.

*Neville Meaney*

# Abbreviations

Adm      Admiralty
ALP      Australian Labor Party
ANA      Australian Natives Association
ANL      National Library of Australia
AWM      Australian War Memorial Library
*BD*      J. P. Gooch and Harold Temperley, eds, *British Documents on the Origins of the War, 1898–1914*
BM      British Museum
Cab      British Cabinet Papers
CDC      Colonial Defence Committee
CID      Committee of Imperial Defence
CofA      Commonwealth of Australia
CO      Colonial Office
CP      Commonwealth Permanent Series, Archives Office, Canberra
CPD      *Commonwealth Parliamentary Debates*
CRS      Commonwealth Record Series, Archives Office, Canberra (A reorganization and reclassification of all Commonwealth records including the Commonwealth Permanent Series.)
DT      Daily Telegraph
FO      Foreign Office
MP      Melbourne Papers, Australian Archives Office, Melbourne
MP      Morning Post
PRO      Public Record Office, London
*SMH*      *Sydney Morning Herald*

# 1
# Problems and Perspectives

In that rather hazy folk-myth which doubles for twentieth-century Australian history it has generally been considered that at least down to World War II Australia possessed neither a defence nor a foreign policy of its own. As rumour has it, on the world scene Australia, an integral part of the British Empire, was but an appendage of Great Britain and consequently its defence efforts and whatever seemingly independent role it played in international affairs were mere adjuncts to the work of the British navy or the British foreign office. Australia saw the world of power politics through British eyes—that is when it cared to raise its own eyes above the outer rim of its island-continent—and was willing to leave relations with the rest of the world in British hands. At the end of World War I Billy Hughes had made a stir about the future of the former German islands which Australia occupied in the South Pacific but this was exceptional and for most Australians happily so. From the foundation of the Commonwealth, as in the preceding era of colonial self-government, the primary tasks of defence and foreign policy—security against the threat of attack from other national powers—had been left to the Mother Country. It was only after Pearl Harbour that Australia, casting off the traditional inhibitions, was forced despite itself to take on the responsibility for its own defence and to fashion a foreign policy to suit its own needs. So runs the myth.[1]

The chief result of this study has been to show that this superficial judgement, at least for the period 1901–22, has little to be said for it, that from the end of the nineteenth century successive

---

[1] See Gordon Greenwood (ed.), *Australia, A Social and Political History,* Sydney 1955. Professor Greenwood wrote of Australian relations with the world beyond its shores, 'Until 1914 Australians enjoyed the luxury of almost undisturbed concentration upon their own domestic affairs' (p. 252), and again 'All political parties were inexperienced in the conduct of foreign affairs and comparatively ignorant of the play of international forces. The reasons are not far to seek. Until 1914 Britain's voice was decisive in shaping foreign policy for the empire; Australia's interest and influence were at best intermittent, being confined to those occasions and those issues which might conceivably affect vital aspects of domestic policy. Isolated by geography from powerful and populous neighbours, sheltered by the might of the British navy, absorbed in the task of developing a continent, Australians by a fortunate combination of circumstances were able to afford the luxury of an almost exclusive concentration upon internal pursuits' (p. 259).

R. M. Crawford in his *Australia,* London 1952, p. 164, Manning Clark in his *A Short History of Australia,* New York 1963, p. 189 and Fred Alexander in his *Australia Since Federation,* Melbourne 1967, pp. 29–30 and 169–70, mention the introduction of compulsory military training and the creation of an Australian navy in the years before World War I. They neither comment on the distinctive character of this legislation nor, apart from vague references to 'nationalism', suggest an explanation for its passage. By default the reader is left with the impression that Australia in those years had no interest in international affairs, that events in Europe and the Pacific had no effect on Australian politicians or policies.

Australian governments, without distinction of party or person, were aware of their peculiar geo-political circumstances and within the formal framework of the British Empire they evolved consistent, cohesive and comprehensive defence and external policies to provide for the security of their own country. From the colonial era to the Washington Conference of 1921–2, Australian governments were acutely alive to the dangers of their Pacific environment. Following the emergence of Japan as the great power in the Far East in 1905 and the simultaneous withdrawal of British capital ships from the Pacific to meet the German challenge in Europe, Australian fears were intensified and Australian governments attempted to re-orient imperial defence and foreign policy to provide more adequately for the defence of their own people and territory. Failing to gain any enduring concessions either in defence or diplomacy from the hard-pressed British, they fell back on their own resources. They adopted compulsory military training for all Australian young men, acquired a fleet unit and by 1914 were embarking on an ambitious twenty-two-year plan to build a substantial navy. During World War I, while contributing to the military efforts of the Empire, Australian leaders were alarmed by Japan's expansionist tendencies and at the end of war the Australian government insisted on keeping control of the German islands in the South Pacific and they set up a foreign section of the Prime Minister's Department to provide an Australian source of advice on Pacific, especially Japanese, affairs.

The defeat of Germany in 1918, the apparent security offered by the League of Nations, and the reaction against militarism which set in shortly after the end of war; all these factors did something to weaken Australian defence-consciousness. In imperial relations, though the war had brought the Mother Country and the dominions closer together, the peace-making had tended to accentuate the great diversity of interests represented by the nations of the empire, and in particular the differences between the Australians and the British on Pacific questions. The *détente* of the Washington Conference then came as a God-send. After the Pacific powers had agreed to accept limitations on naval armaments and had promised to respect the *status quo* in the region, the Australian leaders, beset by grave political and economic difficulties at home, were only too glad of the opportunity to turn away from external problems and to cut back severely on their defence plans and preparations. This then is the outline of the story to be told.

The development of an Australian defence and foreign policy in these years has been obscured by several factors. The fact that Australia was formally and constitutionally a dependent part of the empire, lacking all the appurtenances of a separate international identity, made it difficult to perceive the reality behind the appearance. Moreover, the great majority of Australians were uncomfortable in the presence of the idea of independence. Australians' attachment to their British cultural heritage and to British race patriotism often caused them to overlook the full implications of their strategic analyses and their defence and diplomatic initiatives. In particular, public confidence in the supremacy of the British navy, which was the first canon of the imperial religion, was not easily shaken. Most important of all, when war had come it had been a British and European war. Though the Australians had directed all their energies to preparing for defence against Japan in the Pacific, they found themselves by the accident of history fighting for the empire in Turkey and France. Japan, albeit uncertainly,[2] had remained loyal to the Anglo-Japanese alliance and faith in the British navy had been vindicated. The victory of the British Empire in the war provided the keynote for subsequent interpretations of Australian policy. In looking back it was concluded that the Australian government and people had never wavered in their reliance on the amplitude of British power and only the hysterical had feared Japanese ambitions in the Pacific. Thus, there was for Australia, as far as defence and diplomacy were concerned, a non-policy. To give the lie to this folk-tradition is the aim of the present study.

## Nation and empire

One of the critical problems for this study then is the relation of the Australian nation to the British Empire. This has been probably the chief cause for confusion in understanding the evolution of an Australian policy on external affairs. Historians from Keith Hancock to Russel Ward[3] have agreed that the common experience of occupying and taming the land did bring with it a separate cultural consciousness, and that the radical democratic ethos of the colonies did make for a sense of ideological separation from the aristocratic 'old world' of the Mother Country. Nevertheless, nationalism in terms of sentiment and ideology will not stand up to the most superficial scrutiny as the explanation for the major national decisions such as federation or the major national policies such as those connected with defence and external affairs. In the first place the culture of 'the cabbage-tree hat'[4] variety was introverted and isolationist and tended to shrug off the outside world with a grunt of disdain and a sniff of resentment. The Labor party, before it became a truly national party and added defence and foreign policy planks to its platform, reflected this bias to some degree. In the second place and most important, this distinctively Australian pattern of symbolic allegiance and ideological convictions did not have first call on Australian emotional loyalties. Australia's first response in terms of sentiment was to British race patriotism.

Obviously, as Ward remarks, Australians had to find their own objects of sentimental attachment 'by looking for those things which distinguished them from their British fathers and congeners'.[5] Yet, as Hancock has noted, the relation of the Australian nation to the British Empire was not as simple as this.[6] Australians did not turn their backs on Britain nor reject their British

---

[2] Frank W. Iklé, 'Japanese-German Peace Negotiations during World War I', *American Historical Review*, LXXI, October 1965, 62–76.

[3] W. K. Hancock, *Australia*, London 1930–45, Ch. III, 'Independent Australian Britons', esp. pp. 52–5. Russel Ward, *The Australian Legend*, Melbourne 1958, esp. pp. 179–82 and 214–16.

[4] I have adopted this term because Russel Ward cites the widespread use of 'the cabbage-tree hat' by the 'flash' rowdy elements of the cities to indicate the dominance of the bush-derived mores even in Australian urban life and thus to show that the bush legend is really the Australian legend (p. 11). Perhaps such a caricature does not take the legend as seriously as its literature should require yet on the other hand it reduces it more nearly to its true significance in the Australian mind.

[5] Ward, *The Australian Legend*, p. 193.

[6] Hancock, *Australia*, pp. 56–7.

cultural heritage. If anything the cultural luggage which the British settlers had brought out with them in their emigrant ships grew in Australian esteem and affection as it was handed on to succeeding generations. Australians took inordinate pride in being of British stock. The songs which came most readily to Australian lips were not 'Click Go the Shears' or 'Bold Jack Donahoe' but rather 'Soldiers of the Queen' and 'Rule Britannia'. Though by the end of the nineteenth century the native-born easily outnumbered the new settlers—they were some 82 per cent of the population by 1900—the events in Australia which elicited the greatest public enthusiasm were wars of the empire, Khartoum and the Sudan expedition,[7] the Boer War in South Africa[8] and the outbreak of World War I.

This enthusiasm for empire cannot be explained away as an emotive rationalization of national interests for patently the Sudan and Boer Wars did not involve questions of Australian interest. Indeed the imperial fervour was such that most Australians did not exercise any discrimination either in terms of moral justification or national interest in coming to the aid of the Mother Country. In Edmund Barton's words at the time of the Boer War they were for the empire 'right or wrong'.[9] The imperial cause was all. A man had to be brave indeed to speak out against British policy on these occasions and when he did more often than not, as in the case of Henry Bournes Higgins of Victoria and Professor G. A. Wood of the University of Sydney at the time of the Boer War, it was not from the point of view of an Australian nationalist but an English liberal. It is noteworthy that dissent from the Boer War was much more pronounced and widespread in England than in Australia.

It is a curious thing about Australian nationalism that Australians have so often identified the birth of their nation as an outcome of participation in imperial wars, in the Boer Contingent[10] and

---

[7] B. R. Penny, 'The Age of Empire: An Australian Episode', *Historical Studies*, XI, November 1963, 32–42.

[8] The best general accounts of Australian attitudes to the Boer War are Barbara R. Penny, 'Australia's Reactions to Boer War—a Study in Colonial Imperialism', *The Journal of British Studies*, VII, November 1967, 97–103 and H. C. Grimshaw, *Some Aspects of Australian Attitude to the Imperial Connections, 1900–1919*, MA thesis, University of Queensland. 1958. A more specific study is A. P. Haydon, 'South Australia's First War', *Historical Studies*, XI, April 1964, 222–33. None of these studies explains the relation of imperial feeling to Australian nationalism and the Australian political tradition.

[9] NSW, *Parliamentary Debates*, 1889 session, C, 1495, 19 October 1899. Andrew Fisher had much the same to say on this point when the issue was raised on a later occasion. When W. H. Stead reported in his *Review of Reviews* (July 1911), pp. 25–6, that the Labor Prime Minister when in England had said that if Australia thought a British war unjust it would 'haul down the Union Jack' and separate from the empire, Fisher replied, as both W. M. Hughes and Alfred Deakin believed he would, that Stead's account was 'a grotesque misrepresentation' of what he had said. He denied using the words 'haul down the flag'; rather 'Keep the flag flying is my ambition.' He added, 'There was no suggestion that Australia should break with the Empire' (SMH, 25, 29 and 31 July 1911).

[10] See Henry L. Hall, *Australia and England: a Study in Imperial Relations*, London 1934, p. 238. 'Most saw in this war [the Boer War] a chance for Australia to assert her worthiness to be ranked as a nation.' Hall cites the South Australian *Register*, 27 January 1900, which claimed that children watching the return of the troops 'will remember the occasion as an epoch marking the birth of the Australian nation.'

in the Anzacs at Gallipoli and after. This nationalism of the battle-field was not the result of a revulsion of feeling against the Mother Country brought about by a close association of the troops of the two countries. Rather, it sprang out of the achievement of Australian arms in a British cause and under British leadership, out of the pride that the soldiers, as British-Australians, felt in the part they had played in the imperial war effort. The institutional legacy of the Anzacs, the Returned Servicemen's League, though often called an ultra-nationalistic body, has always been a determinedly British body, loyal to crown and empire.[11] Thus what passed for Australian nationalism in these wars tended to be pride by a section of the empire in its contribution to the empire, a pride which was heightened and sharpened by the fact that as a technically dependent part of the empire it was generally deprived of the opportunity of contributing to the central responsibilities of the British race. Such national sentiment represented then a nationalism within a nationalism; perhaps provincialism might be a better word for it. Hancock writing in the nineteen-twenties came to a similar conclusion. He felt that while Australians might describe themselves as 'independent Australian Britons' most stress was laid upon the last. Putting it another way he asserted that, 'Among the Australians pride of race counted for more than love of country.'[12]

Yet this resolution of the problem, as Hancock himself sensed, fails and its failure is due not to an under-valuing of national sentiment but rather to the neglect of the politics of nationalism. The greatest incongruity for the students of Australian nationalism—an incongruity which when one thinks about it is perfectly clear and yet which somehow to this point has escaped comment— is that while on the one hand British race patriotism had a stronger emotional appeal for the Australian people than 'the cabbage-tree hat' culture, on the other Australians unwaveringly insisted on maintaining an exclusive political control over their own affairs. While Penny and Haydon can report on the great emotional upsurge in support of the imperial cause abroad, B. A. Knox and R. A. Shields have, taking one example of policy, recorded the colonial governments' determination not to accept responsibility for the general defence of the empire nor to allow Australian defence to be merged and submerged in any general scheme of imperial defence.[13]

Similarly, though imperial sentiment and symbol might evoke greater enthusiasm than their provincial counterparts, when it came to the issue of political consolidation Australian federation could be carried through with a minimum of difficulty, while the idea of imperial federation was given short shrift and even denied a fair hearing.[14] Probably the imperial federation movement in

---

[11] G. L. Kristianson, *The Politics of Patriotism: The Pressure Group Activities of the R.S.L.*, Canberra 1966.
[12] Hancock, *Australia*, pp. 56–7.
[13] B. A. Knox, 'Colonial Influence on Imperial Policy 1858–1866: Victoria and the Colonial Naval Defence Act, 1865', *Historical Studies*, XI, November 1963, 61–79; and R. A. Shields, 'Australian Opinion and Defence of the Empire: A Study in Imperial Relations, 1880–1890', *Australian Journal of Politics and History*, X, April 1964, 41–53.
[14] C. S. Blackton, 'Australian Nationality and Nationalism: The Imperial Federationist Interlude, 1885– 1901', *Historical Studies*, VII, November 1955, 1–16. Though Blackton does not really understand the

so far as its aim was political federation—and its very hesitancy on this point bespeaks its weakness—had less influence on Australian politics than its radical equivalent, the republican nationalism of the *Bulletin* school, and the influence of this latter group was negligible. Despite the strength of imperial feeling Australians would accept nothing more than the federal union of their own colonies and nothing less than political autonomy. This Australian position was in part the outcome of a desire to cash in on the economies of a quasi-dependent status but more fundamentally it was the result of an Australian perception of a conflict of interest, of an instinctive Australian sense that the colonies' economic, political and strategic interests were so different from those of the Mother Country that union was impossible. And therein lies the answer to the riddle of Australian nationalism.

As David Potter pointed out in dealing with the South and the American Civil War there is in addition to cultural consciousness another primary source of nationalism which binds 'an aggregate of individuals together, and this is community of interest, not in the narrow sense of economic advantage only, but in the broad sense of welfare and security through membership in society'.[15] This truism has often been forgotten by Australian as well as American historians. Though most historians do allow that a sense of common interest is a factor in the creation of nationalism, nevertheless, taking their cue from nineteenth- and twentieth-century European experience they have tended to give the greatest emphasis to cultural self-consciousness. For example Hans Kohn, perhaps the most influential of the historians of nationalism, defined nationalism as 'first and foremost a state of mind' which recognized the nation state as 'the ideal form of political organisation' and nationality 'as the source of all creative cultural energy'. Nationalism, Kohn said, partook of 'an inspirational and sometimes revivalist character'.[16] It is not surprising therefore that most historians when using this concept have, as Potter put it, 'an extremely strong disposition to equate nationality and culture',[17] and to ignore common interest, the other prime root of nationalism.

The consequence of this bias on the part of historians has often been to invent cultural distinctions or to exaggerate their importance in order to account for the plain evidence of a nation-state. Potter claimed that this is what some American historians have done with the *ante bellum* South. However, 'By stressing conflict of interest [between North and South] as a basic factor', Potter suggests that, 'it was possible to explain the otherwise stubborn anomaly that the sectional crisis grew in intensity even as the Republic grew in homogeneity.'[18] The analogy with Australian circumstances is irresistible. Many Australian historians, working with their romantic European idea of nationalism, have magnified the influence and significance of 'the cabbage-tree

---

evidence, and though he treats the movement too seriously and explains its rejection too simply in class terms the point is clear. Imperial Federation was not an issue in Australian politics.
[15] David M. Potter, 'The Historians' Use of Nationalism and Vice Versa', *American Historical Review*, LXVII, July 1962, 935.
[16] Hans Kohn, *The Idea of Nationalism: A Study in its Origin and Background,* New York 1944, pp. 10, 16, 23.
[17] Potter, 'The Historians' Use of Nationalism ...', p. 935.
[18] Ibid., p. 949.

hat' culture beyond all bounds in order to justify their use of the term with respect to federation and its aftermath. Similarly, Potter's assertion that a feeling of common interest could under certain conditions override cultural sentiment and alone provide the motive power of nationalism offers a means of reconciling the rising imperial fervour in Australia at the end of the nineteenth century with the insistence on an exclusive political independence and the development of distinctive Australian national policies towards the external world.

The development of an instinctive sense of common interest by the Australian colonies has not yet been traced out but the elements are clear. Richard Jebb, in the report of his visit to Australia and the other self-governing colonies during 1898–1901, which he entitled *Studies in Colonial Nationalism*,[19] highlighted these elements, and indeed the book provides by far and away the most percipient introduction to the subject. For Jebb, Australian nationalism was 'colonial' because in terms of sentiment the imperial attachment clearly outweighed the cultural nationalism of the *Bulletin* which he discussed but rightly discounted. However, Jebb saw that nationalism was more important than colonialism in the determination of political relations and in his exposition of colonial nationalism he gave most attention to questions of defence and tariffs. He concluded that in its relation with the mother country neither subordination nor constitutional integration were viable alternatives for the future. The only feasible and proper relation was, in his view, that of alliance.

From this judgement it is difficult to dissent. By the last decades of the nineteenth century the colonies had come to appreciate that they had a set of vital interests which were fundamentally different from those of the Mother Country. Disputes between the Australian and British governments over commerce, immigration, the future of the Pacific Islands and naval defence gave expression, sometimes a bitter expression, to these differences. The conflicts helped transmute instinctive Australian reactions into a self-conscious policy, they paved the way for colonial union and at the same time they strengthened Australian opposition to imperial federation.[20] Australians could not contemplate submitting their interests to the disposition of an imperial parliament and government in which they would be but a small minority and under which they would lose power over the decisions controlling their futures and their fortunes. Australian interests were too different from those of Great Britain to be encompassed and determined by one imperial body and this is how successive generations of Australians have looked upon the question. When the greatest of all British colonial secretaries, Joseph Chamberlain, proposed a form of imperial union in 1897, C. C. Kingston, the South Australian premier, put the Australian position sharply and definitively. He asked whether the British government would be prepared to accept equal representation in an imperial parliament for all

---

[19] London 1905.
[20] Geoffrey Serle, 'The Victorian Government's Campaign for Federation 1883–1889' in A. W. Martin (ed.), *Essays in Australian Federation*, Melbourne 1969, pp. 1–56.

parts of the self-governing empire, irrespective of population and when Chamberlain replied, 'I should say certainly no', then said Kingston, closing the subject, 'Better be as we are.'[21]

## The nature of Australian defence and foreign policy

The movement for national autonomy developed from inside the chrysalis of the British imperial constitution. Lord Durham in his classic report of 1839 had tried to show that colonial self-government and imperial unity in all things needful were not incompatible. He believed that the benefits conferred on the colonies by the imperial connection would, without any external coercion, lead them to accept imperial authority in all essential matters. Durham wrote

> The constitution of the form of government,—the regulation of foreign relations, and of trade with the mother country, the other British Colonies, and foreign nations,— and the disposal of the public lands, are the only points on which the mother country requires a control. This control is now sufficiently secured by the authority of the Imperial Legislature, by the protection which the Colony derives from us against foreign enemies; by the beneficial terms which our laws secure to its trade; and by its share of the reciprocal benefits which would be conferred by a wise system of colonization. A perfect subordination, on the part of the Colony, on these points, is secured by the advantages which it finds in the continuance of its connexion with the Empire.[22]

And yet this 'perfect subordination' did not last. Regardless of whether they gained or were given self-government[23] the Australian colonies, by the end of the nineteenth century, had come to perceive a conflict of interest between themselves and the Mother Country in many important areas and as a consequence they had made considerable inroads into Durham's imperial preserves. Even on questions touching on foreign relations, such as commerce and immigration, the colonies had won effective control.

Notwithstanding, however, this erosion of imperial authority, the colonies at the time of federation were still, in constitutional theory and form, dependencies and the control over the most vital external functions of government, over defence policy in its widest sense and over foreign policy, remained in the hands of the imperial power. The British government determined

---

[21] CO Confidential Print, Miscellaneous No. 111 'Report of a Conference between the Right Hon. Joseph Chamberlain M.P. and the Premiers of the Self-governing Colonies of the Empire, June and July, 1897', p. 107, CP 103/12/1.

See also the reply of Sir Alexander Stuart, premier of New South Wales, 5 January 1885 to 6 October 1885, to Imperial Federationists who suggested, following the crises over New Guinea and the New Hebrides, that the Australian colonies could obtain a say in Pacific policy by participation in some form of imperial council. Stuart opposed the idea saying that even if the colonies were agreed among themselves they would be outvoted and their interest still disregarded. Kathleen J. Melhuish, *Australian and British Imperial Policy: Colonial Autonomy and the Imperial Idea, 1885–1902,* PhD thesis, University of Sydney, 1966, p. 209.

[22] C. P. Lucas (ed.), *Lord Durham's Report on the Affairs of British North America,* 3 vols., Oxford 1912, Vol. II, p. 282.

[23] John M. Ward, 'Commonwealth Historiography in Canada and Australia', *Lock Haven Review,* Series I, No. 5, 1963, p. 79.

the empire's international strategy, the Foreign Office, Admiralty and War Office were its chief advisers in the formulation of that strategy and the diplomatic corps, the British navy and army were the instruments and agents for its execution. This was the last and strongest bond making for imperial unity. Both the Mother Country and the self-governing colonies recognized that the decentralizing and pluralizing of control over these external powers would mean the end of the empire as a unitary international force and neither Britain nor the colonies wished to see such a development. For this reason the British government was especially jealous of its rights in this field and the colonies were exceptionally deferential.

Even so the Australians were not altogether happy with this British monopoly in foreign affairs. The same geo-political factors which had moved the colonies to extend the frontiers of local self-government during the nineteenth century also caused them to question the adequacy of a London-determined defence and foreign policy for the purpose of colonial security in the Pacific. Geo-politics was the determining condition of Australian nationalism. Distance from the Mother Country and proximity to each other enabled the Australian colonies to acquire a sense of possessing a community of interests. Although this set them apart from the British Isles on the other side of the world, it also provided the basis of a common identity, on which they could build, in the words of Edmund Barton's federal slogan, 'A continent for a nation and a nation for a continent'. In no way was geography more important in the development of this instinct for national autonomy than on questions of defence and foreign policy, the questions which more than any others were those of political self-preservation.

From the first many Australian settlers had shown an awareness of their Pacific environment and had spasmodically concerned themselves with the questions of war and peace.[24] However, it was not until after 1870 with the rising tension in Europe and the extension of European conflicts and ambitions into the South Pacific that the now well-established colonial governments began consistently and continuously to seek some degree of influence over those British strategic policies which affected them most nearly. Indeed when, in the pre-Commonwealth years, fear and frustration produced a potent political mixture they even, on occasion, undertook defence and diplomatic initiatives of their own.

The Australians resented the attempts by foreign powers to acquire island empires in the South Pacific. They saw them as bases from which attacks could be launched against the Australian mainland and commerce, as unwarranted intermeddling in their own sphere of interest. The British government could not understand how islands up to a thousand or so miles from Australian shores could be regarded as a menace to the colonies. They refused to complicate their international posture by pressing Australian claims. Rather the British, as good Europeans, were inclined to look upon the islands as pawns which could be used in bargaining over more vital territorial and diplomatic problems closer to home. For the Australians on the other hand the

---

[24] See H. L. Hall, *Australia and England*, pp. 75–122. Duncan MacCallum, 'Defence in the Eighteen Fifties', *Royal Australian Historical Society, Journal and Proceedings*, XLIV, 1958, 71–115. Duncan MacCallum, 'The Early Volunteer Corps—The Origin of the Modern Australian Army', *Arts: The Proceedings of the Sydney University Arts Association*, I, September 1960, 143–66.

Pacific provided their geo-political setting; the Fijian Islands, New Guinea, the Solomons, and the New Hebrides were their buffers against possible aggressors. Australia depended greatly on overseas trade for its economic existence. Because of its extensive coastline and its sparse population the continent was difficult to defend as a garrison-state. Thus Australians accustomed until 1870 to a norm of invulnerability premised on remoteness tried to transpose what had been a gift of nature into a principle of nationalism, and so the rhetoric of Manifest Destiny and of a 'Monroe Doctrine' for the South Pacific rapidly gained currency. Unlike its American model, however, Australian spread-eagleism did not in any significant degree reflect an aggressive and self-righteous democratic morality. Even imperial patriotism, the desire to extend the area of British civilization and order, was but a minor ingredient in Australian motives. The chief object of the colonial policy of annexation was simply defensive, to exclude all other foreign powers from the region.

During the last three decades of the nineteenth century when the Pacific Islands along with the unclaimed territories of Asia and Africa were being fought over and parcelled out among the great European powers, the Australian colonies, often joined by New Zealand, made their first concerted effort to influence imperial policy so as to bring all the islands under British hegemony and undertook their first concerted effort to create a national defence policy. Indeed the need for such a policy was at least a major, if not the chief, motive for the federation movement and for federation. However, in this period the dangers were neither immediate nor fundamental. Australian governments feared raids on their commerce and harbours in time of war. Even in the 1890s when a fear of the Yellow Peril, of the subversion of British colonial society and security had clearly established itself, there was no fear of an invasion supported by the armed might of an enemy power. Although during those years there was a continuing interest in Pacific affairs, nevertheless, except at the high-point of a specific alarm, as in 1884–7, defence expenditure was never a weighty item in the colonial budgets and in the 1890s, when under the pressures of the great strike and droughts some expenses had to be jettisoned, defence generally suffered. Colonial co-operation never achieved anything more palpable than the auxiliary unit attached to the Australian squadron. Even after the establishment of the Commonwealth, the Australian government at first pursued a tentative and uncertain defence policy.

However, the year 1905 brought about a sudden change. With the triumph of Japan over Russia and the withdrawal of the British battle-cruisers from the Pacific to meet the German threat in Europe, the Australian government for the first time sensed the possibility of a primary threat to their territorial integrity and national security. Due to European complications and conflicts Japan was left without a counterbalance in the Far East and the Australians refused to be comforted by the technical fact of the Anglo-Japanese alliance. Instead they increased their pressure for a say in the making of imperial policy, even asserting, as Deakin did in 1907 and Hughes in 1919 and 1921, that in the area of Australia's special interest imperial policy should be an Australian policy. In the face of British reluctance successive Australian governments undertook diplomatic initiatives of their own and they began a substantial defence build-up which gave expression to their own Pacific-oriented Australia-centred strategic analysis and which provided in a more certain way for Australian security. As Alfred Deakin in his last and greatest speech on Australian external policy asserted, 'There are Pacific problems in which the

Australian interest is inexpressible.' As he put it, 'Australia, in spite of herself, is being forced into a foreign policy of her own because foreign interests and risks surround us on every side. A Pacific policy we must have.'[25]

The Australian government then was, despite itself, forced by the desire to preserve that community of interests with which Australians primarily identified themselves and in which they sought their security to adopt a national defence policy and even to move towards the substance of an independent foreign policy. Here was the heart of the matter. Australian policy had evolved from inside an empire to which the race-proud Australians felt deeply attached. There was no political or popular support in the country for 'cutting the painter'. Moreover, most Australian leaders believed that solid defence advantages could accrue from membership in the British empire. They considered that if Australia had a fair share in the determining of imperial defence and foreign policy, then the whole weight of British power and prestige could be marshalled behind Australia in the Pacific, and that Australia, backed by such a sponsor, was more likely and at less cost to achieve its ends. By having a voice in the councils of the empire, Australia might be able also to influence the shaping of Britain's world policy which inevitably caught up the dominions in its consequences. Yet, somehow this theorizing did not work well in practice.

For the most part Britain ignored the Australians' overtures until World War I placed it in their debt and made it dependent on their assistance. Then formal expression was given to the notion of dominion participation in imperial decision-making by the creation of an Imperial War Cabinet which was composed of representatives of the governments of Great Britain and the self-governing parts of the empire. But such a body was not and could not in the nature of things be 'a cabinet of cabinets' as some claimed or an imperial executive council as others, less given to phrase-making, put it. Since the imperial cabinet was made up of representatives of independent governments, it had, in order to act as an executive body, to achieve unanimity in decision-making, a unanimity of equals. Very quickly it was shown in the 1918–19 debates over the future of the Pacific Islands and in the 1921 debates over the Anglo-Japanese alliance that their geo-political interests were too disparate to make this possible. Essentially it was a council of allied governments held together by traditional happy associations in and under the empire, by strong sentiments of British patriotism and to a degree, though this was its weakest link, by a sense of common interest. But as in the case of most alliances where common interests have ceased to be sufficiently identical, sentiment and custom were not strong enough bonds in themselves to ensure the continuance of common action. Thus it was proved beyond doubt what had seemed apparent even before 1914, namely that, despite the best efforts of the imperially-minded, the only area for growth as far as a Dominion defence and foreign policy was concerned was in the extension of self-government to full independence.

This movement towards an independent defence and foreign policy in the first two decades of Australian national life was carried on within the framework of the one empire. Though the federal constitution in 1901 granted the powers over 'external affairs' and 'relations with the Pacific Islands' to the Commonwealth parliament, the British government's exclusive right to treat

---

[25] CPD, LIX, 6,859–60.

with foreign countries and to act for the empire in matters of high policy was seldom questioned. Down to World War II these were the accepted constitutional facts of life, breached only rarely by the more creative political leaders under the spur of national necessity. Down to World War II then the Australian government attempted to achieve its distinctive goals in international affairs primarily by influencing British policy. Thus Australia's major diplomatic efforts were directed towards persuading Britain and the other Dominions to reshape their policies to take into account Australia's search for security in the Pacific.

Accepting the convention of the one imperial foreign policy and the overall responsibility of the London government, the Australian political leaders were inhibited in their ability to educate public opinion and to create the technical machinery necessary for the supply of continuous information and advice on such matters. The first External Affairs Department, 1901–16, restricted itself very much to the question of territorial administration, immigration control and legal aspects of treaty-making. Admittedly the diplomatic dangers brought sharply into focus by World War I, did loosen for a time these inhibitions. From 1914 Australian governments did play with the idea of some form of diplomatic representation in the United States and in 1919 they sent a 'Commissioner' with quasi-diplomatic status to New York. From 1914 also Australian governments became concerned to obtain regular and comprehensive reports on the Pacific situation, especially Japanese aims and activities. In 1919 a Pacific Branch of the Prime Minister's Department was set up to collect, sift and analyse information on Pacific affairs for the Australian government. Its director, E. L. Piesse, envisaged this development as the nucleus of a future Australian foreign office. But the psychological hiatus was too great to be bridged by one war and a European war at that. With the settlement in the Pacific, following the Washington Conference, the impetus to independence waned, the Pacific Branch was abolished and Australians leant as heavily as ever upon the services of the British Foreign Office and diplomatic corps.

Conducting a nation's foreign policy at one remove had some important consequences for Australia's relations with the outside world. Because the Commonwealth did not participate directly in the affairs of the community of nations, and came to the field of foreign policy unwillingly and deferentially, there was a stark realism and egocentricity, an obsessive preoccupation with national security in Australian attitudes. In this period of the Hague Conferences, the Fourteen Points, and the League of Nations, in an age of liberal visionaries and international socialists, one of the striking features of Australian external policy is the lack of interest in questions of disarmament, in finding ways to settle disputes peacefully and in bringing the lion to lie down with the lamb. Except for Andrew Fisher's occasional speech in praise of international arbitration—he thought that the process which had brought industrial peace to Australia might have a broader application—there was scarcely any serious consideration given to idealistic schemes for the elimination of international tensions. Indeed, Australian governments in general, both Labor and conservative, looked on such proposals with a good deal of scepticism and suspicion.

Lacking direct contact with the extra-imperial world, lacking direct access to information on the affairs of foreign countries, Australia, for the most part, did not pursue a policy of subtlety and discretion in its external relations. The niceties of diplomatic negotiations were lost on the Australians. Sensing clear dangers, Australia sought a certain security and this security was not to be found in international organizations nor even in foreign alliance systems. On the contrary Australian governments primarily sought to defend their vital interests by extending their territorial boundaries into the Pacific, thus keeping potential enemies as far as possible from their shores while at the same time endeavouring in co-operation with their empire partners to build up a Pacific defence force, naval and military, which would be so imposing as to deter any would-be aggressor.

Australia's defence and foreign policy during these first two decades of the Commonwealth was the creation of a very few political leaders, specifically of the prime ministers and their ministers for defence. The most notable of these were Alfred Deakin, Liberal prime minister, 1903–4, 1905–8 and 1909–10; John Christian Watson, Labor prime minister, 1904 and Labor leader, 1901–7; Andrew Fisher, Labor prime minister, 1908–9, 1910–13 and 1914–15; Joseph Cook, Liberal defence minister 1909–10 and prime minister, 1913–14, and National Minister for the navy, 1917–20; William Morris Hughes, Labor prime minister, 1915–16 and National prime minister, 1917–23; William Alexander Watt, acting prime minister in the National government, 1918–19; George Foster Pearce, Labor minister for defence, 1910–13, 1914–16, and National minister for defence, 1917–21; Senator Thomas Playford, Liberal minister for defence, 1905–7; Thomas T. Ewing, Liberal minister for defence, 1907–8; and Senator E. D. Millen, Liberal minister for defence, 1913–14. These men varied greatly in their backgrounds and abilities. Four: Deakin, Watt, Pearce and Ewing, were native born; six: Fisher, Cook, Hughes, Playford, Millen and Watson, had immigrated while young to their adopted land. They were nearly all self-educated and, in the broadest sense, self-made, and had risen to eminence through hard work, organizational ability or sheer political talent. Four of them were by trade skilled workers, Cook and Fisher, coalminers; Pearce, a carpenter and prospector; and Watson, a printer-compositor. Fisher, Pearce, Watson and Hughes, a man of many parts, teacher, shopkeeper and itinerant bushworker, had also been union organizers and had, following the success of the Labor movement in the 1890s, attained positions of national power and influence. The others were a very mixed bag, Deakin, a lawyer by training, a journalist by profession and a philosopher by inclination; Watt, a clerk turned businessman; Ewing, a surveyor, civil servant and pastoralist; Playford, a market gardener; and Millen, a journalist with squatting connections. Of them all, only Deakin had attended a university, and only Deakin and Hughes had the fascination with ideas which leads naturally to a general consideration of the problems of man and mankind.

This group of ill-assorted Australians and unlikely national leaders had fashioned a defence and foreign policy which possessed its own inner coherence and logic. It had proceeded, however, not from abstract speculation but from pressing circumstances. Setting aside the strategic appreciations of the prestigious British authorities, the Colonial Defence Committee, the Committee of Imperial Defence, the Admiralty and the War Office, the Commonwealth government had descried in the Pacific a primary threat to Australian security and had proceeded in defiance of British advice and contrary to British recommendations to seek to reorient imperial diplomacy and to build up a formidable local defence force. In defining Australia's strategic position and in determining the appropriate response the politicians gained little support or comfort from their professional military and naval staffs. After the initial battle had been won, two very able men of affairs, Frederic W. Eggleston, secretary of the Australian branch of the

Round Table and Major E. L. Piesse, chief of military intelligence in World War I and the director of the Pacific Branch of the Prime Minister's Department from 1919 to 1923 did advance sophisticated and informed arguments on behalf of Australia's peculiar perception of its position in the Pacific and did offer a more mature basis for Australian policy. It was, however, the political leaders alone who were responsible for the shape and character of Australia's first defence and foreign policy. In their attitudes to international affairs the Australian statesmen were narrowly self-interested and generally indifferent to the wider issues of peace and war, and their analysis of international relations, though for the time in fundamentals 'fair and reasonable', was often expressed crudely and couched in the language of racial intolerance. Yet in the carrying out of the first function of a nation's external policy, namely the safeguarding of its citizens and territory, the Australian achievement will stand comparison with many other countries which had all the advantages of a full and independent international status.

# 2
# Colonial Origins

The first formulations of an Australian defence and foreign policy are to be found in the colonial era.

During the twenty years immediately following the establishment of responsible government in the Australian colonies, the question of defence and foreign policy seemed for the most part very remote and largely irrelevant. For Australians engaged in getting and spending, bent on making their fortunes in the Golden Age, on taking possession of the land and exploring new pastures, war and threats of war were part of the unhappy and dramatic life that they had left behind on the other side of the globe. Only occasionally did alarm over their own security, as at the time of the Crimean War, break through the wall of self-content and lead to a fitful effort to furnish the colonial ports and waters with a minimal defence. On the whole though, as the British colonial secretary pointed out in 1863 when the Home government, in the cause of retrenchment, was bringing home the legions, Australia was not, like Canada, menaced by a foreign power, nor was it, as in the case of New Zealand and Natal, cursed with native wars. Australia in mid-century felt relatively insulated from the troubles of the world.

The Australian colonies therefore offered little opposition to the withdrawal of the British garrisons. Remote from the centres of international conflict, confident in the general supremacy of the British navy, Australians complimented themselves on their advantages. A few leaders of opinion even argued that since war would come to the antipodes only as a consequence of the British connection, the Pacific colonies should assume a quasi-independent status in international affairs and try to extract guarantees of neutrality ahead of time from Britain's potential foes. After pondering the question in 1869, Charles Gavan Duffy, a leading Victorian politician, concluded that Australia should be given a status similar to that possessed by Hanover from 1714 to 1857. By this means the colonies would be able to take up a neutral stand in a British war when they thought the cause unjust or their interests not involved. The report of the Victorian Royal Commission on Federal Union over which Duffy had presided in 1870 reflected these view.[1] But he was unable to marshal any widespread support; Australians, feeling secure, were pleased to let well alone.

With the emergence of new tensions in Europe after 1870 and the extension of imperial rivalries into the Pacific, the Australian colonies were shaken out of their complacency over defence matters and ideas of neutrality were quickly abandoned. In this era of imperial competition British race sentiment overwhelmed the former more-limited outlook and the colonies rushed to offer their aid to the Mother Country when overseas expansion led the empire into war. Further, the efforts of European powers to acquire territories and bases in the Pacific

---

[1] Victoria, *Parliamentary Papers*, 1870, session(2), II, 465–90.

brought the frontiers of European antagonisms to Australia's doorstep. The fever of imperialism had drawn the colonies into the mainstream of international politics. The threat of Russian raiding cruisers operating out of Vladivostok, the menace of French, German and more vaguely American aspirations in the South Pacific Islands, and finally, by the eighteen-nineties, the fear of a southward advance of China and Japan, following in the path of their unwelcome migrants, all these considerations taken together produced during the last three decades of the nineteenth century a new sense of strategic vulnerability and prompted the first moves towards the creation of an Australian defence and foreign policy and with it a federal union.

## A 'Monroe Doctrine' for the South Pacific

The first sign of the Australian colonies' new concern for their external security was to be found in their adoption of a 'Monroe Doctrine' for the South Pacific. This Australian or, since the New Zealand government fully endorsed the same view, Australasian 'Monroe Doctrine' was aimed at excluding all foreign powers from the region and to this end the antipodean colonies began to urge in the 1870s that Britain should annex all the remaining islands in the Melanesian and Polynesian groups.

It is true that from the earliest days of settlement some Australian colonists, such as the Reverend John Dunmore Lang had possessed grand dreams of building an Anglo-Saxon empire in the Pacific, of fulfilling the 'manifest destiny' of the British race in the southern hemisphere. Foreign occupation and seizure of islands even in this early period had been the subject of public criticism. After the French annexed New Caledonia in 1853 the *Sydney Morning Herald* expressed its regret that 'the opportunity of colonizing that fine group has been lost.'[2] But the visionaries had had no impact on government policy, the occasional newspaper reproof had not prompted government action. It was only after 1870, in the light of the new international context, that Australian and New Zealand political leaders came to adopt annexation as a settled object of policy and to press the issue on the British government consistently and continuously. And the colonial governments were, unlike the earlier exponents of the doctrine, driven to this course not primarily by the élan of empire-building, the desire for self-aggrandizement, nor even from the hope of commercial rewards, but rather in order to prevent foreign powers from establishing colonies which could be used as bases for launching attacks on Australian trade and against the Australian mainland. By taking possession of the island groups which stretched in an arc from New Guinea in the north through the Solomons to the New Hebrides and, more distantly, Fiji and Samoa in the east they hoped to erect a natural barrier or 'rampart', as Hughes was later to call it, against potential enemies. As James Service, premier of Victoria, explained in 1885

> It was no lust of territory or expectation of the immediate settlement of the islands of the Pacific [which inspired this exclusive policy]; the object they had in view was to keep the

---

[2] *SMH*, 2 and 3 November 1853.

English people in these distant lands as far removed as possible from the dangers arising out of European complications.[3]

In July 1870 the Australian colonies, alarmed by the breakdown of law and order in Fiji, took their first concerted stand on the Pacific island issue. Fearing that either the German or American government might intervene at the request of their residents the colonial premiers, meeting at Melbourne, passed a resolution urging the British authorities to annex the islands. The resolution asserted 'that it is of the utmost importance to British interests that these islands should not form part of, or be under the guardianship of, any other country than Great Britain.'[4] Individual colonial governments followed this up by making separate representations to London. However, W. E. Gladstone's Liberal ministry was not sympathetic to further colonial expansion and when it was learnt that the Australians were unwilling to contribute to the cost of administering the islands, they were confirmed in their opposition. Three years later in 1874 Benjamin Disraeli's more imperially-minded Conservative government acceded to Australian wishes. It is important to note though that the British government was more influenced by an assessment of its own interest in the islands than by Australian pressure;[5] the Australian colonies were perhaps led by this episode into believing that they had more influence over British Pacific policy than was actually the case.

With Fiji safely anchored in the British lion's paw the Australian colonies began to focus their attention on the two most important remaining island groups, east New Guinea with its associated islands and the New Hebrides, against both of which it was thought that foreign governments had designs. The very next year after their first apparent success, the colonial authorities submitted requests for the annexation of New Guinea.[6] Indeed New South Wales presented the Colonial Office with a very complete shopping list, covering New Guinea, the New Hebrides, the Solomons, Marshall, Ellice and Gilbert islands and had the British government complied with Australian wishes the Pacific island problem would have been disposed of in a rather final way.[7] Even the British Conservatives were not willing to expand willy-nilly and like the liberals before them they were deterred further by the Australians' refusal to share the financial burdens. It has been suggested that had the colonies offered to assist with the costs of

---

[3] James Service's Memorandum for the Governor of Victoria, 6 February 1885, Premier's Department, Melbourne 85/467, cited in Merze Tate 'The Australasian Monroe Doctrine', *Political Science Quarterly*, LXXVI, June 1961, 277; see also Roger C. Thompson, 'James Service: Father of Australian Foreign Policy?', *Historical Studies*, XVI, October 1974, 258–76.

[4] NSW, *Votes and Proceedings of the Legislative Assembly*, 1870–1 session, Vol. II, p.56, No. 12-A, 'Intercolonial Conference. Report and Minutes of the Proceedings of the Intercolonial Conference held in Melbourne in the months of June and July, 1870'.

[5] Ethel Drus, 'The Colonial Office and the Annexation of Fiji', *Transactions of the Royal Historical Society*, 4 Series, XXXII, 1950, 94–108.

[6] Marjorie G. Jacobs, 'The Colonial Office and New Guinea, 1874–1884', *Historical Studies*, V, May 1952, 109.

[7] Great Britain, *Parliamentary Papers*, 1876 session, Vol. LIV, C. 1566, 'Correspondence respecting New Guinea', pp.26–30.

administration, Disraeli would have agreed to the occupation of some strategic point on the New Guinea coast in 1875.[8]

Despite this rebuff Australian interest waxed not waned and after the arrival of reports of articles in German newspapers urging the seizure of New Guinea, the Queensland government, the most nearly affected, took possession in April 1883 of the eastern half of the island on behalf of the British Empire. Simultaneously, Sir Thomas McIlwraith, the Queensland premier, wired London seeking confirmation of their action and offering to help pay the costs of administration. This was the first such offer and reflected the depth of colonial concern. Almost immediately, the Victorian, New South Wales and South Australian governments wired their approval and support.[9] However, Gladstone's Liberal government now back in office could not be convinced. Persuaded by the foreign office that the Germans had no substantial interest in New Guinea, the British in July turned down the Queensland request.

In the Australian colonies there was a dramatic response to this news. Representatives of the Australian and New Zealand governments came together to reassert in the most forthright and clear-cut manner their belief in a British 'Monroe Doctrine' for the Pacific. At an intercolonial convention which met in Sydney during November and December to discuss the new situation the colonial leaders resolved 'that further acquisition of dominion in the Pacific, south of the Equator, by any Foreign Power, would be highly detrimental to the safety and well-being of the British possessions in Australasia, and injurious to the interests of the Empire.' The convention called for the immediate annexation of that part of New Guinea not claimed by the Dutch, and the adjacent islands. At the same time they urged the opening of negotiations with France in order to gain control of the New Hebrides 'in the interests of Australasia'. And finally, in the face of this seeming British indifference they showed the seriousness of their purpose by agreeing for the first time to assume some portion of the financial burden entailed in these annexation programmes.[10]

In London, Gladstone remained obdurate. He derided the 'preposterous proposals of the Convention'.[11] Even after the German government showed unmistakable signs of having ambitions to take New Guinea, and the New South Wales, Queensland, Victorian and New Zealand governments had guaranteed £15,000 annually to defray expenses, the British Cabinet was still unwilling to meet colonial wishes. Britain had other fish to fry. Its occupation of Egypt in 1882 had led to strained relations with France. German support and goodwill were necessary for British Mediterranean and European policy. Thus when the Germans forced the issue in 1884 the British agreed to accept a German protectorate over northeast New Guinea in return for German acknowledgement of British hegemony over the south-eastern portion of the island. Lord Derby,

---

[8] Jacobs, 'The Colonial Office …', p. 109.

[9] Great Britain, *Parliamentary Papers*, 1883 session, Vol. XLVII, C. 3617, 'Further Correspondence respecting New Guinea', pp. 132–3, 138–9.

[10] NSW, *Votes and Proceedings of the Legislative Assembly*, 1883–4 session, Vol. IX, pp. 13–14, 'Intercolonial Convention, 1883. Report of the Proceedings of the Intercolonial Convention held in Sydney, in November and December, 1883'.

[11] Tate, 'The Australasian Monroe Doctrine', p. 278.

the colonial secretary, regretted the necessity of making the concession to Germany but recognized that it was inescapable. 'The question of Egypt' he wrote, 'overrides all others.'[12] The formal settlement was embodied in an Anglo-German agreement of 6 April 1886. The agreement not only provided for the division of east New Guinea but also apportioned the associated islands; Germany gained the Bismarck archipelago and the northern Solomons and Britain the southern Solomons and the more distant Gilbert and Ellice group.[13] At the 1887 colonial conference in London, the Australian colonies in return for contributing to the expense were given a share in the administration of British New Guinea which, until after the establishment of the Federation, was exercised for them by the Queensland government.

The Australians were not mollified by this half-way measure. They saw that Britain's world view differed from their own and they sensed that if they were to make any impression on the London-centred diplomacy of the empire they would have to co-ordinate their policies more effectively and push their Pacific concerns more vigorously and more tenaciously. Thus, the Sydney convention had resolved to put the intercolonial conference on a more permanent footing by setting up a Federal Council of Australasia which would be authorized to act with respect to 'the relations of Australasia with the islands of the Pacific'. At the first meeting of the Federal Council held in Hobart from 25 January to 5 February 1886 the colonial governments followed up their earlier 'Monroe Doctrine' pronouncement by calling on the British to refrain from entering into any further Pacific island deals without prior consultation with the Australians and New Zealanders.[14] Though New South Wales, South Australia and New Zealand were not represented at this council meeting, it was clear that on this question the council spoke for all.

With the settlement of the New Guinea question, Australasian attention turned to French activities further south and from 1884 to 1886 the agents-general of the different colonies in London kept up a running fire of complaint and inquiry about the French policy of sending recidivists to New Caledonia and about French aims in the New Hebrides.[15] The British government, perhaps somewhat shamefaced following the New Guinea episode, promised consultation before agreeing to any new changes in the status of the Pacific Islands, and after the French in February 1886 proposed that they should be allowed to occupy the New Hebrides in return for stopping convict transportation to their Pacific possessions, the British under-secretary

---

[12] Derby to Lord Granville, Foreign Secretary, 6 March 1885, cited in Henry L. Hall, *Australia and England*, London 1934. p. 229.

[13] Great Britain, *Parliamentary Papers*, 1886 session, Vol. LXXIII, C. 4656 (Western Pacific No. 1, 1886), 'Declarations between the Governments of Great Britain and the German Empire relating to the Demarcation of the British and German spheres of Influence in the Western Pacific and to Reciprocal Freedom of Trade and Commerce in the British and German Possessions and Protectorates in the Regions Signed at Berlin, April 6 and 10, 1886'.

[14] 'Proceedings of the First Session of the Federal Council of Australia, 1886', CO 808/66, pp. 24–5.

[15] See, for example, letter, Sir Saul Samuel, NSW agent-general to Sir Patrick Jennings, NSW premier, 26 March 1886 enclosing notes of interview between Lord Granville and the agents-general, 23 February 1886, NSW Colonial Secretary's Papers, NSW Archives, In-letters, Box 157, 4422, cited in Kathleen J. Melhuish, *Australian and British Imperial Policy*, PhD thesis, University of Sydney, 1965, p. 184.

for the colonies announced in the House of Commons that no French proposal for annexation would be considered 'without consultation with the Australian colonies, and without conditions absolutely satisfactory to their Governments [being] secured'.[16]

When the Australians were apprised of the French offer, their reaction was, despite an initial New South Wales hesitance, one of overwhelming opposition. After the French, ostensibly to protect the lives and property of their citizens, landed troops on the islands in July, Australia's attitude hardened as it consolidated and New South Wales swung into line. Though the Jennings government had in April survived a censure motion over its cautious approach to the problem, nevertheless, France's subsequent unilateral intervention left it with no choice and by September it was as insistent as the other colonies that no concession should be made.[17] In Victoria some political leaders were threatening to take the matter into their own hands and to oust the French by their own efforts.[18]

As a result of Australia's united and vigorous protests the British and French governments saw the necessity for a diplomatic solution. By August they had begun to discuss the establishment of a joint naval commission, which, while safeguarding the rights of nationals of both countries, would leave the New Hebrides officially neutral and independent. By October a draft convention was under consideration. Yet, despite the desire of the Colonial Office to sign an agreement before the colonials arrived in London in the spring of 1887 for Queen Victoria's Diamond Jubilee, nothing was done. In the total spectrum of British world policy, neither the Pacific, the New Hebrides nor Australia were that important. In the winter of 1886-7 British diplomacy was given over to the Bulgarian crisis, to keeping Russia out of the Mediterranean and the Near East. As the British colonial secretary, Sir Henry Holland, had feared, the issue became the source of the most bitter exchanges between the Mother Country and her Pacific progeny during the first great colonial conference which was held in conjunction with the Diamond Jubilee celebrations.

What precisely happened during the conference sessions of 26 and 28 April when the New Hebrides were discussed is not known since no verbatim record of the meeting has survived. However, the main elements in the encounter and the main drift in the argument are clear. At the Australians' request the Pacific island question was placed on the agenda. Alfred Deakin, the chief Victorian representative and then only thirty years of age, had announced ahead of time that the New Hebrides was 'by far the most important [item] to Australasia that will come under consideration'.[19] Sir Henry Holland, anticipating trouble, prevailed on the prime minister, Lord Salisbury, to attend on 26 April and expound British policy. Holland hoped that Salisbury's presence would overawe the colonies. He asked Salisbury to point out 'that the Colonists must not

---

[16] Great Britain, 3 *Hansard's Parliamentary Debates*, CCXCV, 971, 12 March 1885.

[17] *SMH*, 21 September 1886. Sir Patrick Jennings, the New South Wales premier, said, 'The action of the Government might be put simply into two statements, viz., to protest against any infraction of the status quo between Great Britain and France with respect to the independence of the New Hebrides and also that French deportation of criminals to the Pacific should cease.'

[18] *SMH*, 2 and 4 October 1886.

[19] J. A. La Nauze, *Alfred Deakin: A Biography*, 2 vols, Melbourne 1965, Vol. I, p. 98.

try and set up the Monro [sic] doctrine over all the Pacific Islands'. Salisbury, as it appears, was already impressed by what he called 'the outrecuidance [overweening conceit] of your Great Britain',[20] and almost certainly went into the conference room with a firm resolve to put the colonists in their place. What he actually said, in so far as it can be put together from the different and sometimes conflicting reports, would seem to bear this out. The British prime minister reproved the colonies for their intemperate demands for the annexation of the New Hebrides. The distances of the islands from Australia, he claimed, showed the extravagant nature of colonial fears. Moreover, France would never agree willingly to surrender its rights there and Britain would not risk war in order to gain this point. Finally, Salisbury asserted that the colonies' ultramontane stand was unreal and irrational, that their rejection of the French offer to end transportation to New Caledonia was the height of foolishness. The burden of the speech seems to have been that if the colonial leaders would give up annexation, Salisbury could still secure for them this one sure benefit. It is curious, as W. P. Morrell has noted, that the British prime minister should have tried to reopen the question of annexation when a draft agreement for neutralizing the islands was under negotiation.[21] Yet, it is not altogether beyond understanding. On the one hand it could have been for Salisbury a useful way of scolding the colonial upstarts and even more plausibly, in the light of the delicate European situation, he might well have thought that if he could convince the Australasians of their foolishness, it might be possible to win French goodwill by making a concession to them in the Pacific.

Whatever Salisbury's motive, the colonial leaders were not moved. The Victorians, led by Deakin, declared their unalterable opposition to French annexation. The Queensland representative, Sir Samuel Griffith, in a more decorous way, made the same point and even the New South Wales premier, Jennings, who lacked the Victorian fervour, went along with his fellow Australians.[22] When, on the other hand, they were told bluntly that British annexation was out of the question, they unanimously approved an Anglo-French convention to provide for the island's independence. Thus, with Australian approval the draft convention setting up a joint naval commission was signed in November and four months later, after the clarification of details, the French troops were withdrawn. This *modus vivendi* continued, more or less satisfactorily, down to the beginning of the new century. Though the Australians had submitted to a policy of combined responsibility and restraint as a temporary solution, they never lost hope that the British would ultimately acquire the New Hebrides. And it was to this end that the colonies directed their diplomacy over the next two decades.[23]

By the 1890s then, the fate of all of the island groups in the immediate environs of Australia had been determined and consequently the colonies did not pursue the 'Monroe Doctrine' theme

---

[20] Ibid., p. 99.

[21] W. P. Morrell, *Britain in the Pacific Islands*, Oxford 1960, p. 203.

[22] La Nauze, *Alfred Deakin*, Vol. I, p. 103; Alfred Deakin, *The Federal Story: The Inner History of the Federal Cause, 1880–1900*, Melbourne 1963, p. 22.

[23] Deakin, *The Federal Story*, pp. 22–3. Deakin claimed that in 1888–9 the Victorian government was prepared to use its own naval force to prevent further French military intervention in the islands.

with the same unity and urgency that had marked the 1880s. However, whenever the *status quo* in the Pacific, even in the outer circumference of islands, seemed to be threatened by foreign ambitions there was a vigorous response. When in the wake of civil war in Samoa during 1893 and 1894 it was feared that Germany would intervene and seize these islands, the Victorian government wrote to the Colonial Office that because of 'the manifest destiny of Australasia to be the controlling Power in the Southern Pacific' Britain ought to annex Samoa.[24]

Similarly, in 1898 after the outbreak of the Spanish-American war placed the future of the Philippines in doubt, the Victorian premier, Sir George Turner, directed his agent-general to represent to the British government that it 'is most important on strategical grounds Philippine Islands should be in possession of friendly power; also, in interests of trade, being on route China and Japan.'[25] In reply to Turner's appeal to the other colonial premiers for support New Zealand and Tasmania expressed their sympathy but New South Wales, South Australia and Queensland considered that, since the Philippines were still in Spanish hands, interference at that stage was presumptuous and premature.[26] From an Australasian point of view the Philippines did not appear to be in danger of falling into hostile hands. Australians, like other British peoples, had since the 1870s come to see the Americans as Anglo-Saxon race cousins and the United States as a friendly power. They expressed great enthusiasm for the American cause during the Spanish-American war. American victories were greeted with rapturous applause and public demonstrations of approval, and when President McKinley decided to annex the Philippines Australians were well pleased. The American acquisition of the Hawaiian Islands in 1898 and of Tutuila in the Samoan group in 1899 was also accepted calmly, indeed even warmly, by those who considered that the further the Americans became involved in the future of the Pacific the better were the prospects for Australian peace and safety.

### Defence forces and defence thinking

Australians, disturbed by the gathering tensions in international relations, by the mounting pressures on Pax Britannica and by the sustained interest of the Great Powers in the Pacific, came to recognize during the latter part of the nineteenth century that a vigorous and vocal pursuit of a 'Monroe Doctrine' policy was not of itself an adequate guarantee of their security. Under the pressure of recurring crises and against a generally unpredictable and forbidding world background they perceived for the first time that defence and diplomacy were twin arms of the one object and that they must take steps to build up their defence capability. Colonial defence expenditure, though still modest even on a per capita basis by British or European standards, rose substantially from 1870 to 1890; Victorian defence appropriations rose from £47,672 in 1870 to

---

[24] Memorandum from Victorian government to Governor, 1 May 1894, CP 309/140, cited in Hall, *Australia and England*, p. 218.

[25] *The Australasian*, LXIV, 1162, 21 May 1898.

[26] *Brisbane Courier*, 18 May 1898.

£78,733 in 1880 and to £350,821 in 1890.[27] However, it was easier to find the finance than to determine how it should be spent. In contrast to Australian diplomacy, there was no simple and obvious defence strategy, comparable with the Pacific 'Monroe Doctrine', around which the colonies could unite their efforts.

Though all the major European powers and, after 1890, a modernized Japan and an 'awakening' China were seen individually and in various combinations as possible or potential sources of danger, nevertheless, the precise nature of the threat against which the Australians should prepare was difficult to pinpoint. The British navy was still supreme at sea and it was highly unlikely therefore that any prospective enemy would, in the foreseeable future, attempt an invasion of Australian territory. All Australian and British analyses agreed upon that. What form then would an enemy attack take? Should they expect raids on the heavily populated coastal cities, a blockade of the main ports or interference with their commerce on the high seas? Furthermore, whatever the answer to this question, another and even more difficult one remained; namely, what were the best steps to take to meet the perceived threat? Australia with its very extensive and sparsely populated coastline posed awkward problems for defence planners. Should limited resources be devoted to fixed port defences which could secure the great cities, to a mobile military force which could move to any part of the continent where the need required it, to a coastal flotilla which could harass raiding vessels and help protect the coasts and rivers, or should Australia make a contribution towards an enlarged British naval squadron which would halt the enemy before they reached Australian waters? The answers were not self-evident. Neither the colonial governments nor their British advisers held to a consistent prescription for Australian defence. They tended to move from expedient to expedient and to change with changing circumstances. Australia's defence policy then as it developed in these years was one of improvisation, composed of a little bit of everything. Yet out of this rough and ready learning experience, certain patterns of the future were beginning to emerge. From locally centred policies, in which each government sought through fixed land-based defences to provide for its own, the colonial leaders moved to adopt co-operative policies aimed at ensuring a more certain and powerful British presence in the Pacific and at bringing about a real co-ordination and uniformity in their forces at home.

Down to 1870 the colonies had relied for their land defence on the British garrison troops supported by ill-disciplined and poorly organized volunteers; at times of crisis, as in the Crimean War, they had also shown a sporadic interest in harbour fortifications. But defence was not a continuing or significant concern in these early years. Under the protection of the British navy and more nearly the Australian squadron which became an independent station in 1859 the colonies had few fears. The withdrawal of the British troops in 1870 did not suddenly shatter this

---

[27] One Victorian liberal apologist for the great increases of 1885–6, when defence expenditure rose from £187,568 to £318,978 could still smugly boast that while Russia spent thirty-three times as much on armaments as on education, France eleven times, Britain four times, Germany three times, Victoria spent three times more on education than on defence. Even the United States, he added, only spent twice as much on education as on defence. *Victoria Year Book*, 1886–7, p. 784.

womb-like sense of security. Only slowly with the growing armaments race in Europe, the movement of Germany and France into the South Pacific, the Russian war scares of 1878 and 1885, the Asian migration fear and the rise of Japan did Australia's complacency give way to a more alarmist view of their strategic position. But by 1899 a conference of Commonwealth naval officers was able to assert with some credibility that 'There is every indication that it [the Pacific Ocean] will play the part of the Mediterranean in the past century as the area of national conflicting forces.'[28]

The Australians looked first to their military forces, and in all colonies at different rates and in different ways governments abandoned their exclusive dependence on voluntarism and built up a more reliable system around a small permanent force backed by a partially- or fully-paid militia. The permanent forces were made up generally of specialist troops, notably artillery corps. But their numbers were small, their opportunities for enterprise very circumscribed. In 1882 South Australia's permanent nucleus comprised one officer and twenty men. New South Wales' professionals never exceeded a thousand and taking Australia as a whole their numbers were always less than 2,000. More attention was paid to reforming the citizen forces. In 1874 New South Wales introduced a 'partial payment' and all other colonies before the end of the century had adopted similar legislation. The crisis over the Pacific Islands and the Russian war threat, which coincided in the years 1883–5, produced the most dramatic changes. Queensland, following a military inquiry passed a comprehensive act in 1884 which established a small permanent corps, provided for partially-paid militia and made all male adults liable to be called up in time of emergency. This was the first law providing for conscription. In 1883 and 1884 Victoria not only created a paid militia but also set up a Council of Defence under a special defence minister, the first such in Australian history.

The more technical questions of artillery, port fortification, coastal and harbour defence required greater expertise and at the request of New South Wales, Victoria, South Australia and Queensland, the imperial government in 1876 sent out Lieutenant-General Sir William Jervois and under him Lieutenant-Colonel P. H. Scratchley to advise the colonies on these aspects of Australian defence. The Colonies, especially fearful of raids by a new class of Russian ship-of-war, the *Rurik*, adopted most of the Jervois-Scratchley recommendations[29] and undertook extensive and expensive fortification at the entrance of Sydney Harbour and Port Phillip Bay. They also

---

[28] 'The Report of Conference of Commonwealth Naval Officers', cited in G. L. Macandie, *The Genesis of the Royal Australian Navy*, Sydney 1949, p. 73.

[29] NSW, *Votes and Proceedings of the Legislative Assembly*, 1876–7 session, Vol. III, No. 353-A, 'Defences. Preliminary Report by Sir W. Jervois, June 4, 1877'; Victoria, *Votes and Proceedings of the Legislative Assembly*, 1877–8 session, Vol. II, No. 46, 'Preliminary Report on the Defences of Victoria, July 20, 1877'; Queensland, *Journals of the Legislative Council*, 1877 session, Vol. XXV, Pt I, 'Defences. Preliminary Report by Colonel Sir W. F. Drummond Jervois'; South Australia, *Parliamentary Papers*, 1877 session, Vol. IV, 'Memorandum on South Australian Defences, December 12, 1877', and also C. Kinloch Cooke, *Australian Defence and New Guinea. Compiled from the Papers of the late Major-General Sir Peter Scratchley*, London 1887.

acquired vessels for harbour defence and for the training of naval brigades. In 1881 the Admiralty, at the instance of the New South Wales government, made a gift to the colony of the 22 gun screw sloop, HMS *Wolverene*, which had been built in 1859. However, it was never fully equipped or commissioned, was manned only during the holidays and rarely put to sea, and in 1889 it was scrapped. The more functional vessels built or purchased by the colonies from 1882 to 1885 had rather more enduring value. Victoria still possessed the *Cerberus*, an armoured plated monitor which the British government had helped the colony to purchase at the time of the withdrawal of imperial troops. South Australia in 1884, under the influence of Jervois, who had become governor of the colony, acquired the *Protector*, a small but heavily armoured cruiser of 960 tons designed to watch over coastal trade. The *Protector* saw service in China waters during the Boxer Rebellion in 1900. Queensland also in 1884 acquired two gun-boats of 360 tons, the *Gayundah* and *Paluma* and the eastern colonies added one or more torpedo-boats over the next few years. This was the great period in the development of colonial naval forces. Nearly all the vessels inherited by the Commonwealth defence department in 1901 dated from these years.

The colonies were not content with a narrow local defence. Their problems were Pacific ones and, after the first shock of recognition, they looked to the imperial government to provide greater and more permanent naval security in the region. With a sufficiently powerful naval force resident in the South Pacific, enemy cruisers would have to think twice about launching an attack on Australia. The threat would be met before it reached Australian shores. At the intercolonial conference in Sydney in 1881 the Australian premiers had unanimously agreed that 'the strength of the Australian Squadron should be increased'. However, while pledging themselves to finance the efficient fortification of Australian ports, they insisted that the expansion of the imperial squadron should be an exclusive charge on the British exchequer. Only the South Australian representative indicated a willingness to assume part of the cost.[30]

The British government did not see the matter in the same light. Disturbed by the changed balance of power in Europe and by the first signs of a continental alliance system it had appointed in 1879 a royal commission under Lord Carnarvon on imperial defence. The commission accepted the general line of demarcation between colonial and imperial defences which had been emerging since the 1860s. It asserted that while the imperial navy had general responsibility for the protection of commerce on the high seas and for intercepting raiders, the colonies were to provide 'at their own cost' for the local forces, forts and batteries. Moreover, looking towards the issue the Australians were raising, the commissioners thought also that the time was approaching when the richer colonies might 'not unreasonably' be called upon to assist 'in some degree in the naval defence of empire', and to make a contribution thereby to the general defence of the empire.[31]

---

[30] NSW, *Votes and Proceedings of the Legislative Assembly*, 1880–1 session, Vol. I, No. 143, 'Intercolonial Conference. Minutes of Proceedings of the Intercolonial Conference held at Sydney, January, 1881'.

[31] Great Britain, *Parliamentary Papers*, 1887 session, Vol. LVI, C. 5091, Pt I, 'Colonial Conference, 1887. Proceedings and Papers of the Colonial Conference', p. 315.

When then in 1884 the Admiralty, deeply troubled by conflicts with France in Egypt and with Russia in Afghanistan, began to reappraise imperial naval defence and to consider embarking on a new naval building programme, they naturally looked to the colonies for assistance. Rear-Admiral Sir George Tryon, who in the following year assumed command of the Australian squadron which had just been raised to flag rank, tried to marry the Admiralty's aims to colonial concerns and prejudices. In March 1885 in a letter to the governor of Victoria he put forward such a scheme. It was a persuasive document. Tryon pointed to the high cost of efficient land and harbour defences, he pointed out that they were of no use for protecting coastal trade and, taking up the suggestion of the colonial premiers, he recommended that an auxiliary squadron of cruiser-catchers should be formed to provide a more effectual defence of colonial commerce. He contended that while such a force would be built, paid for and manned by the Admiralty and be under the commander-in-chief of the Australian station, it should be maintained at Australian expense. These vessels were to be in addition to those normally present on the Australian station and were not to be removed from Australasian waters without the consent of the colonial governments.[32] Tryon revealed equal shrewdness in selling his programme to the British, arguing that through such a scheme the Australians could be persuaded to put aside for the time being any idea of acquiring an independent ocean-going navy of their own, a prospect which the Admiralty dreaded.[33] The Admiralty in general agreed with Tryon's proposals with one qualification. Though they seemed willing enough to accept the colonial veto over the movement of an auxiliary squadron—an issue which was subsequently to grow in importance—they wanted the colonies to pay both the capital and running cost of the additional vessels and at the end of 1885 Tryon was authorized to negotiate on this basis.[34]

After a meeting between Tryon and the New South Wales, Queensland and Victorian premiers at Sydney on 26 and 27 April 1886 the general principles of Tryon's scheme were approved. However, the financial details caused some debate. Though the colonies had retreated from their 1881 position and were now willing to contribute to the costs of further naval defence, they baulked at the idea of assuming the full cost of construction, estimated at £800,000. Victoria wanted to pay only maintenance costs while the other governments were willing to assist with 5 per cent of building costs as well.[35] The deadlock continued until the 1887 Colonial Conference.

---

[32] Macandie, *Genesis of the Royal Australian Navy*, pp. 31–7.

[33] Donald C. Gordon, *The Dominion Partnership in Imperial Defence, 1870–1914*, Oxford 1965, p. 87.

[34] CO Confidential Print, Australian No. 115, 'Correspondence relating to the Naval Defence of the Australian Colonies and the Defence of King George's Sound and Fremantle', CO 881/7. See especially, letter, Admiralty to Colonial Office, 9 September 1885, containing a Revised Memorandum, 9 September 1885, 'Local Defence, and Protection of Floating Trade in the Waters of the Australasian Colonies', and also a copy of a letter addressed by the Commander-in-Chief on the Australian Station, Admiral Tryon, to the respective Governors of the Australian Colonies, 24 December 1885. In the latter letter Tryon sets out the basis for an agreement to establish an Auxiliary Squadron.

[35] Letter, Admiralty to Colonial Office, 23 June 1886, enclosing a report from Tryon on the 'Result of Meeting of Premiers on board Her Majesty's Ship "Nelson" at Sydney, April 26 and 27, 1886', ibid.

By the time of the London meeting, the Admiralty had revised and reduced their financial preconditions for the naval agreements,[36] and the colonists, more than ever alarmed by French and German activities in the South Pacific, were anxious for a settlement. Lord Salisbury, in opening the conference, speaking of colonial fears, appealed for their co-operation not simply on the basis of their attachment to the Mother Country but 'on the most solid and reasonable foundation of self-interest and security'.[37] After considerable bargaining an agreement was reached. The Admiralty was to provide an auxiliary squadron of five fast third-class cruisers and two of the latest torpedo-boats for the Australian station: three of the cruisers and one gunboat were to be kept ready for active duty and the remaining cruisers and gunboat placed in reserve. The Australian colonies, with whom New Zealand was also associated, were for their part to pay the cost of maintenance and upkeep of the ships, £91,000, and 5 per cent of the capital cost, not exceeding £35,000 a year. Thus the colonies committed themselves to an annual expenditure of £126,000 for this added imperial defence. New Zealand's share was £20,000 and Australia's £106,000 was distributed among the colonies in proportion to population. In return the Admiralty recognized the special function of these auxiliary ships in defending the Pacific colonies' trade and territory. They were not to be moved out of the limits of the Australian station without the permission of the colonial governments. The agreement was to last for ten years from the date of arrival of the ships in the South Pacific. In 1891 the auxiliary squadron sailed into Sydney Harbour.

The imperial government, at the very time it signed the 1887 agreement, was beginning to reconsider the principles underlying its global policy of naval defence. In response to the confrontation with France and Russia the British parliament passed a Naval Defence Act in 1889 laying down a comprehensive programme of naval rearmament and adopted a two-power standard as the criterion of naval supremacy. Under the influence of Sir John Colomb and the 'Blue Water' school theorists, the Admiralty was converted to the doctrines of naval concentration and centralization and they began to regret their concession of a veto over the movement of the auxiliary squadron. During the 1897 Colonial Conference the Admiralty endeavoured to convince the colonies to surrender this right in the interest of the general defence of the empire. But the colonial leaders were not to be persuaded. George Reid, premier of New South Wales, retorted that the auxiliary ships had been obtained not to augment the overall British naval supremacy but rather to extend the outer limits of Australasia's own defence perimeter. The colonial representatives agreed that the auxiliary squadron might be directed to any of the Southwest Pacific Islands, without their prior consent, for this was within 'the outer line of local defence'; the islands marked the frontiers of Australasian Pacific security.[38] This was the maximum concession that they would make and in face of such determined opposition the British reluctantly withdrew.

---

[36] Letter, Admiralty to Colonial Office, 25 February 1887, enclosing copy of letter from Admiralty to Rear-Admiral Fairfax, 23 February 1887, ibid.

[37] Great Britain, *Parliamentary Papers*, 1887 session, Vol. LVI, C. 5091, Pt 1, P. 6.

[38] CO Confidential Print, Misc. No. 111, Report of 1897 Conference, pp. 55–7, 63 and 85, CP 103/12.

Thus almost from the first Anglo-Australian co-operation over Pacific naval defence was marred by a conflict of view which reflected a conflict over interest.

The problems of military defence did not lend themselves so naturally to either an intercolonial or imperial solution; they were too intimately associated with provincial feeling and provincial authority. However, having worked together successfully to produce a naval agreement, a number of the colonial leaders in 1887 expressed a desire for closer co-operation in improving their land defences. Samuel Griffith, the Queensland premier had spoken at the Colonial Conference in favour of a regular inspection of colonial military forces by an imperial officer and in the following year, on the initiative of Duncan Gillies, the Victorian premier, the colonial governments requested London to send out a British officer to examine the state of Australian land defences.[39]

As a result Major-General J. Bevan Edwards visited the colonies in 1889 and produced a comprehensive report on the military needs of both the individual colonies and Australia as a whole. It was this latter aspect which made his report so novel and which opened up fresh possibilities for Australian defence. His first premise was that 'a common system of defence can only be carried out by a federation of the military forces of the Colonies'. Edwards was not precise about the dangers which faced the colonies but, impressed by the isolated and defenceless character of much of Australia's coastline, he pointed out that garrisons centred on the capital cities were useless for meeting threats to any other part of Australian territories. He concluded that the colonies should create in addition to the garrisons and fixed defence, a field force of 30–40,000 which could be rapidly concentrated and moved to wherever the enemy might appear. Indeed, considering the magnitude of the task, he wondered whether 'every man on attaining the age of 18 to 20 should not be compelled to join a rifle company'. In the absence of political union he recommended that the colonies pass a uniform defence act which would, among other things, permit the use of the military force of each in the territories of all. Only Queensland to this time had such legislation. Similarly he urged uniform organization, discipline, pay and integrated transport provisions so that in an emergency the different colonial forces could act together with the least amount of friction and difficulty.[40]

The Edwards report was referred to the British Government's Colonial Defence Committee which had been set up in 1885 to advise on overseas defence questions. The Colonial Defence Committee believed that Edwards, as a soldier, had overlooked the protective role of the British navy and had exaggerated both the scale and nature of the attack which Australia might reasonably anticipate. They felt that the Pacific colonies were still the most secure part of the

---

[39] Victoria, *Votes and Proceedings of the Legislative Assembly,* 1889 session, Vol. III, paper No. 57, 'Inspection of Colonial Forces by an Imperial General Officer'.

[40] Great Britain, *Parliamentary Papers,* 1890 session, Vol. XLIX, C. 6188, 'Correspondence relating to the Inspection of the Military Forces of the Australasian Colonies, by Major-General J. Bevan Edwards, C.B.'

empire. Unwilling nevertheless to deter the colonies from improving their military capability the Colonial Defence Committee offered only mild criticisms of the Edwards report.[41]

In Australia the report sparked off a revolution in military thinking. An intercolonial military conference meeting in Sydney in 1894 approved a number of Edwards' proposals. They agreed that Australian defence should be treated as one and not six problems.[42] They accepted that after providing field garrisons for the coaling stations at King George's Sound and Thursday Island and some 10,000 citizen soldiers for the defence of the major ports and cities, the remaining troops should be treated as one field force. Against the background of the depression and the Colonial Defence Committee's criticisms, the colonial military leaders pared down Edwards' numbers and suggested a peace-time field force of 7,300 officers and men which could be expanded in war to 12,200. Though allowing that any new scheme would have to be based on voluntary recruitment, nevertheless they urged the colonial governments to write into the new defence bills the Queensland principle, making all able-bodied men liable for military service in an emergency. Procedures for controlling this intercolonial force were not precisely formulated. On the recommendation of Major-General E. T. H. Hutton,[43] the commandant of the New South Wales military forces, the conference supported the establishment of a Council of Defence made up of two delegates from the two senior colonies and one each from the others. The Council of Defence would take charge at the outbreak of war or in time of general emergency. The relation of the political arm of government to the Council was not spelled out.[44]

In January 1896 when the military officers met again they reaffirmed their conviction that the military forces of each colony should be available for the defence of all and that they should be controlled by a Council of Defence, and out of deference to local opinion they rejected the Colonial Defence Committee's suggestion that the field forces should be liable for service outside Australian waters.[45] Hutton had been annoyed by the colonial leaders' lukewarm response to the

[41] CDC, 40R, 'Remarks on Proposed Organisation of the Military Forces of the Australasian Colonies, May 16, 1890', Cab 9/1.

[42] The British government supported this aspect of the Edwards report and encouraged the military officers to work towards 'a Federation of the Australasian Colonies for Defence Purposes.' See 'Memorandum of Conversation between Mr Robert Meade, Permanent Under-Secretary for the Colonies and Colonel E. T. H. Hutton, March 9, 1893 in the Colonial Office', Hutton Papers, add. ms. 50078, Vol. I, pp. 251–5. Meade was giving the British government's instructions to Hutton prior to the latter's departure for the colonies where he was to take over command of the New South Wales military forces.

[43] Major-General Sir Edward Thomas Hutton, 1848–1923; son of Edward Thomas Hutton, died 1849; educated at Eton; entered army, 1867 (lieutenant, 1871; captain, 1879; colonel, 1892; local NSW rank of major-general, 1892; major-general, 1900; lieutenant-general, 1907); King's Royal Rifle Corps, 1867; Zulu wars, 1879–1881; Egyptian and Sudan campaigns, 1882–5; graduated from Staff College, 1882; raised and commanded a mounted infantry unit, Aldershot, 1888–92; Commander of NSW military forces, 1893–6; South Africa war, 1900–1; General Officer commanding, Australian military forces, 1902–4.

[44] 'Report of Military Conference Held at Sydney, October 24, 1894', Cab 11/23.

[45] 'Report and Schedules of the Inter-Colonial Military Committee Assembled at Sydney, January 29, 1896', Cab 11/23.

initial proposals and in 1895 he seized upon the 'pretext' of the Sino-Japanese war to press the matter. In a minute for the New South Wales government he said that

> The sudden rise of Japan to the position of a naval and military power of the first magnitude has placed the importance of the defence of the Australian continent by mutual agreement between the several colonies in the light of necessity. Australia has now at her doors a maritime power whose fleet, having become mistress of the Chinese waters, has transported and is maintaining an army of 200,000 men through a difficult and bloody campaign. The final result of their successive and momentous victories by land and sea cannot be foreseen …
> The necessity for preparation for such a possibility becomes a question of the utmost importance to Australia, not only in relation to British trade but national future.[46]

However, by the time the colonial premiers came together in March 1896, to consider national defence and 'undesirable' Asian immigration—since the beginning of the decade the two issues had begun to converge[47]—the movement for a federal constitution had overhauled and indeed swallowed up its defence origins. The premiers were not indifferent to Australia's external situation and the long-term threats posed by European imperialism and Asian resurgence but they believed that these threats were not sufficiently urgent or immediate to justify surrendering the strongest argument in favour of a more general federal union. Thus, while the premiers agreed to try and establish uniformity between their respective military forces and to amend their respective defence acts so that the forces of each colony could be used for the protection of the whole continent, they felt that a national defence scheme and a national defence council should be left for the determination of the Australian government which would come into being after political federation had been accomplished.[48]

## Federal union

As a result of harsh experience during the 1870s and 1880s, the Australian colonies had become increasingly aware that in the search for security in the Pacific they shared a common interest and pursued a common goal. Graham Berry, a notable Victorian politician, who had taken part in the 1881–3 intercolonial conferences, declared that it was

> at the time [of the New Guinea dispute] that the idea of federation took a real and substantial hold upon the people—that the colonies began to understand that in order to speak with a united voice, which would be heard in Downing Street, in regard to what were then called 'our foreign relations', it was necessary that we should have a central representative body.[49]

---

[46] Minute addressed by Major-General Edward T. H. Hutton to the New South Wales colonial secretary, 12 March 1895, Cab 11/23. See also, copy of letter, Hutton to Duke of Cambridge, 22 April 1895, Hutton papers, add. ms. 50078, Vol. I, p. 90, and copy of letter, Hutton to George Houston Reid, premier of New South Wales, 27 July 1895, ibid., add. ms. 50084, Vol. VII, p. 101.
[47] Myra Willard, *History of the White Australia Policy,* Melbourne 1923, pp. 99–110.
[48] Resolutions of Premiers' Conference, 4 March 1896, NSW Treasury Papers in letters, Public Officers, 96/5907, New South Wales Archives.
[49] Cited in Gordon, *The Dominion Partnership* …, pp. 80–1.

In 1883 the same intercolonial conference, which had promulgated an Australasian 'Monroe Doctrine' for the South Pacific, decided to form a Federal Council of Australasia to enable the colonies to legislate as a body with respect to the Pacific Islands and at the request of any one or more colonies on defence. In 1885 the British parliament at the instigation of the colonies had passed the Federal Council of Australasia Act setting up the Council and clothing it with appropriate powers.

The Council proved an inadequate vehicle for federal sentiment. It lacked executive and revenue powers, and became caught up in a complex web of inter-colonial jealousies and internal colonial politics. Though the New South Wales delegates at the 1883 conference had approved the plan, the legislative assembly had subsequently by a narrow, and perhaps accidental, vote failed to ratify it.[50] The self-esteem of 'the Mother Colony' then stood between New South Wales and membership of the federal organization and New South Wales steadfastly refused to take its seat on the Council. Yet without New South Wales participation, the Federal Council was inevitably defective. Indeed, due to its unfortunate history, the Federal Council came to be seen not as a symbol of unity, but a source of colonial antagonisms.

Edwards' report in 1889 provided the occasion for a new beginning. For whatever reasons—and those advanced are legend[51]—Sir Henry Parkes, the premier of New South Wales, used the report to appeal to his fellow premiers and his fellow countrymen to establish an Australian government. In his famous speech at Tenterfield on 24 October when he opened his campaign, Parkes asserted that,

> Believing as he did that it was essential to preserve the security and integrity of these colonies, that the whole of the forces should be amalgamated into one great federal army, feeling this and seeing no other means of attaining this end [he denied that the Federal Council was adequate for the task], it seemed to him that the time was close at hand when they ought to set about creating this great national government for all Australia.[52]

Defence was for him the overarching justification for the federal movement, and during the ensuing two years he expatiated on the external dangers which cast a long shadow over Australia's future and made it incumbent on the colonists to adopt a common defence and a federal union. Britain, France, Russia and Germany confronted each other in Asia and the Pacific. A breach of the peace in Europe might very well result in an attempt to invade Australian soil. Even more sinister though was the menace posed by the 'countless millions of inferior members of the human family who are within easy sail of these shores'.[53]

---

[50] Geoffrey Serle, 'Victoria's Campaign for Federation' in Martin, *Essays in Australian Federation,* Melbourne 1969, p. 20.

[51] W. G. McMinn, 'Sir Henry Parkes as a Federalist', *Historical Studies,* XII, October 1966, 415–16.

[52] SMH, 25 October 1889.

[53] See speeches at Australian Natives Association meeting, 8 November 1889, at the Federal conference in Melbourne, 13 February 1890 and in the Legislative Assembly of New South Wales, 7 May 1890, Sir Henry Parkes, *The Federal Government of Australia: Speeches Delivered on Various Occasions (November 1889— May 1890),* Sydney 1890, pp. 36, 126–30, 178–9. Parkes in striving for maximum effect had slipped into the

Parkes' exposition of this latter theme grew ever more explicit and ominous with every repetition. As President of the first national convention, which had been summoned to Sydney in March 1891 to lay down the basis of a federal constitution, he declared

> I think it is more than likely, more than probable, that forms of aggression will appear in these seas which are entirely new to the world… We have evidence abundant on all hands that the Chinese nation and other Asiatic nations — especially the Chinese — are awakening to all the power which their immense population gives them in the art of war, in the art of acquisition and all the other arts known to European civilisation, and it seems to me … that if we suffer in this direction at any time, it will not be by the bombardment of one of our rich cities—it will not be by an attack upon our seaborne commerce—it will not be by any attempt to lay us under a ransom to protect our property and our lives, but it will be by stealthily, … effecting a lodgement in some thinly-peopled portion of the country, where it would take immense loss of life and immense loss of wealth to dislodge the invader.[54]

Here drawn crudely, if boldly, was an outline of the 'Yellow Peril' which was to come to dominate the Australian imagination after the Russo-Japanese war of 1905. The plot of the invasion-scare novel. *The Australian Crisis,*[55] published in 1909, could well have been written in large part to Parkes' specifications. Parkes, the word-spinner and crowd-pleaser, had found a receptive audience for his cry of 'danger' from the north, which encouraged him to make it the chief argument in support of federal defence and federal union.

The hostility to Chinese migrants, the struggle to exclude them from the colonies, and the attempts of the Chinese government to intervene through the British authorities had directed Australian attention to this phenomenon, and while the old fears of Russia, France and Germany remained relatively unchanged, the threat from Asia seemed the portent of the future. The 'Father of Federation' was also and in the same sense, 'Father of the "Yellow Peril"' tradition in Australian foreign policy.[56] The 1880s had been a decade of education and growth in the idea of national

---

language of white racial superiority which had become common currency during the debates of the 1880s over the exclusion of Chinese immigrants. But in the same speech and with even greater emphasis he maintained that he was 'not one of those, … who regards the Chinese people with any feeling of loathing'. He added that he did 'not look down upon them as a people who are in their habits particularly inferior to us'. He believed them to be law-abiding, industrious, frugal and peaceable people. His opposition to Chinese migration had been based solely on his desire to preserve the British character of Australian society. He saw the Chinese becoming an aggressive power through the imitation of the European arts of war and acquisition. Parkes thus also exemplifies well the slipshod and almost casual way in which Australian political leaders came to adopt racial language and imagery in discussing defence and foreign policy issues.

[54] *Official Report of the National Australian Convention Debates, Sydney, 2 March to 9 April* 1891, Sydney 1891, p. 316, 13 March 1891.

[55] See Chapter 6.

[56] McMinn has suggested that Parkes was insincere in his exposition of the 'Yellow Peril' as well as in his advocacy of federation. McMinn argued that 'If the problem was really urgent as he [Parkes] claimed, some direct action was necessary at once', and he points out how Parkes refused to cooperate for that purpose in the Federal Council (McMinn, 'Sir Henry Parkes …', p. 411). This is unfair to Parkes' statement of the

interest. The problems of trade and transport, immigration, defence and Pacific affairs cried for action and it was the sharpening awareness of Australia's vulnerability to external dangers which dramatized the need and gave an urgency to action.

In response to Parkes' overtures 'an informal meeting' of colonial leaders including representatives from New Zealand was held in Melbourne in February 1890 to consider what should be done. Agreeing on the desirability of achieving national union, they decided to recommend to their respective parliaments that they appoint representatives to a constitutional convention. In March 1891 the delegates, coming together in Sydney under the presiding genius of Parkes, adopted four principles as a basis for federation. The first, following the United States model, declared that the colonies or states should retain sovereignty in all fields not specifically handed over to the national government, the second and third dealt with matters of tariff and trade and the fourth asserted 'that the military and naval defence of Australia shall be entrusted to federal forces under one command'. In the draft constitutions drawn up by the 1891 convention and subsequently amended by the 1897–8 convention, the founding fathers gave to the Commonwealth broad powers over naval and military defence (Clause 51, VI), 'external affairs' (Clause 51, XIX) and 'the relation of the Commonwealth with the islands of the Pacific' (Clause 51, XXX).

The content of these sections of the constitution did not change greatly as a result of the debates of the 1890s. In 1897 the national government's authority over naval and military affairs was extended by adding to it 'control of forces to execute and maintain the laws of the Commonwealth.' The reason for this revision is not known. It may have been intended to give the Commonwealth an ability to enforce its own laws internally; on the other hand it may have been designed to avoid the complications of a state militia. If the latter, the amendment was but a clarification of Clause 114 which forbade the states to 'maintain' any naval or military forces without the Federal parliament's consent. On the other hand, the 1897–8 convention weakened the 'external affairs' provision by excising a reference to treaties. This move, as La Nauze has shown, was secretly inspired by the Colonial Office which was a jealous guardian of the imperial prerogatives.[57]

John Quick and Robert Garran, the constitutional lawyers most closely associated with the early history of Australia's fundamental law, have denied that there was any desire to encroach upon the final authority of the British Parliament over imperial foreign policy. They have suggested that imperial legislation and colonial precedent supplied three examples of what 'external affairs' for Australia could be construed to mean. The first was the right to appoint an Australian representative or high commissioner, on the Canadian pattern, to Great Britain. By extension this could be generalized into a power to accredit agents to foreign governments. The

problem. He did not claim that there was an urgent and immediate crisis on Australia's hands. Rather he talked about the changing shape of Australia's future in the region, a future which was as certain as it was undated. Parkes, showman, chameleon, charlatan was more than the sum of his personal weaknesses and policy contradictions.

[57] J. A. La Nauze, *The Making of the Federal Constitution*, Melbourne 1971, pp. 184–5.

exact nature of the Commonwealth's right in this respect came under scrutiny in 1918 when the Australian government wished to send a High Commissioner to the United States. Second, Quick and Garran argued that though Australia had not attained the right to sign treaties independently, nevertheless it could refuse to adhere to British treaties, as in fact all the colonies with the exception of Queensland had done in the case of the Anglo-Japanese commercial treaty of 1894, and they could also ask the British government to negotiate special treaties for them. Third, they considered that 'external affairs' could be considered to include authority over extradition of criminal offenders who had entered Australia from other countries.[58] One may wonder whether the lawyers interpreted accurately the intentions of the constitution-makers. At the least, though, it must be conceded that there was for Australians a tension over 'external affairs' between on the one side the deferential loyalty to the Mother Country and on the other the desire to protect national interests. Under 'external affairs' the Australian founding fathers claimed powers for which there were no precedents in imperial constitutional history. Neither the British North American Act of 1867 nor the Federal Council Act of 1885 had granted such powers to the self-governing colonies. Though the precise origin of the 'external affairs' clause is a mystery, the broad commercial, immigration, defence and diplomatic context out of which it emerged makes it inclusion in the Commonwealth Act comprehensible.

There was no such diffidence in treating 'the relations of the Commonwealth with the islands of the Pacific'. This was a direct expression of Australia's anxiety for security in its own geographical sphere. Its presence in the constitution derived directly from the colonies' diplomatic struggles with the British government in the 1870s and 1880s. The Australasian convention of 1883 had placed this power in the hands of the Federal Council and the imperial parliament, in passing the Federal Council of Australasia Act, had accorded to the Council the right to legislate on Pacific affairs. Again this clause was not altogether self-defining. However, even Quick and Garran, who were professionally cautious in their pronouncements, thought that it might 'mean that the Commonwealth is to enjoy a sphere of commercial and political influence in those islands as far as is not inconsistent with imperial legislation'.[59]

Diplomacy and defence were not at the centre of the national debate which raged around the federal constitution; the squabbles over federal-state relations stole the limelight and consumed the energies of the delegates.[60] However, the relative importance of the factors bringing the colonies to accept political unity cannot be judged from the amount of passion and argument expended on them. The issue of national security, unlike the problems of small versus large states and protection versus free trade, had been determined by a common experience and spoke to an

---

[58] John Quick and Robert Randolph Garran, *The Annotated Constitution of the Australian Commonwealth*, Sydney 1901, pp. 631–6.

[59] Ibid., p. 637.

[60] See the *Official Report of the National Australasian Convention Debates, Sydney, 2 March to 9 April, 1891*, *Official Report of the National Australasian Convention Debates, Adelaide, March 22–May 5, 1897*, Adelaide 1897, and *Official Record of the Australasian Federal Convention, Third Session, Melbourne, January 20—March 17, 1898*, 2 vols, Melbourne 1898.

assured consensus. There was thus little to discuss. In introducing the resolutions setting out the principal conditions of federation at the 1897 national convention, Edmund Barton, Parkes' successor as leader of the federalist movement, passed over that prescribing for federal control of naval and military defence, saying simply that it was 'self-evident'.[61] The 'chief stimulus' to federal union required little explication.

It is perhaps significant that the federalist movement ended as it had begun, in an appeal to unite in the face of external dangers. In the critical month of March 1898, when it seemed that the Victorian government was wavering, Alfred Deakin seized the opportunity of a meeting of the Australian Natives Association to speak with revivalist fervour to his fellow countrymen. In his peroration Deakin pleaded for no further delay. After invoking support for the principles of 'enlightened liberalism' enshrined in the constitution he came to the hard core of his case. He said,

> Let us recognise that we live in an unstable era, and that if we fail in the hour of crisis we may never be able to recall our lost national opportunities. At no period during the first hundred years has the situation of the great Empire to which we belong been more serious. From the far east and the far west alike we behold menaces and contagion. We cannot evade, we must meet them. Hypercriticism cannot help us to outface the future, nor can we hope to if we remain disunited. Happily your voice is for immediate and absolute union.[62]

After this Victoria regained its faith in the cause and though the steps to the final consummation of 1 January 1901, were still crowded with misunderstandings and miscalculations, there was nothing that could not be negotiated. With Victoria's leadership assured in 1898 the movement could not fail.

## Imperial co-operation

Just as the Australians recognized that their external security depended on common colonial policies and actions, so also they acknowledged that their Pacific defence was inextricably bound up with that of the empire as a whole. As part of Greater Britain it was undeniable that their international position must fluctuate with that of the empire at large. Moreover, their deeply-felt British patriotism made it impossible for them to be indifferent to the lot of the Mother Country. However, their responses to the two spheres of involvement were markedly different. Between themselves the colonies perceived an identity of interest and they were willing to submit these common interests to the one federal government. Within the empire on the other hand they steadfastly refused to merge their diplomatic and defence and for that matter trade and immigration interests with those of the wider body. They were eager to gain British assistance in dealing with their own problems, they were prepared to contribute to the cost of strengthening British naval forces stationed in their waters, they were willing to spring to Britain's side in time of

---

[61] *Report of the National Australasian Convention,* 1897, p. 20.

[62] A. Deakin, *Federal Story,* Appendix II, p. 179. The first substantial work on the needs of Australasian defence by an Australian was published in the preceding year and it outlined a darkening future along similar lines. See George Cathcart Graig. *The Federal Defence of Australia,* Sydney 1897.

war. Equally, they refused to take any responsibility for Britain's foreign policy, they would not contribute to the general defence of the empire and they turned down every proposal for an Imperial Council or Imperial Parliament where their voices and interests would be lost in or overborne by the greater voice and interest of Great Britain. Some have argued that the Australians' opposition to these broad imperial schemes reflected a narrow-minded, dependent colonial mentality, others have seen in it parsimony—they wanted their defence on the cheap at others' expense. Though it would be wrong to disregard these factors altogether nevertheless the narrow limit of Australians' concerns were the limits of their national interest and it was evidence of their political leaders' independence that they resisted and defied the demands of the imperial authorities. Further, a cheap defence is the proper goal of every power; it is a mark of able diplomacy when a small nation can without fear of retaliation exploit the world strategy of its great ally to achieve its own security. The reason at bottom for Australian caution was this sense of a conflict of interest, an almost intuitive perception that the British conception of imperial interest did not harmonize with their own.

Consequently, it was London that pressed for closer imperial ties and for contributions to the defence of the empire. In the 1870s the British government had been happy to leave the colonies to build their defences or not as they pleased. In the 1880s world tensions had placed greater burdens on the empire. The 1889 decision to maintain the navy at a 'two power standard' made heavy demands on the British taxpayer and the Admiralty had come to the view that the colonies should contribute to the financing of the expanded fleet. The Franco-Russian alliance after 1892 and the aggressive German policy caused great uneasiness. In 1895 when Joseph Chamberlain became Colonial Secretary in Lord Salisbury's Conservative government there were many who were beginning to think that Britain would have to call upon its daughter nations in the new world to balance the threat from the old. Chamberlain, who was a student of J. R. Seeley's *The Expansion of England*, and Sir Charles Dilke's *Greater Britain*[63] had chosen the Colonial Office, a ministry traditionally lacking in prestige, because he believed that imperial federation would be the salvation of the British race. In his first speech as Colonial Secretary he set forth his faith;

> I am told on every hand that Imperial federation is a vain and empty dream … Dreams of that kind, which have so powerful an influence upon the imagination of men, have somehow or other an unaccountable way of being realized in their own time.[64]

Chamberlain brought a new energy and importance to the Colonial Office.

The successive crises of 1896 with the United States over Venezuela, with the Boers during the Jameson Raid, with the Germans as seen in the Emperor's telegram to President Kruger, all pointed up Britain's perilous position. And in 1897, during the celebrations of the sixtieth anniversary of Queen Victoria's coronation, Chamberlain took the opportunity to meet with the colonial premiers and propose the establishment of free trade within the empire and the

---

[63] J. R. Seeley, *The Expansion of England: Two Courses of Lectures*, London 1883 and 1891; Sir Charles Dilke, *Greater Britain: A Record of Travel in English-Speaking Countries*, 2 vols, London 1868.
[64] *The Times*, 7 November 1895.

formation of an Imperial Council. But the response was disappointing. As with the Admiralty's scheme for colonial grants to the navy and the removal of restrictions on the auxiliary squadron, the Australian colonies saw no merit in the plans. Chamberlain had misread the signs of imperial sentiment which accompanied the grand celebrations. The premier of New South Wales summed up the colonies' attitude very well when he replied that

> the great test of our relations, I submit, will be the next war in which England is engaged… Our money would come; our men would come … that feeling of patriotism, we may call it—it would flame out just as practically in the Colonies, in the hour of danger, as in England; but it is only in those moments that you can make the people one in the sense of sacrifice.[65]

The outbreak of the Boer War in October 1899, gave the imperial federationists fresh heart for the news of hostilities led to an unparalleled outburst of British race feeling throughout the length and breadth of the empire. In Australia offers of help anticipated events. The Queensland government in July offered 250 mounted men with machine guns. After war was declared the other colonies hastened to follow the Queensland example.[66] Three hundred thousand people turned out in Sydney to farewell the second New South Wales contingent[67] and similar crowds attested their loyalty in the other major cities. No such expression of mass emotion had ever before been seen in Australian history. After the news reached Australia of the British reverses, suffered in Black Week, 11 to 15 December 1899, criticism became muted and, excepting a few strong-minded individuals, was almost silenced. For public men to oppose the Boer War or even Australian assistance to the Mother Country was to court political suicide. By the end of the war in 1902, Australia had sent 16,463 men, 10,000 supported from Australian taxes, to fight in the cause of empire.

The response of the British-settled colonies was so overwhelming that Chamberlain, impressed by this great testimony to patriotic sentiment, determined to try again to tighten the links of empire.[68] In early March 1900, the Colonial Secretary asked the self-governing colonies whether, in view of their part in the imperial war effort, they would like to be consulted about peace terms and whether they would support the setting up of a permanent imperial council to co-ordinate the defence policies of the far-flung dominions of the Crown. Chamberlain had always understood that imperial unity could not be built on sentiment alone. He recognized that a sense of common interest would have to underpin any successful venture in that direction. In 1897 he had thought to find this in an imperial *zollverein* or common market but in 1900 as a result of the war he now placed his hopes on defence. Chamberlain wrote to the New South Wales governor.

---

[65] Co Confidential Print, Misc. No. 111, Report of 1897 Conference, pp. 107–8, CP 103/12/1.

[66] Great Britain, *Parliamentary Papers*, 1900 session, Vol. LVI, Cd. 18, 'Correspondence relating to the despatch of Colonial Military Contingents to South Africa, November, 1899'.

[67] *SMH*, 18 January 1900.

[68] Richard H. Wilde, 'Joseph Chamberlain's Proposal for an Imperial Council in March, 1900', *Canadian Historical Review*, XXXVII, September 1956, 225–7.

> It seems to me that the time has come when the defence of the Empire, and its military and naval resources, have become the common concern of the whole Empire and not of the Mother Country alone, and that joint action, or at least joint consideration with regard to this subject should be organised on a permanent footing.[69]

Though Chamberlain at first envisaged only an advisory body, nevertheless he anticipated that a more effective and integrated institution would emerge from such a small beginning. This tentative approach might seem harmless enough but it was an explosive issue. If colonies accepted responsibility for peace terms then it might be implied that they were accepting a continuing responsibility for British policy in South Africa; and similarly if they accepted representation on an imperial council charged with broad defence functions they might find themselves with an obligation to defend all of the empire under all circumstances.

The colonies were not to know that in fact the consultation over South Africa offered by the Colonial Secretary was purely nominal. Chamberlain had told the Canadian governor-general in the very message which contained his request that the British government had already decided to annex the two Boer Republics and 'after an interval' convert them into self-governing colonies.[70] However, the Australians had no wish to share in the responsibility. They had rallied to the empire not because Australian vital interests were at stake but simply out of patriotic fervour. Thus they were not as interested in the peace terms as they would have been had it been a Pacific war. Yet they were flattered by the invitation and in order to strengthen the imperial government's hand in pressing for British supremacy in South Africa,[71] the Australian colonies sent a joint note to Chamberlain supporting annexation of the republics. On the question of continuous consultation there was considerable hesitation and in the event it was ignored. As for the Imperial Council proposal there is no record of any Australian reply. Perhaps the colonial governments felt that since they were on the threshold of federation it was inappropriate to prejudge the issue. Probably Edmund Barton of New South Wales spoke for Australia when at a British Empire League dinner in London on 30 April he declared that

> it would be dangerous to formulate proposals which acted too strongly as obligations and which left, perhaps, less play for a feeling of common patriotism. … It might be as they [the Australians] went on they would have to ask the question, which the premier of Canada asked, whether on all occasions and in all circumstances they were ready to render their assistance in the quarrels of the Empire. They might possibly some day make the answer, if they were to do that, if they were to share the responsibility, they must have some

---

[69] See Chamberlain to Lord Minto, Governor-General of Canada, 2 March 1900, the Minto Papers, XIV, 56, Public Archives of Canada, cited in Wilde, 'Joseph Chamberlain's Proposal …', pp. 227–8. See also Chamberlain to Lord Beauchamp, Governor of New South Wales, 5 March 1900, cited in J. L. Garvin and J. Amery, *Life of Joseph Chamberlain*, 6 vols, London 1932–68, Vol. III, pp. 629–30.

[70] Wilde, 'Joseph Chamberlain's Proposal …', p. 227.

[71] Beauchamp to Chamberlain, 27 March 1900, NSW Treasury Papers, In-letters 00/4199, cited in Melhuish, *Australian and British Imperial Policy*, p. 614.

representation. ... But he was free to admit that ... the general opinion in Australia was that the time had not yet come for anything of the sort to be formulated.[72]

Chamberlain saw Australian federation in the same light that he had seen Canadian federation, as a move towards the greater imperial federation. After the colonial premiers had petitioned the imperial parliament to pass an act establishing the Commonwealth of Australia, Chamberlain had written Barton that federation would 'greatly facilitate the task of rendering the whole force of that "complete union of the British Empire" more readily available and more effective for the defence of its common interests'.[73] After the Colonial Office and Law Office had reported on the proposed bill, he began to have some reservations. The technocrats had thought that the claim to 'external affairs' threatened to infringe on imperial prerogative but their greatest objection centred on the nullification of the right of appeal to the Privy Council in Section 74. A truly imperial court of appeal was one further item on Chamberlain's agenda for developing unity between the Mother Country and the self-governing colonies and he fought the Australian delegation, Barton, Deakin, Kingston, Dickson of Queensland and Sir Philip Fysh of Tasmania, with even more than his customary zeal, to obtain a revision. Barton, Deakin and Kingston stood firm and the most they would concede was that the Australian High Court should be granted a discretionary right to determine whether appeals to the London body should be allowed or not. The imperial federationists had to make do with this.

In introducing the bill into the House of Commons, Chamberlain asserted that by agreeing to Australian wishes they would not divest themselves of the 'powers entrusted to the Imperial parliament and government for the protection of these common interests and the common discharge of these common duties which form the peculiar sphere of the central authority of the empire'.[74] Yet, though formally this was true, though formally the Australian Commonwealth constitution did not revoke the Colonial Laws Validity Act which protected the Crown's reserved powers from local trespass, though the constitution did not directly challenge imperial authority in the sphere of foreign policy, though it did not seek to break up the unity of empire in confronting the outside world, nevertheless, it did represent a defeat for Chamberlain's brand of imperialism and a triumph for the Barton-Deakin brand of nationalism. It codified the inroads made by the colonies into imperial preserves during the nineteenth century and in defence, external affairs and particularly in Pacific relations it adumbrated the future. The Australians at the end of century welcomed increased imperial co-operation through the voluntary, consultative Colonial Conference, as had been shown in 1887 and 1897. They also welcomed bilateral co-operation in matters concerning Pacific defence and diplomacy. On the other hand they had turned their face against anything that smacked of an imperial executive. They had come to recognize that there was a fundamental conflict of view over priorities in defence and diplomacy between the colonies and the Mother Country. Australians in looking to their own were unwilling to be sacrificed for a greater interest with which they could not fully identify and which they did

---

[72] *The Times*, 1 May 1900.
[73] Letter, Chamberlain to Barton, 8 February 1900, Barton Papers, 51/1/381.
[74] Great Britain, 4 *Hansard's Parliamentary Debates*, LXXXIII, 71, 14 May 1900.

not wholly share. It was in response to such a predicament that Sir Patrick Jennings, while supporting the sending of a contingent to Khartoum in 1885, proclaimed that the colonies had reached a stage in their development where they 'had been brought to entertain a foreign policy' of their own with regard to New Guinea, the New Hebrides and French transportation in the Pacific.[75] Such a proclamation was to become the watchword in the evolution of Australia's distinctive defence and foreign policy.

---

[75] *SMH*, 21 February 1885.

# 3
# Between Two Worlds: An Uncertain Beginning, 1901–5

The nation was born while the empire was at war. Australia became a federated commonwealth at a time of great trial for the Mother Country. The Boer War brought to an end an almost century-long era of peace in isolation, under cover of which the British Empire had extended its sway to include one-sixth of the globe's surface and population. The Boer War finally broke the spell of easeful self confidence and providential progress, which had hovered over Victorian England. Untrained, ill-educated, poorly-equipped, Afrikaans-speaking farmers for three years kept at bay the flower of the British army. The war thus became a strain on Britain's physical and psychological resources. Moreover, the European nations, which had in the preceding two decades grown powerful and envious, organized and ambitious, took the opportunity to press their advantage at Britain's expense in the Near East and the Far East. It even briefly seemed possible that the continental countries might sink their differences and unite to pull down the mighty empire from its seat. The British leaders, looking across the English Channel at Europe, felt the limits and dangers of their isolation, and, looking outward at the immense sweep of their domains, they felt the weight of the responsibility they had assumed.[1] In the immediate aftermath of the South African peace settlement, Joseph Chamberlain expressed this feeling well when at the opening ceremony of the Colonial Conference, he told the delegates, 'The Weary Titan staggers under the too vast orb of its fate' and called on the Greater Britain beyond the sea to throw its men and money into the scale in order to help preserve the whole empire from its enemies.[2]

This was the imperial background against which the first Commonwealth government and parliament had to formulate a defence and Pacific policy. They did show some concern for these new developments and in the debates over defence and foreign affairs, the fear of Russian, German, and French raids on Australian commerce and coasts which had been present since the 1870s and the more ominous apprehension of Japan and an 'awakening' China which had begun to surface in the 1890s, were often placed in that context. However, overall, neither the Australian government nor parliament were directly affected by this crisis of empire. Defence debates were not informed by a sense of urgency, the initial defence act provided for a bargain basement army, which was limited in its operation to Australian territories. Though under the naval agreement of 1903 the Commonwealth did increase its subsidy to the Australian squadron from £106,000 to £200,000 and did allow the squadron to be despatched wherever in the Pacific the Admiralty

---

[1] George W. Monger, *The End of Isolation: British Foreign Policy,* 1900–1907, London 1963, pp. 1–20.
[2] CofA, *Parliamentary Papers*, 1903 session, Vol. II, No. 2. 'Papers Relating to a Conference between the Secretary of State for the Colonies and the Prime Ministers of the Self-Governing Colonies, June to August, 1902', p. 6.

thought fit, consent was only grudgingly given. Personal, national, political and strategic factors, all helped shape the Australian response to Britain's call of distress and appeal for aid.

The first federal ministry, which was commissioned on 1 January 1901, was composed of a representative group of eminent and experienced politicians drawn from the several colonies. Of the ten ministers the three most concerned with defence and foreign affairs were Edmund Barton, the prime minister who had taken the portfolio of external affairs, Alfred Deakin, the attorney-general, who had been Barton's closest associate in the federation movement and Sir John Forrest, the Western Australia explorer and premier, who almost by default became minister for defence. Neither Barton nor Forrest had evinced any prior interest in those questions. They were novices in the field and as such tended, either, as in Barton's case, to adjust their tack to every political draught or, as in Forrest's, to submit to Imperial authority. Deakin whose official duties, except when he was acting prime minister, touched least on these questions, had had a deep and continuing interest in these subjects. Though he felt strongly about them and tried to influence the government's attitude on them, he respected his colleague's ministerial prerogatives and went along with their decisions.[3]

The Barton government had to contend with many difficulties in approaching the questions of defence and external policy. Firstly they had to create in the mind of their fellow countrymen the legitimacy of their national purpose. The Australian colonies had lurched hesitantly, if at last definitively, toward federation. The federal movement had attracted solid and persistent support but it had never inspired great public enthusiasm. Despite the heat of the debate a smaller proportion of eligible voters took part in the Commonwealth constitutional referenda than in normal colonial elections. The Boer War evoked a larger and more spontaneous outburst of feeling than the ceremonies marking the proclamation of the Commonwealth or the opening of the first parliament. Over 300,000 people cheered the second South African contingent from New South Wales on its way as it marched through Sydney streets on 17 January 1900.[4] Even with elaborate plans and preparations, only 100,000 to 200,000 Sydneysiders turned out to applaud the founding of the nation on 1 January 1901.[5] In Melbourne, after the firing of a 101 gun salute, the

---

[3] Writing for the *Morning Post* on 3 February, Deakin summarized what purported to be Barton's speech to the ANA on 27 January. In that speech he reported Barton as saying that the government's 'faith is pinned to a naval policy of harbour and coastal defence by means of a local flotilla and a military policy of universal training.' *MP*, 16 March 1901. Yet the Australian press does not record Barton proclaiming such a defence policy, either then or subsequently. *Age*, 28 January 1901. Indeed, in his campaign for the first Federal election, Barton studiously adopted a vague stand on defence issues. At the ANA banquet on 11 February he said that apart from maintaining a small nucleus of a permanent force, 'the defence system would be a volunteer one. That was not saying much—because the whole thing depended in the first place upon what would commend itself to the Federal Defence Minister.' *Age*, 12 February 1901. Probably Deakin thought that he had managed to commit Barton to such a proposal but when his ANA speech was postponed, Barton had a chance for further thought and decided indecision was the best course.

[4] *SMH*, 18 January 1901.

[5] *SMH*, 2 January 1901 and *DT*, 2 January 1901.

worthy citizens retired to the beach.[6] In Deniliquin, following a monster picnic, children were presented with Mafeking medals.[7] No people ever assumed the mantle of nationhood with less sense of occasion, with less puffing of their own distinctive identity; virtue in history often comes wrapped in strange packages. Barton did little to help clarify Australians' thought and feeling on the relation between nation and empire. Responding to the mood of the moment he declared in his policy speech that Australia would not avoid its share of imperial defence; 'whatever we expect the Empire to render to us in the way of assistance for defence, we shall be ready and willing to render to the Empire in return'.[8] Yet in fact, apart from a marginal increase in the contributions for the Australian squadron, Barton's government rejected all imperial proposals, such as an imperial reserve, and legislation permitting the Commonwealth government to send the Australian army overseas in time of war. Barton was never able to state, in clear national terms, the basis for defence policy.

In formulating their policy, the Commonwealth government was influenced more by the constitutional and political realities than any other factor. Defence was a drain on the treasury. Under section 87 of the constitution, the so-called Braddon clause required that in the first ten years of federation three-quarters of Commonwealth revenue from customs and excise, the main source of federal funds, be returned to the states. In practical terms the Commonwealth, unless it resorted to extraordinary measures, would have little to spend on defence. The political restraints on the ministry were even more daunting. Barton had been invited to form his government not because he commanded majority support in a Commonwealth parliament but because of his role in the federal movement. The problems facing the national leaders in trying to achieve that necessary basis for parliamentary government were enormous. The party system in the states themselves were only in a rudimentary stage of development. For Commonwealth purposes, that is in order to try and create a parliamentary basis for government and to give voters sensible choices, inter-states alliances were formed. But platforms were flexible and individual loyalties fluid. In the elections of 29 March 1901 the Barton ministry, united chiefly by their protective tariff programme failed to gain a majority in either house. Neither of the other two identifiable groups, the Labor party or the free-traders, could govern by themselves, and so the Barton ministry had to survive by bargain and compromise. The first parliament was the most open in the history of the Commonwealth. Party discipline was loose. The protectionist and free-trade parties, which agreed among themselves on tariff measures were often divided on social and defence issues, while the Labor party, which was united on social and industrial matters, divided on tariff and defence. In this uncertain state of affairs the government was unable to act with decision and despatch. Most fundamental policies had to be sorted out on an experimental basis. The government had to discover by trial and error what parliament would tolerate. And this was probably more true in defence than in any other field. The government, in announcing its policy on 10 May at the opening of parliament simply said that

---

[6] *Age*, 2 January 1901.

[7] Ibid.

[8] *SMH*, 8 February 1901; also *Age*, 8 and 15 February 1901.

as soon possible … measures would be taken for the judicious strengthening of the defence of the Commonwealth. Extravagant expenditure will be avoided and reliance will be placed to the fullest reasonable extent on our citizen soldiery.[9]

## Theory and threat: the parliamentary debate

The parliamentary debates over the South African War, the Pacific Islands, trade, immigration and most notably defence provide the best guide to understanding the collective mind which shaped Australian defence and foreign policy in this period. Since the first parliament also contained among its members all seven prime ministers and ten defence ministers who held office down to February 1923 the debate is also valuable in giving the background out of which emerged Australia's external policies in the generation of the founding fathers. The debates cannot be neatly tabulated and summarized. The speeches were often complex containing contrary and countervailing elements; individuals in succeeding debates took different stands. Depth of knowledge and feeling has to be taken into account, motive and meaning explored before a proper picture can be attempted.

Only two members of parliament, William Morris Hughes, the Labor member for West Sydney and Henry Bournes Higgins, the radical protectionist member for North Melbourne,[10] produced consistent and cohesive philosophies of international relations. They were both strong-minded individuals who were willing to court unpopularity and opprobrium in order to defend the political and moral judgements which they deduced from their general theories. They took up the cudgels on behalf of two very different world views. Hughes who had been fostered out to relatives at the age of seven and who had early in life been forced to fend for himself took a harshly realistic position;[11] Higgins, the son of a clergyman, who had been brought up in a stern but sheltered family environment and who had proceeded to his legal career by orderly, foreordained steps, held, in contrast, a progressive, optimistic and moralistic outlook.[12]

Higgins was an Australian inheritor of the Gladstonian liberal tradition. His contemporary exemplars were, among others, John Morley and John Burns.[13] His was a world of moral principle and individual conscience. While inveighing against the clauses in the 1903 draft Defence Bill which would have permitted the government to send its regular soldiers to fight outside Australia, he asserted that 'We do not want our men to join in an opium war. We do not want our men to be dragged into a war that may be against their conscience.' A sceptic, wishing to bring the issue

---

[9] *CPD*, 1901–2 session, I, 29, 10 May 1901.

[10] Higgins, who had lost his Geelong seat in the Victorian legislative assembly because of his opposition to the Boer War, had been elected to the federal parliament with the help of the Labor party. The Labor party decided not to run a candidate against him because he had accepted the party's platform 'as applied to federal politics'. *Age*, 8 February 1901.

[11] L. F. Fitzhardinge, *William Morris Hughes: A Political Biography*, Sydney 1964, Vol. I, 'That Fiery Particle', Chapters I and II.

[12] Nettie Palmer, *Henry Bournes Higgins: A Memoir*, London 1931, Chapters 1 to 8, esp. pp. 6, 7 and 62.

[13] *CPD*, 1901–2 session, VII, 8757, 14 January 1902.

down to what he considered a matter-of-fact level, interjected, 'Do soldiers usually consider the rights and wrongs of a war', and 'Higgins rejoined, 'If they do not they ought to do so'.[14] He denounced militarism and jingoism. In criticizing the first Defence Bill he stated that

> Our fathers came to Australia largely with a view to getting rid of burdens and dangers of war which have oppressed the people of Europe for so many years and we should be giving up the best part of our heritage in Australia, if, remote therefore from the centres of excitement we were to start a military system in grotesque imitation of the military system on the continent of Europe… We must keep this country from the ghastly bane of militarism.

He believed that Britain's naval supremacy and Australia's remoteness gave Australia security and meant that 'For many years there is no need to make much of the military system of Australia.'[15] With the lessons of the 'Glorious Revolution' of 1688 in mind, he thought that Australia should rely primarily on the navy for its defence and maintain only a skeleton military force.[16] Higgins was one of the very few who appealed to a 'New World' 'escape' vision and this isolationist argument would seem to run counter to other strands in his thought, his pride in British nationality and his faith in international arbitration.

In answer to those who impugned his patriotism, he declared that should Britain be attacked, he would be among the first to spring to its defence and he did not doubt that Australia would 'spend every man and every shilling' in the imperial cause, a phrase which Andrew Fisher, when faced with this eventuality, was to invoke at Colac on 31 July 1914. Higgins affirmed a deep affection for and attachment to the Mother Country. This loyalty, however, was not prompted by the herd instinct or the call of blood but by Britain's record in promoting 'civilization' and 'liberty'. 'No empire in the history of the world', he said, 'has done so much for civilization and for liberty as has the British Empire'. He set forth a condensed but classical Whig history of British foreign policy. England had been 'friend of the oppressed and foe to the oppressor'. It had led in the struggle against slavery, had given encouragement to Kossuth and Garibaldi in their fight for national independence and had similarly aided Belgium and Poland. It had deviated from the highest standards at the time of the American and French revolutions and had betrayed its principles by prosecuting the Opium War and participating in the Crimean War. But always the true voice of the nation, in the persons of Chatham, Fox, Burke, James Graham and John Bright had spoken out against these aberrations and ultimately their judgement had been accepted. Gladstone had successfully fought the good fight against the jingoes of the 1880s. In Higgins' view the pity of their own times was that they had not thrown up a Gladstone who could, like the prophets of old, bring the people back from the worship of idols. The nation had been misled and inflamed into supporting the Boer War by the 'yellow' press. But Higgins believed that the people would come to their senses and, with popular backing, democracy and morality would be reconciled.[17] Higgins was a child of the eighteenth-century Enlightenment, at least of that utopian

---

[14] *CPD*, 1903 session, XIV, 2534, 23 July 1903.

[15] *CPD*, 1901–2 session, III, 2990–1, 24 July 1901.

[16] *CPD*, 1903 session, XIV, 1999, 9 July 1903.

[17] *CPD*, 1901–2 session, VII, 8757, 14 January 1902.

strand in Enlightenment thought which considered that when popular rule was informed by reason, harmony and happiness would prevail in state and society. He believed that there was a simple set of liberal moral tenets which could and should govern world politics and that the spread of democracy and education meant the increasing adoption of these principles and ultimately the emergence of a new era in international relations where conflict would be settled by peaceful means and war become a thing of the past.[18]

Hughes promulgated a very different doctrine. He perceived a very different world. Unlike Higgins, Hughes owed more to Hobbes than Locke, to nineteenth-century Social Darwinism than to the eighteenth-century Enlightenment. Hughes' ideas however cannot, like Higgins', be so easily type-cast; there was much more about Hughes' philosophy, as about his personality, which was original. Hughes, like Higgins, was concerned for democracy and liberty, but he differed with Higgins as to the basis on which they were grounded, the dangers which threatened them and the conditions necessary for their survival. Whereas Higgins had started from the assumption that since democracy was based on consent, it could be equated with self-reliance, stability and harmony, Hughes on the other hand, considered that democracy, just because it was self-government, was the most fragile form of government, the most subject to self-indulgence, anarchy and decadence, the most prone to be overthrown by despotism. Whereas Higgins saw the Boer War as an aberration, a transitory interruption in a world moving towards peace and morality, Hughes, while paying lip service to the utopian socialist and liberal visions of many in the Labor party, saw such dreams being achieved only in some far-off future time. In the interim, it was necessary to deal with the world as it was, to see international relations as a competition for survival and that meant taking the possibility of war very seriously. Where Higgins, reaching toward the reality which Hughes took as the rule, agreed that, if threatened, a democracy had to defend itself, Hughes considered that the strong and permanent defence forces which were necessary to provide against the normal emergencies of world politics had to have a democratic or even socialist character, lest they become the tool of a military despot. Where Higgins feared the effects of state power, especially military power on individual liberty, Hughes felt that an impotent state would expose the nation to internal and external subversion and that strong government imposing order in a democratic manner could extend and enhance the meaning of democracy in civil as in social and industrial fields. Hughes, if he did not believe that man had 'to be forced to be free', did seem to hold that man had to be compelled to defend and even to extend that freedom.

Hughes, too, argued his case from history. 'If there is any light by which we are to guide the infant footsteps of our nation, it is by the teaching of history.'[19] In contrast to the liberal Whig assumption that democracy was 'the culminating effect of mankind', he claimed that history showed there was no form of government, 'so unstable … so evanescent as democracy'.

---

[18] The League of Nations Covenant and the Kellogg-Briand Pact were grist to his mill. Of the latter he wrote, 'The Pact is a definite declaration against war. It is a definite international covenant. There has been nothing like it in all the history of the world', Palmer, *Henry Bournes Higgins*, p. 227.

[19] *CPD*, 1901–2 session, III, 3296, 31 July 1901.

Democracy was like a triangle turned upside down on its apex. From classical Greece to the French republic democracies had 'abandoned the care of [their] territories, and [their] country and then [they] have gone down'. Louis Napoleon's *coup d'état* in 1851 even illustrated how the 'People can will a dictatorship. It is through the medium, and by the shibboleths of democracy that liberty is stolen from democracy.'[20]

When Higgins pointed to the United States, as an example of an enduring republic and as the cynosure of the future, Hughes, unwilling to be deflected from his goal, dismissed America as a violent and unequal society. Hughes contended that democracies suffered from their virtues. They lacked the order and discipline which were necessary preconditions for the survival of any form of government. Under self-government people opted for the easy choice. When faced with external threats, they brought in mercenaries to fight their wars and this often precipitated the downfall of democracy. To avert such a calamity, Hughes, in 1901 and again in 1903 and 1906, urged that the Commonwealth should adopt compulsory military training for its able-bodied citizens. He further maintained that by this means they would also 'counter the curse of larrikinism'.[21] 'Our people', Hughes said, 'should be taught obedience which is a primary virtue, and an essential of citizenship in a free state.'[22]

Hughes' sense of insecurity in the world followed from his Hobbesian view that international relations was a war of each against all in which the weakest went to the wall.[23] In looking out from the island-continent in 1901 and 1903 he was unable to point to a clear and present danger to the Commonwealth. However, he saw many possible, if not precise, dangers emanating from Europe and Asia and he refused, unlike all other Australian leaders until 1905, to rule out invasion as a contingency against which the Commonwealth ought to arm itself. Neither the isolation of Australia nor the pre-eminence of the British navy could be counted upon with certainty. Should the British navy suffer a set-back or be withdrawn from the Pacific, and these for him were not outlandish hypotheses given the relative decline in the British fleet's superiority over all other navies in the preceding decade, then Australia's isolation would make it the most vulnerable part of the British Empire.[24] He did not believe with Higgins that because of the citizens' pride in self-government, one could rely for defence on spontaneous offers to serve in time of trouble. Paraphrasing Tom Paine's Crisis Paper of 1778, he explained that 'the volunteer is very like snow in summer. He melts away when the glamour and novelty of the thing have worn off, when he

---

[20] *CPD*, 1906 session, XXXIII, 2587, 9 August 1906.

[21] *CPD*, 1903 session, XV, 3094, 23 July 1903. Chris Watson, the leader of the parliamentary Labor party had some sympathy with Hughes' intention but Andrew Fisher, who became the deputy leader in 1905 and leader in 1907, joined Joseph Cook of the Free Trade Party in denying that 'larrikinism' was a serious problem in Australia.

[22] *CPD*, 1906 session, XXXVI, 2587, 9 August 1906.

[23] This assumption was expressed most bluntly at the laying of the foundation stone of the national capital, Canberra, on 12 March 1913. See *SMH*, 13 March 1913.

[24] *CPD*, 1901–2 session, III 3294–5, 31 July 1901; *CPD*, 1906 session, XXXIII, 2580–7, 9 August 1906.

realizes… a good deal of hard work is to be done.'[25] Hence, Hughes argued the necessity of compulsory training. For Hughes it was simply a prudent measure in an uncertain and unpredictable world. In promoting such a measure, he denied that parliament would be doing anything more than exercising its inherent rights for 'every Government has, by the nature of government, the power to call out its citizens in defence of the country.'[26]

Hughes was at pains to show that what he proposed was neither militarism after the fashion of continental Europe nor contrary to liberal and socialist thought. He proposed neither to militarize the nation under a caste system nor to create a standing army which could overrule or overthrow parliamentary government. Rather, he sought to raise a *levée en masse*, a citizen army on the democratic Swiss model, in which, for a limited period each year, all youths and adult males were trained alongside their neighbours to defend their country.[27] Charges that such a system ran counter to the English liberal tradition he dismissed as sentimental sloganeering, which set aside the dictates of common sense. Quoting from John Stuart Mill's *On Liberty*, he asserted that it was 'an essential to citizenship and not inconsistent with liberty that men be forced to defend their countries'. Compulsion was not incompatible either with democracy or socialism. All children were compelled to attend school and in New South Wales the state required that the parties to an industrial dispute submit their differences to arbitration. Moreover, distinguished socialists such as August Bebel, the German Social Democratic leader, had advocated this scheme and the 1896 International Socialist Congress had adopted the replacing of standing armies with citizen defence forces as the first plank on its platform.[28] Hughes concluded that such a defence system would, moreover,

> kill the jingo spirit, the cheap patriotism which makes men throw up their hats and sing patriotic songs… Men who have to fight their own quarrels will be very careful about entering into wars.[29]

---

[25] *CPD*, 1901–2 session, III, 3294, 31 July 1901.

[26] Ibid., 3292.

[27] Ibid., 3396.

[28] Hughes read rather too much into Mill. Mill concedes that there are 'many positive acts which he (the citizen) may be rightfully compelled to perform', including requiring him 'to bear his fair share of the common defence'. Or again he allows that each individual was obliged to accept 'his share … of the labour and sacrifices incurred for defending the society'. J. S. Mill, *On Liberty, Representative Government, The Subjection of Women: Three Essays*, London 1912, pp. 16, 92. Mill did not say anything about forcing men to submit to compulsory military service in peacetime. On Bebel and the Second International, Hughes was more accurate. The 1891 Erfurt Programme of the German Social Democratic Party had adopted universal military education. The substitution of militia for a standing army was the third plank on its platform. (*Manifesto of the Social Democratic Party in the German Empire*, Melbourne Fabian Society, Melbourne 1896, p. 5). The 1889 Congress of the Second International called for the replacement of standing armies with a popular militia and each successive congress down to 1914 endorsed this position. (Julius Braunthal, *History of the International*, 1864–1914, translated by Henry Collins and Kenneth Mitchell, London 1966, p. 325).

[29] *CPD*, 1906 session, XXXIII, 2587–92, 9 August 1906.

Hughes, like the great majority of the Labor party, shared in the British radical liberal tradition and, like most Labor men in the early days of the Boer War, he had opposed sending contingents to fight in South Africa. Hughes criticized the war for being contrary to all that was best in the 'noble tradition of the British race' and, in answer to Barton's call for support for 'the empire, right or wrong', he invoked the names of all the Whig heroes from Chatham and Burke to Bright and Gladstone, appealed to principle and to conscience, and hinted that the causes of the quarrel could be traced to the interests of the great mining syndicates. However, he allowed that

> If it came to this, that we are to choose between one nation and another, we shall never hesitate as to what nation we shall give our allegiance, whether right or wrong, when it is in the last extremity. I join with those who say that when the die is cast, when two nations— ourselves and any others—are engaged in a life and death struggle, it is not the party of any citizen of either of those nations to enquire, 'Why I am fighting?' but to fight.[30]

After 'Black Week' in December, Hughes, perceiving the empire to be in danger, swallowed his scruples and voted for the despatch of reinforcements. When the issue came before the Commonwealth parliament in January 1902, Hughes was paired as an aye vote in support of a resolution to grant 'all requisite aid to the Mother Country'.[31] It had not taken a great deal to overcome Hughes' qualms of conscience. He did, however, have the decency not to become a vocal 'hawk'. Though he voted for the contingents, he left the war oratory to others. In his approach to defence and foreign policy, Hughes was preoccupied with national power and obsessed with social order and as early as the first parliament, the elements which were to inform his authoritarian style of leadership in World War I had become apparent. As the first decade wore on, events conspired to justify Hughes' realism and all parties came to accept the necessity of a citizen army and a Commonwealth navy. While Hughes' influence grew correspondingly, Higgins, becoming politically isolated, gladly accepted a seat on the High Court. After Hughes became prime minister in World War I, the clash of philosophy was brought into the open. Higgins used his position to try and protect industrial and individual liberty against the extreme claims of Hughes' warfare state.[32] But it was Hughes' view that predominated; it was Hughes who dictated the tone and texture of Australian politics and policies during the war and immediate post-war years.

The debates on defence in the first parliament, however, generally lacked the broad compass and inner coherence of Hughes' and Higgins' speeches. Most members agreed that defence, along with trade and immigration, had been one of the most important causes of federation and indeed the defence debates reflecting this judgement were among the most extensive. Forty-three out of seventy-five members addressed themselves to the subject. On two general points, arising out of the experience of the colonial era, there was a consensus of views. Firstly, despite the

---

[30] NSW, 1 *Parliamentary Debates*, 1899 session, C, 1428–36, 16 October 1899.
[31] *CPD*, 1901–2 session, VII, 8800, 14 January 1902.
[32] G. Sawer, *Australian Federal Politics and Laws*, 1901–1929, Melbourne 1956, pp. 178, 198–9.

overwhelming support for the imperial cause in the Boer War[33] the great majority of the participants in the debates spoke against merging the Commonwealth defence forces in an imperial organization or subjecting them in any way to imperial control. Though they would come to the assistance of the Mother Country in its hour of need, they were adamant that Australia's defence policy, in peacetime, should be exclusively concerned with protecting Commonwealth territories and interests.[34] Secondly, the parliamentarians made it clear that they had grasped the importance of the relationship between Australia's geographical position and its defence policy. Yet, while the relationship was noted, there were considerable differences over whether isolation implied security or vulnerability, and if vulnerability, whether the main danger came from European or Asian powers. No one felt there was a pressing threat or the likelihood of an invasion. Australians still trusted in the British navy and this trust was often an unstated assumption in the arguments presented in parliament. For this reason the debates lacked a sense of urgency and the most common piece of practical advice offered the policy-makers was a drastic reduction in defence expenditure. Yet, more than half the speakers spoke with some apprehension of the immediate future and a few painted a very grim picture of the distant prospect.

The Boer War had exacerbated those anxieties about Russian, French, German, Japanese and even Chinese ambitions in the Pacific, which had taken root in the colonial period. Following the great powers' intervention in China during the Boxer Rebellion, the opinion grew that 'the storm centre' of world politics was shifting to the Pacific.[35] Some alarmists were vague and unconvincing. George Reid, who possessed a genius for standing on both sides of issues, asserted that Australia was 'confronted with mighty risks' without defining them, while concluding that national defence could well be left to a volunteer militia.[36] His deputy, Sir William McMillan, representing Wentworth in New South Wales thought that Australians were living through 'the most dangerous period' of their existence but believed nevertheless that the Commonwealth would have to rely upon the British navy for its defence.[37] Hughes, while not wishing to rule out altogether the possibility of an Asian invasion, nevertheless considered that, as a result of the Boer War and Boxer Rebellion, the major threat to Australia came from a coalition of European

---

[33] In January 1902, parliament passed resolutions denouncing charges of inhumanity against British authorities in South Africa and promising 'all requisite aid to the Mother Country'. The first passed both house without dissent and the second passed the House of Representatives forty-five votes to five and the Senate on the voices. The five nay-sayers were Higgins and four Labor men: F. W. Bamford (Herbert, Queensland), the Rev. J. B. Ronald (South Melbourne), J. Thomas (Barrier, NSW), and C. McDonald (Kennedy, Queensland). Hugh Mahon (ALP, Coolgardie, W.A.) was paired against the resolution and Andrew Fisher abstained. *CPD*, 1901–2 session, VII, 8738–800, 14 January 1902 and 9002–30, 22 January 1902.

[34] Those who spoke to this end included George Reid, the leader of the free trade opposition party, *CPD*, 1901–2 session, III, 3102, 26 July 1901 and J. C. Watson, the leader of the Labor party, ibid., III, 2991, 24 July 1901.

[35] *CPD*, 1901–2 session, III, 2989, 24 July 1901.

[36] Ibid., III, 3102, 26 July 1901.

[37] Ibid., III, 3299, 31 July 1901.

powers.[38] A. C. Groom, a free-trader from Queensland, feared that if the continental nations seized the opportunity provided by the Boer War to attack the British Empire, then French, Russian and German cruisers might cause havoc in Australian ports and to Australian trade.[39]

Following the 1902 Colonial Conference at which the Admiralty presented a memorandum demonstrating the growing concentration of French and Russian naval forces in the Far East, the spokesmen for the Commonwealth government and a number of other parliamentarians saw in this development the main threat to Australia. By 1903, against the emerging pattern of Britain's foreign policy, Anglo-Russian tensions in India and the Far East, the Anglo-Japanese alliance of 1902, which was directed against Russian pressure in Manchuria and China, and the beginning of discussion aimed at an Anglo-French detente, this group had come especially to focus its fears on Russia. Barton, in justifying the naval agreement agreed to at the 1902 conference, cited the Admiralty's paper showing that France was strengthening its naval forces in the Far East and that Russia had 'a mighty fleet' of sixty-nine vessels off the coast of China. He considered the latter 'a menacing possibility'.[40] This was echoed by Forrest[41] and other members of the House of Representatives, including Hughes,[42] N. Cameron from Tasmania,[43] A. Poynton from South Australia,[44] G. B. Edwards of South Sydney, W. Knox, representing Kooyong in Victoria, and T. Brown, a New South Wales Labor member.[45] Henry Willis, a New South Wales free-trader also saw the chief threat to Australia coming from a European power, but he feared Germany more than Russia or France. He was concerned that a German-Dutch alliance might give Germany control over the Dutch-East Indies.[46] Senator R. O'Connor, vice-president of the executive council, in presenting the naval agreement to the Senate, gave a similar rationale for Australian naval policy. He not only mentioned the increasing intervention of European powers in the Far East but also referred to the advances made by Japan. He thought that the British Empire might be drawn into war as a result of a Russo-Japanese quarrel. However, the principal danger to Australia arising out of such an eventuality would be 'the interruption of our trade'. Senator E. D. Millen, a leading free-trade representative from New South Wales and Senator G. F. Pearce, a Labor senator from Western Australia, agreed about the pre-eminence of the Russian threat.[47] Pearce's acceptance of the European threat was curious since, in 1901, in his first statement on Australia and the world, he had declared that there was 'a greater fear of foreign aggression from eastern nations than from European nations'. At that time he had identified himself very clearly with the

---

[38] Ibid., 3295.

[39] Ibid., III, 3592, 9 August 1901.

[40] *CPD*, 1903 session, XIV, 1791, 7 July 1903.

[41] Ibid., XIV, 1991, 9 July 1903.

[42] Ibid., XIV, 236, 16 July 1903.

[43] Ibid., XIV, 2331, 21 July 1903.

[44] Ibid., XIV, 2351, 21 July 1903.

[45] Ibid., XIV, 2171–5, 15 July 1903.

[46] Ibid., XIV, 2161, 15 July 1903.

[47] *CPD*, 1903 session, XV, 3707, 18 August 1903; ibid., XVI, 3794 and 3804, 19 August 1903.

'Yellow Peril' camp, arguing that China and Japan would use the White Australia Policy as an excuse to satisfy their 'earth hunger'.[48] Pearce was to return to this theme after the outbreak of the Russo-Japanese War in 1904. His deviation in 1903 probably reflected no more than the general uncertainty of Australians in confronting this problem.

For most of the nineteenth century, Australians had supposed that Britain's European enemies who had bases and cruisers in the Pacific were their most probable source of danger. However, in the 1890s they had become aware of Japan's rising importance and China's potential might and when this was placed against the colonists' determination to exclude Asians from their shores, it was not unnatural that they should also come to fear a military as well as a migratory threat from the north, a fear succinctly defined as the 'Yellow Peril'. In general, the 'Yellow Peril', in comparison with raids by European squadrons, was at this time generally thought of as a long-term danger. However, it raised greater apprehension, for it menaced not only trade and territory but ultimate survival. In the early Commonwealth debates about as many members spoke of the Asian as of the European threat and, in general, those who gave primacy to the Asian threat spoke in the more strident tones and foretold the graver consequences.

Though Senator Pearce and V. L. Solomon, from South Australia[49] had touched on the Asian threat in the address-in-reply, it was in the debate on the 1901 defence bill that these fears were firstly fully developed. R. A. Crouch from Corio in Victoria, a radical protectionist, who opened the attack on the bill, declared that it was not from Europe 'but from the great nations of the East, which we have unfortunately stirred up, and which we are unfortunately teaching European methods of utilizing their military sources', that Australians had 'to expect any great national difficulties'. Referring to Charles Pearson's *National Life and Character: A Forecast*,[50] he foresaw a conflict of the races. He concluded that defence, therefore, was, even before the questions of immigration and the tariff, the nation's first priority and that compulsory drill and military service ought to be instituted.[51] Two conservative protectionists, Allan McLean, who had been premier of Victoria in 1899–1900 and C. C. Salmon, who had been a minister in the McLean government, echoed Crouch's grim prognostication. McLean considered that because of its isolation Australia was essentially insulated against European wars, especially if the Commonwealth were able to gain control of the Pacific Islands. But geography did not provide the same immunity against attacks from the Eastern powers; Japan and an 'awakened' China posed a serious problem for the future. Solomon, applying A. T. Mahan's *The Problem of Asia* to Australia's predicament, similarly saw in 'the contiguity of these Eastern nations ... a position of the very greatest dangers'.[52] Richard Edwards, a conservative protectionist, representing Oxley, Queensland, made the same point rather more moderately; the Commonwealth would face possible dangers not only from Britain's complications in Europe but also because of Australia's

---

[48] *CPD*, 1901–2 session, I, 260, 23 May 1901.

[49] *CPD*, 1901–2 session, I, 507, 30 May 1901.

[50] London 1894.

[51] *CPD*, 1901–2 session, III, 2959, 24 July 1901.

[52] Ibid., III, 2959, 24 July 1901 and 3421, 1 August 1901.

'proximity to China and Japan'.[53] J. Kirwan, free-trade member for Kalgoorlie, Western Australia, turned these fears to good account. He argued that if Britain and Japan should find themselves in opposite camps during a conflict, Japan, because it was 'very ambitious to establish colonies for surplus population' and to acquire an island-based empire in the Pacific, would attack Australia. From this analysis he deduced not only that Australia ought to maintain a 'larger defence force than is necessary for most other countries', but also that the Commonwealth should build, without delay, a Port Augusta-Kalgoorlie transcontinental railway.[54]

The signing of the Anglo-Japanese alliance neither comforted the fearful nor stifled the expression of these fears. The suspicions aroused by Japanese attempts to intervene in the passage of the 1901 Immigration Restriction Act more than counterbalanced any relief which the Anglo-Japanese alliance might have engendered. By 1903 J. C. Watson, the leader of the Labor Party, whose main concern in the early defence debates had been to reduce expenditure[55] had begun to align himself with the preparedness lobby. In supporting Hughes' amendment to the second defence bill, which would have required all men, eighteen to twenty-one years of age to undergo fourteen days' military training annually, Watson held 'that the feasibility of an invasion is such that we ought to make adequate provision to repel it'. He considered that the number of men in the proposed army was 'preposterously low' and he was willing to vote £500,000 to purchase 100,000 rifles to increase Australia's military capability. When pressed as to the source of the anticipated danger, he replied, 'We do not know what Japan might do'.[56]

T. T. Ewing, a conservative protectionist from New South Wales, though he had skirted the issue altogether in 1901, produced in the 1903 debate on the Naval Agreement bill the most vivid picture of the 'Yellow Peril'.[57] Alongside the Asian hordes which stood poised 'to pour down on us in countless numbers', the Russian danger paled into insignificance. It was axiomatic that 'Every man … knows that the white man is superior to the coloured man and that he must maintain his superiority'. It was inevitable that 'Between the white and the yellow man there is racial hatred. … They are destined to be enemies for all time'. When the coloured nations had taken 'a few more steps up the ladder of civilization or advancement', he thought that the White Australia Policy would cause the Asian peoples 'to seek an opportunity for revenge'. There was no sense of imminent crisis. But he predicted that the next generation would experience 'the greatest storm which the world has ever seen when the white man eventually in these latitudes faces the yellow man in deadly war'. This would be 'the great battle of Armageddon' and Australia would be 'right in the vortex of the struggle'. Ewing, who was to become defence minister in 1907–8, despaired about Australia's capacity to resist the onslaught of the alien races. Australians could hold their

---

[53] Ibid., III, 3597, 9 August 1901.

[54] Ibid., III, 3524, 7 August 1901.

[55] *CPD*, 1901–2 session, III, 3191, 30 July 1901.

[56] *CPD*, 1903 session, XV, 3101–7, 5 August 1903.

[57] Dating from the Sino-Japanese war, this had been a continuing preoccupation of Ewing's. See NSW, 1 *Parliamentary Debates*, 1895 session, LXXVIII, 7735, 2 July 1895. 'We must not forget that only a few days' sail from us a great cloud is rising up which may wipe our civilisation out of existence.'

continent only with the assistance of their kinsmen in the British Empire and the United States.[58] J. H. McColl, Victorian free-trader and W. B. Sawers, the member for New England, also anticipated that the White Australia policy would lead to difficulties with Japan which might result in conflict, and possibly even war.[59]

A third and very substantial group of speakers rejected all talk of danger. The essential assumption in their position was that Australia's isolation provided the Commonwealth with a unique shelter against the slings and arrows of international politics. Joseph Cook, a conservative free-trade representative for New South Wales saw Australia 'girt by the great broad sea'. He declared, 'We are away from Europe and the balance of power is so even among the nations that none of them could afford to send a marauding army to despoil' the Commonwealth, which could thus feel 'absolutely free from attack by a European power at present' and equally secure from an Asian threat. Japan was fully occupied with the nations on its doorstep and would, as far as Cook could foresee 'continue to do so'.[60] A number of radical free-traders in the House of Representatives. A. Poynton of South Australia,[61] A. H. Conroy[62] and H. Wilks of New South Wales agreed. Wilks had in 1901 assessed that 'the only danger we have to fear is from an Eastern nation making invasion at remote points',[63] but by 1903 he seemed to be dismissing even that faint possibility. 'I have heard for years that if we do not establish a navy, the eastern nations, such as Japan and China, will come down and eat us all up. I have heard these statements until I am sick and tired of hearing them.' At the least he was depreciating savagely the currency of these fears.[64]

A number of Labor men also shared this point of view. King O'Malley from Tasmania, in keeping with his American origin, took a simplistic Jeffersonian view of defence. Listening to what he called these 'splendid military orations', he said that it seemed as though they were engaged in 'an eternal struggle for … national existence'. Since 1888 he had heard the cry of invasion raised but he had only seen an invasion of rabbits. Falling back on the frontier myth, O'Malley stated that in the unlikely event the Commonwealth was attacked, 5,000 Australians, fighting like the Boers for hearth and home, would be able to defeat 200,000 Japanese, 200,000 Chinese or 200,000 of any other nationality.[65] Even after 1905, when Australian public opinion was undergoing a great change, O'Malley held to this view steadily but by 1907 he was a voice crying in the wilderness. Charles McDonald, from Queensland, who became speaker of the House in 1910, and who, more than any other member, espoused a socialist gospel, also expressed scepticism about external danger. 'A few years ago', he said, 'the cry was that the Chinese were going to invade our shores. Now that nation has been thrust aside and it is urged with much

---

[58] CPD, 1903 session, XIV, 2049, 2056, 14 July 1903.

[59] Ibid., XIV, 2179, 15 July 1903 and XIV, 2244, 16 July 1903.

[60] Ibid., III, 3256, 7 August 1901.

[61] Ibid., IX, 72, 143, 30 April 1902; there was 'no real danger'.

[62] Ibid., III, 3536, 7 August 1901.

[63] Ibid., III, 2989, 24 July 1901.

[64] CPD, 1903 session, XIV, 2334, 21 July 1903; see also ibid., XV, 3101–9, 5 August 1903.

[65] CPD, 1901–2 session, III, 3532, 7 August 1901.

persistency that there is a danger from Japan swooping down for us.' McDonald felt that Australia's isolation was its 'strongest means of defence' and reasonably adduced that given the balance of power of 'armed camps and rivalry' in Europe and the Far East, Australia had nothing to fear from either quarter.[66] Andrew Fisher[67] and the Reverend J. Ronald, the Presbyterian minister from South Melbourne, sided with O'Malley and McDonald in playing down the alarm scenarios. Ronald thought that in contrast to Machiavelli's Florence, Australia was 'fortunate in having no foreign element among her neighbours'. Invasion was 'a very remote possibility'.[68] J. M. Fowler, from Perth, and W. G. Spence, from New South Wales, rejected Ewing's vision of 'a bloody Armageddon'.[69] Spence, in supporting cuts in defence expenditures in 1902, expressed his faith in the progress of mankind and the abolition of war.[70]

Among the protectionists Sir John Quick, a Victorian lawyer, joined Higgins in protesting against militarism. He did not envisage any direct threat to Australia though he thought it possible that Australia might be drawn into war through Britain's conflict with other great powers. Even so, he spoke against compelling men to submit to military training either for the defence of Australian territories or for broader imperial purposes.[71] F. W. Piesse, an independent conservative from Tasmania, perhaps influenced by his own state's defence tradition, felt that Australian security could quite safely be left in the safekeeping of the British navy; a skeleton defence framework was all that was needed in these circumstances.[72] In the Senate, a similar scattering of members from all parties spoke against the scare-mongers, though the Labor Senators were the more numerous. Senator J. C. Stewart of Queensland, who had moved unsuccessfully in the ALP caucus 'that there be no military forces',[73] reiterated McDonald's point that since the great powers were 'fighting among themselves' they were in no position to trouble Australia and further, he did not believe any nation had an inclination to do so.[74] Labor senators, W. G. Higgs from Queensland and G. McGregor from South Australia, and conservative senator Sir John Downer from South Australia and protectionist senator Simon Frazer of Victoria expressed similar doubts.[75]

The first debate over defence was thus a very mixed and confused one. No one argued that Australia faced imminent invasion. The supremacy of the Royal Navy was the guarantee against that possibility. A majority of the speakers were apprehensive about the future but they could not agree about the nature and source of danger. One section of opinion thought that Russian, French

---

[66] Ibid., 3521.

[67] *CPD*, 1903 session, XI, 3107, 5 August 1903.

[68] *CPD*, 1901–2 session, III, 3426, 1 August 1901.

[69] *CPD*, 1903 session, XIV, 2067, 14 July 1903.

[70] *CPD*, 1901–2 session, IX, 12133, 30 April 1902.

[71] *CPD*, 1901–2 session, III, 2968, 24 July 1901.

[72] *CPD*, 1901–2 session, III, 3439, 1 August 1901.

[73] ALP caucus minutes, Vol. I, 17–18, 25 July 1901.

[74] *CPD*, 1903 session, XVI, 3834, 13 August 1903.

[75] Ibid., XVI, 4085, 4106, 13 August 1903 and XVI, 4876–90, 2 September 1903.

or German cruiser raids following an outbreak of war in Europe were the most likely contingency that they had to guard against. Such an analysis had British authority behind it and the Commonwealth government, in so far as it offered a strategic rationale for its policies, adopted this view. Another section slightly less numerous than those fearing European squadrons, felt that Australia's main danger would come from Asia and, specifically, Japan. With the exception of W. M. Hughes, this group included all those who considered that the threat of invasion had to be taken seriously. This scenario was prompted by fear of geographical isolation, fuelled by the determination to exclude Asian races from the Commonwealth and often dressed up in striking and sensational language. The exaggerated nature of its presentation might well be due to the fact that it was a distinctively Australian perception, a perception arising out of an awareness of its geo-political position, a perception which made Australia's own survival the issue at stake. The minority who refused to entertain any thought of threat saw Australia shielded behind a *cordon sanitaire* of wide oceans, patrolled by the British Navy. For Australians, isolation was an ambiguous condition and could be used equally well on both sides of the debates. The lines were not rigidly drawn between the various perceptions and arguments. Very few took up doctrinaire positions. Quite often, domestic political factors influenced the character of the division. Simply because they wished to embarrass or at least oppose the government, free-trade conservative and radical Labor men were more prone than protectionists to play down threat theories, the conservatives pinning their faith on the omnipotence of the Royal Navy and the Labor men on the goodwill of workers and people throughout the world. However, such a schematic description does not do justice to the complexity or individuality of the debates. Overall the parliamentarians did not divide along party or ideological lines. Essentially, what the debates did reveal was national uncertainty about Australia's position in the world. For Australians isolation seemed ambiguous. And, given this uncertainty and ambiguity, it was not altogether surprising that the government down to 1904 failed to provide any clear strategic guidelines for their defence policy.

## Defence forces and defence policy

On 1 March 1901 the Commonwealth government assumed control of the former colonial defence forces. In all, the land forces consisted of some 29,000 men—approximately 1,800 permanent troops, 16,000 partially paid militia and 11,000 volunteers, and an even more indeterminate body of reserves estimated by Forrest to number about 37,000–29,000 rifle club members and 8,000 cadets.[76] The naval forces which were confined to New South Wales, Victoria,

---

[76] There were certain discrepancies in the figures supplied at different times. Forrest, in introducing the first defence bill, stated that the Commonwealth had taken over 28,953 on the active list, made up of 1,487 permanent or regular troops, 18,603 partially paid militia and 8,863 volunteer militia, and 37,887 on reserve, 29,252 rifle club members and 8,635 cadets. CPD, 1901–2 session, II, 2159, 9 July 1901. A Defence Department memorandum of 1909 gave an active figure of 29,205 for 1 March 1901, 1,808 permanents, 16,000 partially paid and 11,158 volunteers, while declining at the same time to make a guess as to the rifle club reserve. 'Memorandum on Australian Military Defence and its Progress since Federation', Melbourne, Department of Defence, 1909, Cab 11/24. The latter figures would seem to be more reliable.

Queensland and South Australia were said to have 1,545 men on their strength, though only 1,000 of these were 'bona fide seamen', the rest being boatsmen and yachtsmen.[77] The Commonwealth also succeeded to a mixed bag of port and coastal vessels, most of which had been acquired following the war scares of the 1880s. The largest and oldest of these vessels was the *Cerberus*, an iron armour-plated turret ship built in 1868. It was by 1901 only suitable for training purpose or as a floating fort in Port Phillip Bay. The most effective and seaworthy was the *Protector,* a steel-protected cruiser, which had been purchased by South Australia in 1884 and which had seen service in the China Sea during the Boxer Rebellion of 1900. In addition, there were five serviceable torpedo boats and a few lesser vessels of dubious worth.[78] The federal government initially saw its task not in terms of developing a defence scheme to meet Australian needs but rather simply to integrate and administer the colonial forces bequeathed to it, while keeping costs inside what the Commonwealth purse could afford. The promise of the Barton government, which appeared in the governor-general's speech, to take steps to bring about the 'judicious strengthening of the defence of the Commonwealth', was never fulfilled. The first federal government, in framing its defence policy, was primarily concerned to avoid 'extravagant expenditure' and to rely 'to the fullest reasonable extent, on our citizen soldiery'. And ultimately they were pushed by parliament into going even further in these directions than they had intended.

The first defence bill, which Forrest introduced into the House of Representatives on 9 July, was aimed at reorganizing the colonial forces for national purposes. The bill was based on a draft submitted by the officers commanding the state forces. The draft owed much to the work of the inter-colonial military committee, which had met in 1894 and 1896.[79] As a result of the imperial enthusiasm aroused by the Boer War, the military officers, encouraged by the Home authorities, followed the CDC lead and urged that Australia form an Imperial Reserve as an element in its military structure and that the Australian government be given the power to send its armed forces to fight overseas.[80] Since the military officers' draft bill was based on the Queensland, South Australia and West Australian defence acts, the cabinet, for the most part, had little quarrel with it, but there were a number of novel insertions which were deleted or amended. After some tart

[77] CofA, Parliamentary Papers, 1901–2 session, Vol. II, No. 27, 'Report of the Conference of Naval Officers Assembled at Melbourne on July 31, 1899, to consider the Question of Naval Defence of Australia'.

[78] Macandie, *The Genesis of the Royal Australian Navy,* p. 23.

[79] Report and minutes of the Military Conference held at Sydney, 24 to 26 October 1894; minute by Major-General Edward T. H. Hutton, commanding officer of the NSW Military Forces to the NSW Colonial Secretary, 12 March 1895; Letter, G. H. Reid, NSW premier to other colonial premiers, 16 April 1895; Report and Schedules of the Inter-Colonial Military Committee assembled at Sydney, 29 January 1896; Remarks of CDC, 21 November 1895, Cab 11/23.

[80] In December 1898 Colonel J. M. Gordon, commander of the South Australian military forces, had put forward a plan for an Australian imperial reserve, and in May 1900 Major-General G. A. French, the commander of the NSW military forces, had suggested a plan for a war reserve of 10,000 men. CofA, Parliamentary Papers, 1901–2 session, Vol. II, No. 31, 'Defence Force and Defence (Memorandum by the Colonial Defence Committee) March 30, 1901'; Cab 8/3; Cab 11/21.

exchanges with the military commanders, the government restricted the power to compel the army to serve overseas, placed the military both in peace and war directly under ministerial control—the military had sought a special relationship with the governor-general and a free hand in time of war—omitted provisions giving permanent officers seniority over volunteer and militia officers and included a clause to provide for Commonwealth control of local naval forces. The final version of the draft, even so, did not achieve a united approach. The military officers deprecated what they considered to be political interference and dissociated themselves from the bill. The ministry itself was divided and the minister himself not fully convinced of the merits of the compromise.[81]

The bill did not then go before the House under the most favourable conditions. It had been hastily revised and contained some poorly phrased and seemingly vague or contradictory provisions. Forrest's poor explication and explanation of the bill did nothing to dispel the doubt and disquiet in the minds of members. He admitted himself that it was a matter 'on which my experience has not been very great' and that he had had little to do with the drafting of the measure.[82] Taking the lessons to be learnt from the South African War, he was optimistic about Australia's relative security and capacity to defend itself. The example of the Boer farmers would 'deter any foreign foes from making a descent upon the shores of Australia', and even if they should attempt it, he believed that Australia would be able to successfully resist such an incursion. This was the closest that he came to offering a strategic guideline for the government's defence proposals. He announced that the government intended to follow the example of the colonies and to make the citizen soldiers, as in Canada and Switzerland, the backbone of the defence forces. This principle had been adopted not merely out of a need for economy but also because the Boers had shown its efficiency. The permanent troops were to have charge of forts, artillery and the other specialist branches of the army. He indicated that the government had agreed that, in harmony with the model state acts, all men between the ages of eighteen and sixty years were to be liable to be called up in time of emergency, but under clause 48(b) the citizen defence force could only be sent 'without the Commonwealth for the defence thereof'. The idea of an imperial reserve as such had been dropped, but a loophole to enable the government to send troops overseas was retained. Forrest argued that the Commonwealth needed this power in order to be able to protect Australian interests in the South Pacific.[83]

In the ensuing debate, members, in addition to criticizing the government for its lack of policy, expressed opposition to compulsory overseas service, to the fostering of 'the dominance of a military caste' or militarism and to wasteful expenditure. There was a general feeling that the Australian defence force should be 'democraticized'. By that term it was intended that unnecessary pomp, ceremonial and gold braid should be dispensed with, that men be able to rise from the ranks and officers selected on merit and not social background. Some of the support for a

---

[81] CofA, Parliamentary Papers, 1901–2 session, Vol. II, A7, 'Further Report of the Federal Military Committee, Assembled at Melbourne, June 21, 1901'.
[82] CPD, 1901–2 session, II, 2159 and 2172, 9 July 1901.
[83] Ibid., 2169.

'democratic' army came from militia officers within and without parliament who feared that a closed professional system, even if based on social caste, would undermine their own positions and privileges. Sir John Quick urged that civilian officers should be represented at the central headquarters of the army.[84] This antagonism between the professional and civilian officers was evident during the term of Major-General E. T. Hutton as Commander-in-Chief from 1902 to 1904 and was in part responsible for the revision of his military organization and for the administrative changes provided for under the 1904 Defence Act. With the exception of Higgins and a few likeminded men, there was no dissent from the principle that all able-bodied citizens should be liable to be called up for military service in time of war or invasion; some members, especially Labor members, felt that the term 'emergency' was too vague and could be defined to include strikes or other industrial disturbances. Opposition to compulsory service overseas came from all factions in the parliament but the Labor party, having in caucus agreed to vote against that clause, presented a solid front against the provision.[85]

During the debate Forrest undertook a tour of inspection of the state's defence forces and left the management of the bill in Barton's hands. Though Barton carried out his task conscientiously—he took detailed notes of the criticisms and passed them on to Forrest—the House did not appreciate the treatment accorded them by the minister. The prime minister made conciliatory gestures to the bill's opponents. In winding up the debate he declared that it was unreasonable to expect a statement of general policy in a bill designed to serve an administrative purpose. On the other hand, he was willing to gratify the desire for a democratic army. He acquiesced in the demand for the abolition of gold lace, a theme which, in his view, seemed 'to run through every speech', and he promised to suggest to the minister, 'that the difference in the uniforms of the various grades of the service shall only be sufficient to enable the troops on parade to know who are their officers to act accordingly'. He also accepted that officers should be able to rise from the ranks, even agreeing with an interjector that it would be 'a very good rule' to require all officers to serve first as privates.[86] However, he said nothing on the topic which had roused the most hostile criticism, namely the assumption of power to compel men to serve overseas. The government had already modified considerably the original recommendation of the military officers. The clause, as it appeared in the bill, was a delicate compromise and rather than stir up a hornet's nest in cabinet, he kept his counsel. The debate had shown up the weaknesses and unpopularity of the bill and rather than risk defeat or piecemeal immolation in committee, the government, on reflection, decided to abandon the bill and postpone the matter until after a General Officer had been appointed to command the Commonwealth's military forces.

On 3 May the Commonwealth government had requested the British authorities to nominate an officer from the active list of the imperial army to take command of Australia's land forces. They sought a man who had 'sympathy for the citizen soldiers', and who had had battle experience

---

[84] Ibid., III, 2968, 24 July 1901.

[85] ALP caucus minutes, Vol. I, 17–21, 25 July 1901. This was one of the first caucus decisions binding the Labor members of parliament.

[86] *CPD*, 1901–2 session, III, 3601–5, 9 August 1901.

in the South African campaign.[87] It was no easy task to find the right man. Eligible British officers recognized that such an appointment would not advance their careers and were loath to consent. Thus, Major-General Pole-Carew refused the offer. The Australian government, for its part, was not easily satisfied; it indicated that it did not look favourably on Lord Dundonald, an aristocrat with a reputation for arrogance.[88] Six months elapsed before agreement was reached, and on 23 November, Colonel Sir E. T. Hutton, the only remaining officer whom Lord Roberts, the British commander-in-chief was willing to recommend, accepted the post.[89] Hutton was promoted to the rank of major-general. However, much to his chagrin, he had to consent to select his aide-de-camp from among the Australian officers and to wait until his arrival in the Commonwealth to determine the composition of his general staff. To allay his misgivings he did succeed in reducing the term of his appointment from five to three years.[90]

Given his background and experience, Hutton was indisputably the most suitable imperial officer to take charge of the Commonwealth military forces. He had had wide experience in the colonies and had a first-hand knowledge of Australian military practice and politics. From 1893 to 1896 he had commanded New South Wales' colonial forces and had attempted to inject into that rather lax, easy-going organization, a degree of professional efficiency and a sense of professional pride. He had been the master-mind behind the 1894 draft scheme for a federal military force and in 1896 had presided over the inter-colonial military conference which adopted a revised version of that scheme. From 1897 to 1899 he had commanded Canada's land forces and had suffered much in trying to reconcile what he considered imperial and professional desiderata with colonial and political prejudices. He had been sent to South Africa in 1900 and given command of the first Mounted Infantry Division, which contained a large Australian contingent. The ability and performance of the Australian troops in the field left a lasting impression on him. Hutton belonged to a new breed of British officer. He held a professional and meritocratic view of what the army should be and felt at odds with a military system which still favoured heavily the aristocrat and the amateur. It may well be that this sense of not quite belonging helped persuade him to accept the Australian challenge. Yet, even though Hutton had a much greater understanding of and even sympathy for the colonial perspective than was common in the War Office, nevertheless, he could not come to terms with the extreme egalitarianism of Australian democracy nor accept the Australian opposition to training troops for overseas service. When Australian politics or even policy infringed on the proper province of the professional, as he

---

[87] Telegram, governor-general, Lord Hopetoun to colonial secretary, Joseph Chamberlain, 3 May 1901, CO 418/9/515.

[88] Telegram, governor-general to colonial secretary, 13 June 1901, CO 418/9/515; telegram, governor-general to colonial secretary, 10 October 1901, CO 418/10/234.

[89] Telegram, colonial secretary to governor-general, 12 November 1901 and telegram, governor-general to colonial secretary, 15 November 1901, CO 418/10/334.

[90] Letter, Lord William Seymour, War Office to Sir Edward Hutton, 22 November 1901; copy of letter, Hutton to Seymour, 23 November 1901; and letter, Hutton to Sir John Brodrick, the secretary of state for war. 24 February 1902, Hutton Papers, add. ms. 50085, Vol. XVIII.

broadly defined it, then he had no hesitation in doing his utmost to circumvent and abort those political purposes.[91]

Hutton was an ambitious man who had a high view of the importance of his role in making an army, and even a nation.[92] In drawing up a defence scheme for Australia, he showed political acumen in trying to accommodate imperial ideas to Australian prejudices. He was a capable organizer who carried out his military policies effectively and expeditiously. He had complete trust in his own judgement of men and methods, and could be quite unrelenting and ruthless when dealing with the unfit and the erroneous. At a time when it was under attack, Hutton did strengthen the self-esteem of the permanent army. Certainly when he returned to England in 1904, he left behind a devoted band of regular officers who considered his principles and example to be the touchstone of orthodoxy. However, the imperialistic mould in which he fashioned these men and the encouragement he gave them to look to the War Office rather than to the Commonwealth parliament or government for policy direction, tended to isolate them from the processes of policy-making, and as a result, the initiative in the shaping of Australia's military policy and the impetus behind its execution down to 1914 came almost entirely from the responsible ministers.

Before departing for Australia, Hutton conferred with Joseph Chamberlain, the colonial secretary, on 19 December and with King Edward VII, Sir John Brodrick and Lord Roberts on 21 December. In reassessing Britain's position, as the costly Boer War drew to its close, the Colonial Office, War Office, Admiralty and Treasury were agreed that the colonies should bear a fairer share of the defence burden and that the total resources of the empire should be reorganized and

---

[91] W. S. Hamer, *The British Army: Civil-Military Relations, 1885–1905*, Oxford 1970. See especially pp. 13–30 for the conflict between the conservatives and the reformers in the army in this period. The 'Old Guard' respected aristocratic privilege, military and regimental tradition, promotion by seniority, and the exclusive, gentlemen's club atmosphere of the officers' mess. The reformers in contradistinction sought a more functional approach to the management of military forces. They valued efficiency, intelligence, organization, training, education, promotion by merit and the development of a general staff. See pp. 31–72 for a discussion of the conflict between the military and civil leaders over questions of general policy and financial control.

[92] Though at the time of his appointment the War Office had made it clear that he could not hope for a higher rank than major-general, Hutton had no sooner arrived in Australia than he began pressing for promotion to lieutenant-general. Copy of letter, Hutton to Brodrick, 24 February 1902, Hutton Papers, add. ms. 50085, Vol. VIII. When in 1915 he was engaged in writing his autobiography, he expressed the view that his defence schemes of 1894 and 1896 were responsible for bringing about federation. Ibid. In accepting his appointment Hutton wrote as Hopetoun put it 'in rather high-faluting language'. Letter, Hopetoun to Barton, 1 December 1901, Barton Papers 51/448. Hutton in taking up his 'grave responsibility' assured Barton that he would 'loyally and truly carry out all the instructions which I may receive from your Government, yourself and my respected minister, Sir John Forrest'. He told Barton that it was his aim 'to place the National Military Service upon a plane above party-political intrigue, and personal influence'. Only then could the military forces be 'effectively organised and maintained'. Ibid., 51/449.

centralized for the security of the whole.[93] Despite Chamberlain's instruction to Hutton that he should regard himself as 'the servant of the Australian government', and should never appear to be acting as the agent of the imperial government, it is evident that both Hutton and the British authorities expected that the commander of the Commonwealth's military forces should exercise his influence in defence planning and policy to advance imperial interests. Hutton at both meetings assured his auditors that he would try to ensure that a clause enabling Australia's forces to be sent abroad was included in the defence act, and he promised Brodrick that he would try to raise a force of 20,000 mounted troops which, when occasion arose, could be employed as an imperial reserve.[94]

Arriving in Australia on 29 January, 1902, Hutton quickly took the initiative in his campaign for a 'broad' defence policy. On 15 February he outlined his view. From his earlier tour of duty in New South Wales, he was well aware of Australia's peculiar anxiety about danger from Asia and he harnessed this fear to his appeal for a vigorous and a 'broad' defence policy. Arguing, with doubtful conviction, that 'the present epoch in the history of Australia was one of immense difficulty and gravity not only to the Commonwealth but to the relations of the empire with the East', he proposed the formation of a force of 20,000 mounted men, equipped and organized for service wherever Australian interests were threatened. He also declared that the empire had learnt three lessons from the Boer War; firstly, that compulsory service was not necessary for the British 'race', secondly, that organization, discipline and training were of paramount importance for efficiency, and thirdly, that a citizen militia could produce fighting troops of a high calibre.

At the request of Barton and Forrest, Hutton on 7 April submitted a Minute on Australia's defence needs which pursued these same themes and laid down the basis of a defence scheme. The strategic rationale was composed of two separate elements. The first just repeated almost word for word the Colonial Defence Committee's position as it had been formulated in 1890 and reaffirmed in the federal defence schemes of 1894 and 1896. According to that analysis Australia, because of its geographical position, was 'less liable to aggression from any foreign power than most parts of the Empire'. The most likely threat was raids by enemy cruisers. The second part, however, expanded upon the Eastern menace theory.

> The rapid and continuous improvement in steam and telegraph communications have now destroyed the former isolation of Australia, and modern developments in the East have brought the states of the Commonwealth upon the arena of old world strife.

To emphasize this change in the balance of power in the East, he recited a catalogue of new developments and national aspirations; Japan was 'an armed power of the first magnitude', Russia had ambitions in China, the United States was established in the Philippines, Guam and Samoa,

---

[93] J. L. Garvin and J. Amery, *Life of Joseph Chamberlain*, Vol. V, 'Joseph Chamberlain and the Tariff Reform Campaign', London 1967, pp. 8–9, 34–6.

[94] Notes of Interview with Joseph Chamberlain, 19 December 1901 and Notes of Meeting with the King, Secretary for War and Commander-in-Chief, 21 December 1901, Hutton Papers, add. ms. 50078, Vol. I; see also letter, Hutton to Sir William Nicholson, Intelligence Division, War Office, Hutton Papers, add. ms. 50086. Vol. IX, p. 251.

Germany in the Solomons and New Guinea, France in Madagascar. He saw these changes as signs of a coming struggle for commercial supremacy. From this it was concluded that Australia should be willing to defend not only the territories of the Commonwealth but also the 'vast interests beyond her shores upon the maintenance of which her present existence and her future prosperity must so largely depend'. To this end Australia's military organization and administration should be divided into two parts, a garrison force to protect forts and to man fixed defences, and a mobile field force which could be sent 'wherever' Australian interests might be threatened; of a military force of 29,571 men, 15,470 would be kept as garrison troops and the remainder would form the field force. In wartime the total strength could be expanded to 44,218 men, with 28,748 being allocated to the field force.[95]

Hutton had moved with a certain cunning to compass his imperial objective. Nothing had been said about an imperial reserve. Recognizing how unpopular such a suggestion would be in Australia, he had argued the case for 'a broad policy' in terms of Australian interests. As he explained to Sir Montague Ommanney at the Colonial Office, 'I have been careful to leave the deduction to be drawn as to what is really comprised under this head "Australian interests"; the keynote is a "Cooperative System of Defence".'[96] Equally the Eastern threat was consciously adopted as a device whereby to coax or coerce the Australian government and parliament into acceding to imperial wishes. Hutton did not take this threat any more seriously in 1902 than he had in 1895.[97] When taxed by the Colonial Defence Committee with deviating from the strategic analysis set down by the imperial authorities, Hutton replied that 'in the condition of public feeling in Australia … to state that invasion by a large and well equipped Force was impracticable, … would have been seized upon as an argument for the abolition of the Military Forces altogether'.[98] He also defended his proposed field force against the Committee's criticism that such a force could not serve a useful purpose within Australia, by pointing out it was intended to be primarily available for employment overseas. The War Office continued to assume that Hutton was forming an imperial reserve which would be available for use at the British government's discretion. They, indeed, read Hutton's defence minute in this light. And Hutton, aware of Australian susceptibilities, had to warn that this was not the case, that the Commonwealth would, on every occasion, have to decide whether or not Australian troops would take part in imperial wars. However, Hutton assured the War Office that the field force of 20,000 mounted men which

---

[95] CofA, *Parliamentary Papers*, 1901–2 session, Vol. II, A36, 'Military Forces of the Commonwealth: Minute upon the Defence of Australia by Major-General Hutton, 7 April 1902.

[96] Copy of letter, Hutton to Ommanney, 8 April 1902, Hutton Papers, add. ms. 50078, Vol. I.

[97] Copy of letter, Hutton to Duke of Cambridge, 22 April 1895, Hutton Papers, add. ms. 50078, Vol. I, 'the Sino-Japanese War and its bearings upon British interests and Australia have given me a pretext for again urging upon the Government of New South Wales the necessity of taking some immediate measures to bring about Federal Defence'.

[98] Letter, Hutton to Lord Tennyson, governor-general, 9 March 1903, enclosed in despatch, governor-general to colonial secretary, 11 March 1902, CO 418/26/151–9; see also copy of letter, Hutton Papers, add. ms. 50087, Vol. I, p. 75.

he hoped to form would be trained for just such an eventuality, and he believed that, when the time came, the Commonwealth government would do its part.[99] Hutton had a keen insight into the Australian political mood. Barton was impressed and complimented his military commander on drawing attention to 'the salient fact that the theatre of the struggle for commercial dominance has shifted eastward; and that in future strife we shall hear the clash and see the shots instead of merely listening to the echoes'.[100] In manoeuvring to get his own way, Hutton was, as Deakin in a later context put it, 'absolutely "slim"'.[101]

The Colonial Conference which was summoned for June 1902 interrupted the discussion of Hutton's defence scheme and the preparation of a new defence bill, and it also provided the imperial authorities with a more direct opportunity to influence the Australian government's thinking. Joseph Chamberlain, in the light of Britain's changed position in the world, had hoped that the conference, being held as it was at the time of the Boer War peace settlement, might take some effective steps towards the political integration of the self-governing colonies with the Mother Country; with this in mind, the defence departments had drawn up proposals for closer co-ordination and more central control of the military and naval resources of the whole empire.

On 25 July Brodrick placed the War Office plans for military co-operation before the conference. The proposals were premised on certain general principles which had been laid down by Lieutenant-Colonel E. A. Altham in a paper of June 1901 on 'The Organisation of Colonial Troops for Imperial Service'[102] and approved by the Colonial Defence Committee in June 1902. These principles were that the defence of the empire had to be taken as a whole, that the totality of its white manpower should be available for the protection of any part, that it was necessary to prepare in peacetime for united action in war and that it was desirable for the colonies to make provision in their defence establishments for special contingents for imperial service. It was also essential, if such a scheme were to be successful,

> That the supreme authority, which is responsible for the defence of the Empire as a whole, should be able to rely with certainty on colonial contingents of definite strength, being available for defensive or offensive operations in any part of the world.

Though the paper recognized that the British government could not command but only recommend, it proposed that Australia should be 'encouraged' to establish a field force of 9,000 men, 'the Imperial Australian Force',[103] as it was to be called, which would be 'at the disposal of the Imperial Government for general service in the case of war between Great Britain and one or

---

[99] Letter, Sir William Nicholson to Hutton, 1 June 1902, Hutton Papers, add. ms. 50085, Vol. VIII, p. 205 and copy of letter, Hutton to Nicholson, 23 July 1902, Hutton Papers, add. ms. 50086, Vol. IX, p. 251.

[100] Letter, Barton to Hutton, 6 April 1902, Hutton Papers, add. ms. 50084, Vol. VII, pp. 16–17.

[101] Letter, Deakin to Barton, 17 June 1902, Barton Papers, 51/578.

[102] Lieutenant-Colonel E. A. Altham was Assistant Quartermaster-General at Headquarters.

[103] It is probable that herein lies the provenance of the term 'Australian Imperial Force', which was used to designate the Australian expeditionary force in World War I; Hutton's Australian disciples, most notably Major-Generals W. T. Bridges and C. Brudenell White, never allowed the imperial dimension to be forgotten.

more European powers'. Brodrick, in putting the War Office proposal, emphasized these principles though laying less stress on specific commitments and more on colonial consent. He added that colonial troops organized for general purposes 'should realise that they are a part of the Army Reserve of the Imperial Forces' and that if the War Office was given power to call upon them at its discretion, then the imperial government would assume the cost of their training. Richard Seddon, the New Zealand prime minister, had already offered a resolution along these lines and Chamberlain hoped that, as in the Boer War itself, New Zealand's initiative would shame the other colonies into making matching offers.[104] But this was not to be. The Canadian premier, Sir Wilfrid Laurier, gave the suggestion short shrift and Barton, who with Forrest was representing Australia, joined the Canadians in opposing it.[105]

Barton understood well the potentially explosive nature of the imperial issue. The debate on the first defence bill had alerted him to parliament's sensitivity on the matter and to its hostility towards any scheme which would remove Australian troops from Commonwealth control or which would compel Australian soldiers to fight overseas. Thus, when he learnt that Seddon had submitted a resolution for the creation of an imperial reserve, Barton became exceedingly wary in his pronouncements on the question. In contrast to his speeches in the early days of federation when he had insisted upon Australia's reciprocal duty to the empire, the Commonwealth prime minister now began to underscore the limits of Australia's obligations. Shortly after hearing the news of Seddon's resolution he asserted that he would do nothing to detract from Australia's constitutional autonomy. He said that the proposed imperial defence schemes sounded 'as matters are at present very much like taxation without representation'.[106] On the eve of his departure for England he reiterated this limited approach to defence questions; Australia would undertake only the defence of its own shores.[107] Barton was so concerned that he asked Chamberlain to meet with him prior to the opening of the conference in order to discuss 'confidential matters affecting Australian relations with the rest of the empire',[108] and it may well be that as a result of this meeting, the British ministers muted and modified somewhat their appeals for colonial co-operation and imperial unity.[109]

At the conference itself, Barton held to his position on colonial autonomy. He explained that while the Commonwealth could be relied upon when the Empire was imperilled, Australian public opinion would not consent 'to reduce any terms of assistance by way of land force to a specific agreement'. Colonial help had to be left to the spontaneous response in time of need and in Barton's view such assistance, tendered freely, was to be preferred. Barton endeavoured to make

---

[104] Garvin and Amery, *Life of Joseph Chamberlain*, IV, 36.

[105] CO Confidential Print, Miscellaneous No. 144, pp. 1–4, 80–93 and Appendix III, 'Colonial Troops for Imperial Services in War: Memorandum by the CDC, June 13, 1902' together with 'The Organization of Colonial Troops for Imperial Service' by Colonel E. A. Altham, 25 November 1901, CO 885/8.

[106] *SMH*, 13 March 1902.

[107] *SMH*, 6 May 1902.

[108] Letter, Barton to Chamberlain, 9 June 1902, Joseph Chamberlain Papers, 17/2/4.

[109] Letter, Chamberlain to Barton, 12 June 1902, Barton Papers, 51/516.

a sentimental virtue out of national necessity. He offered, as an alternative to the War Office and New Zealand proposals, a recommendation urging uniformity of training and equipment throughout the empire and approving the setting up of arms and ammunition factories in each colony. And on this rather anti-climatic note the discussion ended.[110]

On their return to Australia Barton and Forrest found themselves faced with a series of difficulties in their efforts to establish a defence scheme and to draw up an acceptable defence bill. In April and May the defence estimates had come under attack from both the Labor[111] and the free-trade parties. Though the treasurer pleaded that he had cut back the defence submission from £1,250,000 to £937,000, the House was not satisfied and Forrest was compelled to reduce the defence budget by a further £175,000.[112] Under pressure from Watson, who wished to see defence costs pared down to £700,000, Sir William Lyne, the acting minister for defence, agreed in October to cut back the defence estimates at a rate of £62,000 for a full year from December 1902, that is by an amount of £35,000 for the financial year 1902–3.[113] These heavy inroads into the defence appropriations, which were made primarily at the expense of the commander-in-chief's headquarters' staff and the permanent troops, enraged Hutton. The general struggled, both politically and administratively to avoid the consequences of these decisions. But to no avail. In June Deakin, the acting prime minister, had spotted Hutton's 'deep game' and confessed that, as a result of his manipulations, the proposed savings were 'merely illusory'.[114] Again in November, when Forrest insisted on Hutton carrying through Lyne's commitment to parliament, the general resisted but was overborne. Forrest was not to be trifled with. Though Forrest had an inordinate respect and admiration for the Royal Navy, he had little interest in upholding the *amour propre* of the regular army. In Forrest's view, it was the navy which protected Australia from attacks or other incursions. His enthusiasm in enforcing the financial strictures on the army was probably due to the fact that at the Colonial Conference Barton and he had agreed to increase the Australian subsidy to the imperial squadron.[115] Forrest was aghast to learn—with the connivance of Captain R. Muirhead Collins, the first permanent head of the Defence Department — that eighty permanent soldiers were being employed as officer's servants and orderlies. When it was apparent that Hutton was not responding to persuasion, he ordered the general, in precise terms, to carry out the government's decision. 'I have looked through your recommendations', he wrote Hutton

---

[110] Minutes of the Colonial Conference, 1902, CO Confidential Print, Miscellaneous No. 144, pp. 32 and 86, CO 885/8; see also *SMH*, 18 October 1902. Barton, speaking at the Sydney Town Hall, said that he 'did not care to organize and drill any portion of our people for the mere purpose of taking part in European wars according to the judgment of the [British] Government of the day'.

[111] ALP caucus minutes, Vol. I, pp. 56–60, meeting of 30 April 1902.

[112] *CPD*, 1901–2 session, IX, 12090–144, 30 April 1902; ibid., IX, 12, 212, 1 May 1902.

[113] *CPD*, 1901–2 session, XII, 16, 386, 2 October 1902.

[114] Letter, Deakin to Barton, 17 June 1902, Barton Papers, 51/578.

[115] He wrote Chamberlain in November that he was 'taking practical steps to assist to that end, by decreasing the military expenditure so that with £200,000 [promised in naval subsidy] the Defence Estimate will not exceed £700,000 or £750,000 a year'. Letter, Forrest to Chamberlain, 24 November 1902, Joseph Chamberlain Papers, 17/2/9.

'and regret to say they won't do… The rearrangement you propose would result in no way in pleasing Parliament and I would have to admit that I had failed to carry out its wishes.' He then instructed Hutton that there were to be permanent garrisons sufficient only to maintain forts and armaments, that permanent officers, over and above those necessary to supervise these garrisons, were only to be maintained for instruction purposes, and the remainder of Australia's military defence was to be left to the citizen forces.[116] Civilian control of the defence forces was vindicated and Hutton, though he gnashed his teeth, knuckled under.[117] By 1903 Hutton had had to reduce his permanent staff from 135 officers and 1,596 other ranks in 1901 to 91 officers and 1,209 men, and the total strength of the peace establishment from 29,550 to 24,957. There was to be a field force of 12,747 and a garrison force of 12,110. This was the organization which cabinet approved in the Defence Scheme of July 1903.[118]

The drafting of a second defence bill and the passage of a Defence Act also proved troublesome. Hutton, whom Barton and Forrest had requested to draw up a new defence bill, was determined to safeguard the prerogative of the general officer commanding and to provide for the use of Australian troops outside Australian territories. In this latter respect, Hutton recognized that, given Australian public opinion and political temper, neither an imperial reserve nor imperial control were as such feasible options. The only way by which he could achieve his object, at least in part, was to ensure that the Commonwealth government was given power to send Australian troops abroad. This had been the essence of his April 1902 minute. Hutton lobbied directly on behalf of his draft bill. Annoyed by Lyne's failure to argue his case in the estimates debate, Hutton had met privately with the opposition leaders, including Reid and Watson, and expounded his thesis, once again putting the case of the 'broad policy' in terms of Australian interests. He told them that Australia was in a perilous position. It had common frontiers with Germany and Holland in New Guinea, and France in New Caledonia was 'essentially in the direct sphere of Australian interests'. Australia needed to adopt such a policy in order that its South

[116] Letter, Forrest to Hutton, 16 November 1902 and Forrest to Hutton, 24 November 1902, Hutton Papers, add. ms. 50084, Vol. VII, pp. 266–8. Forrest did not hold Hutton's pertinacity against him. Rather he saw it as evidence of character and he respected the general for it. Forrest wrote that he considered Hutton 'a really good man, although naturally being a strong man, he wanted his own way'. Forrest confessed that he preferred 'a man who has a strong view of his own rather than one who looks to me for anything'. Letter, Forrest to F. D. North, 8 April 1903, Forrest Papers, 766A.

[117] Hutton put his defeat down to the weakness and want of character on the part of the government for whom he had great contempt. The ministers were 'reeds broken by the winds', letter, Hutton to Colonel Sir Arthur Bigge, secretary to the Prince of Wales, 6 September 1902, Hutton Papers, add. ms. 50078, Vol. I. He considered that Sir William Lyne 'showed great weakness in dealing with the defence question… He displayed want of confidence in himself and in the power of the Government to carry into effect any Military Defence System… The present Government has shown great weakness all round.' Letter, Hutton to Ommanney, 23 December 1902, Hutton Papers, add. ms. 50078, Vol. I.

[118] CofA, *Parliamentary Papers*, 1903 session, Vol. II, No. 37, 'Annual Report of Major-General Sir Edward Hutton, January 1902–30 April 1903' and ibid., 1904 session, Vol. II, No. 25, 'Second Annual Report of Major-General Sir Edward Hutton'.

Pacific Monroe Doctrine could be realized. Hutton, on whose record we depend, claimed that, as a result of his discussions, the Labor leaders' hostility was modified and Reid was convinced of the wisdom of giving the Commonwealth power to send troops wherever Australian interests might require them.[119]

Hutton found almost as much suspicion of his proposal among the imperial authorities as among Australian politicians. Certainly, the War Office and Colonial Office, by their lack of sensitivity to Australian opinion, embarrassed Hutton in his efforts to salvage something for the imperial dreamers. Hutton was irritated by the failure of the War Office to consult him about the plans for military co-operation which had been placed before the Colonial Conference. Hutton knew how unacceptable they would be in Australia and how such talk, even though ineffectual, would stir up suspicion among the more, as he saw it, paranoid colonials. Against his wishes, the CDC Memorandum on Imperial Reserves was published with the bowdlerized conference report in 1903, in the midst of the debate over the second defence bill. Hutton's position was further undermined by the Colonial Defence Committee's critical comments on his Minute of 7 April 1902, in which he had set down his views as to the proper basis for the Commonwealth's defence policy. The CDC chided him for going beyond the imperial appreciation of the 1890s which had ruled out the prospect of invasion and for suggesting that changing circumstances in the Pacific might endanger Australian security. The CDC, in contradistinction to Hutton, concluded that Australia needed only a minimal local defence, and that this could be achieved by garrisons and forts at the major ports. The Royal Navy would be adequate for all other possibilities. Bringing out in the open Hutton's hidden intent, the CDC stated that the field force could only be justified if it were available to serve in the West Pacific in time of war. 'If it were the settled policy of the Commonwealth to maintain the effective nucleus of a force' for this purpose, 'this force would be a real access to the military strength of the Empire.' Even so, with the Altham blueprint in mind, the CDC thought that the size of the field force suggested by Hutton could be cut by half.[120]

The CDC paper arrived in Australia in February 1903 and Hutton immediately perceived how it could injure his defence scheme and his defence scheming. At Hutton's suggestion, the governor-general wrote privately to the Colonial Office, pointing out the harm which the report might do and asking that he be allowed to keep it from his ministers.[121] The Colonial Office refused, not on constitutional grounds, but because of their belief in the wisdom of the views propounded by the CDC. Inside the Colonial Office, John Anderson, supporting a smaller field force, said, 'Knowing what we do of the discipline of the untrained Australian, the cohesion and efficiency of such a force, serving probably by itself without any stiffening of regulars, would be

---

[119] Copy of letter, Hutton to Lord Tennyson, acting governor-general, 3 October 1902, Hutton Papers, add. ms. 50082, Vol. V, pp. 48–9; letter, Hutton to Tennyson, 3 October 1902 in despatch, Tennyson to Chamberlain, 7 October 1902, CO 418/19/368.

[120] CDC, 301R, 'Minute upon Defence by General Officer Commanding the Military Forces of the Commonwealth: Remarks by the CDC, 22 October 1902', Cab 9/5.

[121] Telegram, Tennyson to Chamberlain, 17 February 1903, CO 418/26/82.

extremely doubtful.' Ommanney and Onslow concurred.[122] They overlooked completely the fact that the CDC remarks, if revealed, would destroy the basis of Hutton's campaign for a 'broad' defence policy. They replied that they could not see any objection to the paper being handed to the Australian government.[123]

On 25 February Hutton submitted his draft bill. He retained in the draft the Commonwealth's right to send the defence forces without the limits of Australia 'in case of national emergency'; the field force was to be available 'for the defence of Australian interests generally'.[124] Despite the Colonial Office's instruction, Tennyson, at Hutton's insistence, agreed that the distribution of the CDC paper should be restricted to Barton and Forrest, who, it was thought, favoured 'some sort of military cooperation with the Imperial government'. On the other hand, there were at least two other members of Cabinet, Charles Kingston, the minister for trade and Sir George Turner, the treasurer, who were believed to be 'violently opposed to such measures'. Moreover, Tennyson and Hutton felt that if the document went beyond the prime minister and the defence minister, it would be leaked to the press and awkward consequences might ensue.[125] Hutton shared his anxiety, at least in part, with Forrest, and Barton was persuaded to withhold the document from the other ministers.[126] Yet, despite these Herculean labours on behalf of the 'broad' policy, Cabinet, when it came to consider the draft bill, restricted further the clause relating to overseas service, making it applicable only to the permanent troops. Hutton, in his first report to parliament on 1 May, made a final appeal for his 'offensive' defence strategy as it had been incorporated into his draft bill. He repeated that a large-scale invasion of Australia was not impossible. He recited again the list of growing threats and geographical responsibilities which Australia faced in the Western Pacific. And in the sharpest thrust of all, he declared that the voluntary principle was not good enough for the protection of the 'Australian Monroe Doctrine of Immigration'. He concluded with an appeal to Australia's sense of duty to the empire and New Zealand.[127]

However, when the bill came before parliament in July, there was no evidence that Hutton's eighteen-month campaign had influenced members either one way or another. Compared with his 1901 performance, Forrest, apart from blustering about imperial patriotism, showed much greater competence in introducing the bill. He assured the House that he had studied the 1901 debates very closely and that the revised bill had taken into account many of the criticisms made of its predecessor. Provision had been made to enable officers to be promoted from the ranks.

---

[122] CO 418/26/83, 19 February 1903.

[123] Copy of telegram, Chamberlain to Tennyson, 27 February 1903, CO 418/26/84.

[124] CofA, *Parliamentary Papers*, 1903 session, Vol. II, No.37.

[125] Copy of letter, Hutton to Sir William Nicholson, 10 March 1903, Hutton Papers, add. ms. 50086, Vol. IX, p. 273; despatch Tennyson to Chamberlain, 11 March 1903, CO 418/26/145–59.

[126] Copy of letter, Hutton to Forrest, 29 March 1903 and letter, Forrest to Hutton, 22 March 1903, Hutton Papers, add. ms. 50085, Vol. VII, pp. 281–2; copy of minute for minister of defence, 26 March 1903, Hutton Papers, add. ms. 50082, Vol. V, pp. 88–9; copy of letter, Hutton to Ommanney, 1 April 1903, Hutton Papers, add. ms. 50078, Vol. I, p. 300.

[127] CofA, *Parliamentary Papers*, 1903 session, Vol. II, No. 37.

'Emergency' had been replaced by 'time of war' or 'danger of war' as the ground for conscripting all able-bodied men. Service overseas was restricted to permanent troops. Forrest maintained that this, like the first bill, was inherently a 'machinery' bill, and that it should be treated as such. He urged that, since the general issues had been canvassed widely in 1901, parliament ought to content itself with a brief debate and give the measure a speedy passage.[128] He blunted the criticism of many of its would-be opponents, a number of whom remarked on the metamorphosis which had taken place. Most speakers accepted the bill's general features. Only two major amendments were forced on the government; the role of the permanent troops in the defence force was strictly circumscribed and clause 42, which authorized the government to send permanent troops overseas, was abandoned. The case against clause 42 was not well argued, but behind the rhetoric was a suspicion of how such a power might be used or abused.[129] Higgins attempted to extend the exemption from compulsory military service to include not only those who objected on grounds of religious belief, but also those who were opposed on the ground of individual conscience. Higgins found only five supporters for his amendment, one Victorian protectionist, R. A. Crouch, and four Labour men, Mahon, Ronald, Tudor and McDonald. The Labor leaders, Watson and Fisher, voted against the amendment. The amendments to require compulsory military training, which were introduced into the house and senate, were easily defeated.[130] Parliament passed the bill in October. Australia's Defence Act was proclaimed in March 1904.

Hutton was distressed by the outcome. It capped the process of deteriorating relations between the commanding officer and political leaders, which had begun in the previous year. In 1903 and 1904 there was continuing wrangling over reductions in the headquarters' staff and the artillery. When informed in the early part of the year that the headquarters' staff must be cut yet again, Hutton, after resisting valiantly, capitulated with a threat. On 4 May he told Forrest that he was 'not prepared to continue efforts which must necessarily be doomed to failure.'[131] Further conflicts developed over Hutton's policy of promoting permanent officers over the heads of their colleagues in the militia or, as he put it, of making efficiency rather than seniority the test in determining advancement. From this, developed a complaint that Hutton was acting arbitrarily and making decisions on appointments before they were sanctioned by cabinet. In March, Hutton passed over a senior militia officer, Lieutenant-Colonel Braithwaite, whom he described as 'weak, ignorant and in-experienced',[132] and gave the command of the Light Horse at the Victorian Easter camp to a permanent soldier. This caused a furore in cabinet, political pressure was brought to

---

[128] CPD, 1903 session, XIV, 2265–78, 16 July 1903.

[129] CPD, 1902 session, XV, 3120, 5 August 1903.

[130] CPD, 1903 session, XVI, 4875, 10 September 1903.

[131] Letter, Hutton to Forrest, 4 May 1903, Hutton Papers, add. ms. 50085, Vol. VII, p. 281; see also letter, Hutton to Forrest, 3 April 1903, ibid., and letter, Hutton to Lord Tennyson, 4 May 1903; 'I am not prepared to continue the Sisyphus task in which I must fail unless I have assistance of an adequate degree', Hutton Papers, add. ms. 50082, Vol. V.

[132] Letter, Hutton to Forrest, 25 March 1903, Hutton Papers, add. ms. 50085, Vol. VIII, p.281.

bear by a number of members of parliament, and, though Forrest and Barton won the fight for Hutton, it went 'against the grain'. 'The difficulty is "the Citizen soldier" is being overlooked', wrote Forrest. They demanded that Hutton make no more announcements of the kind without first gaining cabinet's consent.[133]

Hutton saw that everything he stood for was being repudiated by parliament and the politicians. His authority was flouted and his advice spurned. The nationalizing of the militia in a field force, the development of a professional officer corps, and most important, the 'broad' policy, which would have made Australian forces available for imperial duty overseas had been sabotaged by political parochialism and expediency. Even though he had been worsted in the parliamentary battle, Hutton, as was his wont, fought on with those weapons which remained to him. Reporting on the abandoning of the overseas clause, Hutton wrote Ommanney at the Colonial Office that,

> I have no fear whatever, but that in a National Emergency the major part, if not the whole of the Field Force will volunteer for service abroad. I shall take care that this description of spirit shall be the guiding principle of at least all the troops comprising the Field Force.[134]

The ministerial changes which followed the resignations of Barton and Forrest in September and the general election of December did nothing to repair the relationship between the commanding officer and the Commonwealth government. Hutton was pleased to be rid of Forrest, even though it was Forrest who had often protected him against the wrath of the other ministers, for 'He was never in sympathy with the Troops and had no real interest in the success of any Military Scheme.[135]

The Deakin ministry, which held office from August 1903 until April 1904, persisted with the policies pioneered under Barton and showed no inclination to buckle under to Hutton.[136] Growing Russo-Japanese tensions in Manchuria caused some concern in Australia and Britain. As

[133] Cabinet notes, 31 March 1903, Barton Papers. It was agreed, after confirming the appointment, that the prime minister should 'place a minute on the paper regretting the manner in which the G.O.C. had dealt with the matter'; letter, Forrest to Hutton, 25 March 1903, Hutton Papers, add. ms. 50085, Vol. VIII, p. 281; letter, Tennyson to Hutton, 27 March 1903, ibid., add. ms. 50082, Vol. V, pp. 86–7.
[134] Letter, Hutton to , August 1903, Hutton Papers, add. ms. 50078, Vol. I, p. 304.
[135] Ibid.
[136] When Hutton, irked by the criticisms of Captain Collins, the Secretary of the Defence Department, went over the head of the defence minister and took his grievance directly to the governor-general and the prime minister, Deakin offered no sympathy or support. Indeed he considered that Hutton's attempt to involve the governor-general in the incident was 'utterly indefensible'. His chief concern was to 'shield' Lord Tennyson 'from being in any way whatever officially concerned in purely departmental differences between two public servants'. Even though Hutton had appealed to the governor-general as his commander-in-chief and Tennyson had seemed inclined to meddle, Deakin would have none of it. The supremacy of the civil power over the military and of the responsible ministers over the conduct of government business was vindicated. Hutton was to be left to his minister. 'Were I his minister', Deakin commented caustically, 'he would have a very short reply.' See copy of letter, Hutton to Chapman, 23 November 1903, letter, Tennyson to Deakin, 26 November 1903, letter, Deakin to Tennyson, 27 November 1903 and letter, Tennyson to Deakin, 27 November 1903, Deakin Papers, 1540/6/4734–7.

a result of consultations with Britain's ally, the War Office sent a curious unofficial inquiry to Hutton. In a 'private and personal' letter, Sir Ian Hamilton told the Australian commander that the 'Japanese would like the cooperation of some of our fellows in Manchuria — especially Cavalry' and that he had suggested to the War Council that 'Australia might easily send 3-4,000 mounted men, who would be more than a match for twice their number of Cossacks'. It was quite noticeable how the British view of the fighting value of the Australian soldier altered with changing circumstances. Hutton replied that, as things stood, unless the British Empire was engaged directly in the war, neither the Commonwealth government nor he, himself, as their servant, could do anything to support the raising of a mercenary force to fight for Japan. At the same time, though, he allowed that, if the pay were sufficiently attractive, many Boer War veterans might be induced to enlist for such an operation. The Australian government was aware of the consequences which might follow from a Russo-Japanese war and had already consulted him about the numbers and organization of a force, which might be sent if Britain became directly involved in such a war.[137] Hutton evidently believed that the Far Eastern situation would play into his hands. He expected a modification of 'this narrow policy … in the near future'.[138] But this heady optimism had no basis in Australian political sentiment. When the Commonwealth government decided to send a military observer to report on the Russo-Japanese war, they set aside Hutton's nominee and appointed 'that arch-intriguer and soldier in buckram', Colonel J. C. Hoad. Hutton was deeply offended, for ever since South African days he had been convinced that Hoad lacked the intelligence, decorum and professional loyalty required of an officer, and he had made no secret of his opinion.[139]

Hutton had, by this time, made up his mind to resign at the end of his term of office in December and he, therefore, felt free to speak his piece. His second annual report of 1 May 1904 was a reaffirmation of the principles of his original defence scheme and a statement of the achievements and deficiencies in the Australian defence forces. He deplored the reduction in the headquarters' staff at Victoria Barracks from eight to six officers, which was five less than the number suggested by the Colonial Defence Committee and two below the New South Wales headquarters' staff prior to federation. If the decision was carried through, it would be 'impracticable for the commanding officer to accept the responsibility' for the efficient administration of the military forces. He advised an increase in the artillery and the expenditure of £524,000 for arms, ammunitions and military stores. He warned that Australia needed a military force capable of resisting an invasion of up to 50,000 armed men. The events in the North Pacific were used to illustrate that this was not a theoretical proposition. He foresaw a struggle of

---

[137] Letter, Hamilton to Hutton, sent 25 December, received 2 February 1904, and copy of letter, Hutton to Hamilton, 3 February 1904, Hutton Papers, add. ms. 50086, Vol. IX, pp. 388–96.

[138] Letter, Hutton to Duke of Connaught, Hutton Papers, add. ms. 50078, Vol. I.

[139] Copy of letter, Hutton to Tennyson, 19 April 1904, Hutton Papers, add. ms. 50082, Vol. V, p. 103; copy of letter, Hutton to Sir William Nicholson, 8 April 1904, ibid., add. ms. 50086, Vol. IX. In his confidential report to the minister on his officers he concluded with respect to Hoad that he was 'an officer of limited capacity and military knowledge', MP 729/1.

the great powers for commercial supremacy in the region and contended that, if Australia did not maintain 'a reasonable measure of defence' — the implication being that at that time it did not —, then its interests 'must be seriously compromised, if not imperilled'.[140]

Hutton's autocratic style and devious tactics rebounded on his head. Throughout 1904 the defence ministers, Austin Chapman in Deakin's government, Senator Andrew Dawson in Watson's Labor government, April to August 1904, and Lieutenant-Colonel J. W. McCay in the Reid-McLean coalition government, August 1904 to June 1905, devoted their best efforts to revising the Defence Act, in order to curb the powers of the commanding officer. Though the amendments followed the recommendations of the Esher Committee, which had been set up in 1902 to reform the War Office and, indeed, some of the language in the amending act of 1904 was taken bodily from the Esher report, nevertheless, the main motive behind the revisions was a desire to give the government greater influence over the administration of the defence department by dividing functions and working through collective leadership of a Defence Council and Military and Naval Boards. On 16 August Senator Dawson presented a report which argued that, since the General Officer Commanding was under the 1903 bill, the 'sole responsible officer' of the government in defence matters, the government was deprived of firsthand knowledge of technical questions. It was felt that the minister should be 'directly in touch with the force'. The powers of the commanding officer were thought to be 'too wide'. In order to secure continuity of policy, responsibility should be shared. Finally, and more distinctly in line with the Esher committee's findings, the report urged that new mechanisms were needed to integrate more happily the civil and military, as well as the naval and military, sections of the defence department. The report proposed as remedies that the post of General Officer Commanding should be abolished and that its function be divided between an inspector-general who would have charge of supervising discipline and training and a Military Board, which would have responsibility, under the government, for policy and administration. It further suggested that a Director of Naval Forces should be appointed and a Naval Board set up to administer this arm of the defence forces. Superimposed on the whole structure there was to be a Council of Defence comprising the minister, who would be chairman, the treasurer, the inspector-general, the chief of the general staff and the Director of Naval Forces.

Hutton, who was invited out of courtesy to comment on the report, entered a vigorous dissent. In his submission, he claimed that any failure in the existing system followed from the inadequate means which had been given him. He saw in the proposal a method by which the secretary of the Defence Department would come to dominate the administration of the armed forces. He pleaded for the continuance of the post of General Officer Commanding, arguing that Australian officers did not have the experience and knowledge to provide the material for a colonial model of the Army Council. The inspector-general system could not work under Australian circumstances; the Australian forces required a leader and instructor more than an inspector. In particular, Hutton recommended that an imperial officer should be appointed to succeed him for there was no Australian officer equal to the task. He could accept a Military

---

[140] CofA, *Parliamentary Papers*, 1904 session, Vol. II, No. 25.

Board of Advice, which would co-ordinate civil and military aspects of administration, but its function should be limited to advising the commanding officer and the defence minister.[141]

The Commonwealth government was in no way deterred by Hutton's opposition. Colonel McCay, who became minister of defence in the Reid-McLean government, shortly after Dawson had brought down his report, completely endorsed its sentiments. He was, himself, a militia officer and very conscious of the professional officers' arrogation of power under Hutton's administration. The amending bill, which McCay introduced on 2 November, followed very closely the findings of the Dawson report. It established a Council of Defence and a Military and a Naval Board, abolished the post of General Officer Commanding and provided for the appointment of an Inspector-General of Military Forces and a Director of Naval Forces. McCay also indicated that these administrative changes might well be followed by more wide-ranging policy changes, both for coastal defence and for 'systematic cadet training in schools'. 'We must', the minister said, 'take care to be prepared for the future.'[142] Perhaps the Russo-Japanese War did give a vague strategic reason for the bill. J. Page, a Queensland Labor member, did interpolate the Yellow Peril into the debate. For the first time, he gave voice to the view that 'Australia is now coveted by the overcrowded races of the East; the Japanese are equal to any white race on sea or land, and in a very few years may make the Chinese the same',[143] but he was the only member to try and relate the bill to Australia's fears of Asia. Forrest put his finger on the major cause when, in mildly criticizing the suggested changes, he deprecated making 'a radical change' merely because 'Hutton carried out his duties in a somewhat autocratic manner and centralized the control to a greater extent than is considered desirable'.[144] By the end of December the bill became law and, over the protests of Hutton and the governor-general,[145] the government appointed an Australian officer, Major-General H. Finn, as inspector-general. Captain W. R. Creswell was made Director of Naval Forces. And the First meeting of the Council of Defence was held on 12 May 1905. The administrative revolution had taken place without any consultation with London and when the Colonial Office were informed, they dismissed it contemptuously: 'I suppose, so long as our Fleet is supreme, the Australians can continue to play a game of soldiers under any rules they like.'[146]

On 15 November Major-General Hutton resigned as commander of Australia's military forces. He had come with high hopes and good qualifications. His knowledge and understanding of colonial politics and colonial troops far exceeded that of any other imperial officer. He approved, in principle, of the citizen army as a basis for the colonial defence force. He was less

---

[141] CofA, *Parliamentary Papers*, 1904 session, Vol. II, No. 58, 'Defence Forces of the Commonwealth (Memorandum by a Committee in Regard to the Administration of Military and Naval Forces together with a Memorandum thereon by Senator A. Dawson and Major-General Sir E. T. H. Hutton)'; copy of letter, Hutton to Ommanney, 14 June 1904, Hutton Papers, add. ms. 50078, Vol. I, pp. 312–13.

[142] *CPD*, 1904 session, XXIII, 6383–9.

[143] Ibid., XXIII, 7498, 25 November 1904.

[144] Ibid., XXIV, 7490, 25 November 1904.

[145] Letter, Lord Northcote to Joseph Chamberlain, 20 August 1904, Joseph Chamberlain Papers, 19/1/5.

[146] CO 418/31/604.

class-bound than was the case with the British officer caste in general, though there were limits to his tolerance of the lesser breeds below the salt. In this connection, he was willing to concede that Watson's Labor ministers were honest and well-intentioned, but as men he thought them unimpressive. He adjudged Senator Dawson to be almost illiterate: 'He cannot write a legible letter and has great difficulty in reading. He cannot read handwriting.' He cited in evidence a letter of thanks from Dawson.

> I have yours of the 27th inst. and desire to express my thanks for your kind congratulations. I heartily reciprocate the wish that the relations between yourself and the department will be as cordial as they were before. I have personally resigned from the Select Committee, as has also Senator McGregor. It will sit tomorrow but it is hardly likely in my opinion to take any important evidence.[147]

It was not an elegant composition, but the meaning was clear, and the grammar and syntax compared quite favourably with those often found in Hutton's own works. Like the governors-general, he found himself more comfortable in the company of the anti-Labor ministers and, like them, he looked to a union of protectionists and free-traders to keep the 'enemy' at bay.[148]

In framing his defence scheme and in the execution of defence policy, he pursued professional, national and imperial aims. He sought efficiency and considered that only a well-trained, disciplined and educated army could achieve this. He risked unpopularity in influential circles by ignoring the claims of senior militia officers with long service and by promoting younger and more qualified permanent officers over their heads. He quietly encouraged the fading away of the old 'volunteers', replacing them with paid militia. He recognized that the citizen soldier could only be made amenable to discipline if he were paid for his service. He had, as his national goal, the effective integration of the formerly separate and independent colonial military forces. In order to achieve this end, he maintained a tight control over the work of the states and moved his permanent officers periodically from state to state. Equally, he hoped that the mobile field force would aid in the process of nationalizing the Australian army. Many former colonial officers and soldiers resented the centralized control, the movement of officers, the disturbing of local ties and influence. And this reaction against Hutton's nationalizing and professionalizing efforts, in part, explain the 1904 Defence Act.

However, while the professional and national policies served a justifiable Commonwealth purpose, Hutton also intended that they should serve an imperial purpose. He realized that Australia would never permit an imperial reserve as such, whether it was subject to War Office control or deployed only with the consent of the Commonwealth. He saw that any attempt to foist such a scheme on the Commonwealth would result in the kinds of colonial-imperial conflicts which sparked off the American War of Independence; it was a tax in blood or money without any reciprocal representation. On the other hand, he believed that the empire had to organize on a co-operative basis so that it would be able to call on trained troops from all the dominions, should a great emergency arise. For this reason, he had sought broad powers for the Commonwealth

---

[147] Letter, Dawson to Hutton, 28 April 1904, Hutton Papers, add. ms. 50085, Vol. VIII, p. 36.
[148] Letter, Hutton to Ommanney, 19 August 1903, ibid., add. ms. 50078, Vol. I, p. 304.

government, so that Australian forces could be sent wherever Australian interests were menaced. Of course, since he believed that Australian and imperial interests were one, this was but a device. When war came, he believed that the Commonwealth government would acknowledge its responsibility to assist the empire and he was trying to ensure that it would be free to send immediate aid. He discreetly said nothing about the wider imperial question in the campaign for the adoption of his defence bill. In preparing a defence scheme to encompass this purpose, he also acted independently of the Colonial Defence Committee and the War Office and, in arguing his case, he spoke of the possibility of an Asian invasion which the British authorities thought chimerical, but yet which he knew appealed to a distinctive Australian apprehension.

When cabinet and parliament rebuffed him, he refused to accept their decision. By personally persuading politicians, by instilling into the army a spirit of imperial service, and by public criticism, he still hoped to have his own way. He wrote Lord Roberts that, 'I have done my utmost, officially and unofficially, publicly and privately to induce public opinion to take a broader view of the military necessities.'[149] He was a dogged and determined man, a man in search of a destiny. It was his hope that the Australian defence scheme would become the model for the rest of the empire. He believed unto the last that history was on his side and that Australia would have to adopt his policy. The problem of establishing an effective relationship between imperial and colonial defence forces was a difficult one. Hutton's solution was probably, for its time, the most reasonable of those which confronted the question square on. Buoyed up by the conviction of his rightness and even more by his commitment to the empire, he was willing to act in an arrogant manner and resort to underhand means to gain his object. Even so, there were things that he could not bring himself to do. Holding a high view of the dignity of his post, he would not humiliate himself before the politicians. He could not ingratiate himself with the politicians and, in that sense, he was unable to play politics. His aloofness in the Australian ethos was resented and tended to keep in view his imperial connections.

And the imperial connections could never be severed. With all his experience in the colonies, Hutton could never forget that he was a British officer. He still wrote to the Colonial Office, the War Office, and the commander-in-chief as though he were responsible to them and as though it was his duty to carry out their policies. He inspired a group of junior officers, including Lieutenant-Colonel W. T. Bridges and Captain C. B. Brudenell White with the same deferential imperialism. But these assumptions of superiority and inferiority, of centre and periphery, could not be harmonized easily with the realities of self-government in the colonies. The Commonwealth government was determined to keep control over its own defence forces. It was determined not to do anything beforehand, which would compromise its ability to decide on how its forces should be used in a particular crisis. This sensitivity over sovereignty was in many ways the cause of the introverted military defence policy adopted in the first years of the Commonwealth. The clause limiting the use of Australian soldiers to Commonwealth territories was a symbolic not a substantial one. Nevertheless, symbols, as the 1916 and 1917 conscription referenda demonstrated, do often come to play political roles which were not anticipated by their

---

[149] Letter, Hutton to Roberts, 19 August 1903, Hutton Papers, add. ms. 50085, Vol. VIII, p. 220.

creators. Hutton, no matter how far he bent in order to accommodate himself to colonial susceptibilities, could never go as far as Australia's sense of political nationality demanded.

## Naval policy and naval subsidy

The Commonwealth government had greater difficulty in settling on a naval policy. Naval defence raised complex imperial problems. Whereas the British government had always recognized that the control and organization of local military forces was strictly a matter for colonial determination, their attitude towards local navies had been more ambiguous. When in the middle of the nineteenth century Great Britain had been busily engaged in shedding its responsibility for colonial government, it had been agreed that the self-governing colonies should be able to establish naval forces for local defence. Under the authority bestowed on them by the Colonial Naval Defence Act of 1865, the Australian colonies had thus acquired a collection of naval vessels for harbour and coastal defence. However, the Admiralty opposed the notion of colonies obtaining an ocean-going navy. It was feared that an offensive capacity on the high seas might enable the colonies to entangle Britain in diplomatic incidents and compromise its foreign policy. Moreover, towards the end of the century the Admiralty, having been converted to the doctrine of concentration and mobility, came to regard colonial navies as wasteful and to look at limitations placed on the movements of imperial squadrons which were subsidized by the colonies as unreasonable restraints on its freedom of action. The great weight of the Admiralty's mystique—the mystique of the invincibility and supremacy of the Royal Navy—was thrown behind the centralizing slogan of 'one Empire, one sea, one fleet' and the movement to persuade the colonies to abandon their infant navies and to contribute without conditions to the imperial fleet. In this situation, the Commonwealth government found itself torn between, on the one hand, its respect for Admiralty authority and its need for an economical defence, and, on the other, its doubts whether under the centralizing doctrine the British fleet would protect Australian coasts against raids in time of war and its national sentiment which demanded a local navy for reasons of self-respect.

The Barton government did not give the naval question a high priority in their initial defence planning. In the first defence bill it was almost overlooked.[150] However, the issue could not be postponed indefinitely. The future of the naval forces and vessels taken over from the colonies had to be decided and the 1887 naval agreement, which had expired in 1899, had to be reconsidered. The Commonwealth government, when it came to office, had before them the report of the naval officers' conference of August 1899, and also a memorandum of September 1900 by Captain R. Muirhead Collins, the secretary of the Victorian Defence Department, who became the first secretary of the Commonwealth Defence Department. Both papers urged the importance of building up an independent Australian naval force. The colonial naval officers disapproved of the imperial proposal that Australia should make its contribution to naval defence by establishing a branch of the Royal Naval Reserve. Since such a Reserve would be under the control of the

---

[150] *CPD*, 1901–2 session, II, 2163, 9 July 1901.

Commander-in-Chief on the Australian Station, they pointed out that the Australian sailors would be merely an adjunct to British strength. The naval officers argued that Australia was an island-continent and must, therefore, depend on the navy for its defence. Like Hutton, they knew how to gild the strategic pill in order to make it acceptable to the Australian people. They warned of the growing strength of French, Russian and Japanese naval power and naval bases in the Pacific. They predicted that the Pacific would become the new Mediterranean, the maritime cockpit in which the great powers would struggle for supremacy. Australia had to prepare its defence against the day. It, therefore, needed a naval force of its own. They estimated that if the moneys paid in subsidy for the auxiliary squadron were added to the moneys which the colonies had allocated for the local forces, the federal government would be able to purchase five second-class cruisers and train the reserve necessary to man them in time of war. Piously, they noted that the result would be 'a substantial addition to the fleet of the Empire', even if it were not in the form desired by the Admiralty.[151]

During 1901 the naval officers continued to mount their case for an Australian navy. Captain W. R. Creswell, commandant of the Queensland naval forces became the focal point in this campaign. Creswell, who became the first commandant of the Commonwealth's naval forces and in December 1904, the first Director of Naval Forces, played an important role in the development of the Australian navy. He had retired from the Royal Navy as a lieutenant in 1879, at a time when naval expenditure was being cut and career prospects looked bleak, and emigrated to Australia. In 1885 he had joined the South Australian cruiser, *Protector*, as a lieutenant and in 1895 was made captain in South Australia's naval forces. In May 1900 he had accepted an offer to take command of the Queensland naval force and from August to December was, as captain of the *Protector*, on active service in the China Seas. As a result of his own experience in the navy, Creswell had become disenchanted with the Admiralty, and after twenty-one years in Australia, he had begun to identify himself with colonial interests and the colonial perspective. This combination of factors turned Creswell into a self-assertive and vocal spokesman for an Australian navy.[152]

Sensing that the colonial naval forces were in danger of becoming extinct through neglect, Creswell, on 28 September 1901, thrust a further report on the Minister of Defence, reaffirming the views of the naval officers. A policy of subsidies was 'one of stagnation and continued naval impotence for Australia—tying up for an indefinite time the country's best defensive arm'. He maintained that 'an absolute and complete dependence by Australia upon the British navy' was unfair to the imperial fleet and a denial of Australia's own responsibilities. Following the success of the *Protector*, Creswell recommended the gradual acquisition over a period of ten years of five cruisers specially adapted to Australian circumstances. The cost would run to approximately

---

[151] CofA, *Parliamentary Papers*, 1901–2 session, Vol. II, No. 27, 'Report of the Conference of Naval Officers Assembled at Melbourne to consider the Question of Naval Defence of Australia'; Macandie, *Genesis of the Royal Australian Navy*, pp. 75–6.

[152] Sir William Rooke Creswell, *Close to the Wind: The Early Memoirs (1866–79) of Admiral Sir William Creswell*, Paul Thompson (ed.), London 1965, esp. the introduction and Ch. XVI.

£300,000 or £350,000 a year, the greater proportion of which would be covered by existing appropriations for local forces and subsidy. He felt that to request such a sum out of a total defence budget of £850,000 was not unreasonable, since the navy was the first and only real line of defence in Australian circumstances. He was content that the cruisers in time of war should be placed at the disposal of the admiral on the Australian station for service in local waters.[153] In an article published in the press later that year, Creswell expanded on the political and strategic basis for his scheme. He described the imperial attitude to colonial navies as one of 'discouragement and aloofness'. He cited the failure of the auxiliary squadron to furnish the promised training facilities for naval reserves in the colonies. He implicitly questioned the wisdom of deferring to the Admiralty's opinion on such matters. While accepting the imperial view that Australia was free from fear of invasion, he contended that fixed defences were not sufficient to ward off raids on Australia's commerce and coastline. The prospect of such raids had increased over the years. He reiterated the naval officers' strategic outline, Europe had come to Asia. Japan had risen 'to a forward place among naval powers'. More modern types of cruisers and the potential conversion of fast mail-steamers to naval purposes introduced naval dangers into the picture. The auxiliary squadron was out of date. The Commonwealth needed a larger, more modern naval force, and it needed one which was Australian, both in its composition and control. This was the substance of Creswell's case. Creswell was, like Hutton, something of a publicist and a politician,[154] but in both capacities he proved to be the more successful. Perhaps the reason for his greater influence was simply that he had chosen a cause which jelled with national needs and national sentiment.

The stand taken by the naval officers on behalf of an Australian navy is easily explained. The colonial officers were fighting for their professional lives. They were inherently no greater nationalists than the imperial army officers who had been seconded to the colonies or who had taken up posts in the land forces. They were nearly all retired Royal Navy officers. And even given a certain resentment among men like Creswell, it was still not possible for them to doubt the British navy's invincibility. They indeed evinced some difficulty in finding plausible arguments to justify their demand. Heedless of the Admiralty's protestations to the contrary, they had to assert that an Australian flotilla would relieve the Mother Country of the responsibility for local naval defence, and that it would, in addition, offer a useful addition to the total strength of the imperial navy. The protagonists of an Australian navy had no answer to the Admiralty's doctrine of concentration and flexibility. They could not counter the claims that the British navy had a responsibility for the security of the whole empire and that this entailed unity of operation and command. They indirectly suggested that a local naval force would offer a sure defence of ports and trade, that it would be permanently stationed in Australian waters. They did not explain why

---

[153] C of A, *Parliamentary Papers*, 1901–2 session, Vol. II, No. 52, 'Report by Captain Creswell on the Best Method of Employing Australian Seamen in the Defence of Commerce and Ports'; Macandie, pp. 87–104.
[154] His talent for gaining publicity manifested itself early in his Australian career. In 1886, appalled at the lack of interest in naval defence in the colonies, he wrote a series of articles for the South Australian *Register* and from that time became a fast friend of J. Harvey Finlayson, the editor of the newspaper, see *Close to the Wind*, p. 196.

a revised naval agreement, producing through subsidy a bigger and better auxiliary squadron, could not more effectively and cheaply satisfy the same purpose. Nevertheless, there was something in the lure of independence, the sense that a nation cannot either decently or safely leave its defence entirely in the hands of great and powerful kinsmen, which enabled the naval officers to strike a responsive chord in parliament and among the public. But it was not until a palpable threat appeared on the immediate horizon that the Australian political leaders and people were willing to give substance to sentiment and bear the cost of their feelings of national self-respect.

In the debate on the first defence bill, many voices were raised in favour of an Australian navy; Creswell's influence, even at this point, was apparent. Sir John Quick wondered whether as 'a self-relying, self-governing people', Australia ought to leave its naval defence to Britain.[155] George Reid spoke up for preparing for an 'independent Australian navy'.[156] Joseph Cook vaguely supported forming the nucleus of a future Australian navy.[157] Hughes, alone of them all, offered a possible strategic justification for such a force. He argued that Britain was struggling to maintain its margin of superiority over its naval rivals and he stated if war ever came, Britain would indubitably withdraw its warships from Australian waters. Australia would then be helpless; invasion would not be impossible. But he did not press home his point and demand immediate provision of an Australian navy.[158] Perhaps he thought that his plan for compulsory military training had more merit. A small number of Labor men, including Watson, indeed opposed an Australian naval force on the grounds of expense.[159] Only one member sought a larger contribution to the British navy.[160] The prime minister, in winding up the debate, answered the navy lobby by declaring that such a project was financially impracticable and that the only alternative open to them was to reallocate the contributions paid under the 1887 agreement for the development of a local force or to renew the agreement on better terms.[161]

The Commonwealth government proceeded quite unperturbed by the public campaign. On 10 June Barton turned to the commander-in-chief on the Australian station, Sir Lewis Beaumont, for advice on the naval defence of Australia. To Barton the most important consideration was economy. He informed Beaumont that the government had to keep down costs and, therefore, limit the permanent nucleus of a local force. Even had Beaumont been so minded, such strictures must have inhibited him from recommending the development of an autonomous Australian navy.

---

[155] *CPD*, 1901–2 session, III, 2966. 24 July 1901.

[156] Ibid., III, 3102, 26 July 1901.

[157] Ibid., III, 8526, 7 August 1901; see also G. A. Cruikshank, a New South Wales protectionist, ibid., III, 3427, 1 August 1901; McDonald ibid., III, 3520, 1 August 1901, R. Edwards, ibid., III, 3592, 9 August 1901.

[158] Ibid., III, 3791, 30 July 1901.

[159] Ibid.

[160] Ibid., 3515, 7 August 1901, W. B. S. C. Sawers of New South Wales.

[161] Ibid., III, 3592, 9 August 1901.

Beaumont's reply followed very different lines. He deprecated the idea of building up an independent local navy upon the basis of the colonial organizations. Sidestepping the broad strategic questions, he recommended that the Commonwealth should increase its contribution to the auxiliary squadron and subsidize a squadron of at least six cruisers, two first-class and four second-class, in commission, and two second-class cruisers in reserve. The squadron would remain under the command of the Admiral on the Australian station and the men enlisted in these ships would serve under the same conditions as those in the Royal Navy.[162] This report was presented to parliament on 15 August and Creswell's submission in the following month might well have been provoked by the publication of Beaumont's view.

For financial reasons, Beaumont's proposal was not altogether acceptable,[163] but he had more influence than Creswell over the government. On 7 November, at a meeting with Barton and Forrest, Admiral Beaumont put forward a much modified version of his earlier scheme. In the new version the Commonwealth would not be required to pay the total cost of the eight-cruiser squadron. The cost was to be shared between Britain, New Zealand and Australia, Australia's share being £140,000. At the same time, prompted by the Australian ministers, Beaumont agreed that a local naval reserve should be trained in order to provide a reservoir of sailors in time of war and he thought that the older cruisers of the auxiliary squadron might be transferred to the Commonwealth for the purpose. The overall cost to the Commonwealth for such a naval policy would be £234,000.[164]

Again, Creswell responded. Crumbs from the master's table did not meet his conception of Australia's role in the empire. He stirred up support in the newspapers. The Brisbane *Courier* on 21 December, the *Sydney Morning Herald* on 20 December, the *Argus* on 18 December, the *Age* on 20 December, the *Register* on 13 March 1902, all approved his scheme for an Australian naval force. Questions were asked at his instance in parliament. Sir Langdon Bonython, a South Australian friend, asked that Creswell's report be printed.[165]

As the Colonial Conference approached, the government was compelled to accelerate its thinking on the matter.[166] This was clearly the occasion for discussing naval defence with the imperial authorities. The Colonial Office had indicated their intention of raising the matter and New Zealand had given notice of a resolution endorsing Beaumont's scheme. Under such pressure, Forrest drew up for the prime minister a minute on the Commonwealth's naval defence needs. Forrest took his cue from Beaumont. In his introduction he agreed that British naval supremacy protected Australia from invasion and Australia's responsibility was limited to securing its ports and commerce from enemy raiders. He regarded the existing local force as 'of small value

---

[162] CofA, *Parliamentary Papers*, 1901–2 session, Vol. II, A12 'Rear Admiral Sir Lewis Beaumont's view on Naval Defence for Australia'.

[163] *SMH*, 12 September 1901.

[164] Macandie, *Genesis of the Royal Australian Navy*, pp. 79–81.

[165] *CPD*, 1901–2 session, IV, 4800–1, 12 September 1901 and VII, 8715, 13 December 1901.

[166] *Age*, 18 February 1902; *SMH*, 18 February 1902.

for naval defence'. An Australian navy was too costly and inefficient to be seriously entertained. Forrest looked toward a thorough-going imperial solution. Australians had to

> altogether get rid of the idea that we have different interests to those of the rest of the Empire, and we must look at the matter from a broad common standpoint. … There is only one sea to be supreme over, and we want the fleet to be mistress over that sea.

He had made the dictum of the Blue Water school his own However, he super-imposed on that the Chamberlain definition of empire; indeed, Forrest was such a pedantic imperialist that he refused to use the world 'nation' in referring to Australia. He said that: 'Our aim and object should be to make the Royal Navy the Empire's navy.' And what this entailed was not only contributions of men and money from all parts of the empire, but also adequate representation of the 'British Dominions beyond the Seas' at the Admiralty. He had come to share Chamberlain's imperial vision. In the meantime, he recommended a revision of the naval agreement and, after negotiating the numbers and classes of ships to be supplied and the contribution to be paid, its renewal for a further ten-year period. The local forces were to be trained as reserves for the imperial squadron. The permanent naval force of the Commonwealth was to be reduced to a skeletal staff for training the reserves. Expert advice was to be sought on the future of the colonial vessels.[167]

Forrest consulted Hutton about his paper on naval defence. Hutton gave his assent to the general drift of the argument. He had no desire to compete with local naval officers for limited defence funds. Moreover, such a scheme comported with his own view of imperial co-operation. Joseph Chamberlain had informed him before he left England that Australia would not need a navy 'as long as the Old Country kept control of the seas'.[168] Hutton, too, was more acutely attuned to colonial sensitivities and more appreciative of the full import of Chamberlain's imperialism. Thus, he suggested, to Forrest, that the Australian naval militia should have 'its own identity and training ships' and that instead of representation at the Admiralty, Australia should seek participation in policy making in 'a Council of Nations and Defence, of which naturally the dominating elements would be the Imperial representatives of the Army and Navy'.[169] Forrest, perhaps, encouraged by Beaumont, did not amend his draft to meet Hutton's major points, but rather, on the advice of Barton, 'launched it on a sea of criticism' inside the cabinet.[170] Surprisingly the document survived this process. It is hard to believe that Kingston, and even Deakin and Lyne, would have let a statement on policy, which was so out of keeping with Australian attitude to defence, escape their notice. Yet Forrest was able, with or without cabinet's approval, to present the minute, unaltered, to the colonial conference and to have it printed as a conference document.

However, it was Barton and not Forrest who took the lead for Australia in the defence discussions and negotiations at the conference. Forrest was ill for most of the conference and

---

[167] CO, Miscellaneous Print No. 144, 'Report of 1902 Colonial Conference', Appendix V, pp. 253–7, CO 885/8.

[168] Notes on Interview between the Colonial Secretary and Sir Edward Hutton at the Colonial Office, 19 December 1901, Hutton Papers, add. ms. 50078, Vol. I.

[169] Copy of letter, Hutton to Forrest, 11 April 1902, Hutton Papers, add. ms. 50084, Vol. III, p. 248.

[170] Letter, Forrest to Hutton, 10 April 1902, Hutton Papers, add. ms. 50084, Vol. VII, p. 244.

Barton acted without even consulting his colleague. Barton's approach to defence policy was never well worked out. He did not on naval questions, any more than on military, follow any clear principle—whether imperial or national, strategic or political. Barton's naval policy was dominated by one concern, the poverty of the federal purse. He managed to shroud all his utterances on defence policy in that flabby language which is the resort of politicians who do not understand the issue or who have not made up their mind where they stand with respect to it. But this continued vagueness gave him great flexibility in manoeuvring. In preparing for the conference he had a wide range of opinions to draw upon, the local naval officers, the commander-in-chief on the Australian station, his defence minister and Lord Hopetoun, the governor-general.

Of them all Hopetoun's views probably weighed most heavily with Barton. In a letter which Barton received just before his departure for London, Hopetoun confirmed Barton's feelings about the Creswell scheme. 'Those who talk as glibly about a fleet of second-class cruisers for the Commonwealth hardly appreciate or wilfully ignore the huge cost of such an undertaking.' In order to be able to meet and match the French and Russian warships in the Pacific, Australia would have to arm itself with the most powerful modern cruisers at a cost of £1,000,000 each. The governor-general then went on to back the recommendations of Beaumont and Forrest. He supported a policy of increased subsidies in return for a more substantial imperial Australian squadron. As a sop to the naval-minded in Australia, he favoured the adoption of Beaumont's plan for a local 'citizen sailor' force which could be used as an imperial reserve in time of war.[171]

The Admiralty had also been preparing for the conference. In their submission which summarized a decade of thinking about imperial naval strategy and organization, the Admiralty drew attention to the growth of the French, German, Russian and American fleets, which they took as an augury of a coming struggle for naval supremacy. According to their analysis, the outcome of this struggle would depend upon the capacity of the different nations to concentrate their forces at the decisive point. In order to survive the challenge, the British Empire had to have 'a single navy, under one control'. The paper demonstrated how Britain was bearing an unreasonably high proportion of the cost of protecting colonial commerce in the Indian and Pacific Oceans. It clearly implied that the colonies should contribute more towards the costs of their defence. In the case of the Commonwealth the Admiralty had calculated that it should contribute £387,490 towards the upkeep of the Australian squadron and also provide £100,000 for training a colonial reserve.[172]

Lord Selborne, the First Lord of the Admiralty, elaborated on these themes on 14 July when he opened the debate on naval policy at the conference. He explained that, since the primary

---

[171] Letter, Hopetoun to Barton, 29 April 1902, Barton Papers, 51/497.

[172] Co, Confidential Print, Miscellaneous No. 144, Appendix IV. A, CO 885/8; see also CO 323/474/131–41; see also paper on 'Colonial Navies—Colonial Contributions' by H. O. Arnold Forster. secretary of state for war, for Lord Selbourne, 12 February 1902, 'Colonies should be induced to contribute in men and money to relieve the immense strain upon the U.K. … It seems scarcely possible to hold any other view than that the formation of separate Navies would be a calamity. …' Arnold Forster Papers, add. ms. 50294.

object of the navy was to search out and destroy the enemy, there could be 'no allocation of ships, to protect the mouth of the Thames, Liverpool, Sydney or Halifax'. Expanding upon the Admiralty's point that Russia possessed an Atlantic and a Pacific fleet, he disclosed that the French president had issued a decree strengthening France's naval forces in Eastern seas and bringing them under a single command. Against this background he commended Forrest's memorandum and urged that a new agreement be drawn up to provide a more modern and powerful squadron on the Australian station and to provide for the training of an Australian branch of the Royal Naval Reserve. In the light of the need for concentration, he thought the revised agreement should also permit the ships of the Australian squadron to serve anywhere in the Eastern oceans. Here the application of the doctrine of concentration was a regional one. Indeed, down to World War II, the Admiralty thinking with respect to this problem, oscillated back and forth between regional and world-wide concentration. In general, as the pressure of events in Europe brought danger closer to the British Isles, regionalism gave way to a more exclusive concentration around the British Isles. British resources were not able to afford equal and adequate protection in both theatres simultaneously and when faced with the choice, 'concentration' was reinterpreted to the disadvantage of Pacific security.

Though having considerable sympathy with the Admiralty's proposals, Barton found the specific recommendations unacceptable. In reply to Selborne, he said that because of the cost, he had no intention of creating an Australian navy, that that was a 'matter entirely for future consideration'. For a similar reason, it was impossible for Australia to be as generous as the Admiralty thought proper. He also expressed disquiet over the suggestion that the squadron which Australia would rent should be able to leave Australian waters without the Commonwealth government's consent; such a provision would be unpopular in Australia. Since the responses of the colonies were so disparate—Laurier resisting any kind of co-operation at all—it was decided that interested colonies should individually pursue the matter with the Admiralty.[173]

After Barton had reported back to Melbourne the substance of the Admiralty's proposal, the Australian cabinet went further than its prime minister in their criticisms. They complained that an increased naval subsidy could only be found by cutting back military expenditure and that had already been pruned severely. Further, they denounced the subsidy principle, believing it to be unpopular in the country. Instead, they wanted to put all the Australian effort into training a locally controlled naval reserve on vessels lent by the Admiralty. Their alternative proposition bore a striking similarity to that advocated by Kingston at the 1897 Colonial Conference.[174] Despite this radical advice, when Barton met with the Admiralty, he proceeded to negotiate along the lines which Hopetoun, Forrest, and he himself had agreed upon. The Admiralty grudgingly accepted a lesser increase in the Australian contribution than they had sought. Under the terms of a new ten-year agreement, Australia was to contribute £200,000 and New Zealand £40,000 annually for a reconstructed Australian squadron which would consist of one armoured cruiser, two second-class cruisers, four third-class cruisers and four sloops, all of the most modern type.

---

[173] CO, Confidential Print, Miscellaneous No. 144, pp. 18–39, CO 885/8.
[174] Copy of telegram, acting Prime Minister Deakin to Barton, 16 July 1902, Deakin Papers.

The Admiralty's resentment of colonial parsimony was understandable. The British parliament appropriated more than £31,000,000 each year to maintain the Royal Navy; the colonial subsidies were a very small fraction of that sum. The Australian taxpayer paid only one shilling each annually for naval defence compared to the British taxpayers' fifteen shillings. The Australian subsidy only met about half of the annual maintenance costs of the Australian squadron. The Admiralty took pleasure in drawing Australian attention to the fact that countries of comparable size, such as Argentina and Holland, spent between £920,000 and £1,400,000 annually on their navies. However, the Admiralty never grasped the full significance of colonial self-government, that in a polycentred empire the interests, power and responsibility of its constituent parts were not one. Under the agreement the Admiralty also promised to provide vessels for training 700 men and 25 officers in a branch of the Royal Naval Reserve. Barton, on his side, agreed that the Admiralty should be free to despatch the Australian squadron to any part of the Indian or Pacific Oceans. The Admiralty congratulated the Dominions on their 'improved understanding of naval strategy'.[175] Returning home, Barton had to convince the parliament and people to accept the terms of the new agreement.

Barton's government had only a precarious hold on parliament. It had somehow to contrive a different majority for almost each piece of legislation. The diversity among its own supporters had to be respected. Labor could not be too directly offended. Even the bridges to the free-traders had to be kept in some kind of repair. As Deakin reminded Barton while he was in London, it would be an extraordinary feat if they were able 'to survive the session'.[176] At home Barton hoped, by convincing public opinion, to convert parliament. He defended the naval agreement in terms of a qualified imperialism. He stood for what he called 'a reasonable Imperialism' which, while it avoided 'reckless engagements' in overseas quarrels, nevertheless supported unity 'by all reasonable and wise means, consistent with the preservation of our autonomous governments'.[177] Australia should bear a fair proportion of imperial defence, but this did not mean paying on a per capita basis equal to that of the British taxpayer. Neither the 'Braddon blot' nor Australian interests could allow so much. The unity of naval defence was, however, important, since the unity of the empire depended on control of the seas.[178] In an address to his West Maitland electors, Barton set out the official position of the government. He had wrung a reluctant consent from his cabinet,[179] and in return he had to stress that subsidies were simply a temporary expedient. For financial reasons an 'independent navy' was ruled out for the present, but the

---

[175] CO, Confidential Print, Miscellaneous No. 144, Appendix VIII, 'Memorandum by the First Lord of the Admiralty, August 7, 1902', p. 263, CO 885/8.

[176] Letter, Deakin to Barton, 3 June 1902, Barton Papers, 51/513; see also letter, Forrest to Joseph Chamberlain, 18 September 1902, Joseph Chamberlain Papers, 17/2/7, 'I think we will [be able to pass the Naval Agreement Act], though we have a queer house to deal with and the Government cannot be called brave or bold, some at least being very timid and easily scared'.

[177] SMH, 13 October 1902.

[178] SMH, 18 October, 11 and 29 November 1902.

[179] MP, 6 January 1903.

government expected that, once the difficulties created by the Braddon clause had been overcome, steps would be taken to establish an Australian navy. The naval reservists who were to be trained under the agreement would supply the manpower.[180]

This campaign of explanation and justification was necessary. Reid was on the hustings lamenting the fact that the Commonwealth had surrendered its control over the movements of the Australian squadron. He asserted that the new agreement destroyed the 'distinctive Australian character' of the squadron.[181] The Commonwealth Labor Conference resolved that any money available for naval defence should be spent on establishing a local force 'owned and controlled' by the Australian government.[182] Watson thought that if Australia shared the burden of imperial defence, it should have a say in imperial policy-making.[183] Senator A. P. Matheson, a Labor senator from Western Australia, spoke at the Royal Colonial Institute against the new agreement and published a pamphlet calling for an Australian navy.[184] Deakin reported these events in the *Morning Post*.

> The idea of a specially Australian navy manned by colonial sailors and under our own executive direction has been so assiduously preached of late that it has 'caught on' with the masses … there is a prevailing distrust of the 'British bureaucracies', the War Office and the Admiralty.[185]

Notwithstanding this barrage of criticism, Barton and Forrest determined to push the measure through. Forrest who had formed a firm friendship with Chamberlain wrote him of their difficulties and promised to do his 'level best' to gain parliament's consent for the agreement and to have it vote 'the pittance' of a subsidy.[186] Chamberlain, on the strength of Forrest's information wrote Barton in March 1903 to strengthen his resolution. Chamberlain exhorted him to remember that the agreement represented 'a principle the rejection of which would be disastrous'.[187] The government and the governor-general were perturbed by the widespread opposition. The prime minister adjudged that the passage of the naval agreement would be 'difficult and doubtful'. To try and make the bill more palatable Lord Tennyson with Barton's consent proposed on 24 April that the Admiralty should supply six torpedo-boat destroyers in

---

[180] Cabinet notes, 20 November 1902, Barton Papers: *SMH*, 25 November 1902.

[181] *SMH*, 18 October and 3 December 1902 and 14 January 1903.

[182] Official Minutes and Proceedings, Commonwealth Labor Conference, Sydney, 1–4 December 1902.

[183] *SMH*, 11 March 1903.

[184] *SMH*, 16 April 1903; 'Australia and Naval Defence', *Proceedings of the Royal Colonial Institute*, XXXIX, March 1903, 194–246.

[185] *MP*, 6 January 1903.

[186] Letter, Forrest to Chamberlain, 18 September 1902, Joseph Chamberlain Papers, 17/2/7; see also letter, Forrest to Chamberlain, 24 November 1902 and 22 February 1903, ibid., 17/2/9 and 18/2/6. Forrest was the only Australian politician to carry on a frequent or extensive correspondence with Chamberlain. Chamberlain replied that he and Forrest were 'absolutely in sympathy on the matter … that you and I are the only true Imperialists in the British Empire'. Copy of letters, Chamberlain to Forrest, 12 October 1902 and 1 April 1903, ibid., 17/2/8 and 18/2/7.

[187] Letter, Chamberlain to Barton, 21 March 1903, Barton Papers, 51/587.

place of one third-class cruiser. There would be one torpedo-boat destroyer for each capital city, they would be officered and manned by Australians, and the colonial crews were to be paid out of the £200,000 subsidy. The governor-general, at the same time, probably informed the Colonial Office that while Reid had given his personal assurance that he would vote for the bill, he felt that some concession should be made to local sentiment. Neither the Admiralty nor the Colonial Office were sympathetic to the appeal. Lord Selborne poured scorn on the proportion. The torpedo-boat destroyers could serve no useful purpose since there were no foreign torpedo-boats within 4,000 miles of Australia. The Colonial Office said that 'it would never do' to let Australia, because it grumbled, obtain advantages over New Zealand 'which did not grumble'. Ommanney repeated the constant refrain of the imperial opponents of colonial navies. 'The Australians do not seem to be able to grasp the principles of local defence.' On 19 May they replied that it was impossible to renegotiate the terms of the agreement.[188]

Forrest had not associated himself with the Tennyson proposal. His full-blooded and simple-minded imperialism had caused him, more than any other member of the cabinet, to identify closely with Chamberlain's recentralizing scheme. He thought that the 'paltry contribution' offered by Barton at the Colonial Conference reflected badly on Australia's loyalty to the empire. He believed that the Commonwealth should have agreed to a naval subsidy of 'at least £250,000'. To meet local problems and quieten local agitation, Forrest considered that it would be better to add to the existing terms rather than to alter them and he sent to Barton a plan which, while it recognized local feeling, would integrate local naval defence into a united imperial organization. He wanted the Commonwealth to acquire three torpedo-boat destroyers, one for Sydney, one for Melbourne and one for New Zealand. They would be under Admiralty control but the Commonwealth, through its High Commissioner in London, would have *ex officio* representation on the Admiralty board when matters concerning the Australian squadron were under discussion. Under Forrest's scheme all officers in the former colonial naval detachments would be given positions in the Australian squadron or on the destroyers. By these means Australia would, inside the larger imperial framework, gain a local naval interest, a say in policy affecting the Australian squadron and a solution to the problem of the former colonial naval forces.[189] Though an ingenious scheme, Barton vetoed it on grounds of cost and control.

Nevertheless, as the time to submit the bill to parliament drew near, Forrest's anxieties continued to grow. Committed as he was to its success, he made a further attempt to gain a concession from the Admiralty which he could use to buttress his case against the bill's detractors. Since the Admiralty had already indicated that they would not consent to any variation of the number of class of vessels to be placed on the station, Forrest sought a nominal right to consultation. He asked that the Admiralty agree to consult the Australian High Commission about

---

[188] Letter, Tennyson to Barton, 16 April 1903, Barton Papers, 51/590; telegram, Tennyson to Chamberlain, 24 April 1903, CO 418/26/332–34, and 251–4; copy of telegram, Chamberlain to Tennyson, 19 May 1903, CO 418/29/34–5.
[189] Letter, Forrest to Barton, 26 April 1903, Barton Papers, 51/593.

the 'Australian naval reserve'.[190] What he intended by this was unclear. At the most, it did not amount to much. The Admiralty, perceiving this, were thus happy to accede to the request.[191] Working indirectly, Forrest had also approached Chamberlain privately to see whether the Admiralty could be persuaded to grant the Commonwealth government the same power of veto over the movement of the new Australian squadron as the colonies had had over the auxiliary squadron. When consulted, Selborne replied that he would 'rather that the Commonwealth started a local navy of its own and that there was no naval agreement' than that the Admiralty should in any way surrender control over the squadrons in Eastern waters. 'To speak frankly', he wrote, 'I do not trust the Commonwealth Government or any other Colonial Government in such a matter as this'.[192] Under the schemes presented to the Colonial Conference, the Admiralty had expected the colonies to have absolute trust in its wisdom in deploying the concentrated naval forces of the empire, but the Admiralty for its part had no confidence whatsoever in the colonies' judgement, even in the most marginal area of naval policy. Chamberlain, while not endorsing wholeheartedly this lack of trust, agreed with the general principle involved, and advised Forrest that his suggestion could not be entertained.[193] Despite their best efforts, neither Hopetoun, Barton nor Forrest had been able to wrest a bargaining bid from the Admiralty. They had to defend the naval agreement before parliament in the terms in which it had come originally from the Colonial Conference.

Barton, who had had charge of the negotiations at the conference, took control of the naval agreement bill when it came before parliament on 7 July. He gave a very succinct exposition of the history of Australian colonial naval initiatives and described clearly the new arrangements. He emphasized that Australia would be obtaining greatly increased naval protection at little extra cost and that, under the scheme, Australian officers and crew would man one of the second-class cruisers and, through a local branch of the Royal Naval Reserve, Australian seamen would be trained for naval service. By outlining Australia's strategic situation, he hoped to show why the Admiralty should be allowed the right to despatch the Australian squadron to any part of the Far East. Adopting almost the words of the Colonial Defence Committee and the Admiralty, he said that 'The position of Australia is extremely isolated and it is not much in danger of any other invasion than a raid by armed and fast cruisers'. Since the Russians had assembled a fleet of sixty-nine vessels in the North Pacific and the French were concentrating their naval forces in the region, it was important that the Admiralty should be able to unite all the empire's naval squadrons speedily to meet a threat from either source. He acknowledged that there was a 'spirit of local patriotism' abroad which desired to create an Australian navy immediately. Such a development would undermine the principle of unity of imperial control. But his main objection

---

[190] Telegram, Tennyson to Chamberlain, 1 June 1903, CO 418/26/393.
[191] Copy of telegram, Chamberlain to Tennyson, 16 June 1902, CO 418/29/45.
[192] Letter, Selborne to Chamberlain, 22 July 1903, Joseph Chamberlain Papers, 18/2/13.
[193] Copy of letter, Chamberlain to Forrest, 19 July 1903, Joseph Chamberlain Papers, 18/2/10.

was cost. Using Admiralty figures he admonished the nationalists that such a navy would cost £2,500,000 to build and £1,000,000 annually to maintain.[194]

Crouch, who opened the attack, summarized the argument of those who opposed the bill. Though assuring the House that he was as willing as any Australian to attest to his loyalty to the empire, nevertheless, he denied Barton's assumption that an Australian had 'equal power with an Englishman in England'. The British government determined policy, including naval policy, for the whole empire. Australia's authority was limited to local self-government. Therefore, the Australian taxpayer, unlike his British counterpart, had no say in the way in which his contribution to the imperial navy would be used. He saw, in such a state of affairs, the danger of imperial-colonial conflicts, like those which had led to the American War of Independence, arising to disturb Anglo-Australian relations. Like the American colonists, what Crouch sought was not representation in an imperial parliament but, bolstering his case with quotations from Creswell and the colonial naval officers, a separate Australian navy responsible to the Commonwealth government.[195] Sir John Quick,[196] S. Mauger of Melbourne Ports,[197] Higgins,[198] J. N. H. Hume Cook from Victoria,[199] McMahon Glynn,[200] Sir Langdon Bonython,[201] McDonald,[202] Page,[203] L. E. Groom,[204] A. Paterson of Queensland,[205] Brown,[206] also quoted from Creswell and argued for an Australian navy. Others such as Reid,[207] J. Cook,[208] A. McLean[209] and Salmon[210] looked to the development of an Australian navy in the distant future. Colonel McCay thought the time was not ripe for such an experiment. True to his military background he took issue with Creswell and claimed that land, not sea, defences were of first importance to Australia.[211] Watson and Batchelor, though sympathizing with the nationalist aspirations, felt that due to the cost, the beginning of an Australian navy would have to be postponed until a later time. Any available

---

[194] CPD, 1903 session, XIV, 1773–92, 7 July 1903.
[195] Ibid., XIV, 1802, 7 July 1903.
[196] Ibid., 1905, 8 July 1903 and 1968, 9 July 1903.
[197] Ibid., 1982, 9 July 1903.
[198] Ibid., 199, 9 July 1903.
[199] Ibid., 2034, 14 July 1903.
[200] Ibid., 2059, 14 July 1903.
[201] Ibid., 2151, 15 July 1903.
[202] Ibid., 2160, 15 July 1903.
[203] Ibid., 2246–50, 16 July 1903.
[204] Ibid., 2259, 16 July 1903.
[205] Ibid., 2261, 16 July 1903.
[206] Ibid., 2418, 22 July 1903.
[207] Ibid., 1968, 9 July 1903.
[208] Ibid., 2077, 14 July 1903.
[209] Ibid., 2424, 22 July 1903.
[210] Ibid., 2431.
[211] Ibid., 2131, 15 July 1903.

funds should be used on harbour defence and military equipment.[212] Forrest[213] led a small band who championed the bill philosophically and politically. Forrest, Sawers,[214] Ewing[215] and Cameron[216] argued, on grounds of imperial unity, that Australian and British interests in naval defence were one and that only an integrated naval defence could counter the combination of powers which might be brought into play in the Eastern Seas.

At the conclusion of the debate, Barton offered the critics an olive branch, a sop to national feeling. He indicated his willingness to insert a provision in the bill specifically spelling out Australia's right to establish coastal and harbour defences under its own control. However, the dissidents thought the palliative to be potentially too constricting, that in effect it might ultimately be used to limit Australian naval progress, and so they turned it down. Barton, nevertheless, gave it as his opinion that, while the empire must remain the first line of defence, Australia, as it grew wealthier, might go beyond its land forces and acquire torpedo-boats and even cruisers of its own for local defence. Calling the bluff of many of the theoretical nationalists, he said that, if parliament would approve the money for torpedo-boats for local defence, the government would welcome the gesture. When the vote on the bill was called, a number of the Creswell men, such as Bonython and Quick, went with other protectionists and free-trade doubters into the government lobbies and the bill passed the House by thirty-eight votes to twenty-four.[217] The senate divided along the same lines and gave the government an equally comfortable majority of fifteen to nine on 25 August.[218] A naval agreement providing for subsidies to the British fleet thus became the foundation of the Commonwealth's first naval policy. Barton, in his last policy statement as prime minister, declared that following the passage of the naval agreement bill, the government intended to scrap the old colonial war vessels and look to the imperial squadron for its naval protection.[219]

The solid support for the policy of imperial contributions was not, however, all that it seemed. A small minority accepted the ideology underlying the agreement and had voted accordingly. But the great majority of those who had voted for the bill had done so for other reasons. Given the straitened circumstances of the federal treasury, they saw no other way at that time of providing Australia with naval defence. Some, like Reid and Cook, did not wish to give the Mother Country a 'slap in the face' by rejecting the scheme after it had already been negotiated. Others, such as Quick and Hume Cook, regarded the bill as a test of confidence in the government and were unwilling to challenge the Barton administration. The naval agreement, insofar as it embodied a clear policy, did not have firm roots in public or political opinion.

---

[212] Ibid., 2045, 14 July 1903 and ibid., 2161, 15 July 1903.

[213] Ibid., 1991, 9 July 1903.

[214] Ibid., 2244, 16 July 1903.

[215] Ibid., 2049, 56.

[216] Ibid., 2331, 22 July 1903.

[217] Ibid., 2433, 22 July 1903.

[218] CPD, XVI, 4117, 25 August 1003.

[219] SMH, 31 August 1903; CPD, 1903 session, XVI, 4500–1, 21 September 1903.

Throughout 1904 and 1905, as governments succeeded one another in rapid succession, the Commonwealth pursued a querying, querulous approach on the topic of the naval agreement and naval policy in general. In the election campaign at the end of 1903 Watson had nailed Labor's colours to the nationalist cause and had asserted that the time had come to build a 'purely Australian navy'.[220] Since the debate on the Naval agreement, he had adjusted his views to the temper of predominant Labor and popular opinion. After Labor came to office in April 1904 Watson looked again at the question and he asked the Admiralty to loan the Commonwealth two or three torpedo-boat destroyers, which would be manned and maintained locally, on condition that Australia paid the interest to cover the cost of construction and a sinking fund. Even though Watson, unlike Barton, offered to help with the cost of the destroyers and would not make any dent into the £200,000 contribution to pay the crews, the Colonial Office and Admiralty rejected the proposal. Ommanney, at the Colonial Office, warned that, 'This would be the first step towards … a local naval force, tied to Australian coasts, and, therefore, useless for the defence of Australia.' The Admiralty repeated what they had told Barton the previous year, namely that such vessels would, in Australia's strategic situation, serve no useful purpose. To be sure that their answer was understood, they added that they did not have any destroyers which could be loaned to the colonies.[221]

Though Labor failed, they did lay the groundwork for a reorganization of the administrative structures of the Defence Department which gave a formal recognition to the idea of a separate Australian naval force. The Reid government gave legal effect to this work and passed a comprehensive defence administration act in November 1904. Subject to the general supervision of a Council of Defence, Australian naval forces were to be administered by a Naval Board and a Director of Naval Forces. Captain Creswell, at the end of the year, was appointed to this latter post. Though he presided over a skeletal body of men and an outdated and outmoded collection of vessels, nevertheless, as a result of the act, the principle of independence had been inscribed in legislation and gave promise of a future for an Australian navy. However, these actions of the Watson and Reid government were still only straws in the wind. They marked no radical new developments. The Reid government showed no desire to tamper with the naval agreement. They consented readily to an Admiralty request to re-order the composition of the Australian squadron, though they, at the same time, demanded to know when the Admiralty was going to bring the squadron up to the strength prescribed under the agreement.[222]

At the first Council of Defence Meeting held on 12 May 1905, McCay, the minister of defence, who presided, intimated that the government did not think an Australian navy to be an urgent question. He said that they 'proposed to postpone' such a development 'as being the one which could best bear to be postponed'. Creswell presented a case for an Australian flotilla which would be under Commonwealth control in peacetime and under the Admiralty in war. Creswell's

[220] *SMH*, 13 November 1903.

[221] Telegram, Northcote to Lyttleton, colonial secretary, 22 June 1904, CO 418/31/278–9 and letter, Admiralty Board secretary to under-secretary of state, Colonial Office, 16 July 1904, CO 418/31/60–1.

[222] Telegram, Northcote to Lyttleton, 24 January 1905, CO 418/34/85–9 and 418/36/47; see also CP 290/15/1.

was a rather woolly argument and he did little to advance his cause on this occasion. McCay and Turner, the treasurer, asked what additional protection such a local force would afford Australia and, when Creswell replied that it was 'simply a proposal to add to the strength of the [imperial] Navy', McCay reported that Creswell was advocating the Mahan theory of concentration, a theory of 'ultimate Imperial welfare by total local sacrifice'. Creswell urged the diverting of defence funds from land to sea defence, stating that since Australia was an island, its first line of defence, like that of Great Britain, must be the sea. With McCay's well-known predilection for the military in mind, Creswell maintained that if the British navy were defeated, then all our military forces would prove of no avail 'against, say, Japan, which had put 600,000 men into Manchuria'. To this McCay and Turner replied that the logical consequence of Creswell's argument was that no nation would bother to arm itself unless it was able to secure itself against the whole world. McCay derided the analogy between Great Britain and Australia. Britain had world-wide responsibilities; Australia, through military defence, could become a self-contained fortress. Turner thought that, given Creswell's assumption, the Australian government would be better advised to contribute a further £500,000 to the imperial navy and to abandon the notion of an independent naval force of its own. Under Creswell's scheme Australia 'would be left defenceless' at the very moment it needed naval protection most; 'the increased strength might be taken away at the very time we needed it.'

McCay considered that for Australia the only alternative to concentration on land forces, was 'to make herself a sea power, irrespective of British naval power'. Manifestly the Commonwealth could not afford such a policy. McCay demanded of Creswell whether it was Australia's duty to share in imperial defence or to devote itself to local defence. Answering his own question, the minister of defence said that 'As a matter of fact, I may say that there is no hope of getting Australia to take any more generous view of Imperial defence than she takes at the present time. She is ready to take part in local defence.' Though McCay had declared himself for a national defence policy, he had demolished Creswell's argument for an Australian navy. The meeting ended on a desultory note. Creswell was to reply to a series of questions posed by the political and military leaders. Creswell did not report back to the Council of Defence.[223] Succeeding governments did not find the Council of Defence, as a policy-making body, suited to their needs. It was revived on special occasions in order to enable a distinguished visitor to discuss a broad problem in a proper setting. For the rest, prime ministers and their defence ministers found it more convenient to consult their military and naval advisers individually. Through this means the political leaders were able more easily to retain the initiative in the creation of new policies. In the formation of an Australian navy, Creswell was ultimately the beneficiary of political perspicacity and persistence.

---

[223] Council of Defence Minutes, Vol. I, pp. 1–30, CRS A2032. For the background to Creswell's differences with the military authorities see letter, Creswell to McCay, 2 November 1904 and Creswell's critique of Hutton's strategic analysis and defence recommendations in letter and report, Creswell to McCay, 3 December 1904, MP 729/1, File 04/6486. McCay's military predilections and preferences are set out clearly in the minute circulated for the first meeting of the Council of Defence, 25 April 1905, ibid., File 06/58.

Down to 1904 and 1905 the Commonwealth government was distracted by the multiple demands and difficulties of federalism. There was no clear and present danger to cause the nation's leaders to focus their attention on defence. Though time and events were closing around the empire, the British navy still ruled the seas. The most serious threats that anyone foresaw in the immediate years ahead were raids by cruisers on coasts and commerce. The Commonwealth's future in the Pacific had taken on a more ominous appearance, but for most Australians there was time enough to ponder its shape and meaning.

The problems of local as against imperial defence were beginning to be understood. While Australians had a sincere attachment to the empire, they also possessed a jealous regard for the rights of self-government and an awareness that British and Commonwealth interests were not necessarily identical. In establishing their military forces, the Commonwealth parliament, while employing a British officer as the commander, refused to participate in an imperial reserve and even declined to give the Commonwealth government the power to compel Australian troops to serve overseas. Turning to naval defence, they had reluctantly agreed to pay more for imperial naval protection on the Australian station while surrendering any say over how the hired help should be deployed. There was considerable talk of the need for an Australian navy, but the requirement of economy, reinforced by the mystique of the Admiralty, overrode nationalist sentiment. However, in both respects, these first military and naval policies were false starts. They were expedients, contrived out of a complex set of circumstances, but only vaguely determined by a perception of Australia's defence needs.

Caught between two worlds, the worlds of colony and Commonwealth, of nation and empire, of nineteenth-century security and twentieth-century anxiety, of European predominance and Asian preoccupation, no Australian government could have in this period, given a clear direction to defence policy. Even so, it is doubtful whether Barton and Forrest, who carried the major burden for decision-making, were the best men for the task. They did not, even in the murky situation in which they found themselves, make the most of the possibilities. They rather let the possibilities engulf them, and defence policy became the plaything of imperial conspiracy, domestic politics, federal penury and bureaucratic wrangling. It was an uncertain beginning.

# 4

# 'External Affairs' and Pacific Policy: France and the New Hebrides, Japan and Immigration, 1901–5

Under the federal constitution, the Commonwealth had been entrusted with powers over 'external affairs' and 'relations with the Pacific Islands'. Indeed, one of the major motives inspiring the federal movement in the 1880s and the 1890s had been the desire of the Australian colonists, as part of a wider concern over defence, to exercise a greater influence in Pacific affairs. However, the first Commonwealth government, coming to office at a time of crisis for the British Empire, was initially unwilling to press its claims in those areas lest they should hamper the Mother Country in the prosecution of its war-time diplomacy. Moreover, Barton, who had assumed the 'external affairs' portfolio and who had evinced in the past little detailed interest in these subjects, did not wish to rush into these unchartered waters while there were so many other purely domestic federal problems awaiting his attention.

Very soon after taking office, Barton declared that Australia could have no 'foreign policy' of its own.[1] What Barton clearly meant by this assertion was that the empire should face the world as a single entity, speak with one voice in the international arena and be represented abroad by one diplomatic corps, and to this end Barton was content to rely upon the British foreign service and to work through the British government to achieve Australia's 'external affairs' goals. Barton's 'external affairs' department, therefore, did not attempt to exercise the central function of a foreign office; they rarely prepared a submission to the government on a diplomatic or strategic question. Though the 'external affairs' department had responsibility for relations with the British government and the Pacific Islands, the greater proportion of its time was given over to other matters, including Commonwealth-state relations, territories, and immigration.[2]

Even so, Barton and, more decidedly, other ministers and political leaders, considered that the Australian government had a right to press the British government to protect what they identified as Australia's 'external' interests, especially in the Pacific, and also, in some cases, to carry on direct negotiations with foreign governments. They expected that the British government would adopt the Australian and New Zealand point of view on the Pacific Islands and make the Australasian view the basis of imperial policy in the region. As things developed, it was the prime minister who formulated and conducted negotiations on these questions with the British authorities and, where applicable, foreign governments. In the Labor and Cook governments, when the prime minister did not hold the external affairs portfolio, the external

---

[1] *SMH*, 15 February 1901.

[2] K. A. MacKirdy, 'The First Australian Department of External Affairs, 1901–1916', *Canadian Journal of Economic and Political Science*, XXV, February to November 1959, 502–7.

affairs minister played a very small part, if any, in the shaping of these policies. When in 1911 a Prime Minister's Department was carved out of external affairs, the new department took over the responsibility for relations with the British government. The dissolution of the first external affairs department in 1916 had, therefore, no symbolic or practical significance for the continuing interests of Australian government in foreign affairs. Though Cabinet and individual ministers were sometimes consulted, it was the prime minister who pre-eminently made Australia's foreign policy.

Barton, while formally eschewing a 'foreign policy' for Australia, nevertheless, in the early days of his administration, declared that Australia must have 'a national policy on the Pacific Islands'.[3] He said that 'the future interests of the Commonwealth, not only trade but in other respects as well' were 'vastly ... concerned in the question of the occupation, the management and government of the Islands.' Moreover, he suggested that the close proximity of Australia to the Pacific region, made it inevitable that the Commonwealth should have a keener and clearer appreciation of the problems faced there; 'We are much nearer than our fellow citizens in the United Kingdom. We have the eyes to see and the ears to hear, and I hope we have the mind to forecast the future development that may occur there.'[4]

Other Australian leaders were making the same point even more sharply. For many, federation had promised the realization of an Australian Monroe Doctrine for the South Pacific.[5] Deakin, in reporting on the inauguration ceremonies marking the foundation of the Commonwealth, had made much of these aspirations.[6] Deakin, himself, had little faith in either Lord Salisbury, the Colonial Office, or the Foreign Office as 'jealous custodians of colonial rights' in the region,[7] and called for a vigilant pursuit of Australian interests in the area. After allowing Barton the first public word on the subject, Deakin had, in opening his election campaign at Ballarat on 6 March, stressed along with the need for 'racial purity' and protectionism, 'a policy of firm, consistent and constant pressure upon the Imperial government to prevent further aggression on the part of foreign powers in the Western Pacific.'[8] W. A. Watt, who was himself to become acting prime minister in 1918 felt that in substance Barton held the post of minister of 'foreign affairs' and, through that office, he should now achieve a more direct say in the affairs of

---

[3] *Age*, 12 February 1901.

[4] *Age*, 15 February 1901.

[5] Hutton, in his efforts to persuade Australians to agree to allow the government to send Commonwealth troops overseas had appealed to their desire for a Monroe Doctrine for the South Pacific. Writing to the governor-general, he declared that 'For many years and throughout all the discussions. which preceded the establishment of the Commonwealth, the hope was widely and sincerely held that as time went on, the Federal Government would be able to exercise a direct and growing influence over the islands forming part of His Majesty's Dominions in the South Pacific.' Letter, Hutton to Tennyson, 30 September 1903 in despatch Tennyson to Chamberlain, 7 October 1902, CO 418–19/320–3.

[6] *MP*, 12 February 1901.

[7] *MP*, 12 and 19 March 1901.

[8] *Age*, 7 March 1901.

the Pacific Islands.[9] Isaac Isaacs, the Victorian attorney-general and later federal minister and governor-general, pressed the same argument.[10] There was emerging a crusade, spearheaded in Victoria, for action in the Southwest Pacific.

Barton, who did not share Deakin's distrust of the imperial authorities and who had a greater sensitivity for imperial diplomacy in the midst of the Boer War—no other minister had actually declared himself for 'the empire right or wrong'—was not moved by a sense of urgency. Even while recommending 'a national policy on the Pacific Islands', he declared that

> however firm might be the policy of the Ministry, … [the subject] required a very great amount of prudence and reserve in the exercise … of that policy so the result of the policy entertained might not be embarrassing to the Empire, of which we are a part.[11]

And to those who said, 'To be pacific, we want the Pacific', he replied that the Commonwealth's policy 'must be Pacific both in its tone and in its aims'. Australia had to remember that in pursuing its policy it made representations

> not to a foreign power but to the friendly and all-embracing government of an Empire which has no desire to do anything but assist us, but which is placed in a position of extreme delicacy of management, and is, at all times, required to prevent misunderstandings with other powers.[12]

Barton's aim was to dampen down the public agitation for a defiant and self-assertive policy. In bringing down the policy of the government at the opening of parliament, the governor-general declared that

> The relations of the Commonwealth with the Islands of the Pacific have been occupying the earnest attention of ministers, who have taken such steps as seem to them prudent for the protection of Australian interests in this respect, without in any sense embarrassing the international relations of His Majesty's Government.[13]

The Commonwealth's attitude toward its ocean and island environment reflected these perceptions and aims. With experience and disappointment the Commonwealth policy became tougher and, after Barton's resignation, the government took up a much more belligerent stand in asserting its demands and expressing its complaints. The Barton government approached the problem in a thorough and comprehensive manner. In September 1901, indeed, they sought and obtained from the British government a political map of the South Pacific showing the existing claims of the European powers in the region.[14] Australia's regional interests were quite widespread

---

[9] *Age*, 30 January 1901; He endorsed Deakin's view that 'in order to be pacific we want the Pacific', *Age*, 27 February 1901.

[10] *Age*, 13 March 1901.

[11] *Age*, 12 February 1901.

[12] *Age*, 15 February 1901.

[13] *CPD*, 1901–2 session, I, 29, 10 May 1901.

[14] Despatch, Hopetoun to Chamberlain, 13 September 1901, CO 418/10/43. Some Colonial Office officers thought it undesirable to furnish the map but Chamberlain believed it impossible to refuse the information.

and it would appear that the Australian ministers studied the map with microscopic care. The Commonwealth government desired to take over the administration of British New Guinea in which they were ultimately successful, and to take over the administration of the Solomon islands in which they were not. They were anxious about French ambitions with respect to the Kerguelen islands in the Indian Ocean,[15] but the Admiralty assured them that the islands had no strategic value and it was futile to press the matter.[16] They expressed a wish to have the governor-general made High Commissioner for British island possessions within the immediate vicinity of Australia, which was likewise rejected.[17] They complained about German discrimination in the Marianas and Carolinas against the Australian Pacific Island trading firm of Burns Philp which the Commonwealth subsidized.[18] However, of all these Pacific problems, the most important, the most enduring, and the most contentious were the New Hebrides.

## The New Hebrides, Australia's 'Channel Islands'

The Australian colonies had never regarded the 1888 Anglo-French agreement, under which both countries agreed to respect the property and rights of each other's citizens in the island and a joint naval commission was authorized to supervise the enforcement of these provisions, as a satisfactory or final resolution of the question. The New Hebrides were the only major group of islands whose sovereignty had not been settled in the nineteenth century. Geographically, they formed a strategic link in the island chain to the northeast of Australia and Australians had never abandoned hope of acquiring them. In the years following the inauguration of the Commonwealth, Presbyterian missionaries seeking protection for their missions and the natives, settlers needing security of land tenure, traders wanting assistance in combatting their rival, the French New Hebrides Company, pressed the federal government to take action to bring the island group under British or Australian control. But above and beyond all these pressure groups, the fundamental motive which caused the Commonwealth government to undertake a campaign to secure better protection for British rights and then to demand annexation was strategic. As Deakin explained in his first contribution to the *Morning Post* on the subject, Australia's ambition to acquire these islands was not inspired chiefly by 'earth hunger', missionary pressure or trade, but rather by the fact that 'the far-seeing ... noted that they [the New Hebrides] contained splendid harbours, the possession of which might prove hereafter of great value for naval

---

[15] Despatch, Hopetoun to Chamberlain, sent 16 April 1901, received 30 May 1901, CO 418/9/485–503.

[16] Despatch, Chamberlain to Hopetoun, 17 July 1901, CO 418/15/138.

[17] Despatch, Northcote to Lyttleton, sent 2 February 1904, received 7 March 1904 and despatch, Lyttleton to Northcote, 7 June 1904, CO 418/31/60–2. H. B. Cox minuted to on March 19 'I can conceive of nothing more likely to embitter our relations with France than to let the Commonwealth put its finger into the New Hebrides pie. Australian feeling is that every island in the Pacific ought to belong to them and not understanding anything about foreign relations or diplomacy, they would land us in serious difficulties before six months were past.' The Colonial Office replied that 'no change is desirable'.

[18] Telegram, Northcote to Lyttleton, 1 August 1905 and 8 August 1905, CO 418/37/14–21; *MP*, 22 November 1904; *SMH*, 9 November 1904 and 28 March 1904.

operations.'[19] The overriding aim of Commonwealth policy was to prevent the New Hebrides coming under French control and so enabling a potential enemy to build bases from which they could launch attacks against Australia.

Within weeks of the swearing in of the Commonwealth government, a deputation of Presbyterian missionaries was waiting on the prime minister. They complained that the French New Hebrides Company was seizing land from the natives and that the joint naval commission, which had been established to mediate Anglo-French differences, was powerless to act. Since occupation of territory was nine points of the law in settling sovereignty disputes, they feared that the islands were liable to come completely under French rule unless something was done to protect British interests. Barton consulted with the New Zealand premier, Richard Seddon, and on 6 February reported to the Colonial Office that there was 'considerable unrest in Australia on the subject arising from the suspicion of French designs to absorb these valuable islands.'[20] When two days later the cabinet considered the issue, Deakin treated his colleagues to a pointed and painted summary of the history of Anglo-Australian negotiations over the New Hebrides. The outcome was that they determined to seek the appointment of a tribunal to deal with 'the most important disputes', those affecting maintenance of order and conflict over land rights. Barton in forwarding the Australian request on to London pleaded urgency on the ground 'that the future settlement and government of important and valuable islands in the Pacific is a matter of greatest importance to the Commonwealth and New Zealand.'[21]

The colonial secretary had noted on Barton's first telegram that 'The matter must now be dealt with', that 'delay might lead to serious trouble'. Even so, there was inordinate delay in producing answers, let alone results. The Commonwealth continued to bombard the Colonial Office with a stream of complaints and requests for remedies. They protested against the French New Hebrides Company taking land from Burns Philp, they expressed concern over increased French settlement and over the appointment of two more minor French officials to work in the islands, and they besought the British government to station a resident high commissioner in the islands to counter French influence.[22] Only in the latter respect were they satisfied.

By the end of the year Barton had become fully converted to the Australian mission in the south seas. In a report to his West Maitland electors on the state of the nation, he assured them that the New Hebrides had been 'the subject of constant care to me, and almost daily communications since the Commonwealth was instituted'. He explained his concern in geo-

---

[19] *MP*, 12 March 1901; compare J. A. La Nauze, *Alfred Deakin: A Biography*, Melbourne 1965, p. 441

[20] Telegram, Hopetoun to Chamberlain, 6 February 1901, CO 418/9 133–42.

[21] Ibid., 12 February 1901, CO 418/9/158–70.

[22] Despatch, Hopetoun to Chamberlain, 30 March 1901, CO 418/9/375–438; telegram, Hopetoun to Chamberlain, 11 July 1901, CO 418/9/639; despatch, Hopetoun to Chamberlain, 11 August 1901, CO 418/10/74, telegram, Hopetoun to Chamberlain, 10 August 1901, CO 418/10/78; despatch, Hopetoun to Chamberlain, 22 August 1901, CO 418/10/87; despatch, Hopetoun to Chamberlain, 1 October 1901, CO 418/10/240; telegram, Hopetoun to Chamberlain, 11 November 1901, CO 418/10/379.

political terms, 'Situated at no great distance from our coast, they are a sort of no man's land.'[23] During the Colonial Conference in 1902 the Australian and New Zealand prime ministers held talks with Lord Onslow of the Colonial Office on the Pacific island question. Though there was no mention of the New Hebrides in the report of the meeting, Barton did agree 'in principle' with Seddon that British possessions in the area should ultimately come under the control of the Commonwealth or the Dominion. His practical reservations seemed to have been based on fears that New Zealand might pre-empt some island groups which, in his view, should properly come under Australian jurisdiction. He had already had occasion to protest against the extension of New Zealand's island frontiers.[24] Though Fiji, for example, was closer to New Zealand than to the Commonwealth, he insisted that its economic and cultural ties were primarily with Australia.[25]

It was almost two years before there was any sign of movement in Anglo-French negotiations over the issues raised by the Commonwealth in early 1901. The British blamed this lack of progress on the French failure to co-operate. The Foreign Office had put proposals to the French government in 1901 and 1902, but the French did not reply. It would seem probable that Barton, during his stay in London, instigated inquiries and pressed for action, for on 17 July Lord Lansdowne, the foreign secretary, wrote the French ambassador, seeking a reply to the British proposals. The British government was very anxious that there should be no further delay in coming to an agreement.

In January 1903 the British approached Australia for its views on alternative forms of control and administration of the islands, in particular on a French suggestion of a joint protectorate. The Commonwealth government, in their reply, for the first time outlined a general policy on the New Hebrides. They recounted the history of Anglo-Australian exchanges over the Pacific Islands, they recalled the disappointment over Germany's annexation of northeast New Guinea, and they reminded the Colonial Office of the long-held hope that the New Hebrides 'would be secured to the Empire'. They interpreted the French suggestion as an argument from weakness. French commerce was declining and the number of British settlers, then 188, was slowly overhauling that of the French, estimated at 266. Neither the number of settlers nor the commercial interest at stake could justify by themselves so much intense diplomacy on Australia's part. They had to be seen within a wider framework. The Commonwealth government appealed to the British to see the matter through their eyes. The New Hebrides were 'at the very door of Australia'. Though 'the distance of 1400 miles, which separate it from our shores, may seem considerable, yet Australia is

---

[23] *SMH*, 10 January 1902.

[24] Despatch, Hopetoun to Chamberlain, 2 December 1901 enclosing minute from Barton, 28 November 1901, CO 418/10/476–81.

[25] CO, Confidential Print, Miscellaneous No. 144, 1902 Colonial Conference Proceedings and Papers, p. 515, Appendix XXIX, 'Memorandum by Earl of Onslow, 11 August 1902 of interview with Sir Edmund Barton and Mr. Seddon to discuss Pacific Islands', CO 885/8; see also Barton on Fiji, *SMH*, 29 November 1902. The absence of any reference to the New Hebrides is even more surprising in the light of Deakin's urgent plea that Barton 'should press all you can for the acquisition of the New Hebs. by exchange—and that this should be known afterwards—whatever the result.' Letter, Deakin to Barton, 20 May 1902, Barton Papers, 51/535.

a country of vast distances, and in the eyes of Australians, the group is as near to them as the Channel Islands are to the inhabitants of Great Britain.' Thus, Australians looked to acquisition as the only truly satisfactory settlement. They thought that France could be brought to acquiesce 'by some readjustment whether of territory or of privilege elsewhere'. Should the British be successful in this direction the Commonwealth government was prepared to ask parliament for the cost of administering the islands. Facing up to unpalatable alternatives, they allowed that if such a solution eluded them, then a joint protectorate would be 'less, but only less, unpopular than a partition of the Group between the two Powers'. Somehow they felt that a joint protectorate, unlike a fixed division, would still leave the door to annexation slightly ajar, and so, in this extremity, it was to be preferred.[26]

The Colonial Office was unsympathetic to the Australian plea. On 30 April John Anderson minuted that Barton knew there were 'no loose ends of Empire for a deal'. He was impatient with Australia's failure to appreciate the burden of empire. He commented that 'Newfoundland thinks it a shame we don't sacrifice the New Hebrides for French fishing rights.' France's equal rights in the islands had long been admitted. Acquisition, from the imperial point of view, given the options open to the Colonial Office, seemed out of the question. It would be Britain that was called upon to make the countervailing concession. Chamberlain agreed that Australia had 'no case'. There was no chance of evicting France. As far as other alternatives were concerned, since New Zealand wanted partition and Australia preferred a joint protectorate, the Colonial Office concluded that they had no choice but to do what came most naturally, and to leave things as they stood.[27]

In July 1903 Anglo-French relations entered a new and more cordial phase and this brought about a new desire on both sides to settle outstanding colonial difficulties. The French who were seeking suzerainty over Morocco solicited British backing in order to neutralize possible German interference. Britain, for its own part, had since 1902, in a reaction to Germany's minatory tone, been adopting a softer approach to French colonial claims. More especially, though, by mid-1903 the British, becoming concerned that they might be drawn into a Russo-Japanese war, were hoping, by reaching an accommodation with France, to place a restraint on France's Dual Alliance partner.[28] And so when on 7 July the French foreign minister, during a visit to London, declared that 'all outstanding colonial issues' were now 'capable of settlement', Lord Lansdowne had responded favourably.[29]

---

[26] Telegram, Tennyson to Chamberlain, 17 February 1903, CO 418/26/80–1; despatch, Tennyson to Chamberlain, 17 March 1903, containing despatch, Barton to Tennyson, 13 March 1903, CO, 418/26/163–90.
[27] Ibid.
[28] George W. Monger, *The End of Isolation: British Foreign Policy, 1900–7*, London 1963, pp. 126–8.
[29] Confidential despatch, Lansdowne to Sir E. Manson, British ambassador to France, 7 July 1903, G. P. Gooch and Harold Temperley (eds), *British Documents on the Origins of the War, 1898–1914*, 12 vols, HMSO, London 1927–38, Vol. II, 'The Anglo-French Treaties of April 8, 1904', p. 294.

After spending three months clarifying issues, Lansdowne managed to convince his cabinet colleagues to agree to opening formal negotiations.[30] While France looked to Britain to support its Moroccan ambitions, Britain, in return, expected France to recognize its own paramount position in Egypt. These were the central concerns of the two great powers. However, it had been envisaged from the outset that the negotiations should attempt to encompass all colonial questions, not just Morocco and Egypt, but also French fishing rights in Newfoundland, Siam, West Africa, Zanzibar, Madagascar and the New Hebrides. For the New Hebrides the French favoured partition.[31]

The Australian government in early July had gained an inkling of the new French initiative. In response to an article in the *National Review* by M. Etienne, a former French under-secretary for the colonies, in which he had advocated the division of the New Hebrides between Britain and France, the Commonwealth government had informed the Colonial Office that they hoped nothing would be done to encourage the French in this idea 'unless in the last resort to prevent complete French annexation'.[32] In reply to a question in the House of Representatives, Barton assured the members that the Australian government would resist the partitioning of the island.[33]

Even before this new chapter in Anglo-French relations had opened, the Australian government had been searching for a way to break the impasse in negotiations on the New Hebrides. Following up a rumour that France was willing to sell its interests in the New Hebrides for a figure of £250,000, Barton had in June urged the British government to investigate the story and to try and secure the islands for Australia and the empire. Again, he promised that, if they were successful, he would ask the Australian parliament for the cost of administration and development.[34] Chamberlain thought it possible that France might be induced to part with the New Hebrides for a price, but Britain had no interest in them and consequently Australia should pay for their purchase.[35]

The Australian government, as was its wont, at first argued that acquisition was an 'Imperial' interest and therefore that the British should pay the cost.[36] However, after they realized that the

[30] Despatch, Lansdowne to Cambon, 1 October 1903, ibid., II, 311–15.
[31] Despatch, Lansdowne to Manson, 29 July 1903, ibid., II, 305.
[32] Despatch, Tennyson to Chamberlain, 16 July 1903, CO 418/26/585.
[33] *CPD*, 1903 session, XIV 1761, 7 July 1903.
[34] Despatch, Tennyson to Chamberlain, sent 1 June received 6 July 1903, CO 418/28/401–8.
[35] Telegram, Chamberlain to Tennyson, 10 July 1903, CO 418/26/407; see also letter, Chamberlain to A. J. Balfour, undated, but from internal evidence sometime early in July 1903, Balfour Papers, add. ms. 49774, 49–50. In the letter which was written apparently before Chamberlain knew that Egypt was to be tied to Morocco, Chamberlain said, 'As regards the New Hebrides, we can come to no conclusion until we hear definitely from Australia. But I think partition is not possible, I would not pay a penny from the Imperial Exchequer and I doubt whether Australians would pay either. If they will not or if the French refuse compensation we must again [as for Newfoundland] fall back on Morocco. Thus we must say that the Moroccan agreements depend on a fair offer in regard to the New Hebrides. This should take the form of pecuniary compensation. Thus if the Colonies refuse to pay, we should throw responsibility on them'.
[36] Despatch, Tennyson to Chamberlain, sent 20 July 1903, received 25 August 1903, CO 418/20/596–8.

whole colonial question was in the melting pot and their advice was sought on the New Hebrides, they took a much more positive attitude and, in order to make acquisition more palatable to the British, they offered to find 3 per cent per annum interest on a maximum sum of £250,000 in addition to the administrative costs.[37] The Australian government, in reply to the Colonial Office's general inquiry, reiterated the stand it had taken in February, listing its preferred solutions as '1. Acquisition of the group by treaty or by pecuniary compensation … 2. joint Protectorate with a tribunal to settle land claims … 3. Partition.' The Colonial Office considered Australia's offer to contribute to the 'cost of purchase', a much more 'reasonable' response. But as Chamberlain noted, in sending the Australian telegram on to the Foreign Office, 'The real question' was whether the Foreign Office had 'enough in hand to tempt the French to be liberal in the matters in which we are concerned.'[38]

All was now left to the Foreign Office. Though Morocco and Egypt claimed the centre of the diplomatic stage, the other colonial questions were not ignored. In a position paper, following Lansdowne's conversation with Cambon, the Foreign Office had stated that 'Our only object is to gratify Australian and New Zealand sentiment, and, if we fail to do that, we had better leave the question alone.' They dismissed French claims that the New Hebrides were important to them because of their strategic connection to New Caledonia. They attributed French interests largely to 'manufactured French sentiment in regard to it'. They concluded that 'If we are to treat the New Hebrides question at all, to do any good it must be on the basis of total surrender of any political rights of France in the group.'[39] For these reasons the British government, in the terms presented to the French on 1 October, ruled out partition as a basis for settling the New Hebrides problem, and sought simply an arrangement to provide for settlement of land disputes and for the supervision of native affairs.[40]

On 5 February 1904, Lansdowne, in a more decided effort to satisfy Australian and New Zealand aspirations and in response to a French request for the cession of the Isles de Los, which were situated off the West African coast just opposite French Guinea, the British sought the New Hebrides as a makeweight on the other side of the scale. However, when the French objected, 'Quant aux Nouvelles—Hebrides il [Delcassé, the French foreign minister] ne peut admettre qu'à ce propos il en soit question', the British government on 25 February knuckled under and agreed to cede the Isles de Los without further compensation. The long-feared Russo-Japanese War had broken out on 9 February and perhaps this made the British more conciliatory and more anxious to bring their negotiations with the French to a successful conclusion.[41]

---

[37] Cabinet notes, 17 August 1903, Barton Papers.

[38] Telegram, Tennyson to Chamberlain, 26 August 1903, CO 418/26/722–4.

[39] CO, Confidential Print, No. 160, 'Notes on Colonial Questions referred to in Lord Lansdowne's Recent Conversation with M. Cambon, August 19, 1903,' CO 885/8.

[40] BD, despatch, Lansdowne to Cambon, 19 November 1903, II, 315; ibid., II, 327.

[41] Despatch, Lansdowne to Cambon, 5 February 1904, ibid., II, 343; despatch, Cambon to Lansdowne, 18 February 1904, ibid., II, 343–5; despatch, Lansdowne to Manson, 25 February 1904, ibid., II, 346.

Though the British and French governments were able to reach a satisfactory settlement of nearly all the colonial questions at issue, a solution of the New Hebrides, for some reason which was not immediately apparent, evaded them. On 6 April, Lansdowne discussed the New Hebrides once more with Cambon but without making any progress. Since neither the French nor the British wished to let the New Hebrides stand in the way of the overall settlement, they signed the general Declaration two days later. With respect to the New Hebrides, the Declaration in Article III simply expressed the intention of the two powers to draw up an agreement which, while leaving the political *status quo* intact, would provide for an effective judicial control over the native people and for a commission to resolve land disputes between French and British settlers.[42] A further two years were to elapse before the New Hebrides agreement was signed.

The Australian government first heard of the signing of the Declaration from the press. In response to an inquiring telegram, the Colonial Office on 14 April wired a summary of the New Hebrides article to Melbourne.[43] In a despatch posted the following day, the colonial secretary explained that the Agreement in no way altered the *status quo* in the islands. He assured the Australian government that no agreement would be signed on land or native jurisdiction questions until their views had been received.[44]

The Watson Labor government which came to office on 23 April showed somewhat less interest in the Pacific Islands; their policy was rather more exploratory than exhortatory. Even so, the new government was disconcerted by what it discovered. Watson, in a minute of 22 June quite accurately observed that the Declaration of 8 April did not advance negotiations beyond the point that they had already reached in 1901. He wanted to be kept informed of subsequent discussions and thought that if land titles of three-year duration or more were not to be questioned, then that provision should apply from no later than 19 June 1902. Further, if the Commission was to have only two members, one British and one French, he was willing to leave the conduct of the empire's case solely in British hands, believing that on this matter, the British commissioner would 'regard Australian interests as those of the Empire'. However, if there were to be more than one, he thought that an Australian representative should be included in the British delegation.[45]

In the House of Representatives feeling ran high. W. E. Johnson, a New South Wales free-trader, on 28 July sponsored a resolution calling on the Commonwealth government to encourage Australian settlement in the New Hebrides and to press the British to fight for 'a more satisfactory agreement with the French respecting their control'. Johnson stressed 'the strategical importance' of the islands to the safety of British and Australian commerce in the Pacific. When in August the Reid-McLean coalition succeeded the Labor government, they took up the same position as their predecessors. Reid was besieged by interested groups, Presbyterian missionaries, chambers of

---

[42] Despatch, Lansdowne to Manson, 6 April 1904, ibid., II, 363; Final Text of the Declaration between the United Kingdom and France, 8 April 1904, ibid., II, 397.

[43] Telegram, Northcote to Lyttleton, 13 April 1904 and telegram, Lyttleton to Northcote, 14 April 1904; CO 418/31/208.

[44] Despatch, Lyttleton to Northcote, 15 April 1904, CO 418/31/209–24.

[45] Despatch, Northcote to Lyttleton, 27 June 1904, CO 418/31/311-14.

commerce and the Australian Natives Association, seeking action on the New Hebrides. Reid spoke fair word in reply, assuring them of the government's concern for the future of the islands.[46] However, in bringing the matter before the British authorities, Reid merely confirmed the position taken by Watson in June.[47] Under Reid Pacific policy, like other policies, languished.

With the return of Deakin to power in July 1905, the Anglo-Australian exchange over the New Hebrides assumed an intense and fiery character. Deakin reproached the Colonial Office for its indifference to Australian interests and for its dilatory behaviour in carrying on negotiations. The Colonial Office, on the other hand, resented the Commonwealth's importunity and considered that Australia failed to make sufficient allowance for the complex context within which the negotiations took place. It was against such a framework of Anglo-Australian relations that the Anglo-French negotiations finally came to a head, producing a settlement for which the Australians would accept no responsibility.

Deakin's first act as prime minister was to seek a report on the progress of the Anglo-French discussions with respect to the New Hebrides and to remind the Colonial Office of the Commonwealth government's desire to be represented on any commission which should be set up to deal with the question.[48] The Commonwealth government's resolve was stiffened by a House of Representatives resolution urging the renewal and strengthening of Australian representations to London and asserting that the control of the islands would have to be decided in Australia's favour. Those members speaking to the resolution were particularly agitated about the fact that the ports could be used as naval bases and that the islands lay strategically between New Caledonia and the Australian mainland.[49] Deakin assumed a tougher attitude than any of his predecessors and was prepared even to try and restructure Australia-Imperial relations as they affected foreign policy decision-making in order to attain more satisfactory results in the New Hebrides. In responding to a parliamentary deputation, Deakin explained that seventy-two notes had been sent to London on the subject and that clearly 'more representations were necessary'. He deprecated the fact that Britain had acted 'more as a mediator or ambassador than as principal', and maintained 'that the whole Empire of Great Britain was as much a principal as Australia was or could be'. He found it a matter for regret that Britain did not in the Pacific region identify Australian interests with imperial interests.[50]

In August the Commonwealth government sent two despatches to London reviewing the history of the negotiations, setting forth a statement of the Australian attitude as to the future of the islands and specifying the problem with which it had to contend in respect to the New Hebrides. Following the passage of the House resolution and the reception of a Presbyterian Church deputation, Deakin wrote the Colonial Office putting before them the substance of the complaints. Deakin maintained that despite the hopes of the colonies at the time of federation it

---

[46] *SMH*, 26 August 1904 and 5 September 1904; *MP* 4 October 1904.

[47] Despatch, Northcote to Lyttleton, 3 September 1904, CO 418/31/445.

[48] Telegram, Northcote to Lyttleton, 29 July 1905, CO 418/36/360.

[49] *CPD*, 1905 session, XXV, 811, 10 August 1905.

[50] *SMH*, 3 August 1905; compare La Nauze, *Alfred Deakin*, Vol. II, p. 447.

appeared that the Commonwealth was not able to exert any greater influence over Pacific policy than had the individual colonies, and that its failure in this respect was beginning to affect the prestige of the empire in the region. In particular, he emphasized the fears expressed in parliament about the strategic importance of the New Hebrides; 'The possession of these harbours has been described as of great value to the Empire.' On 29 August he followed this up with an enquiry about the possibility of a joint protectorate. He recalled that in 1903 the Australian government had told the British authorities that if annexation were impossible, a joint protectorate would be their reluctant second preference. In the existing circumstances the Commonwealth government considered that 'a permanent Joint Protectorate ... would certainly be preferable to the state of affairs that now obtains'. Under such a settlement they could be assured that 'The harbours of the group, while open to commerce, would not, in the event, become the bases of hostile action in the Pacific.' Deakin ended with a plea for Australian and New Zealand participation in the processes of approving conditions for such a protectorate.

On 3 November the Colonial Office despatched a curt reply. They denied that the New Hebrides had any strategic or defence value, and assured the Australian government that the actions they had taken and were taking in regard to the islands were 'solely at the wishes of Australia and in her non-military interests'. H. E. Dale lamented the Australian obtuseness. 'It seems impossible to induce the Australians to believe H.M.G. when they say that the New Hebrides are of no strategic value.' The Australian government never received a reply to its second despatch. The reason for this discourtesy was not far to seek. The Australian proposal had been overtaken by events. Anglo-French negotiations for establishing a land commission had been at last set in motion. The idea of a joint protectorate cut across the smooth flow of the negotiations. The Colonial Office disliked it both for itself and its inconvenience at a time when Anglo-French diplomacy seemed to promise some kind of a settlement. Sir Montagu Ommanney on 19 October commented, 'I do not believe a Joint Protectorate will ever work and I think the proper course is to press on the Land Commission with all the strength we can command'.[51] They referred the Australian suggestion to New Zealand and by the time the New Zealand answer surfaced the Anglo-French commission had been appointed and a reply to Australia seemed no longer necessary.

In 1905 Franco-German tension over the future status of Morocco provided the first test of the Anglo-French *rapprochement*. The British government, curiously enough, initially saw it as their role to strengthen the French will to resist German pressure and then subsequently at the end of the year to clamp down on French bellicosity. By September the British, for the first time since the Napoleonic wars, were considering the circumstances under which they would send an expeditionary force to the continent. The British, therefore, desired to do all in their power to

[51] Despatch, Northcote to Lyttleton, sent 23 August and received 25 September 1904, and copy of despatch, Lyttleton to Northcote, 3 November 1905, CO 418/37/54-66; despatch, Northcote to Lyttleton, sent 29 August and received 3 October 1905, CO 418/37/82-99.

convince the French of their good faith and so they hurried on the process of settling outstanding questions such as the New Hebrides.[52]

Sir Edward Grey, foreign secretary in Campbell-Bannerman's Liberal government, which came to office on 4 December, carried forward the French policy which Lansdowne had pioneered. He had stated on 21 October prior to taking office, that 'Nothing we do in our relations with Germany is in any way to impair existing good relations with France.'[53] It was Grey who on 10 January 1906 authorized Anglo-French military conversations to prepare the ground for possible British intervention in a continental war against Germany.[54] And on 16 January the Algeciras Conference met to determine the Morocco question. This was for the British no time to quibble over New Hebrides details merely to please the antipodean colonials. When the French in September had offered to enter into expert talks on the land disputes in the New Hebrides, the British accepted readily. In early December Britain and France had appointed their technical representatives, and on 9 December at the instance of the French, the British had agreed to extend the scope of the Commission to take in all contentious matters.[55]

The commission began its deliberations on 1 February and on 27 February a draft convention was signed. The agreement dealt with all the questions at issue. Without precisely asserting a joint protectorate over the islands, the two powers did, in order to discourage other nations from making political claims, declare their joint 'paramount rights' in the islands. They provided for the exercise and operation of both British and French law and set up a joint court presided over by a Spanish arbitrator to resolve land and other bi-national disputes. The native peoples were placed under the jurisdiction of British and French officials. All this had been carried through without either informing or consulting the Commonwealth. It was understandable, therefore, that when the news of the agreement reached Australia, it was greeted with a certain degree of consternation, not to say hostility.

In his innocence Deakin, while the negotiations were underway, had sent the new colonial secretary, Lord Elgin, an overview of Australia's attitude to Pacific affairs. He calculated that if the new Liberal broom were to sweep any crumbs in their direction, then it would be necessary to ensure that the sweeper knew of their existence. Once again, he told his story. Federation had been prompted in large measure by the Australian colonies' desire to speak with one voice in external affairs and so gain 'better understanding and greater celerity in action' for their Pacific

---

[52] Monger, *The End of Isolation* …, pp. 188–92, 196–9, 202–15.

[53] Ibid., p.260.

[54] Ibid., p.249.

[55] Letter, FO to CO, 21 September 1905, despatch, Lansdowne to Cambon, 5 October 1905. The British agreed to bilateral semi-official expert discussion, letter, CO to FO, 6 December 1905 and the CO designated H. Bertram Cox, the Assistant Under-Secretary of State to represent the British side. He was to be assisted by H. G. Dale of the CO and FH Villiers of the FO, letter, CO to FO, 9 December 1905 and Lyttleton agreed to a French proposal to extend the scope of the discussion, CO 418/37/81–99; see also CofA, *Parliamentary Papers*, 1907 session, Vol. II, No. 15, 'New Hebrides — Correspondence Relating to the Anglo-French Convention'.

policy. Australians had been dismayed to see Britain let slip an opportunity to annex the islands in former, less complicated times, but they still believed that if the British would bestir themselves and show 'a keen interest … a substantial part of the wishes of Australia could be realised'. Deakin complained that two years had passed since the signing of the Anglo-French Declaration and that the New Hebrides was still an item on the agenda for Anglo-French discussions. He asked for regular reports on the British government's progress in handling the Pacific island question. The Colonial Office bureaucrats were critical of Deakin's presumption. 'The Australians who have never had to face any diplomatic difficulty seem to think that we can treat France as if she were Tonga or Samoa', H. B. Lucas wrote on 19 March. Ommanney concurred, 'We cannot tell Australia of the progress of negotiations—cannot be sure that anything we tell them will not find its way into the newspapers.' Lord Elgin regretted 'the tone of Mr. Deakin's letter'.[56] Clearly, it had touched a tender spot in the Colonial Office's tough hide. The Colonial Office's reply was, in contrast to its private remarks, quite conciliatory, if evasive. It blamed foreign governments for the delays and assured the Australians that British policy was 'to keep Colonial Governments informed of the progress of negotiations affecting them in any important respect'.[57] But by the time the British reply arrived, the principles it avowed were not relevant as far as the New Hebrides were concerned.

Three days before Deakin's Pacific policy paper had reached London, the Colonial Office had despatched a copy of the Anglo-French draft agreement with a short explanation of its contents. Though the colonial secretary asked for Australia's views on the draft, he made it clear that there was no prospect of persuading the French to accept any modification in principle, and that modification, even in 'minor details', would necessarily involve further delay. Making nonsense of the request for Australia's comments, he concluded that 'The draft Convention must therefore be confirmed or rejected practically as it stands.'[58] They hoped to railroad it through. Lord Elgin, writing personally to the governor-general re-emphasized that it was 'practically impossible to get more from the French'. He reported that Forrest, who was in London, had adjudged it to be 'on the whole satisfactory and fair' and Elgin hoped that the Commonwealth government would take the same position.[59]

Deakin was angered by this *fait accompli*. In order to prevent the Colonial Office from playing off slight differences in the Australian and New Zealand responses Deakin consulted with the Dominion's government and reached an accord with respect to the answers that should be made. It was not until 14 June that the Australian reply was sent off. Deakin remonstrated against the British government's failure to inform them about the scope and nature of the talks and to consult them while the talks were proceeding. He rejected Elgin's assertion that no important step had been taken or any important information received without it being communicated to the

---

[56] Letter, Lord Elgin to Northcote, 6 April 1906, PRO 30/56/1.
[57] Despatch, Northcote to Elgin, sent 7 February 1906 and received 12 March 1906 and copy of despatch, Elgin to Northcote, 26 April 1906, CO 418/44/96–112.
[58] CofA, *Parliamentary Papers*, 1907 session, Vol. II, No. 15, despatch, Elgin to Northcote, 9 March 1906.
[59] Letter, Elgin to Northcote, 12 April 1906, PRO 30/56/1.

Australian government. Manifestly, this had not been done 'in this case which is a most crucial incident deeply affecting Australia'. He expressed Australian resentment at being told that the draft had to be accepted or turned down as it stood. The Australian government was 'unable to take the responsibility of advising the Colonial Secretary to confirm the draft in its present form'. And in defiance of Elgin's admonitions, it submitted an extensive list of proposed revisions to the draft articles.[60] Anonymously in the *Morning Post*, Deakin was freer to vent his true feelings. Once again, he saw the British failure in the New Hebrides as part of a pattern of malign neglect dating from Germany's outwitting of Lord Derby over New Guinea in 1883–4. The outcome of the negotiations testified eloquently to what he called 'the supineness of the British Government and the wilful indifference of "Downing St." to all Australian affairs'.[61]

Deakin followed up his despatch with telegrams advocating the immediate proclamation of a joint protectorate. After the onset of the Moroccan crisis in early 1905 Australia had become perturbed by German activities in the South Pacific, and when reports reached Melbourne that the Germans were trying to purchase plantations in the New Hebrides, the Commonwealth leaders feared that this might give them a pretext for intervention in the islands. Thus, the Australian government had urged immediate action on the question in order to preclude any political interference from Germany.[62] The British government replied on 4 October that the French would not agree to a joint protectorate and were pressing for ratification. The colonial secretary said in the cable that the major amendments put forward by Australia, such as a common code of laws for the islands, were impracticable and that lesser matters could be sorted out after the agreement had been formally adopted. The British government urged immediate confirmation of the convention and asked for Australian consent for such action.

Deakin was placed in an impossible position. He retorted that since Australians had had no part in the negotiating of the convention, and since Australian amendments did not have British approval, and since the Commonwealth government was unable to judge for itself how much delay might result from persisting with their desired revisions, they had decided to 'leave the whole responsibility with His Majesty's Government'. The Australian government had effectively washed its hands of the matter. On 20 October the British government, exercising the discretion delegated to it by the Australians, ratified the Anglo-French agreement.[63] The recriminations between the Australian government and the Colonial Office over the procedures adopted in reaching the settlement continued into the following year. Australia refused to be pacified. Deakin aired his grievances openly.[64] However, by early January 1907 Deakin, while not retracting one

---

[60] Despatch, Northcote to Elgin, sent 14 June, received 24 July 1906, CO 418/44/360–402; see also the New Zealand reply, CofA, *Parliamentary Papers*, 1907 session, Vol. II, No. 15.

[61] *MP*, 19 July 1906.

[62] Telegram, Northcote to Elgin, 31 August 1906 and telegram, Northcote to Elgin, 8 September 1906, CO 418/45/183 and 207.

[63] CofA, *Parliamentary Papers*, 1907 session, Vol. II, No. 15, telegram, Elgin to Northcote, 4 October 1906 and telegram, Northcote to Elgin, 13 October 1906.

[64] *SMH*, 23 October, 3, 10 and 29 November 1906, and 16 January 1907.

word of his indictment of the British action, recognized that it was futile to continue with these acrimonious exchanges and he informed the Colonial Office accordingly.[65]

This episode in Anglo-Australian relations left a deep and abiding impression on Deakin. Having to pursue its interest in the New Hebrides at one remove from the bargaining table or through an intermediary, as Deakin described Britain's role, had been a less than satisfactory experience. There was some truth in the Colonial Office complaint that, because Australia had no direct acquaintance with international affairs, it failed to appreciate the broader context into which imperial policy had to be fitted and tended to assume that France and other great powers were more malleable than was the case. There was more truth, however, in the Commonwealth's counter claim that Britain lacked any understanding of Australia's perspective on world affairs, arbitrarily ignored Dominion representations when they were likely to prove embarrassing and used its control over the machinery of imperial diplomacy to ensure that imperial policy served Britain's own purposes.

Australian antagonism did not stem primarily from having its proposed amendments to the Anglo-French agreement rejected. None of the amendments had great substance; the substance of the question for the Commonwealth from the beginning had been strategic, a desire to prevent any other power from acquiring the islands and using them as bases to hit out at Australian trade and territory. Australia's Pacific concerns had been sacrificed to British interest in Europe and the Mediterranean. And it was this that rankled. It rankled not simply because Australia had failed to have its own way on the New Hebrides issue but also because of the manner in which the diplomacy had been conducted. As a result the Commonwealth government became convinced that its initiatives, requests and protests had not received the consideration to which they were entitled.

This sense of being betrayed, of being treated in an off-hand and peremptory manner, of being the victim of a campaign of studied evasion, was partly due to the cumbersome nature of the communication and administrative procedures which were employed. Too often Australian and British messages were sent by sea mail despatches which took five weeks or more to reach their destination. On the British side, too, the Colonial Office bureaucracy took things in order and took time to consider and comment. Frequently, the advice of the Foreign Office, the Admiralty or the War Office was required before a reply could be sent. In the case of the New Hebrides, it was necessary for the Colonial Office to ask the Foreign Office to approach the French government before an answer could be drafted. Tedious, time consuming routine vitiated the impact of an Australian initiative on the decision-making process.

At the beginning of Anglo-French negotiations in 1903, the British government had kept in mind Australian wishes with respect to the New Hebrides. However, when they ran into difficulties, they went ahead and agreed in the 1904 convention without further consultation with Australia to create an Anglo-French commission to settle the question of land disputes and native jurisdiction in the islands. The Australians had no choice but to accept what had been done and to

[65] Despatch, Deakin to Northcote, 5 January 1905, enclosed in despatch, Northcote to Elgin, 7 January 1907 and copy of despatch, Elgin to Northcote, 7 March 1907, CO 418/51/14–17.

insist on being given an opportunity to influence the determinations of the commission. The British reaffirmed their frequently stated position that nothing would be done without consulting Australia. After two years of silence the Anglo-French commission had met and decided terms of a settlement in secret. The Commonwealth government was not informed of the commission's mandate, was not invited to send a delegate to sit on the commission and was not consulted about the deliberations that ensued. At the end the Australians were presented with a token request to give their consent. Since it had been made clear that no amendments would be practicable, Australians hands, even at this stage, were tied and, though they refused to take any responsibility for the agreement, they left the British free to ratify it. Thus, the New Hebrides settlement was, despite the Australian government's earnest and persistent efforts, foisted on them in a very arbitrary and devious manner. Perhaps, had Joseph Chamberlain still been colonial secretary, Australian interests would have been treated with more respect, but under Lord Elgin the Colonial Office was more easily able to go its own way. Had the Colonial Office permitted Australia to take a full and active part in the negotiating of the New Hebrides arrangement, they would undoubtedly have had to deal with a much more complex situation and to have been called upon to pursue an agile and dexterous diplomacy. Failing to do so, however, they left the Australians feeling angry and resentful at what they considered to be a further example of the Colonial Office's wanton disregard for the Pacific Dominion's interests and of the metropolitan government's supercilious presumption of omniscience, as well as of omnipotence.

The New Hebrides episode did much to influence the attitude of the Commonwealth government, and especially of Deakin, to imperial relations and to imperial defence and foreign policy down to 1914. It left Australians with the suspicion that the Colonial Office and, through them, the British government, could not altogether be trusted to watch over Pacific security. As a result of the New Hebrides experience, Deakin went to the 1907 Colonial Conference determined to try and transfer control over Dominion affairs from the Colonial Office to an imperial secretariat which would be representative of and responsible to all the self-governing nations in the empire. He looked towards Australia taking an active and energetic part in the shaping of imperial defence and foreign policy where its interests were affected. However, by 1910 he had become so discouraged by British policy and practice that he felt that the Commonwealth, 'despite itself', might very well be forced to develop and pursue an independent policy of its own for the Pacific.

## *Japan and immigration*

The other and more ominous Pacific question, which loomed over the infant Commonwealth was that of Japan. The Commonwealth had inherited from the later years of the colonial period a certain apprehension concerning Japan's future role in the region. At the least, Japan, as the early defence debates illustrated, was commonly viewed as one among a number of possible threats to Australia's future security, and a vocal minority considered that Japan's emergence as a great power would, in the long term, be the most important factor in Australia's international position. However, in these first years of the Commonwealth, the Australian government's policy was not, in any direct way, influenced by those strategic considerations. Rather, the chief issues disturbing Australian-Japanese relations were the Commonwealth's immigration policy and with it the question of the Commonwealth's responsibility to observe, as far as Queensland was concerned, the provisions of the Anglo-Japanese treaty of commerce which that colony had adhered to in March 1897, and which it had, through the protocol of October 1900, defined for the purpose of admitting Japanese residents.

The Australian colonies had as one of their goals in seeking federation the securing of a uniform law for immigration control which would keep Australia safe for British white settlers and for other Europeans who might be readily assimilated into a 'British race' culture. In particular, they desired to set up an impregnable wall against all coloured migration. Following the Chinese influx into the goldfields in the 1850s, the British Australians had become convinced that coloured immigration inevitably produced a conflict of cultures and, in particular, they saw in this conflict a threat to the white man's standard of living. The colonists' uncertain hold on their new land and their insecurity in their own cultural setting, unformed and derivative as it was, intensified this feeling of unease with and animosity towards the Chinese and led them very quickly to generalize the Chinese problem into a colour problem and to portray the problem in simple racial terms.

From laws aimed at restricting Chinese immigration, the colonies moved in the 1890s to laws intended to exclude not only Chinese, but also Japanese and all other coloured peoples from entering Australia.[66] The British government had attempted to restrain the colonies from adopting an overt racial barrier, and Queensland had, as a result, in giving practical form to its adherence to the Anglo-Japanese treaty of 1894, worked out a gentleman's agreement in October 1900 with the Japanese government. Under the agreement the number of Japanese residents in that colony was not to exceed 3,147 and, in return for the Japanese consenting to regulate this quota, the Queensland government exempted the Japanese from the provisions of their discriminatory immigration law.[67] But the British intervention and the Queensland experience only served to strengthen the colonists' determination to seek a national solution to the problem. In the first federal election of March 1901, all parties and leaders gave their support to a White Australia Policy.[68] It was the task of the Barton government to give legal expression to what was the undoubted will of the people.

In framing an immigration restriction bill, the Australian government could not avoid its imperial and international dimension. In 1897 the Japanese government had protested against colonial immigration bills which discriminated against coloured races as such. The Japanese took it ill that they were being treated like the Chinese and 'other less advanced populations of Asia'. The British government, in turn, had protested both on behalf of the Japanese and also on behalf of India and other British coloured subjects,[69] and had persuaded the Australian colonies to

---

[66] Myra Willard, *History of the White Australia Policy,* Melbourne 1923. Sections II, III and V.

[67] Queensland, *Votes and Proceedings,* 1901 session, Vol. IV, pp. 1140–1, A. 56, 'Admission of Japanese into Queensland (Further correspondence relating to)'.

[68] A. T. Yarwood, *Asian Migration to Australia: The Background to Exclusion,* 1896–1923, Melbourne 1964, pp. 5–22.

[69] Ibid.

accept the 'Natal' or European language dictation test as the technical device for controlling entry into the colonies. In the midst of the Boer War, the British government was especially concerned that nothing should be done which might offend its coloured subjects, particularly in India, or which might antagonize Asian nations. Britain, in its hour of trial, had experienced the shortcomings of 'splendid isolation' and, in seeking to check Russian interests in the Far East, had by 1901 perceived in Japan a friend who shared the same fears and a potential ally who was worth cultivating.[70] Consequently, the colonial secretary, anticipating the Commonwealth's promised immigration bill, warned the Australian government on 1 May against bringing down legislation which would openly discriminate against the empire's coloured subjects or, even more intolerable, which would antagonize the Japanese. Chamberlain told the Australians that Japan's feeling had to be given 'peculiar force at the present time owing to the position of affairs in the Far East.'[71]

The Japanese themselves did not wait for the Commonwealth to propose its bill before pressing their interest in the matter. They launched a two-pronged attack, one prong prodding the Commonwealth government through H. Eitaki, their consul in Sydney, and the other prodding the British through their minister in London, Baron Tadasu Hayashi. On 14 May the Japanese consul, in a letter to Barton, stressed that the Japanese would resent any attempt to control immigration through an overt racial or colour test. He said that the Japanese would feel it as a 'reproach' if they were lumped together for such a purpose with peoples possessing inferior standards of civilization such as the 'Kanakas, Negroes, Pacific Islanders, Indians or other Eastern Peoples'. He suggested that, since Japan was 'under no necessity to find outlets for her population', his government would be willing to enter into an arrangement which, while erasing the public stigma of being associated with inferior cultures, would enable Australia to achieve its aims. Indeed, he dangled the possibility of increased trade before Barton as a further inducement to the Australians to try and meet Japanese wishes.[72] On 4 July the Japanese minister in London, as instructed by his government, asked the British to advise the Australians against adopting a migration measure which would be 'unfair' to the Japanese.[73] Since the British government had already expressed its concern and had no definite knowledge of Australian intentions, it simply sent the Japanese note to Melbourne for the information and edification of Commonwealth ministers.[74]

Without consulting the British, Barton presented his immigration restriction bill for a first reading on 7 August. In its crucial clause, clause 4a, it authorized the Australian government to require any would-be immigrant to take a dictation test in English. This modification of the 'Natal' test, from a European to an English language test, was intended as a gesture to Japanese

---

[70] Monger, *The End of Isolation ...*, pp. 21–34; Ian H. Nish, *The Anglo-Japanese Alliance: The Diplomacy of Two Island Empires, 1894–1907*, London 1966, pp.127–34.

[71] Cited in Yarwood, *Asian Migration to Australia*, p. 27.

[72] Copy of letter, H. Eitaki to Barton, 3 May 1901, CO 418/10/287.

[73] Copy of letter, Hayashi to Lansdowne, 4 July 1901, CO 418/16/75–6.

[74] Copy of despatch, Chamberlain to Hopetoun, 20 July 1901 enclosing copy of letter under secretary of the Colonial Office to the Foreign Office, 20 July 1901, CO 418/16/177–8.

and imperial protests. Since such a test did not ostensibly differentiate between European and non-European countries, the points raised by the imperial and Japanese authorities would seem to have been met. It was a modification which, on the surface, the Australian government reasonably expected would also commend itself to the colonials' 'British race' patriotism.[75]

The British authorities were not happy with Barton's attempt at a compromise. When the governor-general inquired whether, under his instructions, he should withhold the royal assent from the bill, the British government replied, with the approval of the Foreign Office, that he should reserve the bill 'if it passes as it stands at present', and that, in the meantime, he should urge the substitution of 'a European language' for English as the mode for carrying out the exclusion policy. That is, the Commonwealth should be encouraged to stick to the Natal test, even though it appeared, on the face of it, to be more offensive. The only reason given in the Colonial Office for preferring the European language was that 'it [the clause in the Barton bill] is clearly contrary to the policy of equality between all white men.' The minute continued, 'We cannot give up the Natal test as the Japanese ask.' Thus, even though the British were seriously engaged in alliance discussions with the Japanese, they were too European to be willing to endorse a gesture to Japan which might seem to undermine the theory of white racial supremacy, and so perhaps hurt their relations with the European powers. So much for Chamberlain's vaunted policy of treating all races and colours within the empire alike, on a basis of equal dignity and right.[76]

Though the Japanese were willing to acquiesce in the English language test, the parliamentary debate which gave rise to amendments using racial language stimulated them to renew their efforts to influence the character of the Australian immigration act. On 7 September, Watson, supported by McMillan, the acting leader of the free-trade party, had expressed his dissatisfaction with Barton's test clause. For him the device was too unpredictable in its effects and he gave notice of his intention to move an amendment which would explicitly prohibit the entry of coloured migrants into Australia.[77] Eitaki was distressed by this turn of events and, on instructions from Tokyo, reminded Barton that the Japanese government was prepared, in order to avoid 'friction and irritation', to give assurances and to come to an understanding which would effectively control Japanese immigration into Australia.[78]

Subject to criticism and pressure from the Commonwealth parliament, the imperial authorities and the Japanese representative, the Australian government found itself in a difficult position. Deakin, on 12 September exerted his great rhetorical skill in an attempt to appease all parties by drawing out even more distinctly the conflicting aims of the test device in the bill, while at the same time, attempting to show how these aims had been reconciled within the one clause.

---

[75] *CPD*, 1901–2 session, IV, 4812, 12 September 1901. Deakin admitted that the clause had been adopted out of consideration for Japanese and imperial feelings.

[76] Telegram, Hopetoun to Chamberlain, 20 August 1901, minute by H. E. Dale, 22 August 1901, letter, under-secretary, CO to under-secretary, FO, 31 August 1901 and copy of telegram Chamberlain to Hopetoun, 9 September 1901, CO 418/10/81–6.

[77] *CPD*, 1901–2 session, IV, 4628–36, 6 September 1901.

[78] Copy of letter, Eitaki to Barton, 11 September 1901, CO 418/10/289–90.

On the one hand, he allowed that the clause had been drafted in this particular way to take into account the submissions of the British and Japanese and that Japan, in the government's view, was justified in taking umbrage at 'any unnecessarily offensive legislation on the part of another nation.' On the other, he emphasized that the object of the legislation was to maintain 'the purity of our race' and that powers delegated to the government under the act, for the purpose of applying the test, were intended, first and foremost, to 'exclude alien Asiatics as well as the people of Japan against whom the measure is primarily aimed.' Deakin attempted to resolve the seemingly contradictory aims by asserting that the Japanese had to be excluded 'in the most considerate manner possible and without conveying any idea that we have confused them with the very uneducated races of Asia and untutored Asians who visit our shores'. Being as considerate as possible, Deakin added that the Japanese had 'to be absolutely excluded … because of their high abilities.'[79]

Hughes, for the opposition, refused to permit Deakin's exercise in sophistry to remain unchallenged. Bringing to bear his great forensic abilities and stiletto — like logic he built up a strong case for substituting Watson's openly racialist amendment for the government's ambiguous circumlocution. Hughes restated the objection to the English test clause in itself, namely that it would discriminate more against Gaelic and Welsh-speaking Britons than it would against educated Japanese. More arrestingly though, Hughes attacked the government for its confessed subservience towards Britain and Japan and for framing the central part of Australia's immigration bill simply out of deference to their views. He denied fears that Britain would withhold royal assent. He claimed that British opposition to a direct prohibition of Asian migration was due to the fact that 'today Britain stands almost without an ally. She is now driven into a corner, and she is dependent upon the support tardy and reluctant of Japan.' The Australian parliament should not regard matters altogether from a British standpoint. 'We want a White Australia and, are we,' he asked, 'to be denied it because we shall offend the Japanese or embarrass His Majesty's ministers?' In determining Commonwealth policy, Australian interests must be paramount. 'We have come to the parting of the way. We have to decide now at the beginning of our new nation whether we are to go on inspired by the victories which our forefathers have won for us in this country and in England.' Hughes' answer was clear. Allowing that no more than 5 per cent of the population wanted separation, he asserted that for himself 'while I do not wish it, I do not fear it.' If Britain thwarted the Commonwealth in the pursuit of its national interest and identity, then he threatened that Australia might be impelled to follow the example set by the Americans in 1776.[80] In response, Barton played his hand very cagily. He announced that if the Watson amendment were rejected, he would submit an amendment of his own to replace the English language test with a test in any European language.[81] By this stratagem Barton managed to bow to British wishes while at the same time offering a sop to those wavering members of

---

[79] *CPD*, 1901–2 session, IV, 4812–16, 12 September 1901.
[80] Ibid., 4819–25.
[81] Ibid., 4834.

parliament who felt that the English language test was not a sufficiently formidable or fair, that is fair to Europeans and Britons, device.

The debate itself and Barton's proposed concession drew further complaints from Eitaki. The consul confessed himself to be puzzled and disturbed by Deakin's speech. He queried whether Deakin could be 'serious' when he said that Japanese must be excluded 'because of their good points', while saying simultaneously that they were the most dangerous of all Asian peoples. Directed by his government, he expressed Japanese opposition to Barton's tabled amendment. The replacement of the English language by a European language test would tend to place the Japanese on a lower level than the Turks, the Russians and the Greeks. The Japanese had found the public declarations of Barton and Deakin, that the bill was aimed at the Japanese, to be offensive. Eitaki urged once more the desirability of a gentlemen's agreement between the two governments. He also protested the postal bill which parliament was considering at the same time and which restricted employment in the postal service to white labour. He hinted that if Barton persisted with these measures, the Japanese government might well seek the intervention of the British authorities.[82] After the narrow defeat of Watson's amendment in the House on 25 September Eitaki wrote yet again, warning against substituting the Natal test for the English language one.[83]

However, the Japanese consul's pleas went unheeded. Barton proceeded on the course that he had indicated and the House accepted his amendment on 5 October. Eitaki duly recorded his dissatisfaction. He denied Barton's claim that since Japan had not protested when New South Wales, Western Australia, South Australia and Tasmania had adopted the Natal test in their colonial legislation, the same provision, embodied in Commonwealth legislation, could not reasonably be construed as an affront to that nation. Circumstances had changed and the Japanese government found the European language device almost as offensive as direct racial discrimination.[84] Throughout the continuing barrage of protest and complaint, Barton had remained his usually phlegmatic self. Not until after his amendment had been safely passed did he vouchsafe the consul an answer and even then he merely reported what he had done and repeated the observation with respect to the colonial legislation which Eitaki had already discounted.[85]

The centre of the diplomatic contest then reverted to London. On 5 October Eitaki, on orders from Tokyo, appealed, as he had threatened to do, over the head of the prime minister to the governor-general. He explained that Barton had ignored his appeals with respect to both the immigration restriction bill and the postal bill, and he stated that the Japanese government considered the educational test 'racial, pure and simple'. He conveyed Tokyo's 'high dissatisfaction with these measures'. It was manifestly his intent, by approaching the governor-general, to persuade him to exercise his powers of reservation.[86] Hopetoun was perturbed by the controversy.

---

[82] Copies of letter, Eitaki to Barton, 18 September 1901 and 20 September 1901, CO 418/10/291–5; copy of letter, Eitaki to Barton 18 September 1901, CO 418/10/301.

[83] Copy of letter, Eitaki to Barton, 28 September 1901, CO 418/10/297–9.

[84] Copy of letter, Eitaki to Barton, 10 October 1901, CO 418/10/307–8.

[85] Copy of letter, Barton to Eitaki, 17 October 1901, CO 418/10/300.

[86] Copy of letter, Eitaki to Hopetoun, 5 October 1901, CO 418/10/306.

After the bill had passed the House of Representatives, he wrote Home once again, requesting instructions. He admitted that Barton, in compliance with the wishes of the British government, had altered clause 4 from an English to a European language test. However, since the bill was 'distasteful' to Japan and since it was essential to avoid friction with that nation 'in the immediate future'—a clear reference to the Anglo-Japanese alliance talks—Hopetoun wanted to know whether the bill, even in its new form, should be reserved.[87]

In London the Japanese minister, informed of the impasse which had been reached in Australia, began almost at that moment to take up the cudgels. Eitaki, the ever dutiful watch-dog, had kept the Japanese foreign ministry fully aware of the developments in Melbourne and of his failure to influence them. For a nation which had only recently been initiated into the mysteries of Western diplomacy, the Japanese on what for them was but a secondary issue exhibited a high degree of efficiency. Indeed, it was in Japan's bureaucratic virtues that the greatest danger to Australian policy lay.

On instructions from Tokyo, Hayashi complained of the European language test and the Commonwealth ministers' statement that the test was to be used against Asians. He appealed to the British to 'induce the Government of Australia to so modify these clauses as to place Japanese subjects on the same footing with those of European nationalities.' He essayed to show why Japan, which had not previously objected to the Natal clause, now felt unable to accept it. He weakly argued that in contrast to earlier colonial legislation this act was 'to apply in all parts of Australia and maintained that therefore the Commonwealth act would have effects "of practical importance".' Politely alluding to ongoing alliance negotiations, he explained Japan's motives in terms of its desire 'to remove the obstacles in the way' of promoting relations, 'which have every prospect of further development in the future.'[88] The Colonial Office was not very sympathetic. In 1894 the Colonial Office had, following Japan's protests, urged the Australian self-governing colonies to adopt the European language test and to use the Natal legislation as a model. The secretary of state noted that both Great Britain and the colonies had understood that 'to be the wish of the Japanese Government in the matter.' Chamberlain did not see how they could ask more, especially since 'there was no prospect that the C'wealth [sic] would be able to entertain the suggestion.' Assuredly, Chamberlain was also constrained by the fact that the Commonwealth had revised the clause in order to oblige the British government. And so the Colonial Office did no more than to forward the Japanese memo with an addendum pointing out to Hopetoun the position that had been taken in 1897.[89] The governor-general then, after the immigration bill had passed both houses, decided that in terms of the advice he had received, he could not reserve it. The British government approved his decision.[90]

---

[87] Telegram, Hopetoun to Chamberlain, 12 November 1901, CO 418/10/394–5.

[88] Copy of letter, Hayashi to Lansdowne, 10 October 1901, CO 418/16/217–74.

[89] Copy of letter, H. B. Cox, under-secretary of state for the colonies to under-secretary of state for foreign affairs, 18 October 1901 and copy of telegram, Chamberlain to Hopetoun, 18 October 1901, CO 418/16/279–80, 282.

[90] Telegram, Hopetoun to Chamberlain, 12 December 1901, CO, 418/10/491.

The Japanese government, having been informed of the passage of the bill, was unwilling to let the matter stop there. They made one final effort to try and secure British intervention. Hayashi on 16 December made the chief bone of contention not the bill itself but 'the purpose' of the bill, not how it looked, but how it was to be used. To this end, he quoted accurately from Barton's and Deakin's speeches in which they said that it was 'not aimed at European nations', that 'the ... test should exclude alien Asiatics as well as the people of Japan, against whom the measure is primarily aimed.' Hayashi thought these 'monstrous declarations' and he urged the British government, in his stilted English, 'to dispense with these legislations quite unfair to one of the friendliest nations with the United Kingdom.'[91]

This new note of protest came at an inopportune time. The Anglo-Japanese alliance talks had entered their final and most delicate stage.[92] Lansdowne, who had been apprised of Chamberlain's approval of the immigration bill and who was worried about the repercussions on his major diplomatic undertaking, asked 'whether it would not be possible to dispense with the discrimination with which it is proposed that the Educational Test should be applied.' Lansdowne had no understanding of the Australian mind or, in that context, the immigration issue. He did not seem to appreciate that for the Australians the whole purpose of the bill was to provide an inoffensive mechanism through which they could discriminate on a racial basis. Lansdowne's only concern was to placate the Japanese. It was the Foreign Office view that 'The passage of such a Bill in the face of a protest from the Japanese Government would be most unfortunate at the present time.[93]

Chamberlain, however, was not to be moved. He pointed out that the Japanese no longer objected to the form of the legislation but to the intention ascribed to it in the parliamentary debates. For his part, it was the law itself and not the debate which had to be considered. Since the law conformed with the prescriptions of the Japanese as they had been set out in 1897, and since disallowance might result in the Commonwealth adopting 'an even more drastic measure', he contended that they had no choice but to leave things as they stood.[94] The royal assent was not withheld from the Commonwealth's immigration bill and no disastrous consequences followed. The Anglo-Japanese treaty of alliance, which committed each of the parties to come to the aid of the other in defence of their Far Eastern interests, should either be attacked by more than one power, was signed on 30 January. Even after the bill had become law and the alliance had come into effect, the Japanese did not altogether give up the struggle. In June when the Australian prime minister was in London for the Colonial Conference, the Japanese government sought through its minister to take the opportunity to reopen the question in order to try and come 'to a satisfactory

---

[91] Copy of letter, Hayashi to Lansdowne, 16 December 1901, CO 418/16/389–90.
[92] Nish, *The Anglo-Japanese Alliance* ..., pp. 204–16.
[93] Letter, under-secretary of state, FO to under-secretary of state, CO, 25 December 1901, CO 418/16/404.
[94] Copy of letter, under-secretary of state, CO, to under-secretary of state, FO, 4 January 1902, CO 418/16/391–4.

arrangement' with respect to Japanese immigration.[95] But Barton would not be drawn and replied, through Chamberlain, that 'the present temper of the Australian people' would not countenance any amendment. And the matter was left there.[96]

A subsidiary question arising out of the Immigration Restriction Act was the future of the Queensland-Japanese agreement, which had been signed following Queensland's adherence to the 1894 Anglo-Japanese commercial treaty. Under the 1900 protocol Queensland had agreed to allow the entry of Japanese pearl fishermen and labourers as well as Japanese having other occupations up to a limit of 3,247, which was the number resident in the colony at that time. It was also agreed that the Japanese government would control the flow of immigration by issuing permits. Thus, in order to remove the slur of inferior treatment, the Queensland government handed over the responsibility for administering its immigration policy to the Japanese. In return, Queensland had gained the most-favoured-nation tariff advantages under the commercial treaty. After the Commonwealth came into being, the federal government, reflecting public opinion, did not look kindly on this arrangement, which seemed to detract from the nation's ability to exercise an absolute and unqualified jurisdiction over this subject. The fearful saw the Queensland concession as 'the thin end of the wedge', an argument which was to be used by many Australian political leaders down to the nineteen sixties against modifying Australian discriminatory immigration practices. The Commonwealth, though adamant in its rejection of the 1900 protocol, did not wish to be unreasonable in bringing about its termination. When Eitaki complained that clause 10(a) in the immigration bill could be interpreted so as to negate the rights which Japan had under the Queensland agreement and to cancel contracts and permits already issued by the Japanese government, Barton consented to amend the clause to prevent it from being applied retroactively.[97]

The Australian government waited until the immigration bill had become law before tackling the question of the Japanese-Queensland agreement. On 23 January 1902, Deakin took the first step and announced that, in the view of the federal government, the Commonwealth was not bound by the agreement.[98] The attorney-general's opinion was not in accord with the general conclusions of a majority of international law commentators who maintained that successor-states assumed all the international obligations of their constituent members.[99] The Colonial Office argued that since neither the Australian colonies nor the Commonwealth was an independent international entity and since the British government had assumed treaty obligations on behalf of

---

[95] Copy of letter, Lansdowne to Sir Claude MacDonald, British minister in Tokyo, 11 June 1902, CO 418/23/579–82.

[96] Copy of letter, under-secretary of state, CO, to under-secretary of state, FO, 10 July 1902, CO 418/23/584.

[97] Copy of letter, Eitaki to Barton, 3 October 1901 and copy of letter, Barton to Eitaki, 10 October 1901, CO 418/10/304–5.

[98] CPD, 1901–2 session, VII, 9150, 23 January 1902.

[99] L. F. L. Oppenheim, International Law: A Treatise, 2 vols, London 1905–6, Vol. I, p. 121.

Queensland, a 'mere alteration of the internal constitutional relations of the Australian colonies' had no effect on the validity of the treaty.[100]

The legal niceties, however, were set to one side. The Japanese themselves broke the deadlock. Though they held that the understanding was still in force, they were willing to meet the Australian government's wishes and agreed not to exercise their rights in the matter, provided that the Commonwealth would honour the entry permits which had already been granted.[101] Barton conceded the point for the sake of peace and on 13 February he informed parliament that the Japanese were going to allow the Queensland agreement to lapse.[102] By proceeding in this way, by reaching a gentlemen's agreement to set aside the gentlemen's agreement, Queensland was still able to retain the commercial advantages of the Anglo-Japanese commercial treaty. This anomaly was, however, within a few years to become, as a result of international developments, state jealousies and Japanese diplomacy, the starting point of a new round of tortuous Australian-Japanese negotiations.

It was through the diplomacy surrounding the immigration bill that the Commonwealth gained its first experience of the pressures and practices of international politics. The Japanese had asserted forcefully their interest in the question. As their bargaining position with the British government had grown, they had raised their demands. No longer content with the Natal Act of 1897, they insisted that the device of a dictation test in a European language was unaccepted and they pressed for a special bi-lateral arrangement. Similarly, when they were unable, logically, to explain this change in the nature of their objection, they altered the ground of their argument and explained that their dissatisfaction stemmed not from the act itself but from the anti-Japanese construction placed upon it by the Australian ministers. The Japanese, failing to gain any substantial concession in Australia, exploited the opportunity afforded by the alliance negotiations, to try and achieve their object by working through the governor-general and the British foreign secretary.

Considering the conflicting pressure brought to bear upon him, Barton followed a firm but judicious course. Though his English language clause would seem to have offered the least difficulty for the Japanese, he agreed, after the Colonial Office had indicated its disapproval and the Australian parliament had highlighted its defects, to substitute the Natal Test. From this position, he would not shift. The British government, recognizing that Australian opinion was firmly set on achieving a racially discriminating policy and accepting that they were in fact responsible for the Natal Test amendment, kept the Japanese at bay and took the risk that the Japanese, when so rebuffed, would not scrap the alliance negotiations in retaliation. The British government was probably not unmindful that many Australians, as Hughes had pointed out, saw the right to determine the composition of their population as a fundamental right of nationhood

---

[100] Telegram, Northcote to Chamberlain, 18 January 1902 and copy of telegram, Chamberlain to Hopetoun, 29 January 1902, CO 418/18/52; Arthur Berriedale Keith, *The Theory of State Succession with special reference to English and Colonial Law*, London 1907, p. 97.

[101] Telegram, Hopetoun to Chamberlain, 31 January 1901, CO 418/18/113.

[102] *CPD*, 1901–2 session, VIII, 10041, 13 February 1902.

and probably not unaware that any British interference with Australia's sovereign powers in this respect would imperil the bonds of empire.

The Commonwealth government's immigration policy was shaped primarily by social, cultural and racial factors. There is no evidence that it was in any way influenced by considerations of trade or defence as such. The Japanese consul-general had endeavoured to tempt Barton to make concessions by holding out the prospect of a growth in Australia-Japanese trade. But this had not elicited any response. Trade with Japan amounted to only a small proportion of Australia's total exports and imports. The federal government, like nearly all the colonial governments before it, was indifferent to the commercial advantages which would accrue from adhering to the Commercial Treaty of 1894. Their racial fears were such that they would not sacrifice one iota of their power to regulate migration in order to gain a trade advantage. It was due to an accident of diplomacy and Japan's good graces that Queensland retained its tariff privileges.

When Deakin had spoken, in the immigration debates, of Japan as 'the greatest danger', he was not thinking at that time of Japan as a military or strategic threat. He was primarily speaking of economic competition and cultural tensions inside Australia, though he and others did recognize that, if a large group of Japanese were to settle in Australia, this would have defence and diplomatic implications. They anticipated that a substantial minority of Japanese inside Australian society could provide Japan with grounds for intervention in the Commonwealth's domestic affairs and that in case of conflict such a minority might prove to be a fifth column. But these thoughts were only in the background. The Australian political leaders, when apprised of the Anglo-Japanese alliance—they were never consulted about it—welcomed it. Barton greeted the news of the treaty 'with satisfaction'. He asserted that Australia's immigration policy was not affected by it and that, with respect to defence, it was more 'beneficial than otherwise'. He evaluated Australia's interest in it in terms of how it would alter the empire's position in the world. Since the alliance placed the empire in a stronger position, it would diminish risks of rupture with other powers and consequently there was 'nothing in the treaty' which would 'increase the risk of attack on Australia'.[103] Watson agreed with the prime minister,[104] and Reid, while approving, hoped that the United States might also be associated with the treaty. Reid, curiously, argued that 'if the United States were a party to the treaty', then Australians would be able 'to welcome another great advance and important stride towards … the ultimate fusion of the Anglo-Saxon race'.[105] Perhaps Reid, like Theodore Roosevelt, thought of the Japanese as 'honorary Anglo-Saxons'. The more probable explanation was flaccid thinking and expression.

Overall, the Australians responded to the alliance as loyal members of the empire. Considering that the alliance represented a great innovation in British foreign policy, considering that it was intended to have a great influence on Pacific policy and considering that the Australians themselves had just been engaged in a dispute with the Japanese over immigration, it

[103] *SMH* and *Age*, 14 February 1903.
[104] *Age*, 17 February 1902.
[105] *SMH*, 14 February 1902.

was rather surprising that the Australian reaction was so limited and so subdued. The reason for the modest response lay in the fact that Australians did not see Japan as an immediate menace to their security. Indeed, the Australian government, in 1902 and 1903, accepting the British authorities' judgement, had concluded that Russia posed the greater threat to Australian and imperial interests in the Pacific. In returning to Hutton a letter from the British minister in Tokyo, which outlined Japan's military progress and which had been lent by Hutton as part of his campaign to enlist 'the Yellow Peril' behind his defence policy, Barton in 1903 commented that 'In the present position of affairs, Japan as a Power is of even more interest to all who revolt from the idea of submitting to Russian arrogance!'[106] In his judgement, Japan's military might in 1903 was to be applauded, not feared, since it acted as a counter to Russia's ambitions in the Far East. It was not until the Russo-Japanese war that Australian opinion began to shift definitely and decisively on this question and that the Australian government came to assume a perspective on Japan, which both cut them off from the British and forced them to adopt a defence posture of their own.

The most important consequence of the New Hebrides and immigration diplomatic episodes was to bring out in sharp relief the problems involved in trying to protect Australia's external interests, while still formally subject to an imperial foreign policy. As part of the British Empire, Australia accepted that the Dominions and the Mother Country should face the world as one, and should speak to the world with one voice. It followed from this assumption that Australia had to pursue its distinctive external interests primarily through London. The Commonwealth government, in facing up to the implications of the constitutional realities, came to believe that working as a junior partner inside such an intimate alliance might have its advantages as well as its disadvantages. The Commonwealth leaders thought that they should be able to use British power as a lever for their own ends. They considered that the British government should adopt Australian policy as the empire's policy in matters directly touching Commonwealth interests in the Pacific and should press it as assiduously as if it were their own. Though this had been Australian theory in the New Hebrides case, it had broken down in practice. The British who had control over the making of imperial foreign policy refused to accept that, even on South Pacific questions, Australian interests should have the dominant say in determining policy. Rather, as in all areas of policy-making, colonial perceptions and petitions were overborne by the requirement of British interests. The British locked Australian wishes into their own system of priorities and refused to sacrifice their own interests to appease a colony. The New Hebrides question was negotiated strictly within the confines of Britain's European concerns. Despite their failure in the New Hebrides, successive Commonwealth governments continued to operate on the basis of the lever theory. On some rare occasions, as at the Paris Peace Conference in 1919, Australian governments did, through these means, achieve some success.

The Commonwealth also came to see that having Britain as an intermediary in conducting its external affairs could be exploited not only to secure favours but also to block 'feelers'. The

---

[106] Letter, Barton to Hutton, 30 September 1903, Hutton Papers, add. ms. 50084, Vol. VII, p. 17.

intermediary could be used as a barrier to deflect unwanted attentions and to filter and diffuse foreign complaints. In the case of Japan and immigration, this point made its mark. Barton, embarrassed by the tenacity of the Japanese consul on his doorstep, recommended in 1902 that 'communications on international matters between the Representatives of the United Kingdom and Japan should, as far as practicable, be made through the regular diplomatic channels in London and Tokio.'[107] The British government, for its own reasons, readily concurred, the Colonial Office noting that direct negotiations tended 'to withdraw the foreign relations from the control of H.M.G.'.[108] Direct negotiations endangered British supremacy in imperial foreign policy. The Japanese, when informed of the British decision, saw how their diplomacy's effectiveness might be impaired by such restrictions and they urged the continuance of the existing practice of direct intercourse between the local consuls and the colonial governments. The British, given their opportunity by Barton, held fast to the centralist view of policy-making. The only exception they made was, where the Japanese had a complaint, to permit them to seek a direct explanation from the colony concerned. When this failed to satisfy, negotiations were to be conducted on routine lines through the Foreign Office.[109] By insisting on the letter of the constitution and urging that Japanese approaches be routed through London, the Australian government successfully headed off and dissipated Japan's diplomatic offensive.

Britain's central control of imperial foreign policy machinery could be used to delay and defeat unwelcome overtures and complaints; the cumbersome system, by its very nature, lent itself to such exploitation. The Commonwealth found, however, that while it was an efficient mean of obstruction, it was a hopeless channel for initiative. Since the Australian government had generally to operate through Whitehall to achieve its foreign policy aims, the frustration, especially arising from the New Hebrides experience, caused some soul-searching, and various expedients were proposed from time to time as panaceas for the imperial foreign policy problem. Some thought that the appointment of an Australian High Commissioner to London would go far to solve the problem. Senator Drake, a member of Barton's cabinet, argued in 1901 that a High Commissioner should discharge the duties of 'a diplomatist rather than an agent representing commercial and producing interests.' An Australian High Commissioner 'above all things should be possessed of the qualities which will enable him to ably represent the great Commonwealth of Australia amongst the diplomatists from all parts of the world.'[110] However, others thought that he should be no more than a booster for Australian trade and commerce. A High Commission bill

---

[107] Telegram, Hopetoun to Chamberlain, 18 January 1902, CO 418/18/52.

[108] Letter, under-secretary of state, CO to under-secretary of state, FO, CO 418/18/85.

[109] Copy of despatch, MacDonald, British minister in Tokyo to Lansdowne, 21 May 1902, CO 418/23/599; copy of letter, Baron Komura Joutaro, Japanese foreign minister, to Lansdowne, CO 418/29/*passim*; copy of letter, Hayashi to Lansdowne, 23 June 1904 and letter, under-secretary of state, CO to under-secretary of state, FO, 16 August 1904, CO 418/34/389–91. The Colonial Office considered that it was 'not desirable to extend the Canadian precedent [with respect to Canadian-American direct diplomacy] unless we are obliged to do so.'

[110] *CPD*, 1901–2 session, III, 3447, 2 August 1901.

was not passed until 1909 and the first High Commissioner not appointed until 1910. It would be difficult to contend that his appointment made any essential difference to the efficiency of Australian diplomacy. A further intermediary was no answer to the problem of intermediaries.

Another solution with a long history was that the self-governing colonies should be given a direct voice in the shaping of imperial foreign policy. It emerged in the debates over the South African War and in the debates over admitting Chinese coolie labour into the Transvaal.[111] This suggestion appeared merely as a subterranean murmur of dissent when contentious imperial and international issues were raised. Both attempts in 1904 to influence broad imperial policies, a resolution condemning the introduction of Chinese labour into South Africa and another urging the granting of 'home rule' to Ireland had little effect. Under Deakin, after 1905, this view was pushed energetically; the structural reforms he pressed upon the 1907 Colonial Conference looked towards a greater participation by the Dominions in imperial defence and foreign policy. Much emotional and intellectual energy, much constitutional skill and political know-how were invested in such efforts down to World War II. But, this was a blind alley. Apart from a brief period at the end of World War I, those efforts failed to produce machinery which would work.

---

[111] *CPD*, 1901–2 session, Vol. VII, 9029, 22 January 1902; CPD, 1904 session, XVIII, 696–719, 17 March 1904; ibid., 729–55, 18 March 1904.

# 5

# 'The Commonwealth Crisis': The Perception of an Asian Threat and the Emergence of a National Policy, 1905–7

Against a background of revolutionary changes in international relations, nearly all Australia's men of affairs came, in these years, to distrust the comforting assurances of security emanating from the British Colonial Defence Committee and Committee of Imperial Defence, and to adopt a distinctive strategic scenario of their own which betokened a time of crisis for the Commonwealth. The confusions and uncertainties of the earlier period were, under the pressure of events, replaced by a clear conviction that Australia, as a result of the sudden shift in the world power balance and alliance system, was placed in a vulnerable position and was exposed to attack and even invasion from Asia, in particular from the greatest Asian power, Japan. With perhaps the exception of a brief period of modest reappraisal in the 1920s, Australian defence and foreign policy was to be governed by this fear of Japan until well after the end of World War II.

A series of new developments in international affairs had produced this radical change in Australia's perspective on defence and foreign policy. Those developments included the Japanese victory over Russia in the war of 1904–5 and the emergence of Japan as the undisputed great power in the western Pacific; the renewal of the Anglo-Japanese alliance in 1905 and the increasing British dependence on Japan's goodwill for the safeguard of their interests in Asia and the Pacific; the German challenge to British naval supremacy and the withdrawal of British cruisers from the Pacific to augment the strength of the Royal Navy in the North Sea; the Anglo-French entente and confrontation of and threat of war with Germany in the Moroccan incident of 1905 and 1906; and finally the Japanese-American tensions in 1906 and 1907 arising out of American discrimination against Japanese residents on the west coast of the United States.

In the light of these developments Australians came to believe that they were in a perilous position and to foresee an impending crisis. Following the Russo-Japanese war, the Russians were no longer able to act as a counterpoise to Japan and Japan became the dominant power in the Far East. The British, completely absorbed in their efforts to meet the German challenge in Europe, were concentrating their naval forces around the Home Islands and were no longer able to protect adequately imperial interests in the Pacific.[1] Sir John Fisher, who was First Sea Lord from 1904 to 1910, described this change in British policy in these words, 'The German people have chosen to embark on a scheme of naval aggrandisement. … The English Channel and the North Sea have

---

[1] Arthur J Marder, *From the Dreadnought to Scapa Flow*, 4 vols, London 1961, Vol. I, 'The Road to War, 1904–1914', p.42.

become the frontier of the British Empire.'[2] In early 1905 Fisher recommended that the five British battleships in the Pacific should be moved to the North Sea where they were 'so urgently needed to redress the balance of naval power nearer home.'[3] And later in the year this was done. In these circumstances Australians doubted whether the Anglo-Japanese alliance, at least in the medium to long term, could be relied upon to assure the security of the Commonwealth. Rather, they felt that Japan, seizing the opportunity afforded by Britain's preoccupation with European affairs, might very well attempt to extend its hegemony in the western Pacific. They saw Japan's intervention in 1906 and 1907 in California's attempt to discriminate against Japanese residents, as the prefigurement of their own situation. They feared that they might be left alone to cope as best they could with Japanese diplomatic pressure to modify their immigration laws, with the expansion of Japanese influence southward into the archipelagos which guarded the approaches to Australia, and in the most extreme case, with a Japanese invasion of their continent. From the beginning of the period the different strands were to be found in piecemeal form in the various speeches, debates, papers and letters, which worried at the problem. Within three years, however, they had been woven into whole cloth. They had been brought together into a systematic analysis which gave coherence and meaning to Australia's strategic position. And it was this analysis which was to underpin and to sustain the Commonwealth government's new defence and foreign policy.

### The awakening to danger: the 'menace' of Japan

By the time of the Battle of Tsushima in May 1905, when Japan inflicted a crushing blow on the Russian navy, Australian political leaders had become aware of the great changes affecting power balances and arrangements both in Europe and Asia. Anglo-German naval rivalry had already begun.[4] On 1 April, Emperor William II had indicated Germany's intention of halting the spread of French influence in Morocco, and the British had joined with its Entente Cordiale partner to resist German demands.[5] In Asia, Japan, through its signal victory over the Russians, had achieved a dominant position. This transformation in international relations made a profound impression on Australian statesmen, and most especially on Alfred Deakin, who from 1903 to 1910 was the chief architect of Australia's defence and foreign policy. In an interview granted to *The Herald* of Melbourne on 12 June, that is within two weeks of the Battle of Tsushima, Deakin expressed his anxiety at these novel developments and suggested their importance for Australia. He pointed out that since Napoleonic times, Britain had held undisputed control of the seas and that 'the whole history of Australia had therefore been peaceful'. For this reason, 'no war in which the mother country was engaged has involved direct risks to ourselves in our own homes.' However, he warned that, 'the march of events during the last few years' had drastically altered this comfortable state of affairs, and with 'the striking growth of three new naval powers — the United States,

---

[2] P. K. Kemp (ed.), *The Papers of Admiral Sir John Fisher*, 2 vols, London 1960, Vol. II, pp. 301–16. This quotation originally appeared in an article by Fisher in the *Fortnightly Review* (September 1905).

[3] Ibid., II, p. 81.

[4] Marder, *Dreadnought to Scapa Flow*, Vol. I, pp. 110–14.

[5] Monger, *The End of Isolation*, pp. 186–201.

Germany and Japan,'[6] Australia was obliged 'to review the whole situation in the light of the possibilities now present.'

In Deakin's view, the most significant change in Australia's strategic position proceeded from the fact that, as a result of the Russo-Japanese war, Japan had become by far the greatest naval power in the Far East. 'What we have to estimate for the future', he said, 'is that instead of two fleets in the China Seas belonging to separate—even opposing—powers, we shall now have one fleet, only it will be probably as strong as the two former fleets, and will operate under one flag.' Australia could no longer 'depend on its isolation for security.' The Pacific offered 'the amplest field for future naval [enemy] developments.' The strategic revolution combined with the technical improvements, which had extended the range of modern navies, had placed Australia within striking distance of 'no less than sixteen foreign naval stations', and he named ports ranging from San Francisco to Hawaii and Samoa, from New Caledonia to Saigon, and from Shanghai to Port Arthur and Yokahama. This was of course a gross exaggeration intended to fill out and heighten the sense of impending crisis which he wished to convey. However, it was Japan that preyed on his mind. The precise point which he was endeavouring to make was that, 'As a fact, Japan is the nearest of all the great foreign naval nations to Australia. Japan at her headquarters is, so to speak, next door, while the Mother Country is many streets away, and connected by long lines of communications.' He focused on Japan not because of racial differences or immigration problems, but because of that country's strategic ascendancy in the Pacific and its evident ambition. 'This result', he said, 'would have been obtained if the same decisive victory had rested with Russia, as has been achieved by Japan.'

In this situation he concluded that Australia had to cease debating defence primarily in terms of administration and organization. Australia had to look to purposes underlying policy and relate proposed policies to the perceived needs. He was circumspect in presenting Australian defence requirements for the new era. The development of an Australian navy would depend on Admiralty co-operation and compulsory military training was a politically divisive issue. Such defence programmes would involve much greater federal expenditure, and since no party controlled parliament, this could only be obtained in response to a groundswell of public opinion. He did make three suggestions. Firstly, he urged that harbour defences should be attended to, in order that Australian ports might be able to resist raids perpetrated by a small squadron of fast cruisers. This proposal was still based on the presumption of limited threats which the British government had advised and which in the first years of the Commonwealth the Australian government had accepted. Secondly, he doubted whether the existing naval agreement would be adequate in the new circumstances, and contended that Australia should acquire its own naval force to protect its coastline and coastal trade. Finally, fixing his attention on the possibility of invasion, he asserted, 'emphatically', that it was 'the duty of ablebodied men to fit themselves for defence work.' He saw, however, as his immediate task, the awakening of public opinion.

---

[6] The inclusion of the United States was not because Deakin feared American naval power but rather because he did not wish, for diplomatic reasons, to point the finger too specifically at the Japanese and German dangers.

Australians had to be shocked out of their complacent attitude towards defence, which 'the long period of peace' had induced and to be alerted to 'the risks and responsibilities' which surrounded them.[7] In the following two years the press and publicists gradually began to co-operate with the politicians to achieve this end.

This sense of Australian vulnerability in the changing powerscape of international affairs and this concentration on Japan as the prime threat to Australian security had, as we have seen, begun much earlier. In the 1890s, especially after the Sino-Japanese war of 1895, the cry of 'Yellow Peril', especially as it was embodied by Japan, had been raised. In the early Commonwealth debates on defence, too, a vocal minority had aired similar fears. But until at least the end of 1903, the Japanophobes were in a minority in parliament and they exerted little influence on government policy. The Russo-Japanese war had presaged a new situation. Australians not only came almost without dissent to accept the reality and pre-eminence of the Japanese menace, but their fears also attained an intensity without precedent in the nation's history. For the first time, Australians came to entertain seriously the fear of invasion.

There are certain practical difficulties in trying to pinpoint the time and degree of this change in popular and political attitudes towards Japan. Because Japan was bound to Britain in alliance and because, during the Russo-Japanese War, it was always possible that Britain might be drawn into the fray, Australia's leaders and the press probably masked, at least to some degree, their true feelings about Japan. Nevertheless, there was evident a certain unease about what a Japanese victory might mean, and even, in some quarters, open hostility towards the Japanese cause. Australian political leaders sometimes spoke with two voices but it need not necessarily be construed from this that they were in two minds: with one voice they would speak as Pacific-minded Australians and with the other as imperial diplomats. Deakin himself, during the war years had made seemingly conflicting statements about the new developments in Asia. In December 1903, when Russia and Japan stood on the brink of war, Deakin had said that Australia

---

[7] *Herald*, 12 June 1905; the interview was also printed in CofA *Parliamentary Papers*, 1905 session, Vol. II, No. 31, 'Hon. Alfred Deakin—Statement re Present Condition of Defences of Commonwealth, communicated to the Herald on 12 June 1905—Return to Order'. Though the politicians, the press and the publicists responded to Deakin's warning the professional military officers did not. In reply to a request from the treasurer, Sir George Turner, for comments on Deakin's critique of Australian defences, the Chief of Intelligence, Lt Colonel W. T. Bridges, replied that he saw nothing new in the analysis and that, with the completion of the Hutton scheme, Australian defence needs would be adequately met and Captain W. R. Creswell, while acknowledging in vague terms the increasing threat to Australia in the Pacific (Japan's tutelage over China, Russia pressing down on India, the German Empire absorbing Austria and Holland, most especially a Russo-German alliance) used the occasion to once again hit out at the military dominance of Australian defence, asserting that the field force which could serve no useful Australian purpose had been 'organised with a view of Imperial overseas service' and urged the development of an Australian naval squadron. See 'Report by the Director of the Naval Forces upon the Matters Referred to in the Interview Regarding "Defence" Appearing in the Melbourne *Herald*, of the 12 June, 1905', 8 July 1905—and 'Remarks by Chief of Intelligence', 29 June 1905, MP 729/1, Files 05/6276 and 05/5018.

needed a navy as a 'defence from hordes of Asians'.[8] On the other hand, when asked about a prediction in the *Spectator* that if Japan were victorious, 'she would be likely to seek predominance in the Southern archipelago' and so threaten Australia, Deakin had replied that he thought it 'a novel view', that once established on the Asian mainland, Japan would have more than enough to hold its attention and consume its energy.[9] By placing the New Zealand prime minister's answers to the same questions alongside those of the Australian prime minister, certain doubts about Deakin's candour must be raised. Richard Seddon had said that, if Japan won, 'he was not sure that New Zealand would not have cause for anxiety. Japan was ambitious and with a powerful navy. She might compel New Zealand to receive Japanese immigrants.' He thought the Dominion should be prepared to pay to strengthen the naval squadron.[10]

Again at the end of 1904 Deakin had shown a similar ambiguity. In the *Morning Post* he spoke of 'disquieting evidence that the West Pacific is to become a theatre of conflict', but in giving concrete form to the disquiet, it was Germany and German commerce which he named. On the other side, while addressing his imperial preference bill in parliament in December he had anticipated his *Herald* interview of June 1905. Here he pointed to the troubled condition of the world which marked 'the end of the era of relative peace which we have enjoyed', and he coupled the 'opening up of wider possibilities for all the Asiatic populations' with 'naval developments' in Europe to explain his anxiety. 'They foretold the clash of martial arms that may ring around this planet and determine the fate of nations.' He continued,

> Therefore it befits us, if we wish to defend what we have, and to hand it down to our children to consider all the means possible by which, while time is allowed to us, we may strengthen the position we occupy, making ourselves, more desirable as friends to those who look favorably upon us [This is a reference to imperial tariff preference and the unity of the British Empire] and more dangerous foes to those who regard our prosperity with jealous eyes.[11]

Neither the Watson ministry nor the Reid-McLean ministry, which were in office for nearly the whole period of the war, pronounced on the problem. In bringing down the defence reorganization bill on 2 November 1904, McCay, the minister of defence, had stated Australia 'must take care to be prepared for the future'. He also said the government considered it 'a central matter of importance' that the fixed and floating port defences should be completed and that 'a more efficient and more widespread system of training our youth' should be established.[12] Only one member, J. Page, the Labor member for Maranoa took the opportunity to relate the implication of the Russo-Japanese war to Australian defence needs. He remarked that 'Australia is now coveted by the over-crowded races of the East.' He said that 'The Japanese are equal to any

---

[8] *SMH*, 12 December 1903.

[9] *SMH*, 6 January 1904.

[10] *SMH*, 7 March 1904.

[11] *MP*, 5 January 1905 (despatched from Australia 22 November 1904); *CPD*, 1904 session, XXIV, 8099, 8 December 1904.

[12] *CPD*, 1904 session, XXIII, 6395, 2 November 1904.

white race on sea or land, and a very few years may make the Chinese the same.'[13] Page was a level-headed member, not given to histrionic ranting, and it is worthy of speculation whether he had spoken what many others thought and felt. The governor-general, who at the beginning of the war, had noted, 'a great dread of Japanese immigration here which checks any strong pro-Japanese sentiment',[14] was by the end of 1904 commenting on what he described as Australia's 'curious indifference to the Russo-Japanese war'.[15] On the surface, this did, indeed, seem to be the case. But that there were doubts, suspicions, and antagonisms, swirling beneath this placid appearance, can hardly be denied. During the senate debate on a resolution dealing with the Russian fleet's attack on British trawlers, these subterranean feelings briefly emerged into the light of day.

Following the Russian attack on the British trawlers off the Dogger Bank, the Australian parliament dutifully passed resolutions expressing 'profound indignation at the cruel and wanton attack' and supporting British demands for satisfaction, even though they knew that this might bring the British Empire into the war on Japan's side. Whereas the resolutions were passed without debate in the House, in the Senate the leader of the government only consulted with the leader of the Labor opposition minutes before bringing the matter before members, and the senators, taken by surprise, expressed views which demonstrated widespread hostility to Japan. A group of Labor senators complained that Russia was being condemned unheard, that, as in the Boer War, the press was conspiring with British authorities to whip up the people into a warlike, and in this case, anti-Russian and pro-Japanese, mood. Moving from this fair-minded ground of objection, one member went on to assert that their sympathies were 'enlisted on behalf of the European and not the little brown Asiatic nation'. Two Labor senators, Senator Pearce and Senator H. Turley of Queensland, indicated that, even though they would vote for the resolution, they, too, sympathized with the European power. No one spoke up for the Japanese and, of course, the issue of the war was not directly germane to the resolution under consideration. But a hurried lobbying brought the wayward Labor men back into line, the amendment was withdrawn, the resolution passed and British race patriotism vindicated.[16] That such antipathies and fears were present can also be deduced from the fact that Hutton, in his last campaign for his defence scheme in 1904, had made a direct appeal to the 'momentous changes taking place in the balance of power in the

---

[13] *CPD*, 1904 session, XXIII, 7498, 25 November 1904.

[14] Letter, Northcote to Chamberlain, 14 February 1904, Joseph Chamberlain Papers, 19/1/3.

[15] Letter, Northcote to Balfour, 20 November 1904, Balfour Papers, add. ms. 49697/49.

[16] *CPD*, 1904 session, XXIII, 6258–60, 28 October 1904; see also editorial in the *Bulletin,* 14 January 1904, 'no European power would attempt such a wanton and dangerous enterprise as an attack on Australia. But in one respect struggle between Japan and Russia would touch our interests closely and enlist Australian sympathy for Russia' for a Russian victory would 'by humbling the growing arrogance of a mushroom Asiatic power' remove the danger from the 'yellow race' and the 'unnatural alliance between Britain and Japan … the only possible foe that this section of "the Empire" has reason to dread.'

East', and hinting at Japanese and Chinese ambitions for expansion in the region.[17] His motives and sincerity might be questioned, but his political acumen must be conceded.

The reticence which Australians, for the most part, had shown during the war, ceased with Japan's vanquishing of Russian naval power at the Battle of Tsushima on 28 May. Deakin's arresting statement of 12 June began a movement among Australian political leaders to redefine and restate Australia's world position, and in doing so, they discarded fears of Russia and France, set aside British advice, relegated the German threat to a secondary status and concentrated their attention on Japan's role in the Pacific. McLean, deputy prime minister in the Reid-McLean coalition, who had already in the 1901 debates identified himself as a Japanophobe, on the day after Deakin's interviews were published, echoed and amplified his remarks. 'The stupendous struggle in the East', he said,

> must awaken the people of Australia to the fact that we have been living in a fool's paradise, when we have assumed that our great distance from the military nations gave us immunity from foreign invasion. … Japan has astonished the world. … We now find one of the great naval and military powers within a very short distance of our shores. That puts us in a very different position from that which we considered we occupied before.

And, like Deakin, he warned that 'in a future scheme to provide for the effective defence of Australia we must take cognizance of these altered circumstances'. Though it was fortunate that 'the great Power which has recently arisen in the East' was allied to Great Britain, he thought it was possible that 'that condition of things might not always continue and we must be prepared for what might happen'.[18]

Similarly, McCay, the defence minister, addressing the Navy League in Adelaide, declared that 'We are close — too close for safety to a new Power which has arisen,[19] unless we are prepared for any danger that may exist. Australia is not now in the vanguard, but the advanceguard' of danger.[20] Reid, however, true to his style, reacted ambiguously. He thought Australia should cultivate friendly relations with Japan while preserving 'the integrity of the race'. He envisaged the development of an Australian navy, which would act 'as a bulwark of self-defence', standing alongside 'the Old Country' in Britain's greatness or decay — high-sounding phrases sufficiently imprecise in meaning not to commit him but sufficiently relevant to attract those fearful of Japan, while not offending the British government and those Australians who deferred to British judgement.[21] Reid was fighting at this time for the survival of his government.

---

[17] CofA, *Parliamentary Papers,* 1904 session, Vol. II, No. 25; see also *West Australian,* 2 August 1904 and *SMH,* 14 November 1904.

[18] *Herald,* 13 June 1905.

[19] This was a standard circumlocution for referring to Japan. It was intended as a diplomatic gesture to the existence of the Anglo-Japanese alliance.

[20] *Advertiser,* 28 June 1905.

[21] *SMH,* 13 June 1905; see also *SMH,* 26 June 1905. Reid proclaimed that broadening the bases of the citizen defence forces was of the greatest urgency, but that there was a difficulty in carrying out any system of general conscription in military service in any British community.

At the ALP Commonwealth Conference in July, Watson told the delegates that in the preceding twelve months it had been brought home to him that 'the developments to the North, colloquially known as the Far East', necessitated Australia acquiring a great population. He was at that time willing to believe that, for possibly twenty years, China and Japan would be taken up with their difficulties, with Russian reprisal and revenge. But within that relatively short space of time, Australia's position would deteriorate. He feared that Australians were lulled too easily into a false sense of security. A resolution favouring compulsory military training was only narrowly defeated.[22] In November, Senator Pearce asserted that Australia had very little or no reason to fear European aggression against its territories. However, he thought that it would be 'foolish if we took that [Anglo-Japanese treaty] to be a guarantee for all time.' He continued,

> Japan has shown that she is an aggressive nation. She has shown that she is desirous of pushing out all round. What has always been the effect of victory and of conquest upon nations? Do we not know that it stimulates them to further conflict? to obtain fresh territory? Has not that been the history of our own race? ... Is there any other country that offers such a temptation to Japan as Australia does?[23]

Though the Anglo-Japanese alliance was renewed and strengthened in August 1905, Australian anxieties about the new power constellation in the Pacific were not allayed. In this atmosphere of gathering crisis voluntary associations sprang up to 'ginger' public opinion and, if need be, politicians, into taking the necessary actions for self-defence. On 5 September, the National Defence League was founded in Sydney,[24] and the Victorian branch held its inaugural meeting on 1 December.[25] The National Defence League was influenced to a certain degree by Lord Roberts' campaign in Britain for compulsory military training. But it differed in some significant ways from its British counterpart. The Australian movement sought a system of universal training based on the Swiss militia system rather than a system of full time national service, following the more common continental model. The Australian movement, also unlike the British, was supported by many leading Labor and liberal politicians; Watson, Hughes, Deakin and T. T. Ewing, who became defence minister in 1907, were among its active supporters. Finally, the Australian movement was, in contrast to the British, inspired by fear of an Asian, not a European, threat. In his inaugural address the first president, Sir Normand Maclaurin, the chancellor of the University of Sydney, justified the setting up of the League by pointing to the 'recent events', which had shown that Australia was no longer isolated from the rest of the world. 'We know not', he said, 'when the din of battle and clash of arms just ceased in the East, would be at our doors.'[26] The League's journal, *The Call*, subsequently spelt out these Asian fears in a more precise form. Australia had to contend with 'the far more serious danger of invasion by a colonising army, vast in numbers, from Asia, since China is now arousing herself to warlike

---

[22] Official Report of the Commonwealth Political Labour Conference, Melbourne, July 1905, 8–12.
[23] *CPD*, 1905 session, XXIX, 5346, 22 November 1905.
[24] *SMH*, 6 September 1905.
[25] *Age*, 2 December 1905.
[26] *SMH*, 6 September 1905.

organization and Japan is the possible, if not probable, enemy of the future.'[27] At the same time, Deakin and Watson helped establish an Immigration League which had as its aim the stimulation of a vigorous British or, less certainly, European migration policy and programme. The League held its first meeting in the Lyceum Theatre, Sydney on 14 October.[28] It was felt that by spreading settlement and building a larger population, Australia would be more secure. The Commonwealth's thousands of miles of unsettled coastline was 'a constant temptation to our rivals among the nations.'[29] Dr Richard Arthur, who became the first president of the Immigration League, advocated a more energetic migration policy specifically to counter the threats to Australia, caused by the rise of Japan and the withdrawal of British battleships from the Pacific.[30]

After Deakin had forced Reid from office on 5 July 1905, Reid and the freetraders, in opposition, gave the Japanese 'menace' theses rather less support than the other factions in parliament. One free-trade senator, Senator E. Pulsford, after the renewal of the Anglo-Japanese alliance, denounced Australian fears and published a pamphlet in order to give wider currency to his views.[31] However, most free-trade leaders, while accepting the general assumption of Deakin's strategic analysis, tended in so far as they threw doubt on the Pacific threat, merely to question the immediacy and urgency of the crisis. The free-traders' questioning was due not only to the fact that they were in opposition, but also because they included in their number the conservatives who felt a deferential loyalty to the empire and who, like Pulsford, accepted the British evaluation of the Anglo-Japanese alliance. McCay, on 29 August, allowed that Australia was no longer remote from the theatre of the world's wars, 'as it was … even a short time ago' but he was not certain where the great war was 'to take place, in the Atlantic or the Pacific.'[32] A month later, McCay, in justifying his former defence estimates was playing down risks altogether, 'I say the least risk … is that of an invasion of Australia.'[33] At a later point, he added, 'There is only one power — I need not name it — from which such a movement [invasion] towards any part of Australia could possibly be anticipated, and the probability is that that power will not for a generation carry out such an enterprise, even though it may think of acting in such a manner.'[34] Joseph Cook, Reid's deputy, similarly said in September that 'We are all coming to recognize more and more our vulnerability to attack from the East' and that increased population was necessary

---

[27] *Call*, II (November 1906). The relatively moderate statement on Japan might well be another formal gesture to the Anglo-Japanese alliance; see also J. C. Watson, *Call*, 1 (August 1906), p. 6.

[28] *DT*, 16 October 1905.

[29] *Age*, 9 September 1905; Deakin repeated this theme in *MP*, 5 December 1905 and *SMH*, 30 January 1906.

[30] *Age*, 13 September 1905; see also for a more extended version of Arthur's fear of Japan in a Pacific denuded of British naval power, *SMH*, 8 August 1905.

[31] *The British Empire and the Relations of Asia and Australasia* (Sydney 1905). It was also intended to answer a scare-mongering pamphlet *Flashlights on Japan and the East* (Melbourne 1905), which had been written by the Labor member for Melbourne, Dr W. R. H. Maloney.

[32] *CPD*, 1905 session, XXVI, 1624, 29 August 1905.

[33] Ibid., XXVI, 2138, 12 September 1905.

[34] Ibid., XXVIII, 3909–10, 20 October 1905.

to give Australia security.[35] A month later, though, he played down the character of the danger by asserting that Australia, 'for some years', would not face any grave contingency.[36] Reid, for the most part, avoided the topic. On one exceptional occasion when an interjector interrupted him, in the midst of a public address, to ask, 'What about the Japanese navy?' he riposted, 'the knowledge that the British flag was intertwined with the flag of the navy of Japan made Australians sleep much more soundly in their beds.'[37] Though it is difficult to know how much weight should be given to such an emotional and rhetorical retort, it would be accurate to say that not until after Reid resigned from the leadership of the party in 1908 were the senior free-trade members won over completely to the doctrine of the Japanese menace and the Yellow Peril.

Despite these nominal and confused reservations of some free-traders and the opposition and scepticism of a handful of Labor men[38] in the eighteen months following Deakin's *Herald* interview, expressions of apprehension about Asian, and particularly about Japanese, ambitions and Australia's future, became the commonplaces of defence debates and speeches. The very fact that parliament saw fit in August to have the Deakin statement printed, testified to the impact that it had made on the Commonwealth. It had become the starting point and the guideline for a revolution in Australian strategic thinking.

The Commonwealth government, after July 1905, exhibited a new sense of purpose and a new vigour in action in the conduct of Australia's defence and external policies. With Deakin at the helm, the federal government responded to the great changes taking place in international relations in those years. Even though, due to financial stringency, imperial obstruction and a lag in public opinion, Deakin did not achieve great things in this time of transition, his efforts and initiatives did lay the groundwork for the momentous expansion of Australia's defence forces and for the self-assertive posture of Australian diplomacy in the period from 1908 to 1914. Deakin's new defence and external policies took three main forms; firstly, in tentative overtures to Japan, to try by revision of rules and procedures to make Australia's immigration law less offensive to the Pacific's dominant power, secondly, by acquiring more substantial harbour and coastal protection, including a local navy, and by moving towards compulsory military training to create a more substantial defence capacity, and thirdly, by developing more co-operative imperial institutions to enable the Commonwealth to have greater influence in the shaping of imperial policies in the Pacific.

## *Appeasing Japan*

It may well be that Australia's conciliatory approach to Japan over immigration was instigated by the British authorities. In appraising the proposal to renew the Anglo-Japanese alliance, Sir

---

[35] Ibid., XXVI, 2383, 15 September 1905.

[36] Ibid., XXVIII, 3890, 20 October 1905.

[37] *SMH*, 8 May 1906.

[38] See O'Malley and Fisher, *CPD*, 1905 session, XXVII, 2747, 26 September 1905. When O'Malley denounced the new crisis of what he called, 'war, war, war', Fisher scoffed in sympathy, 'it is a new craze'.

George Sydenham Clarke, the secretary of the Committee of Imperial Defence and former governor of Victoria, told the British prime minister that,

> If such a Treaty as this came into existence our Colonies, Australia especially, will have to put the Japanese on precisely the same footing as Frenchmen or Germans. Discrimination against the Japanese, as a colonial people, would not be possible. It might be necessary to speak plainly to Australia, but Australians are not without sense, and their position is one of peculiar weakness except for our support, so that they would find it necessary to swallow their race prejudice as regards the Japanese.[39]

On the basis of this letter, Balfour prepared a submission for Cabinet on 31 May, in which he remarked on the 'obvious difficulties—not to say absurdities—in allowing Australia and other Colonies to treat our Japanese allies as belonging to an inferior race.' However, he thought it 'doubtful whether this is a subject on which we either can or ought,' to coerce self-governing Colonies', and considered that though 'There is much to be said for trying to get this question put on a satisfactory basis before the treaty is signed, … it may be one of the difficulties which is best to ignore in the hope that during the currency of the Treaty, it may not arise in an acute form.'[40] The matter would appear to have been left there. There is no direct evidence that the British did 'speak plainly' to the Australians.

Observing the tide of battle during the Russo-Japanese war, Commonwealth leaders hardly needed British prompting to realize that the Japanese could not be treated like a weak and defenceless Asian or African people. Indeed, as soon as the news of the opening of hostilities reached Melbourne, voices were raised in favour of mitigating the discriminatory immigration controls in so far as they affected Japan. It was felt that such a mark of respect should be extended to Britain's ally. Negotiations were opened with Japan on 16 April 1904, and four months later the Reid government instituted new procedures to enable Japanese merchants, students and tourists to obtain visas from British consuls and so escape the humiliation of exemption procedures applied at the port of entry against coloured persons.[41]

The success of Japan in the war convinced a number of political leaders that even greater concessions should be made. The governor-general reported to Chamberlain that Sir William Lyne and George Reid had both approached him separately and privately to say that 'out of compliment to Japan, Japanese should again be allowed to settle in Australia, and that should be done forth-with.' Lyne had maintained that 'the majority of the Labour Party could be induced to agree.'[42] These purported remarks of Reid and Lyne ran so counter to firmly entrenched Australian attitudes on race and immigration that it is difficult to give credence to Northcote's

---

[39] Letter, Clarke to Balfour, 27 May 1905, Balfour Papers, add. ms. 49701/209/11.
[40] Notes of A. J. Balfour on Anglo-Japanese alliance renewal, dated 31 May 1905, Cab 1/5/28.
[41] CofA, *Parliamentary Papers*, 1905 session, Vol. II, No. 61, 'Immigration Restriction Act, 1901. Correspondence Respecting Proposals to Modify the Administration of the Act in Regard to Visits of Asiatic Merchants, Travellers, etc.' (dated 16 April 1904 to 1 August 1905).
[42] Letter, Northcote to Chamberlain, 4 May 1905, Joseph Chamberlain Papers, 20/1/4.

version of the conversations.[43] Nevertheless, the Australian government, after the announcement of the signing of the new Anglo-Japanese alliance in August 1905, did take steps to try and work out a gentleman's agreement with Japan which would enable the Commonwealth government to exclude Japanese from the dictation test procedures while at the same time, through Japan's own self-regulation, keep Japanese settlers from entering Australia.[44]

In December parliament amended the Immigration Restriction Act to replace 'European' with 'any prescribed language' in the dictation test clause, thus striking the offending phrase from the law, and to provide for the exemption of citizens of foreign countries from the requirements of the test where the governments of these countries had reached an agreement with the Commonwealth to control the emigration of their own citizens to Australia.[45]

Deakin, who had learnt well the New Hebrides lesson, had negotiated these issues directly through the Japanese consul-general. The British government was perturbed by Deakin's flouting of the rules which Barton had invoked and the Colonial Office confirmed in 1902 and 1903, and, chiding Deakin for his temerity, insisted that all diplomatic correspondence and communications be conducted through London. Deakin attempted to placate the British. He said that he agreed 'in principle' with the convention but nevertheless claimed a right to carry on 'preliminary and, to a large extent, unofficial discussions'. In arguing that such 'preliminary' and 'unofficial' discussions could be carried on without consultation, he was, in a sense, using British New Hebrides explanations against the Colonial Office and the Foreign Office. Deakin claimed that in this particular case the informal advice and counsel of the Japanese consul-general, who had 'given so much attention to the subject', was important.[46]

Though the Colonial Office did not like this departure from the established procedures which gave them almost total control over the colonies' foreign relations, they put the best face they could on the matter. 'In the special circumstances', they refrained from objecting, but urged that in any future case the Colonial Office be sent copies of correspondence 'immediately it takes place'.[47] Elgin, writing to Northcote, expressed his displeasure with Deakin's actions. He contended that 'if the Colonies are to remain part of a great Empire, there surely must be occasions when the actions of a Colonial government may conflict with imperial interests. Are we not then to be allowed to ask for information?' He pointed out that Britain's special interest in the immigration question arose out of its alliance with Japan. 'Noone', he wrote, 'would dream of swamping Australia with Japanese—or any other coloured race—but I do think it is reasonable that we who are responsible to our allies should be consulted when legislation which may affect

---

[43] It would seem probable that he interpreted a desire to remove the causes of friction to mean a willingness to open the floodgates and to remove all barriers.

[44] See Deakin's statement, *CPD*, 1905 session, XXVIII, 3886–8, 20 October 1905.

[45] Ibid., XXX, 6361, 6 December 1905; ibid., XXX, 6705 and 6788, 12 December 1905.

[46] Despatch, Northcote to Elgin, 3 January 1906 enclosing despatch, Deakin to Northcote, 29 December 1905, CO 418/44/19–26.

[47] Copy of despatch, Elgin to Northcote, 2 March 1906, CO 418/49/329.

them is proposed.'[48] Deakin found it to be advantageous to negotiate directly with Japan and set aside the Barton principle which had been formulated in order to try and keep the Japanese at bay. A British intermediary in the circumstance of 1905 would have been an obstruction and not a facility. This difference over diplomatic procedures in the Japanese case when superimposed on the New Hebrides row started the Australian government off on a very bad footing with the new Liberal administration in Whitehall. It was a bad beginning from which they never properly recovered.

The Commonwealth government's approaches to Japan and their modifications of the Immigration Restriction Act had been motivated by a desire to improve Australian-Japanese relations. After the act had been revised and the dictation clause changed, Deakin endeavoured to turn the immigration concessions to commercial account. In May 1906 he asked the British government to ascertain whether the Japanese would be willing to allow Australia the commercial benefits of the Anglo-Japanese treaty of 1894 without requiring the Commonwealth to make any further alterations in its immigration policy. Anglo-Japanese trade had been increasing, even though it was but a small proportion of the whole, and Deakin believed that it was 'capable of considerable expansion'. He explained that Australian exports to Japan suffered from American competition, and New South Wales, Victoria, South Australia, Western Australia and Tasmania suffered in comparison with Queensland. He hoped that the visa concession made in 1904 would satisfy the Japanese and he stated that the Commonwealth government would be happy, under the provisions of the revised act of December 1905, to enter into a convention with Japan formalizing the procedures which regulated the entry of Japanese citizens into Australia. Since Japan had permitted Queensland to continue to profit from its adherence to the 1894 treaty, even while allowing its immigration rights with respect to the 1900 protocol to lapse, Deakin was sanguine that such a *modus vivendi* might be extended. However, Deakin made it clear that, in order to gain this favour, parliament would not relax its barrier against Japanese immigration one iota, not even to the limited extent that Queensland had consented in 1900.[49]

The Colonial Office was grateful that Japan's success in the war of 1904–5 and Australia's search for new trade opportunities was making the Commonwealth more tolerant of Britain's Asian ally, but they doubted that anything could be gained by stirring up this issue once more.[50] The Colonial Office's doubts were justified in the event, though it seems probable that the British foreign secretary, Sir Edward Grey, did not put the Australian proposal in its best light nor use the British government's best offices in pressing it. The Japanese government was in a strong bargaining position. Canada had signed the Anglo-Japanese commercial treaty without reservations, and created for the Australians an unhappy precedent. Japan was only willing to enter into negotiations for the Commonwealth's adherence to the treaty if, as the Japanese foreign minister put it, 'the Australian government have no objection to the putting of proper restrictions

---

[48] Letter, Elgin to Northcote, 12 April 1906, PRO 30/56/1.
[49] Despatch, Northcote to Elgin, 7 May 1906, enclosing despatch Deakin to Northcote, 1 May 1906, CO 418/44/319–23.
[50] Minute by H. B. Cox, assistant under-secretary of state (legal), 7 July 1906, CO 418/44/317–19.

upon the unrestricted right of legislation possessed by the Australian Parliament in regard to Japanese immigrants.' The British minister, Sir Claude MacDonald, wrote that the Japanese considered the arrangement of 1904 'altogether too stringent and would insist on terms at least as liberal as those acquired under the 1900 Queensland protocol.'[51] This cooled the Australian ardour for a settlement with respect to immigration and commercial issues. When the Japanese revived the question of their immigration rights under the Queensland agreement and the Law Officers rejected Deakin's opinion that the Queensland act was not binding on the Commonwealth, the prime minister took steps to give notice of termination. In June 1908, the notice was given and at the end of twelve months the Commonwealth government was rid of this embarrassing anomaly.[52]

Treating with the Japanese had proved a frustrating process. At all events, it was much the slightest strand in the pattern of the Australian response evoked by Japan's triumph at Tsushima. It was in defence policy rather than in diplomacy that the major impact was felt.

## Towards an Australian navy and compulsory military training

Deakin, in alerting the nation to the new international context in which it had to take its place, had called for a thorough re-examination of Australia's defence needs. He had dismissed the existing defence force as 'inadequate in numbers, imperfectly supplied with war material, and exceptionally weak on the naval side.' He looked towards the Commonwealth acquiring a naval flotilla of its own and the refurbishing of harbour defences, both fixed and floating, and he saw in the training of all adult male citizens for military service the only sure means of protecting the country against invasion. In office, Deakin, as prime minister, found the task of translating these vague aspirations into precise policies a difficult and frustrating one. Since all such measures involved increased appropriations, the Commonwealth government, being still inhibited by the Braddon 'Blot', had to reckon up the costs very carefully. A more important reason for hesitation and delay, though, was the conflicting advice which the government received concerning defence policy. The British governments and its specialist agencies, the Colonial Defence Committee, the Committee of Imperial Defence, and the Admiralty, made recommendations which were very much at odds with those being urged by the Australian military and naval officers who were themselves divided on what should be done. Deakin at first felt that for practical and political as well as imperial reasons, he could only introduce a new defence scheme, especially a new naval policy, with the co-operation of the British authorities. However, since the British rejected the strategic and logistical assumptions which prompted Deakin to press forward with the naval proposals, the Australian prime minister found the process of extracting a positive response from London a very painful and trying one. Ultimately, in December 1907, under pressure from the

---

[51] Copy of telegram, MacDonald to Grey, 6 October 1906 and despatch, Elgin to Northcote, 7 December 1906, CO 418/49/561 and 601–6.

[52] Law Officers' Views, CO 418/52/262–7; letter, F. A. Campbell, under-secretary of state, FO to Cox, under-secretary of state, CO, 30 November 1907, CO 418/57/428–57; despatch, Northcote to Elgin, 17 March 1908, CO 418/60/134–5; telegram, Northcote to Lord Crewe, colonial secretary, 17 June 1908, CO 418/60/359.

press and public opinion, he unilaterally proclaimed a new defence policy, committed his government to creating an Australian coastal flotilla and to instituting a system of universal and compulsory military training.

Deakin's first move, in what became a sustained campaign to bring about a revolution in Australia's defence policy, was to approach the British government with the aim of bringing about a revision of the 1903 naval agreement. In August 1905 he seized on the remarks of the commanding officer on the Australian station, vice-admiral Sir Arthur Fanshawe, that the naval defence of Australia and New Zealand was inadequate and sent a despatch to London, urging that, since the naval agreement was as unsatisfactory for the Admiralty as it was for Australia, it ought to be reconsidered. He maintained that the defence of Australia and of its coasts 'was accepted as a duty and a necessity of our national self-respect' and that the Australian squadron, as it was then constituted and controlled did not meet Australia's requirements. Recognizing that Australia's national feeling would be more readily understood in Great Britain than its distinctive geo-political perspective, Deakin did not question the strategic justification for the naval agreement, but rather deplored the failure of the agreement to elicit any distinctive Australian sentiment or support. 'Our £200,000 a year would seem in part repaid if we were enabled to take a direct and active part in the protection of our shores and shipping.' He suggested to the Admiralty that the subsidy might be devoted to purchasing first-class mail steamers, which in peacetime 'would confer a boon upon producers', by helping to foster trade between Australia and Britain, and which in war could be quickly converted to naval purposes. Ommanney, now under-secretary of state at the Colonial Office, remarked that if Deakin's proposition were accepted 'Australia would get all she now has and a subsidised mail and passenger service in addition', and this would seem fair comment.[53]

Deakin followed up his request for a revision of the naval arrangement with complaints about the Admiralty's failure to furnish a squadron for the Australian station in strict conformity with the provisions of the agreement. Creswell drew up a list showing the discrepancy between what was promised and what was provided, and there seems little doubt that he instigated a rash of questions in parliament to press home the issue.[54] The matter itself was rather petty. Undoubtedly, as the Colonial Office surmised, Deakin was using it 'to help undermine' the naval agreement and so 'pave the way' for his own naval policy. It was also probably intended as a protest against Britain's decision to withdraw its five battleships from the Pacific. There had been some press agitation on the subject, and Dr Richard Arthur, who was to become the first president of the Immigration League, in an article in the *Sydney Morning Herald* on 'Australia and International Relations', had said

---

[53] Despatch, Northcote to Lyttleton, sent 28 August 1905, CO 418/37/71–81.

[54] Despatch, Northcote to Lyttleton, sent 23 October 1905, and received 27 November 1905, enclosing a memorandum Creswell to Playford, 12 October 1905, CO 418/37/274; *CPD*, 1905 session, XXV, 462, 3 August 1905, ibid., XXVIII, 3437, 12 October 1905; ibid., XXVIII, 3919, 24 October 1905; despatch, Northcote to Elgin, sent 27 April 1906 and received 2 June 1906, CO 418/44/290–6.

> I am beginning to realise that we must have our own Australian fleet. The withdrawal of the British battleships from China has put a different complexion on affairs. In the Naval Defence agreement it was always postulated that these ships would be available for the defence of Australia. But now they have gone and will probably be prevented by circumstances from ever returning. The situation has changed and we are face to face with the question of battleships of our own.[55]

Deakin could scarcely have failed to link the two matters.

The Colonial Office was willing to wash its hands of the naval agreement and so avoid the friction which it was heir to and which the disputes over fulfilment of detailed provisions so well illustrated. Lyttleton was willing to reach some compromise, and, for the sake of peace, to allow the Australians to develop a local force of their own. But the Admiralty remained intransigent. Despite Deakin's appeal for an early cabled answer, it was not until almost a year later that the Admiralty's reply reached Melbourne. It said simply that the Admiralty was content with the agreement as it stood and considered mailsteamers a very costly and inefficient form of naval defence.[56] The brevity of the Admiralty's response was not primarily due to indifference or hostility but rather to the fact that, while the question was still being considered, Deakin has set on foot a more far-reaching investigation of coastal and commercial defences which superseded the August inquiry and in effect made it irrelevant.

In parliament Deakin and his defence minister, Senator Playford, had during September and October 1905, come under pressure to produce their defence policy. There was considerable agitation on the subject. W. H. Kelly, a conservative free-trader from New South Wales, had on 7 September moved a resolution that all Australian naval appropriation be spent on the imperial navy and that the Australian contribution to the Royal Navy be doubled. This was a vain effort to head off the expected move to establish an Australian flotilla. In his speech supporting the resolution, Kelly showed that even conservative and subservient imperialists shared the common anxiety. They simply differed about the remedies. 'We have in this part of the world', he said, 'a new problem to consider in dealing with the defence of Australia. We are now within striking distance of one of the world's great naval powers. ... Now Japan has a very powerful fleet and as it has [since Tsushima] no other fleet to watch in the Eastern waters, it can be sent anywhere.' He cited with approval an article by E. W. O'Sullivan, a radical New South Wales political leader, who had claimed that with Japan's victory over Russia and the weakening of British naval power on the China and East Indies stations, Australia had become exposed to the danger of invasion from the north. Though Kelly, as a good imperialist, thought that the Anglo-Japanese alliance could be relied upon, nevertheless, as a good Australian, he urged that the best way to insure against

---

[55] *SMH*, 8 August 1905; see also editorial in *SMH*, 9 August 1905, on the question of the Pacific.

[56] Cable, Elgin to Deakin, 7 June 1906, CofA, *Parliamentary Papers*, 1906 session, Vol. II, No. 98, 'Naval Agreement with Australia and New Zealand. (correspondence between the governments of the United Kingdom and the Commonwealth—Dated 28th August, 1905 to 23rd May, 1906)'.

menace in the Pacific was to help build up the British fleet.[57] Senator Playford, in answer to criticism, explained that the government was perplexed and, to a degree, hamstrung by the conflicting opinions tendered by the experts. Nevertheless, he stated that Australian policy had three objectives, firstly, to meet the possibility of invasion, secondly, to provide defence against raids on coastal shipping and harbours, and thirdly, to seek to guard against attacks by fast cruisers on ocean-going commerce. He was convinced of the necessity of starting 'to establish the nucleus of an Australian navy'.[58] Limited though it was, this was a statement of policy.

When, in early October, the Australian government received from the Colonial Defence Committee a memorandum on the 1904 defence reorganization in which the British authorities rejected the first and third objectives, Playford, who was somewhat incensed by British perversity, asked his own naval and military officers for their comments. The Colonial Defence Committee evaluation of Australia's strategic position and defence needs had in no way been affected by the Russo-Japanese war or the German threat to British naval power in Europe. They still considered that the British navy gave Australia a blanket protection against invasion and therefore they had concluded that the Hutton military defence scheme, as modified in 1904, 'answers to no definite war requirements'. The only danger to which Australia was exposed was raids by fast cruisers and it was believed that these could be handled effectively by fixed defences, fort garrison and local militia. They could see no justification for Hutton's Commonwealth field force and recommended that it be disbanded and the troops allocated between the fort garrisons and local militia.[59] Both the Australian military and naval officers queried the assumptions in the report. Lieutenant-Colonel Bridges asked, 'Is the Commonwealth to make no preparation for resisting possible territorial aggression?', and Creswell bluntly pointed out that, if the Colonial Defence Committee's views were accepted, there could be no justification for an Australian naval force.[60]

The Colonial Defence Committee was clearly out of step with Australian strategic thinking. Playford ignored their findings. Instead, he asked Creswell to submit a paper on the establishment of an Australian navy and the role it could play in the defence of the Commonwealth. On 10 October Creswell reported back. He repeated the recommendations which he had laid before McCay, following the abortive meeting of the Council of Defence on 5 May. He urged the creation of a naval force comprising three cruiser destroyers, sixteen torpedo-boat destroyers and fifteen torpedo-boats. He estimated that the capital cost of constructing the force, which he thought should be spread over seven years, was £1,768,000, and that the cost of manning and maintenance would be £120,000 annually. He rejected submarines because they were still untried. A covey of

---

[57] *CPD*, 1905 session, XXVI, 1987–2000, 7 September 1905; see also Senator Matheson, who agreed that in time of trouble the British squadron would be withdrawn to European waters, leaving Australia undefended, and who called, as he had in 1902 and 1903, for an independent Australian navy, *CPD*, 1905 session, XXVII, 2776, 27 September 1905.

[58] *CPD*, 1905 session, XXVII, 2823, 27 September 1905.

[59] *CDC*, No. 377R, Cab 8/7.

[60] Copy of letter, Bridges to Playford, 11 October 1905 and copy of letter, Creswell to Playford, 10 October 1905, Deakin Papers, 1540/38/467.

fast destroyers could provide intelligence of enemy movements, and serve a useful purpose in hindering attacks on ports and protecting commerce especially in the immediate environs of the ports.[61] In his first annual report to parliament, Creswell elaborated on the justification for an Australian naval force. Creswell, like nearly all of his fellow naval and military officers, did not, at this time, share the political leaders' fear of invasion from the north. He accepted the Colonial Defence Committee's view that Australia would only be drawn into war on the cot-tails of the Mother Country, and that it could only reasonably anticipate cruiser raids, and though he stressed the decreasing value of isolation he seemed to have European and not Pacific threats in mind. It was not until 1907 that Creswell predicated his case for an Australian navy on the grounds of a threat from Japan. In the meantime, he differed with the British authorities not on ends, but means.[62]

Deakin was placed in a quandary by the inopportune arrival of the Colonial Defence Committee's report, and he wrote his old friend, Sir George Clarke, for advice. Clarke suggested that Deakin place the problem of coastal and harbour defence before the Committee of Imperial Defence. The Committee of Imperial Defence had been set up in 1904 on the recommendation of the Esher Committee to co-ordinate the defence resources and to integrate the strategic policy not only of the relevant departments of the British government, but also of the constituent elements of the empire.[63] Deakin gladly acquiesced and cabled the CID on 11 November in almost the very word formula given him by Clarke. The Commonwealth government asked the Committee to nominate ports in need of defence, to state the level of defence and the 'local naval defence' required in such cases. Here, Deakin's statement deviated from Clarke's, whose wording had been 'Local naval defence to be also considered and its scope laid down, if it is considered desirable'. Deakin asked that the scheme be presented as 'a harmonious whole'.[64]

To assist the Committee in its deliberations and to complete preparation for bringing down a new comprehensive defence policy, the Commonwealth government sent its senior naval and military advisers to London. Creswell was, in the light of his recommendations of the previous October, to study recent naval developments, especially with respect to harbour defence. Since a copy of his naval scheme had been forwarded to Whitehall Deakin expected that the Committee of Imperial Defence would consult the Naval Director about port and coastal defences. Bridges was instructed that after completing his work for the Committee of Imperial Defence he should

---

[61] CofA, *Parliamentary Papers*, 1906 session, Vol. II, No. 66, 'Defence of Australia. Reports by Captain Creswell, Naval Director (a) In reply to Question asked by Minister of Defence as to the Formation of an Australian Navy; (b) upon Australian Defence; (c) Re Submersibles or Submarines; see also Creswell's memorandum for the Council o Defence, 7 June 1905, Macandie, *The Genesis of the Royal Australian Navy*, pp. 123–30.

[62] CofA, *Parliamentary Papers*, 1906 session, Vol. II, No. 44, 'Report of the Director of Naval Forces for the Year 1905', submitted 1 January 1906.

[63] F. A. Johnson, *Defence by Committee*, London 1960, pp. 66–70.

[64] Letter, Clarke to Deakin, 6 October 1905, Deakin Papers, 1540/2/1136; Letter, Clarke to Deakin, 10 November 1905, Deakin Papers, 1540/2/1138; copy of telegram, Deakin to Clarke, 11 November 1905, Deakin Papers, 1540/38/461.

visit Switzerland and study its system of compulsory and universal military training. Deakin took the trouble to warn Clarke, however, with respect to Bridges that, 'he was closely associated with Sir E. Hutton in preparing our present military organisation and is naturally biased in respect to it or anything affecting a scheme for which he receives full credit in the force'.[65] In commending Bridges and Creswell to the Colonial Office, Deakin informed the British authorities that there was in Australia 'a strong public opinion … in favour of some action in regard to local naval defence', and he asked that the Committee of Imperial Defence's scheme be sent to him before the end of April so that the government would be able to put its defence proposals before parliament when it reassembled.[66]

The Committee of Imperial Defence completed its work in May. Though the Colonial Defence Committee had been incorporated into the Committee of Imperial Defence's network of sub-committees, its attachment to the larger body had done nothing to modify the strategic assumptions upon which it based its prescriptions for Australian defence. The Colonial Defence Committee's report which was approved by the Committee of Imperial Defence and despatched to Australia on 1 June, showed that the changes in organization had in no way altered the British authorities' views on Australian defence. In 1905 and 1906 it would appear that they had learnt nothing and forgotten nothing. The strategic assumptions and the recommendations were identical to those found in the Colonial Defence Committee report of June 1905. The key to imperial defence was the concentration of the British navy. There was only 'slight prospect of any, but transitory success' for any attack on Australian coasts and commerce. The maximum possible act of aggression against which Australia ought to prepare itself was a raid of no more than three or four unarmoured cruisers, carrying 500 to 1,000 men. In specific terms, they projected a scheme of defence which was essentially in accord with the recommendations made the previous year, namely fortified harbours, garrisoned forts and a militia force. Creswell's idea of a local naval force was condemned for being 'based upon an imperfect conception of the requirements of naval strategy'. Given the nature of the attack to which Australian forts were exposed, the Committee of Imperial Defence adjudged that the cost involved was out of proportion to the protection which such a force could offer; seeing no merit at all in Creswell's proposal, they had refused to invite him to discuss it with them during his visit to England. The fixed defences would guarantee the safety of harbours. The protection of commerce had to be left to the British navy. The colonies

---

[65] Letter, Deakin to Clarke, 8 January 1906, Deakin Papers, 1540/38/461, and also *CPD*, 1906 session, XXXIII, 2586, 9 August 1906; CofA, *Parliamentary Papers,* 1906 session, Vol. II, pp. 65–80, No. 81, 'Instructions of Minister for Defence to Captain W. R. Creswell, Director of Naval Forces, relative to his visit to England, to inquire into the latest naval developments'; Macandie, *Genesis of the Royal Australian Navy,* p. 159.

[66] Despatch, Northcote to Elgin, sent 3 January 1906, received 5 February 1906, enclosing despatch, Deakin to Northcote, 28 December 1905, CO 418/44/3–7.

could assist with the defence of commerce by increasing their contributions to the existing Australian imperial squadron.[67]

The Committee of Imperial Defence had run roughshod over Australian sentiment. They had ignored Australia's clearly expressed views. Sir George Clarke, overlooking Deakin's explicit statements in his letter of 8 January, was full of self-congratulations in telling Balfour of the Committee's conclusions. 'As Mr. Deakin expected to have to pay about £500,000 for new harbour defence, he will perhaps be surprised to receive an estimate for about £170,000, which is an ample provision.'[68] But, as Deakin had made clear, economy was no longer the pre-eminent factor in shaping Australian attitudes to defence. A revolution in Australian strategic thinking was the motive force pressing on the frontiers of defence. Thus, when the report came under Australian scrutiny, the Committee of Imperial Defence received little thanks for its efforts.

As in 1905, the colonial military and naval officers, while accepting the British estimates of the most likely level and description of attacks against which Australia ought to prepare, differed as to the extent and kind of defence needed to meet the situation. The military officers thought it 'unwise' not to provide for the possibility of temporary loss of control of the seas, and therefore thought provision should be made for a more substantial aggression against Australian territory.[69] The naval officers also contended that when the Australian squadron was called away, land defence would prove inadequate against marauding attacks on coastal commerce and ports. They reiterated their demands for a local naval force of destroyers and torpedo boats. Undeterred by the CID's remarks, they sought a local flotilla composed of four ocean-going destroyers, sixteen coastal destroyers and four first-class torpedo boats, which in terms of cost, tonnage, manpower and maintenance far exceeded their 1905 scheme.[70] The arguments put forward by both services did not, in themselves, carry much conviction. In the case of the military, they could be seen merely as an attempt to justify the existing military establishment, while in the case of navy, their recommendation represented a desperate attempt to find an assured role in the Australian defence structure. In this sense, the Commonwealth's responsible ministers were no more influenced by their local experts' advice than they were by the Committee of Imperial Defence. The rationale for Australia's new defence policy came rather from the political leaders' own independent assessment of the Commonwealth's strategic situation.

Australia's statesmen in 1906, as in 1903, found themselves to some degree embarrassed in making public their critique of the assumptions of the Committee of Imperial Defence for their

---

[67] CofA, *Parliamentary Papers,* 1906 session, Vol. II, No. 62, 'CID Report upon a "General Scheme of Defence for Australia"'

[68] Letter, Clarke to Balfour, 29 May 1906, Balfour Papers, add. ms. 49702/209.

[69] CofA, *Parliamentary Papers,* 1906 session, Vol. II, No. 87, 'Report of a Committee of Officers appointed to consider and report upon the Scheme of Defence for Australia, submitted by CID, September, 1906'.

[70] CofA, *Parliamentary Papers,* 1906 session, Vol. II, No. 82, 'Report of the Director of Naval Forces, 6 August 1906'; ibid., No. 86, 'Report of a Committee of Naval Officers of the Commonwealth assembled at Melbourne to consider the Memorandum of the Committee of Imperial Defence and report as regards the Naval Defence of Australia, September 12, 1906'. See also MP 729/1, File 06/60.

critique required them to question the wisdom of the empire's most distinguished defence and foreign policy authorities, it threw doubt upon the key article of the imperial faith, the all-saving power of the Royal Navy, and it implied that Japan, Britain's ally, could not be trusted. Deakin, as prime minister, felt under special restraints. He had, after all, authorized the report and he recognized that, since any local force would only be brought into existence with Admiralty assistance, too vigorous a dissent might embitter relations unduly. There was no question but that he was dismayed by the Committee's recommendations. He, perhaps, felt especially aggrieved in that back in January he had explained to Clarke that the Australian government supported a local navy and was looking towards the introduction of compulsory military training.[71] Writing in the *Morning Post* on 20 August, he asserted that the Committee of Imperial Defence had ignored 'a sentiment of the duty of self-defence', which was growing stronger the more Australians realized their 'strategically perilous position south of the awakening Asian peoples', and he declared that, in its turn, 'This sentiment will, on this point, ignore the report.'[72] In a more discreet way, he hit out at the issue a week later, when he said that Great Britain 'by no means grasped the special features of Australian circumstances', with respect to defence. The Commonwealth government, beginning in the schools with a system of compulsory cadet training, would ultimately make Australia 'a dangerous country to tackle' and it would also build a local navy force, which could defend its ports and shores 'when the Admiralty deprived them of the British fleet.'[73]

Having promised a new defence policy for so long, Deakin felt compelled when bringing down the defence estimates on 26 September to fly in the face of the Committee of Imperial Defence and pledge his government to establishing a local navy. Deakin steered a tactful course. He paid his formal respects to the authority of the Committee of Imperial Defence and accepted their recommendation for harbour fortifications, which would enable the Commonwealth to save £330,000 from the amount originally sought by its own military advisers. However, while recognizing that the Committee could see no strategical justification for the creation of a local flotilla, he considered that no part of the empire could be indifferent to the German challenge to Britain's naval supremacy. The growth of the German navy 'must lead to an alteration of the greatest moment of the battleship sea power of the world.' In these circumstances, if British control of the seas were 'in any respect shaken, it is more certainly not too much for us now to consider our own conditions, and the possibility of an attack of a more serious nature than had

---

[71] Letter, Deakin to Clarke, 8 January 1906, Deakin Papers, 1540/38/461. Indeed in his reply Clarke had maintained that 'In present naval conditions, all idea of the invasion of Australia can be dismissed. Ommitting [sic] the U.S. an invading force must come from Europe or from Vladivostok. Either supposition is, in present naval conditions, untenable. A raid on the other hand, though improbable, cannot be regarded as impossible.' Letter, Clarke to Deakin, 14 February 1906, Deakin Papers, 1540/38/461. Clarke had designedly avoided any reference to Japan. Clarke was well aware of Australian apprehensions and yet he made no attempt to put the case against them. Rather he tactfully took his stand within the current British assumptions, hoping that the authoritative view implied in his silence would shame the Australian government into giving up its supposedly irrational fears of Japan.

[72] *MP*, 6 October 1906.

[73] *SMH*, 27 August 1906.

hitherto been contemplated.' He announced that the Australian government intended to embark on a three-year naval programme. Though the Commonwealth could not commit itself at that point to the more ambitious five- to ten-year scheme of the naval officers, he indicated that they would obtain in this first stage, four first-class torpedo boats and eight coastal destroyers. Deakin proposed asking for £1,300,000 for defence, amounting to a 50 per cent increase over the preceding year.[74] In answer to a question, he made it clear that the Australian naval force would be 'under the sole control of the Commonwealth government.'[75]

The Labour party endorsed Deakin's policy. De Largie had at the opening of the 1906 parliamentary session spoken of the rise of an aggressive and expansionist power in the Pacific and called for 'a bold and well-defined plan of Australian defence.'[76] Hughes, in moving a resolution to support compulsory military training, in August, had foreshadowed, in rather blunter language, Deakin's speech. The British were 'scarcely powerful enough in view of the ever increasing effort of Germany to attain naval supremacy.' It followed that 'as each year passes our reliance on the British Fleet becomes less and less warranted.' When challenged, the British fleet would be withdrawn from Australia's shores and the Commonwealth would be left defenceless. Hughes contended that, with a nation in arms, 'Not even the innumerable hordes of Asia, now awakening', could, with any hope of success, land a force on Australian soil.[77] In December, Labour's election manifesto claimed that since the emergencies of war would 'inevitably cause its [the British navy's] withdrawal … it was necessary for Australia to provide its own coastal defence.'[78] The free-traders were somewhat less enthusiastic. McCay, whose devotion to the army remained undiminished, 'wanted universal cadet training'. Joseph Cook, too, was sceptical about an Australian naval force, but would support it if he could be convinced that it could achieve efficiency with economy.[79] In his policy speech, Reid made no reference to Deakin's naval scheme and straddled the fence on compulsory military training.[80] Defence was not an important issue in the election itself, and, on 12 December, the parties were returned in much the same strength, Deakin retaining office with Labor support.

## The Colonial Conference of 1907

After the election, Deakin was able to apply himself single-mindedly to preparing for the Colonial Conference, called for April and May 1907. For Deakin, this was an occasion of critical

---

[74] *CPD*, 1906 session, XXV, 5564–75, 26 September 1906.

[75] Ibid., XXXVI, 5686–7, 28 September 1906.

[76] Ibid., XXXI, 631 and 643, 22 June 1906.

[77] Ibid., XXXIII, 2980–3592, 9 August 1906; see also *SMH*, 14 November 1906. Following the outbreak of Japanese-American strife over the discrimination in the Californian public schools, Hughes had declared that 'there was a possibility of the Chinese and Japanese becoming a menace to the whole of the western nation'.

[78] *SMH*, 5 October 1906.

[79] *CPD*, 1906 session, XXXVI, 5695, 28 September 1906.

[80] *Age*, 24 October 1906.

importance for the future of Australia and the empire. Since 1901 all major Australian initiatives in defence and foreign policy had come to nothing. Over questions of the Pacific Islands, most particularly the New Hebrides, on questions of diplomacy, such as Japanese immigration and commerce, in intra-imperial affairs, notably the importation of Chinese coolie labour into South Africa, and on naval defence, Australian interests had been ignored, its intentions thwarted. Australia pressed its case insistently, but, despite this, had had to accept defeat when faced with British stone-walling. The British government in their diplomacy had failed to urge the colonial view with sufficient vigour and conviction. The colonial requests, in being processed through the cumbrous 'proper channels' of the imperial bureaucracy, were subject to a system which unduly distended and complicated the issue. The machine was happy to lose the impulse to action in its maze of cogs and wheels. This, of course, was a well-tried device of institutionalized authorities in dealing with unwelcome demands for reform or change from the dependent and innocent. And these mechanisms had been used effectively by the British to block Australian policy objectives. The Australian government, sheltered from the responsibilities of imperial power as perceived and exercised in London, were unable to understand why the British would not make the antipodean cause their own or fight the good fight as though it were their own. From Melbourne, it was difficult for Australian leaders to appreciate the intricacies of imperial policy, the repercussions which Australian demands must have on Britain's world posture, its European relationships and colonial policy generally. Deakin raged inwardly against what appeared to him to be simply British indifference and Colonial Office obstruction, and certainly, after all allowance for colonial myopia is made, he did have grounds for complaint. The British authorities did not like to be troubled by colonial importuning and rarely attempted, with an impartial hand, to weigh Australian interests against British interests in the imperial scale.

Deakin was provoked by British actions into re-examining the nature of imperial relations and imperial organization and, on the basis of his reflections and experience, he produced resolutions for the Colonial Conference, which were aimed at meeting the perceived deficiencies in the existing imperial constitution. The essential purpose of these resolutions was to acquire for the self-governing colonies a say and a share in the making of imperial policy. Through the recentralizing of imperial institutions so that they represented all the autonomous governments of the empire, he hoped that the colonies would achieve a direct influence over those imperial defence and external policies which affected them. Deakin was groping towards a new theory of empire, which discarded both the traditional superior-inferior relationship between metropolitan and colonial governments and the old British race patriot dream of federation inside a unitary, integrated Greater Britain. What he sought were institutions which would combine the rights of self-governing colonies with a co-operative empire of co-ordinate parts.

Deakin was always attracted by the 'large' questions, and for his day, the large questions were Australian federation and imperial unity. It was natural, therefore, that in the 1880s he should have become a foundation member of both the Australian Natives Association and the Victorian branch of the Imperial Federation League. Deakin had come to believe that the movement of history was ineluctably towards the reorganization of political entities into more extensive nation states or imperial units and that the Mother Country and the colonies could resist the tides of history only at their peril. The meaning of this for the Australian colonies was clear—political union inside a federal nation. Its application to the empire was more elusive. Deakin never espoused political integration inside an imperial nation. In short, geo-politics had placed too many barriers between Britain and its colonies. The desire for participation in a Greater Britain arising out of the demands of culture and sentiment had to be satisfied in a form which did not swallow up the political autonomy of the parts. The search for proper means by which to achieve this end troubled the minds of many British and Dominion leaders for half a century until time dissolved the desire and showed the problem to be impossible of resolution.

From the first Colonial Conference of 1887, which he had attended as a Victorian delegate, Deakin had taken an earnest and continuous interest in imperial questions. In an exchange with Lord Salisbury on that occasion over the New Hebrides, it had been brought home to him, in a palpable way, how far apart British and Australian perspectives were on the empire in the Pacific and how helpless the colonies were before the Mother Country's obduracy. The British failure to carry out the Australian Monroe Doctrine for the South Pacific remained for him a lasting lesson in imperial relations, a lesson which he never hesitated to revive and recapitulate whenever the opportunity allowed. In speaking on imperial preference in December 1904, Deakin had expressed his dissatisfaction with the existing imperial structure as it affected the self-governing colonies. It was in its existing condition 'unstable, untrustworthy, unpermanent and requires to be replaced gradually, but surely, by a fuller and more complete organisation of ourselves and of the sister communities under the Crown.' However, though he viewed 'amity' alone as an inadequate basis for imperial relations, on the other hand, he discounted any scheme of reorganization, which interfered with the autonomy and independence of the individual parts of the empire.[81]

Two days after giving his interview to the Melbourne *Herald* on the ominous developments in the world politics. Deakin had delivered his presidential address to the Imperial Federation League, and in that address he had spoken of the need to cultivate closer relations between Great Britain and the Dominions. The link between the two statements was clear. The safety of the empire in the emerging pattern of international affairs depended on a strong and united empire. The problem for him was, 'how to reconcile the unity of the whole Empire with the self-government of its parts.' He could not see how this was to be accomplished apart from 'some form of federation'. He used the term 'federation' very loosely here. What he had in mind was 'the voluntary union of states', something approaching what the Americans in the War of Independence had called a Confederation, an intimate alliance of states rather than a union of specified powers inside what the American and Australian founding fathers called a federation.[82] This distinction became more evident in the revised statement of objectives adopted by the Victorian Imperial Federation League, while Deakin was still president. The League redefined its federal aims as, 'the maintenance of a United Empire, and the development of constructive principles, securing the permanent co-operation of the United Kingdom and all the Dominions.'[83]

---

[81] *CPD*, 1904 session, XXIV, 8094–110, 8 December 1904.

[82] *SMH*, 15 June 1905.

[83] La Nauze, *Alfred Deakin*, Vol. II, p. 477.

In Britain, the Boer War had given new impetus to those who had felt since the 1880s that the bonds of empire needed to be held together by more than history and sentiment. The South African War had demonstrated dramatically the dangers of isolation. Joseph Chamberlain, at the 1902 Conference, had tried to rally Britain and the colonies to the cause of a political and customs union. Failing to make any progress, he had in 1903 resigned as Colonial Secretary in order to rouse public support for tariff or imperial preference, which he regarded as the first and necessary step to political unity.

With Chamberlain's energies fully taken up on the tariff question, the leadership in the debate over political reconstruction fell to others. Interested groups, composed of old-style Imperial Federationists, Lord Milner's 'Kindergarten' from South Africa, and Fabian-style reformers who saw the need for large-scale planning in the new world, came together to promote the idea. Under the leadership of Sir Frederick Pollock, Professor of Jurisprudence at Corpus Christi College, Oxford, these men found focus and direction. However, despite their earnest interest in the topic, they found themselves almost as bamboozled as Deakin in trying to reach an agreed formula for achieving their aim. They wrestled with a rather different problem. They felt that they had not only to respect colonial feelings about local autonomy, but also to avoid infringing on the British government's ultimate responsibility for imperial policy. After discussing a variety of possibilities, the so-called Pollock Committee, towards the end of 1904, proposed to bring about constitutional reform by elevating the status of the Colonial Conference. They would entitle it an Imperial Council, place it under the presidency of the British prime minister, instead of the colonial secretary, and they would create a 'Department of Imperial Intelligence' which would be responsible to the prime minister. An Imperial Commission would be attached to the Department for the purpose of giving advice to the colonial secretary on matters affecting the Dominions.[84]

Lyttleton, who had taken a keen interest in the deliberations of the Pollock Committee, was impressed by its findings. Looking towards the next Colonial Conference, which, following the 1902 decision to hold quadrennial meetings, was due to meet in 1906, Lyttleton adapted a version of the Pollock recommendations to place before the colonial governments. Under the Lyttleton version the Colonial Conference would become an Imperial Council under the chairmanship of the prime minister and a commission, made up of persons nominated by the British and colonial governments roughly in proportion to national populations, would be set up to advise the Council on questions referred to it.

The British prime minister considered that the time was ripe for the development of centralizing institutions for the empire as for defence. Balfour had been primarily responsible for the creation of the Committee of Imperial Defence. Indeed, he had at times envisaged the Committee having a larger function, including an imperial one. However, the committee's ambit could not easily be extended to incorporate the defence and foreign policy of the whole empire in a meaningful way. Other institutions were needed. Balfour, who was less of a visionary than Chamberlain and who was a more sceptical and pragmatic practitioner of the art of politics,

---

[84] John Edward Kendle, *The Colonial and Imperial Conferences, 1887–1911: A Study in Imperial Organization*, London 1967, pp. 56–63.

recognized fully the difficulties and the reluctance of the colonies to be drawn into such arrangements.

Nevertheless, he felt that the trend of events favoured the Lyttleton scheme. As he wrote to Austen Chamberlain in the latter part of 1904,

> There are other reasons lying altogether outside party politics which tended in the same direction [that is, towards imperial unity and common imperial defence and foreign policies]. It seems quite impracticable to leave the Colonial question exactly where it is. The possibility of new commercial relations between Canada and the United States—the awakening of Australasia to her increased need for the protection of a powerful, and therefore imperial fleet in the face of a victorious Japan, … all these considerations point to the extreme desirability of having a full and free discussion with our colonies on the present position and future organisation of the empire.[85]

Balfour, therefore, approved Lyttleton's proposal in principle, though his analytical mind was puzzled as to how the Commission would actually work. It was, as Lyttleton had described it, to be a 'cross between an ordinary Government office and a Royal Commission'. Balfour thought it should be simplified and recommended that it be a permanent office attached to the Imperial Council and that there be only one representative from each government on it.[86]

When Lyttleton referred the matter to his departmental officials, the reaction was rather cool. The department felt that they would lose control over the affairs of the self-governing colonies. They did not wish to encourage reforms which might end in the Dominions acquiring 'the status of Independent States and their representatives the status of ambassadors'. In deference to their views, Lyttleton dropped his suggestion that the British prime minister should preside over the meetings of the Imperial Council and agreed that it should be made clear that the Commission was not to 'supersede but support' the work of the Colonial Office. And on 20 April 1905, when suggesting to the self-governing colonies that a conference be held in June 1906, he also took the opportunity to lay this proposal before them for their consideration.[87]

Deakin had been kept in touch by the Pollock Committee with these discussions and debates on imperial reorganization. He approved of the Colonial Conference becoming an 'Imperial Council' and of the establishing of a Commission of Investigation. However, since both the Australian and Canadian governments found the time of meeting inconvenient, the conference was postponed until April 1907.[88] Since the Canadians also objected to the title of 'Imperial Council', the Lyttleton proposals were left over for the determination of the 1907 conference. In response to the colonial secretary's invitation to submit items for the conference agenda, the

---

[85] Copy of letter, Balfour to Austen Chamberlain, 10 September 1904, Balfour Papers, add. ms. 49735/94–6.

[86] Copy of letter, Balfour to Lyttleton, 13 January 1905, Balfour Papers, add. ms. 49775/22–6.

[87] CofA, *Parliamentary Papers*, 1905 session, Vol. II, No. 60, 'Despatch from Secretary of State as to previous Colonial Conferences, and suggesting formation of an Imperial Council in place of a Conference, together with a permanent advisory Commission on matters of joint concern, and reply thereto from Prime Minister of the Commonwealth'.

[88] Ibid.

Australian government in October 1906, submitted a very extensive and comprehensive list of resolutions. They reflected Deakin's imperial concerns. The most important arose out of Australian experience and reflected the prime minister's musings over the structure of the empire. The three most significant resolutions were firstly, that supporting the idea of an Imperial Council and calling for a permanent secretariat to execute Council decisions and to keep Dominions informed between meetings; secondly, that advocating imperial preference which would 'by promoting the development of the resources and industries of the several parts, strengthen the Empire'; and thirdly, that seeking colonial representation on the Committee of Imperial Defence and the re-examination of the 1903 naval agreement. Other resolutions, reflecting Deakin's disenchantment with the Colonial Office and his view of the defence needs of Australia, urged that the Colonial Office staff should acquaint themselves directly with 'the circumstances and conditions' of the colonies, that 'all possible means of strengthening British interests in the Pacific' should be adopted, and that the British government should co-operate with the colonies to encourage British settlers to migrate to the Dominions rather than to foreign lands.[89]

In explaining the Commonwealth's agenda items, Deakin told parliament that, with respect to the imperial secretariat, Britain had failed in the past to keep them informed of treaties and other matters germane to their interests, and he hoped that a secretariat would, in the future, prevent this neglect of Australian feelings and interests. However, the prime minister emphasized that while conscious of close ties with all scattered branches of the British race and of the need to cement those ties so that they could give effect to common responsibilities, nevertheless he was 'equally impressed by the absolute contrast in the problems and condition of the problems we are severally called upon to face', and he was therefore unwilling to cede any of the freedom and elasticity in the existing structure of relationships between the Mother Country and Australia.[90]

Australia's particular problem was Japan. The Japanese-American tensions over California's discriminatory action against Japanese residents, which had gained considerable publicity at the end of 1906, gave a cutting edge to Australian fears and added impetus to the parliamentary support for Deakin's programme at the Colonial Conference. Joseph Cook, responding for the opposition, endorsed Deakin's position. While characterizing the government's policy, not altogether unfairly, as 'ludicrous' and 'tortuous', he said that he did not know any man who was against an Australian navy. Australia valued its independence and would not suffer the rest of the empire to tamper with its White Australia Policy or impede its Pacific island policy. He pointed to a dark cloud of 'menace … gradually closing around us'. These themes were given even more colour in the upper house, where senator after senator, representing every party and state, spoke, some in guarded tones, others more openly, of the emerging threat from Asia and Japan.[91]

---

[89] Great Britain, *Parliamentary Papers,* 1907 session, Vol. LIV, Cd. 3337, 'Despatches of the Secretary of State for the Colonies with Enclosures respecting the Agenda of the Colonial Conference, 1907', pp. 6–8.
[90] *CPD,* 1907 session, XXXVI, 123–9, 21 February 1907; see also *SMH,* 7 March 1907.
[91] *CPD,* 1907 session, XXXVI, 130–5, 21 February 1907; ibid., XXVI, 12 and 72. The senators included Tasmanian free-trader, Lieutenant Colonel Cameron, New South Wales free-trader, Dobson, Victorian Labor senator, Trenwith, Western Australian Labor senators, Pearce and Needham, and Queensland free-

On the eve of Deakin's departure for London, Creswell presented him with a secret memorandum which was intended to stiffen the resolve of the prime minister in pressing for a separate navy. Creswell's paper was intended also to answer the Commander-in-Chief of the Australian Squadron, Sir Wilmot Fawkes, who had criticized Deakin's naval policy speech of 26 September, urged the doctrine of concentration and contribution and assured the prime minister that the British naval disposition in the Pacific was adequate to meet any feasible contingency.[92] For the first time Creswell showed that he had grasped the strategic picture which the political leaders had been putting together since the Russo-Japanese war. Perhaps the Japanese-American confrontation had finally lifted the veil from his eyes. In any event, Creswell produced for the occasion one of the most compelling and complete statements of the 'Commonwealth Crisis'. He now rejected the Committee of Imperial Defence's view of a limited threat and based his naval scheme on the vulnerability of Australia to a Japanese invasion. In his answer to Fawkes, Creswell, adopting Deakin's own warnings of July 1905, noted that Australia was no longer insulated from the changes taking place in the international power balance. Rather, he believed that 'we shall be vitally affected by those most probable to occur, and already in the middle distance of our outlook.' The time perspective of fear was shrinking. British naval dominance had, relatively speaking, been declining, and with the naval building programmes being undertaken by both European and Pacific powers, it seemed likely that Britain's naval position would continue to deteriorate. 'The value of the two powers standard would be much reduced, perhaps disappear if a European and an Extra-European combined against Great Britain.' He could not see the United States becoming Britain's enemy, but it was 'not inconceivable' that Japan might one day find it to its advantage to take sides against the British Empire. During any European complications, 'there would be very earnest attention to, perhaps compliance with, the wishes of any Extra-European power'. It was possible that the development of German bases in the South Pacific, and more remotely that German acquisition of the Dutch East Indies, might pose difficulties for Australia, but, in both those cases Britain's predominant naval strength in European waters would effectively shield the Commonwealth from any serious consequences.

However, if a Pacific power were to enter the fray against the empire, then Britain's

> advantages of European position and command of the Eastern trade routes disappear. In the distance of each power from the main base to the common objective— Japan to attack, England to defend—the advantage would be with Japan. ... The marvellous power of secrecy of the Japanese [referring to their surprise attack on Port Arthur] would be equal to making the delivery of the attack its first intimation. ... [He concluded] Combination against England between a European power and Japan (or China) would make the defence of the Commonwealth a matter of extreme difficulty, or, it may be frankly admitted, impossibility,

---

trader, St Ledger. Cameron declared that 'there is danger before us, that it is imminent'. They had to face the fact that 'Japan can dictate to 85 million Americans how Japanese children should be treated'. Needham asserted that if the British fleet were occupied in European waters, Australian 'would be left to the tender mercies of our neighbours, the Mongolian hordes'.

[92] [92]Macandie, *Genesis of the Royal Australian Navy*, pp. 168–72.

unless we earnestly profit by the interim years of shelter and safety to develop our powers of resistance. … Attack from main bases in the North Pacific is a new factor. … [It] must gradually enter more and more into our defence calculations.

Since Japan and China, revivified by the example and leadership of Japan, needed room to expand in order to solve their population problems, they might well challenge the White Australia Policy, which Japan already found offensive, and cast their eyes on the empty lands of northern Australia. The Commonwealth, to survive, would thus have to acquire self-sufficiency both in its land and sea defences.[93] Deakin scarcely needed instruction on his own thesis. He had already replied to Fawkes' criticism, asserting that 'the unity [of the navy] ought to accompany that of the Empire and could only be completely achieved when we have established a unity of Imperial political control'.[94] Profoundly affected by the political and strategic dilemma facing Australia and the empire, the Commonwealth prime minister went to great lengths during the Colonial Conference to try and find an imperial solution to Australia's problems.

Deakin struggled against formidable odds. With the advent of the Liberals to power, the British government's interest in experiments in imperial structures had declined. The imperial visionaries and planners, the protégés of Chamberlain and Milner, had much greater access to and influence with the Unionists than the Liberals. The Liberal government had no desire to share power over the empire with the self-governing colonies. They were happy to leave matters to sort themselves out in their own good time. Lord Elgin allowed himself to be dominated much more by the Colonial Office men and their mentality than had been the case with his Conservative predecessors. The Liberal colonial secretary joined with the Canadian Liberal prime minister to quash Deakin's efforts to raise the status of the self-governing colonies and to give them a greater say in decision-making.

As Elgin had no interest in Lyttleton's reform proposals, and Laurier had little liking for them, the mantle of leadership in the movement to restructure the empire fell on Deakin's shoulders. In moving Australia's resolution calling for the British prime minister to become president of an Imperial Council, he insisted that, unlike the colonial conference, the Council should be seen as a meeting between government and governments and not between the metropolitan master and the dependent colonies. Deakin did not mince words in expressing his dissatisfaction with existing practices. He stated that there were 'some matters of foreign politics for instance', which touched closely the interests of the self-governing colonies and that, in these instances, the Dominions should be able 'to make such necessary enquiries in regards to foreign politics as may appear to us to be urgent and important', and 'to make them direct'.

To further enhance the status of the Imperial Council and the position of the Dominions in the imperial constitution, Deakin urged that a colonial secretariat should be established to execute the resolutions of the Council, to keep the Dominions informed between meetings and to provide machinery for direct communication between all member governments. It would be the agent of the Council itself, while practically, for all day-to-day purposes, under the supervision of

---

[93] Creswell's Memorandum of 6 March 1907, CP 103/12/6.
[94] *MP*, 22 December 1906.

the British prime minister. It would assume many of the functions of the Colonial Office. Deakin's criticisms of the Colonial Office were, like his objection to Japanese immigration, offered in a way that was intended to take the sting out of the attack, while securing the fullest impact. Thus, as with the Japanese, he taxed the Colonial Office with their virtues, in this case, courtesy, patience and civility. What Australia complained of was that 'our representatives ... are met neither with an understanding of the real causes from which they sprung or of our precise intentions.' The Commonwealth government felt itself frustrated by 'an attitude of mind'. And he defined that attitude as 'A certain impenetrability of a certain remoteness, perhaps geographically justified; a certain weariness of people much pressed with affairs, and greatly overburdened.'[95]

Deakin, however, found he had an uphill battle on his hands. Laurier, fearful of the least implication of greater responsibility, vetoed the term 'Council'. The title 'Imperial Conference' was agreed to as a compromise. Elgin, on behalf of his department, opposed the creation of any new body which would derogate from the powers of the Colonial Office. At the most, he would agree that the British prime minister should become ex-officio president of the conference and that the Colonial Office should be reorganized in order to separate the business of the self-governing colonies from that of the crown colonies. It was a symbolic gesture towards the goals Deakin had in view but, in itself, it meant little. It was but a reshuffling of the old pack of cards. Once again, Deakin could feel that he was out-manoeuvred by the Colonial Office.

On Imperial Preference, the self-governing colonies joined forces to reaffirm the 1902 resolution which urged all governments to accept the principle. Deakin was, as Northcote described him, 'a fanatical Chamberlainite' on this subject. He portrayed imperial preference as a means of consolidating imperial organization, of compacting the parts together in 'cooperative relations', and so preparing them to act together in 'a day of trial'.[96] Such a policy was, however, anathema to the party of free trade, and Elgin indicated that the Liberal government would be unable to assent to the resolution.[97]

The topic which had most immediate relevance to Australia was defence. The British government opposed Deakin's proposal to give the Dominions the right to permanent representation on the Committee of Imperial Defence. They would only agree that the Dominions should have the right to seek advice and to have a representative present when their problems were being discussed. On military matters, R. B. Haldane, the minister of war, who had a greater interest in imperial integration than any other member of the cabinet, introduced a proposal for establishing an Imperial General Staff. Behind the smoke screen of words the War Office's plan

---

[95] Great Britain, *Parliamentary Papers*, 1907 session, Vol. LV, Cd. 3523, 'Minutes of the Proceedings of the Colonial Conference, 1907', pp. 27–8, 42–3, 71–2. Deakin illustrated this lack of understanding in discussing the Pacific Islands and the New Hebrides, ibid., pp. 548–60.

[96] Ibid., p. 238; Deakin also pressed his emigration resolution in a similar way. British emigration to the colonies would not only increase trade between the colonies and the Mother Country, but also help guarantee 'the permanence of the control of those great territories, by our own people and our own race'. Ibid., p. 154.

[97] Ibid., p. 429.

would appear to be yet another form of the 1901–2 imperial reserve idea. Through these means, in time of war, the military power of the whole empire would be mobilized speedily for action. Laurier and Deakin were on the alert for such traps. They would merely agree to ensure uniformity of armaments, organizations and methods of training, and to send to London representatives who would join the so-called Imperial General Staff in an advisory capacity. They would not consent to place their troops under the control of an imperial general staff which was of necessity tantamount to placing them under the control of the War Office. They would not allow that their troops should be available to be sent wherever the War Office should think fit in time of war. They would not, before the event, compromise their freedom of action. Australia's defence policy and planning was directed exclusively towards resisting attacks on the Commonwealth.[98]

The naval question was a more complex issue. Lord Tweedmouth, the First Lord of the Admiralty, wanted the colonies to place their confidence 'in the Board of Admiralty and in the present Government, for the future safety of the Empire'. In offering the Admiralty's co-operation for the purpose of establishing colonial naval forces, Tweedmouth attached three conditions to this promise of assistance. He insisted firstly that the Admiralty should have 'charge of the strategical questions, which are necessarily involved in Naval Defence', secondly, that the Admiralty should have control over the empire's naval forces, and thirdly, that they should have complete freedom in the distribution and movement of ships. Tweedmouth recognized that Australia desired to establish its own naval service and the Admiralty was willing that they should acquire small crafts, such as torpedo boats and submarines, which could both reinforce the imperial squadron and be used for local coastal defence. In this latter respect, the submarine was especially commended to the colonies as 'probably the most important and most effective weapon'.[99]

Deakin expressed some bewilderment with respect to imperial naval policy. On the question of a naval defence of all the different parts of the empire, he had never been able to find 'any scheme of responsibility in particular or in general'.[100] He was also troubled by the reserve powers which the Admiralty wish to exercise over local navies. In the full conference on 8 May, Deakin, in rejecting the Admiralty's claims, coupled the constitutional arguments with 'the sense of insecurity' in Australia.[101] When, however, he met with the Admiralty officials to discuss privately his wish to end the naval agreement and to obtain the Admiralty's co-operation in forming a local flotilla, Deakin, knowing that the Admiralty did not appreciate Australia's strategic concerns, argued the case for a local navy on national and constitutional grounds. He pointed out that the subsidies were seen as tribute and further maintained that the government which raised the taxes should control and manage its own defence forces. Defying the Admiralty, he declared that the Commonwealth would retain command over its naval force. In responding to Tweedmouth's

---

[98] Ibid., p. 128.
[99] Ibid., p. 129.
[100] Ibid., p. 132.
[101] Ibid., p. 474

assurances of co-operation, he asked for the Admiralty's advice on the vessels most suited to local needs and also requested that Australian officers and men should, in order to facilitate training and to provide career opportunities, have access to the Royal Navy.[102] Despite Tweedmouth's assurances, the Admiralty did not respond any more warmly to Deakin's plans when presented in person than they had when stated in a despatch. Deakin left the conference with vague promises of benevolent interest and concern but without agreement on the vessels to be acquired or on the conditions under which an Australian force would operate.

## 'A *defence of the people, by the people, for the people*'

Deakin was greatly disappointed by the conference. The resolutions and decisions were 'insufficient to call for congratulations'.[103] His greatest regret was the failure to achieve any substantial changes in the imperial political and administrative structure. Though some progress had been made in remodelling the Colonial Conference to make it appear more like a conference between 'governments and governments', this principle had not been carried over into imperial policy-making and administrative control. Between conferences, the Dominions remained subject to the Colonial Office. It was the almost inescapable intermediary between the Australian and British governments. Deakin, in speaking on this topic to a receptive audience, said that Australia 'did not want Government by the Colonial Office'.[104] When the colonial secretary informed Deakin that, in accordance with the wishes of the conference, the Colonial Office had been reorganized and the Dominions were now to be permitted to correspond directly 'on all matters of routine' with the secretary to the Imperial Conference, the Australian leader spurned the news. In his view, the concession did 'not even satisfy the compromise resolution ... agreed to at the Conference.'[105] The conference had, however, done something to define more sharply Deakin's views on what reforms were desirable or practicable. His secretariat, as he explained to Jebb, would not in any way detract from the right of self-government. It would be able to do '*nothing executively except by consent, nothing legislative, except thro* (sic) *the several legislatures*.'[106] The secretariat was to be responsible to the Imperial Conference. He implored Jebb, who had in an earlier period so ably put the case for colonial nationalism, to turn his talents to advocating this '*doctrine of recentralisation*'. Deakin wrote, 'We must have an Imperial Organisation.'[107] Until this transmogrification took place, Australia had to deal, as best it could, with the emerging crisis in the Pacific.

---

[102] CO, Confidential Print, Dominion No. 12, 'Memo of A. Deakin's meeting with representatives of the Admiralty, April 24, 1907', CO 886/2.

[103] SMH, 22 May 1907.

[104] SMH, 26 June 1907.

[105] CofA, *Parliamentary Papers,* 1907–8 session, Vol. II, No. 170, 'Colonial Office, Copy of Despatch from the Prime Ministers of the Commonwealth Dated 19th November, 1907, Relating to the Organization of the Colonial Office'.

[106] Letter, Deakin to Jebb, 10 September 1907, Deakin-Jebb Correspondence, 339/1/15A.

[107] Letter, Deakin to Jebb, 29 May 1907, ibid.

Returning to Melbourne, Deakin's attention turned again to defence. During 1907 friction between Japan and America intensified. The discriminatory legislation passed in California in 1906 was supplemented by similar additional legislation in 1907 and this was followed by anti-Oriental riots in San Francisco. The American press whipped up a war scare and, on 1 July, it was announced that President Roosevelt was sending the United States Atlantic fleet around Cape Horn to the West Coast. These events inflamed further Australia's racial fears and antagonisms. It was against this background that Deakin, on 29 June, put the rhetorical question whether 'we or our children might have to meet no ordinary foes'. Pursuing the theme, he said, 'It [the putative crisis] might mean peril to all we hold most dear, our family, our industrial life, and perhaps the religious faith we cherish'. The Asian threat could not have been identified more clearly without actually naming Japan. 'Therefore', he concluded, 'the time was ripe to make provision to supplement the strength of the Empire in the Southern Seas'. Until Australians took such action in their own defence, they 'were only tenants in this continent'.[108]

As Japanese-American relations continued to deteriorate, and the prospect of war became ever more pronounced, Australian politicians spoke to the crisis mentality. Hughes, in submitting his compulsory military service resolution a fourth time, produced the bleakest picture yet of Australia's future. No longer was the Commonwealth crisis in the conditional future. 'We shall', he said, 'have to depend, as we ought to depend now — upon ourselves alone.' The Japanese-American troubles offered a salutary lesson, illustrating what well might happen in Australia.[109] On the other hand, some saw that the Japanese-American confrontation might prove advantageous for Australia. Roosevelt's decision to send the fleet into the Pacific was welcomed. Watson hoped that 'that fleet will always remain in the Pacific'.[110] The search for Anglo-Saxon solidarity in the Pacific, which was to be so important to Australians in 1908 and 1909, was beginning to gather support. Joseph Cook repeated his warning about 'the menace' which was 'gradually closing around us'.[111] The New South Wales free-trader, W. H. Wilks, who had been an unbeliever in 1901–3, confessed to his conversion.[112] A cross-section of other members including a number elected for the first time in 1903 and 1906 voiced the same feelings.[113] Only one member, J Hutchinson, who held the South Australian seat of Hindmarsh for Labor, denounced the fear-filled scenario. He called it 'humbug to talk of hordes of Asiatics invading the Northern Territory'.[114] The Australian political parties and leaders had arrived at a consensus on the need

---

[108] SMH, 30 June 1907.

[109] CPD, 1907–8 session, XXXVIII, 1282–9, 1 August 1907.

[110] Ibid., XXXI, 3600, 30 September 1907.

[111] Ibid., XXXVII, 95, 4 July 1907.

[112] Ibid., XXXVIII, 2253, 22 August 1907.

[113] G. Fairbairn, Victorian protectionist, ibid., 2260; Knox, ibid., XXXIX, 3601, 20 September 1907; W. E. Johnson, New South Wales free-trader, ibid., 3601; E. K. Bowden, New South Wales free-trader, ibid., 3605; E. S. Carr, New South Wales, ibid., 3609.

[114] Ibid., XXXIX, 2939, 5 September 1907.

for a greatly augmented defence effort. The ensuing debate ranged round how best to achieve this object.

Worn out by his crowded schedule and his arduous endeavours on behalf of the new imperialism, Deakin, after his return from London, had to rest for two months before taking up the reins of government and preparing his defence scheme. Public expectations were high. The government in 1906 had already laid down the basis for a naval policy for which Deakin had hoped to gain Admiralty approval during the Colonial Conference. In amplifying his naval policy, Deakin had to consider three things, the future of the naval agreement and the uses to which the subsidy should be put, the connection between an Australian naval force and the Royal Navy, and the kind of vessels which would make up the flotilla. Though the Commonwealth had been vainly debating these issues for two years, the Colonial Conference had done little to clarify the matter. Nevertheless, Deakin was determined to act. On 23 September, he cabled the Admiralty suggesting that, in accordance with his understanding of the London talks, £100,000 of the subsidy be allocated for the purpose of training 1,000 seamen, 'Australian if possible', on the Australian station; the remaining £100,000 would be used to help pay the cost of an Australian force of submarines or destroyers. Modifying Creswell's recommendation, he also suggested that the Admiralty retain two P-class cruisers manned by 400 to 1,000 Australian seamen in Australian waters, whether in peace or war, and that it loan two further P-class cruisers for the training of a local naval militia.[115]

Deakin's proposal was provocative. It assumed that Britain would, at least in the short term, continue to keep its squadron in the Australian station at its own expense and that, in addition, it would provide for Australia's use, again at the Mother Country's expense, four modern cruisers. Sir John Fisher, the First Sea Lord, was incensed by Deakin's effrontery. 'The colonies, one and all, grab all they possibly can out of us and give us nothing back.'[116] The Admiralty did not accept that the scheme was part of a general understanding arrived at while Deakin was in London, and they rejected it as a basis for renegotiating the 1903 agreement. The Admiralty informed Deakin that the British government could not assume a greater financial burden in respect to the Australian station and would not consent to be bound to keep specific ships under all circumstances on any station.[117] Moreover, they considered that the Commander-in-Chief of the imperial squadron should be able to take control of a local flotilla at the outbreak of hostilities.[118] Despite Deakin's

---

[115] CofA, *Parliamentary Papers*, 1907–8 session, Vol. II, No. 113, 'Naval Defence of Australia. (Correspondence in reference thereto, between the Commonwealth Government and the Admiralty)'; letter, Deakin to Northcote for despatch to Elgin, 16 October 1907; CO 418/52/599–603; Macandie, *Genesis of the Royal Australian Navy*, pp. 189–92.

[116] Letter, Fisher to Tweedmouth, 1 October 1907, Arthur J. Marder (ed.), *Fear God and Dread Nought: The Correspondence of Admiral of the Fleet, Lord Fisher of Kilverstone*, 2 Vols, London 1956, Vol. II, p. 139.

[117] Letter, C. I. Thomas, secretary, Admiralty to Ommanney, under-secretary of State, CO, 2 December 1907 CO 418/56/1; telegram, Elgin to Northcote, 7 December 1907, CO 418/52/680–94; despatch, Elgin to Northcote, 13 December 1907, CO 418/56/66–70.

[118] Telegram, Elgin to Northcote, sent 13 December 1907, received 16 December 1907, CO 418/56/75 and CofA, *Parliamentary Papers*, 1908 session, Vol. II, No. 6, 'Naval Defence Further Correspondence between

urgent pleas, he could not secure the Admiralty's approval for his scheme, and, given its nature, this should not have been surprising, least of all to him. And as time ebbed away, the prime minister with his defence minister, T. T. Ewing, who had replaced Playford after the latter's defeat in the 1906 election, set about devising a defence policy of their own, without reference to the imperial authorities.

On 13 December, Deakin presented the Commonwealth government's revolutionary defence proposals to parliament. It was a grand theme and Deakin spoke to it grandiloquently. The justification was strategic, a reiteration of his 1905 *Herald* statement.

> There was a time not long since, when it was confidently maintained that Australia was outside the area of the world's conflicts. … That comfortable outlook has by now passed away. No one can contend that Australia is outside that area today. On the contrary, every decade brings it into closer and closer touch with the subjects of other peoples planted in our neighbourhood [presumably German and French] and with the interests of other peoples more or less antagonistic to our own [presumably Japanese and Chinese].

If Australia's first line of defence, the British navy, were removed from their waters, the White Australia Policy would be imperilled. The world-wide arms race set against this geo-political context requires Australia to undertake its own preparedness programme and Deakin spread out before an attentive House, proposals to revamp and strengthen every aspect of the Commonwealth's defence on land and sea. With respect to coastal defence the government intended to carry out the recommendations of the Committee of Imperial Defence for the arming and modernizing of shore forts. More important, though, he reaffirmed the 1906 decision to acquire a local flotilla for harbour and coastal defence. Deakin reported that the First Lord of the Admiralty had accepted the decision in principle, though the questions of how it was to effect the naval agreement and how it would mesh in with the Royal Navy had still to be resolved. He announced that the Australian government would purchase nine C-class submarines and six torpedo-boat destroyers over a three-year period. The vessels would be built, manned and maintained by Australia, and Deakin insisted, despite the Admiralty's opposition, that Australia would retain control. Even in time of war, though it was probable that Australia would place its ships under the command of the Royal Navy, the Commonwealth government would reserve the right to place conditions on the transfer of control.

Turning to defence on land, Deakin for the first time committed the Commonwealth government to bring in a system of universal military training for young men. The government would adopt a modified version of the Swiss system; all youths, nineteen to twenty-one years of age, would spend sixteen days annually in camp. It was to be carried through in the most frugal manner. There would be 'a spartan simplicity of uniform and habit. … We cast aside meretricious display, or glitter of gold lace, or glamour of a separate caste.' As Ewing had said in the August debate on Hughes' resolution, officers would be selected only for their capacity to lead. They

---

the Commonwealth Government and the Admiralty in regard to the Naval Defence of Australia', 16 December 1907 to 20 August 1908.

would be drawn from Toorak or Footscray, regardless of their social background or even formal education. Though Deakin attempted to put an ideological gloss on this decision for simplicity, asserting that it was 'in harmony with the political principles on which our government is based and our social life is based', nevertheless it was clear that the more compelling reason was economy. Even so, economy would not have forced such a break with British traditions had the Australian social ethos not permitted it. A school for training instructors was to be established and an Intelligence Corps organized. Within eight years it was predicted that Australia would have a National Guard of 200,000 trained men with arms and ammunition, and with equipment for field artillery and cavalry available. Ultimately, the military forces including trained reserves would grow to an army of 800,000 men. 'We are at the very beginning of a period of development', said Deakin, 'which I trust will be as thorough and complete as that of Japan.' In winding up, he dedicated the programme to democracy. Paraphrasing Lincoln, he declared, 'Our idea is a defence of the people, for the people, and by the people.'[119]

Deakin had captured and captivated his audience. Andrew Fisher, the newly elected leader of the Labor party,[120] rose to congratulate the prime minister, assuring him that the Australian people would respond to the call. Gone was Fisher's easy 1906 dismissal of defence as 'the new craze'. He, too, was now convinced of its necessity. The debate was adjourned to allow members to study the proposals.[121] Pearce congratulated Deakin on this policy for which the country had waited 'so impatiently'. He commiserated with Deakin over the Admiralty's obstinacy and obstruction and encouraged him to 'stand firm'. Citing a report of a speech by Count Okuma, leader of Japan's Progressive party, in which he had urged Japanese businessmen to seize the opportunity of an Indian boycott of British goods to move into that market and also 'to go to the South Seas', Pearce warned, 'Above all we must watch to the North' and keep Australia safe for the white race.[122]

Deakin's naval scheme was still dependent on British goodwill for its success. Deakin forwarded it to the Admiralty, requesting their co-operation in bringing it into being. He also asked whether the Admiralty would agree to allow the naval subsidy to be used for training 1,000 seamen and to help with the purchase of the local flotilla.[123] The Colonial Office was scornful of Deakin's pretensions and concerned about the consequences which might flow from his plans. W. S. Churchill, the parliamentary under-secretary of state, minuted.

> They will never provide any ships of any serious value. ... They will never pay the money
> necessary for a proper squadron. But a few ineffective vessels under an Australian flag may

---

[119] CPD, 1907–8 session, XLII, 7509–35, 13 December 1907.

[120] ALP caucus minutes, Vol. II, 30.

[121] CPD, 1907–8 session, XLII, 7536, 13 December 1907.

[122] Letter, Pearce to Deakin, undated, Deakin Papers, 1540/4152; from internal evidence (see the Age, 25 December 1907 in which the Okuma speech appears) the letter must have been written on 25 December 1907.

[123] Telegram, Northcote to Elgin, 24 December 1907, CO 418/52/570; telegram, Northcote to Elgin, 1 April 1908, CO 418/60/195–209.

easily cause nasty diplomatic situations. We might give Mr. Deakin a measure of control in Foreign Policy exactly proportionate to Australia's contribution to Imperial defence without much risk.[124]

The Admiralty, following its accustomed practice, prolonged the agony. Deakin, unwilling to let the 1907–8 session close without making provision for the defence scheme set aside under the Surplus Revenue Act of May 1908 the sum of £250,000 in a trust fund.[125] He intended by this means to prevent the money, earmarked by the Commonwealth for defence, being returned to the states, as would otherwise have been the case under the Braddon formula. He also hoped to impress the Admiralty with the seriousness of Australia's purpose. His foresight did not serve him very well. When the Admiralty finally relented and gave the proposal its grudging and guarded approval, Deakin's government was about to fall and the initiative fell into other hands. Thus Deakin left office in November 1908 without having translated either of the two major elements in his defence policy into legislation.[126]

From 1905 to 1907, Australians, looking out on a world wracked by national tensions and conflicts, saw in the changing power balance and the developing pattern of diplomacy, a convergence of factors which threatened their security and even possibly their survival. The Russo-Japanese war, which had left Japan supreme in Asia and the West Pacific, the Tangiers incident in Morocco, which had threatened to bring war between Britain and Germany and which had been followed by Britain's withdrawal of its capital ships from the Pacific, the Japanese-American dispute over Japanese immigration and the rights of Japanese residents on the west coast of the United States, these events taken together presaged a crisis for the newly-founded Commonwealth. With Britain preoccupied with Germany in Europe, Japan, unchecked by any other power, was free to satisfy its ambitions and extend its sphere of influence in Asia and even possibly the South Pacific. Should Japan make demands on Australia and attempt to use force to impose its will, the Royal Navy, chained as it was to the North Sea, would not be able to come to Australia's rescue. The Japanese, given their antipathy to Australia's immigration law, would have no difficulty in finding a pretext to justify their actions. For the first time, Australians felt themselves exposed to the possibility of invasion and, what was more, they recognized that they might be left to face the crisis alone.

This was Australia's distinctive view of world politics and of its place in the disturbed pattern of international relations. The roots of this view lay in the nineteenth century. But, in its full form, it was a product of the immediate preceding years. The Australians rejected the assumptions of imperial foreign policy as they applied to the Pacific and the strategic arguments of the imperial authorities as they affected the dangers confronting the Commonwealth. In the nineteenth century the Australian colonies had allowed that British diplomacy defined the empire's friends and enemies, and for their part the colonists' only fear of attack derived from a recognition that

---

[124] Minute, 15 February 1908, CO 418/52/739–40.

[125] *CPD*, 1907–8 session, XLVI, II, 409, 27 May 1908.

[126] Despatch, Earl of Crewe, Colonial Secretary to Northcote, 21 August 1908, enclosing Admiralty letter of 20 August 1908, received 21 September 1908, CofA, *Parliamentary Papers*, 1908 session, Vol. II, No.6.

they would be caught up in the spin-off from Britain's European embroilments. Their differences with London arose merely over how best, in these circumstances, to provide for the defence of the colonies against marauding European raiders. The conflict of views between the Australians and the Mother Country over the importance of Pacific security and the best means of achieving it was even then evident. But from 1905 to 1907 a new picture had emerged. Australia, while recognizing that Anglo-German rivalry threatened the whole empire, refused to accept the assurance of the Japanese alliance and indeed saw its greatest danger in the menace from the north. In defiance of British advice, they had adopted a defence policy of local naval forces and compulsory military training which was primarily aimed at meeting an Asian invasion.

This novel analysis of the Commonwealth's strategic position and the new defence policy which proceeded from it were almost exclusively the work of Australia's political leaders. It owed little to the press and almost nothing to the Commonwealth's naval and military advisers. Though some specialist weekly papers like the *Bulletin*, the *Worker*, the *Advocate* and the *Tocsin* did sound the alarm early, the daily press in general followed a vacillating and uncertain course in their editorials on external dangers, torn between their deference to British judgement on such matters and the demands made upon them by Australia's special geo-political character.[127]

Similarly, down to 1907 both the military and naval officers, in supporting their submissions for defence appropriations, had based their recommendations on a strategic framework taken directly from the Colonial Defence Committee and Committee of Imperial Defence formulations. Indeed, they had shown very little interest in the larger questions of defence and foreign policy. Major-General Hutton, at a time when political and public opinion was against increasing military expenditure, had tried to invoke fear of Japan in order to bolster the case for his defence scheme. He had smelt the Australian aroma of this particular fear, but he had raised the cry before the events in Europe and Asia had convinced the majority of political leaders that there was a clear and present danger. In this respect, as in a number of others, Hutton was a maverick. His disciples, Bridges and Brudenell White, did not accept the Japanese threat as a basis for defence planning until well after the government's new policy had been adopted and implemented. Captain Creswell, the Director of the Naval Forces, in his campaign for an Australian navy remained until March 1907, singularly blind to the most powerful argument that could be marshalled in its favour. Once he had, however, broken through the intellectual barrier, he became a perfervid exponent of the doctrine. Creswell wrote to Jebb on 31 July 1907, 'Germany and the North Sea are important enough but they are not the beginning and the end of all things', and again on 24 March 1908, 'a German-Japanese alliance would be our death knell'.[128] But

---

[127] *SMH*, 2 September 1905. The editorial stated that with the renewal of the Anglo-Japanese alliance, 'The immediate menace to the East has been removed'. The *Age*, 18 September 1906, urged an Australian navy as an auxiliary aid for the Imperial Fleet in meeting the challenge of Germany. Compare *Age*, 30 December 1907; see also D. C. S. Sissons, *Attitudes to Japan and Defence, 1890–1923*, MA thesis, University of Melbourne, 1956, pp. 38–45.

[128] Letters, Creswell to Jebb, 31 July 1907 and 24 March 1908, Jebb Papers, 813/1/36 and 42.

essentially Creswell in his strategic thinking showed himself to be no more than an apt pupil of his political mentors.

Deakin, in trying to translate strategic principles into a defence policy, had found himself confronted by a complex problem. In his pursuit of a local naval force he had in Creswell a determined and active ally. However, Creswell's enthusiasm was itself something of a disadvantage, since it made him *persona non grata* at the Admiralty, and Admiralty co-operation was necessary for any venture to succeed. Thus, Deakin and Ewing had gone over Creswell's head in proposing the naval section of the 13 December policy speech, and they had, without informing their Director of Naval Forces, accepted Admiralty advice and decided on a flotilla of submarines and torpedo boats.[129]

In making their military plans, the Commonwealth government had a different problem. The chief staff officers, remaining loyal to Hutton and imperial consolidation, had no appreciation of the Australian government's Pacific anxieties and were opposed to compulsory military training. Bridges' report on the Swiss system, which he had inspected in 1907, was less than approving; 'The Swiss army affords a proof … that a democratic form of government and an efficient military system are incompatible.'[130] Consequently, Deakin and Ewing ignored the Military Board and worked with a more junior officer, Major J. G. Legge, who did to some degree share the government's apprehension,[131] in preparing their National Guard scheme. In sending a copy of Deakin's defence speech to his old chief, Bridges commented,

> You will be no more pleased than I am. I can say, however, that the Board have never been consulted. The suggestions are, I believe, due to Legge, who has been working directly under the Minister. … I have up to the present been able to still maintain your principles of organization but I cannot answer for the future.[132]

Bridges exhibited a dog-like loyalty to his old master, but as a result he was unable to serve the Australian government in bringing down their policy. It took a number of years before the Hutton men were won over to the new course. On 3 September 1908, Brudenell White wrote Hutton explaining that 'the existence of so many nations in arms' now made compulsory military training necessary.[133]

What had produced this transformation in the Australian political leaders' outlook on defence? Certainly, national sentiment had played a rôle, but it was a subsidiary rôle. Indeed,

---

[129] Macandie, *Genesis of the Royal Australian Navy*, pp. 206–7.

[130] CofA, *Parliamentary Papers*, 1907 session, Vol. II, No. 129, 'Report on the Swiss Military System, compiled in the Department of the Chief of Intelligence, 1907'.

[131] In a paper delivered to the United Services Institute, Major J. G. Legge had advocated compulsory military training on the ground that invasion would be 'a military undertaking of no serious difficulty' when the European powers were engaged in war, 'The Organisation of a Reserve for the Land Defences of Australia', *Journal and Proceedings of the United Service Institute of New South Wales*, XVII, 27 June 1905, 87–99.

[132] Letter, Bridges to Hutton, 17 December 1907, Hutton Papers, add. ms. 50089, Vol. XII, p. 58–9.

[133] Letter, Brudenell White to Hutton, 3 September 1908, ibid., add. ms. 50089, Vol. XII, p. 68.

during the first decade of the Commonwealth, the more aggressive tones of colonial nationalism evident in the 1890s were muted to some degree and the radical and Labour elements in Australian society which had spear-headed the nationalist movement became, if anything, rather more imperial in their sentiments. Canada, which led the Dominions in expressions of national self-consciousness, remained relatively indifferent to defence. It seems equally true that there was no great socio-political crisis which prompted the national leaders to impose order through appeals to an external threat and by the authoritarian mechanism of the military. Hughes' contribution to the debate over defence in the early years does suggest such a motive, but he is almost alone in providing such a justification. Even he dropped this argument as his goal became more realizable. Other societies, such as Canada and the United States, were more divided and discontented in these years and yet the forces of order did not seek to resolve their problem in this way. The answer to the question, then, would seem to be the answer which the political leaders themselves gave, that the Commonwealth was confronted with an international situation fraught with unparalleled danger for Australian security and, accordingly, they took precautions to meet those dangers. Admittedly, the sense of threat to national survival, whether through Asian immigration or invasion, often led from fear to hysteria. And Australians, drawing upon their nineteenth-century immigration experiences and attitudes, had ready to hand the racial slogans and stereotypes which could be employed to interpret and intensify the threat from the North. For the most part, though, the political leaders couched their arguments in strategic and power terms. Australia's response to the 'Commonwealth Crisis' was that of a small nation actively working inside an intimate cultural and political alliance, to develop its own defence capability and to gain greater influence over the policy of the empire as a whole.

# 6

# The Promise of Security, 1908–10: An Australian Defence Force, an Imperial Pacific Fleet and an American 'Entente Cordiale'

What Australians had to this time seen as through a glass darkly, they now saw face to face, white face to yellow face. The Japanese-American war 'scares', arising out of the racial troubles and riots in California, and the President's decision to move the United States fleet into the Pacific had added the last piece to the jig-saw of fear. These events brought home to the 'lonely kangaroos'[1] in a very striking way their isolation and vulnerability. In these terms, the 'Yellow Peril' came to possess the public imagination, and popular writers and the press, in novel and poem, article and editorial, gave expression to the scenario of dread.

The most interesting and impressive of the fictional representations of the new mood was an invasion story, 'The Commonwealth Crisis' which first appeared in October 1908 as a serial in the *Lone Hand*,[2] a literary offshoot of the *Bulletin* and which was republished in book form under the title, *The Australian Crisis* in 1909.[3] It was written by Frank Fox, the first editor of the *Lone Hand*, under the pseudonym Charles H. Kirmess.[4] Unlike earlier invasion 'scare' tales appearing in the

---

[1] 'Dryblower' Murphy, one of the numerous popular balladeers inspired to verse in August and September 1908 by the visit of the United States fleet to Australia, used the phrase to explain the warmth of the welcome accorded the Americans. Franklin Matthews, *Cruise of the United States Atlantic Fleet from San Francisco to Hampton Roads, 7 July 1908–22 February 1909*, New York 1909, p. 107.

[2] See *Lone Hand*, October 1908 to August 1909; III, 638–91; IV, 65–76, 185–96, 303–13, 421–32, 547–61, 671–81, V, 70–81, 169–84, 321–35, 437–45.

[3] Melbourne, 1909.

[4] [Since *Search for Security* was originally published I have discovered that I was wrong about Kirmess being a pseudonym for Frank Fox. This invasion scare novel, it now appears was written by someone, about whom we know very little, called Charles H. Kirmess. Kirmess's close relation with Frank Fox and the role of the book in the story of Australia's growing fear of Japan , however, still remains significant. The full account of the discovery of this confusion and how it affects the understanding of *The Australian Crisis* is set out in a long footnote 5 to my chapter on '"The Yellow Peril": Invasion Scare Novels and Australian Political Culture' in Ken Stewart, *The 1980s: Australian Literature and Australian Culture* (St Lucia: Queensland University Press, 1996).]

[Original footnote] The evidence for Fox's authorship, though circumstantial, is overwhelming. Fox knew Deakin very well and admired him as a man, a littérateur and a political leader. Deakin stayed with Fox during a visit to Sydney in 1906, expressed a great interest in the success of the *Lone Hand* and, under the guise of advertising Australia, had used Commonwealth funds to help underwrite the first issue of the magazine. (Letter, Fox to Deakin, 10 October 1906, Deakin Papers, 1540/3/1881; letter, Deakin to Fox, 23

June 1907, ibid., 1540/3/1881, 'I don't believe you. You cannot keep it up to the first two numbers. I am genuinely surprised at the variety and general excellence. ... Total effect of both numbers far beyond my expectations. Very much indebted for your help on Bulletin against inexcusable stupidity of one's own party', *CPD*, 1907–8 session, XLV, 10652, 29 April 1908; ibid., XLV, 10753, 1 May 1908; ibid., XLV, 10786, 5 May 1908; despite accusations of personal favouritism, Deakin refused to cut his friend, letter, Deakin to Fox, 6 April 1908, Deakin Papers, 1540/3/1856, 'Do not be distressed—I asked you to dine with full intentions of acceptance of consequences. The "natural side of private life" is my own and will remain so.')

Fox identified himself closely with Deakin's programme of radical reform, political nationalism and self-respecting imperialism. Like so many of Australia's writers and poets Fox was excited by the issue of colour and race—indeed the literary imagination in dealing with political subjects seems naturally drawn to such ideological and emotional exaggeration—and readily perceived in the emergence of Japan the outline of a 'Yellow Peril'. Writing to Deakin shortly after the Prime Minister had announced his ambitious defence policy in December 1907 Fox called 'for a strenuous, aye an alarmist attitude in this matter of defence'. He warned: 'We should be spending £s when we spend shillings. Note the growing feeling in England that they're not going to endanger what they consider "Imperial interests" for the sake of what they consider our "fads". For the sake of Australia bleed every £ you can out of Parliament for defence and send a High Commissioner to London who can say something on the other side as regards a White Australia.' (Letter, Fox to Deakin, undated but from internal evidence written soon after 13 December 1907, ibid., 1540/3/1922. Deakin refused to allow racial prejudice to override a rational assessment of the diplomatic situation and so he cautioned his friend, 'I don't pour cold water on "alarmism" for we shall need it all but the cables now appearing re China and Japan in Manchuria ... indicate that we have less to fear there at present than many think', letter, Deakin to Fox, undated but probably January 1908, ibid., 1540/3/1847). Despite the view of the *Lone Hand's* founder, J. F. Archibald, who had intended that the journal should be a literary venture balancing the economic and political bias of the *Bulletin*, Fox had had other ideas. He had nailed his colours to the mast in announcing in the first issue a political platform of 'an Honest, Clean, White Australia', and in that and all subsequent issues he made Australian defence and foreign policy a central preoccupation of his magazine.

In the initial issue there was a short story concerning the appearance of a hostile 'Asiatic' squadron off Sydney Heads. It defeated and dispersed the local British Squadron and held the city to ransom. The day was saved by a young Australian who had been on 'a drunk' the previous night. He had been imprisoned and had lost face in the eyes of his family and friends. In order to regain his self-respect and the respect of those whom he had wounded, he offered to risk his own life and try to raise the siege. By dint of his heroism and ingenuity he succeeded in blowing up the squadron and, *dictu mirabile*, was restored to his family and rehabilitated in the eyes of his fellow citizens. (*Lone Hand*, I, May 1907, XXI and 61–5). Fox commissioned L. Esson to report on the Asiatic menace and during 1908 a series of articles was published under the headings, 'From the Oldest World: Japan's Ju-jitsu Diplomacy' (II, August 1908, 395–9), 'The Asiatic Menace: Japan the Gamester' (III, September 1908, 514–17), 'The Asiatic Menace: Japanese Imperialism' (III, October 1908, 617–19), 'The Asiatic Menace: The Awakening of the Dragon' (IV, November 1908, 1–4) and 'The Asiatic Menace: Celestial Politics' (IV, December 1908, 121–2). Amidst a plethora of articles on Japan and Asia in this period, the *Lone Hand* only once in these years mentioned Germany and Europe. The magazine espoused compulsory military training, an Australian navy (I, June 1907, 206–10) and even the development of an air force. (C. L. Garland, 'The Aerial Defence of Australia', V, August 1909, 394–400). It feared for '"Our" Pacific Ocean' (G. Collingridge, I, May 1907, 115), suspected that it was fast becoming 'A

press[5] which were merely adaptations of British models. Fox made Japan, not Germany, the aggressor and he based his plot on that distinctive perception of threat which Australia's political leaders had come increasingly to adopt and develop in the years following the Russo-Japanese war.

Fox wrote the novel as a warning to his fellow countrymen. 'Apparently', as he put it in the preface, 'the Commonwealth can be roused to a sense of danger only by patient investigation of its real position in the world and of the possibilities among these. That has been my purpose.' He set

---

Japanese Pond' (VIII, December 1910, 156–61) in which the ocean hue would become increasingly 'Browner' (R. Bedford, 'White, Yellow and Brown: The Present Situation of White Australia in the Pacific that is … becoming Browner' (IX, July 1911, 224–8). It looked kindly on the visit of 'Our Big Brother: The American Fleet' to Australian waters (III, August 1908, 353–89) and extended a 'Friendly White Hand' of welcome (III, August 1908, 351–2). External assistance from white kinsmen, whether British or American, could not, however, be relied upon and the *Lone Hand* advocated a greatly increased Australian defence build-up as the only sure means of 'Guarding our Northern Gate' (V, August 1909, 446–8). The *Lone Hand* addressed itself, and often under the cover of pseudonyms or unsigned contributions, to all the themes which appeared in *The Australian Crisis*. But that the author of the latter was Fox rather than any of his colleagues is most completely demonstrated by comparing his novel *Beneath an Ardent Sun* (London 1923) which was published under his own name with *The Australian Crisis*. Though the central plot of *Beneath an Ardent Sun* deals with the love of an Australian prime minister for a married woman, the themes of *The Australian Crisis*, namely an Asian threat to White Australia, a domestic political crisis and the bush mystique, provide the background for the story. As in *The Australian Crisis*, the events related in *Beneath an Ardent Sun* take place in the years 1912–14. However, Fox, writing in 1923 after he had made his home in Britain and after the defeat of Germany in the Great War, was able to envisage in *Beneath an Ardent Sun* a happy outcome to Australia's Asian dilemma. Likewise the style in the latter novel, though still urgent and action-packed, is not so breathless and hysterical. The staccato style though of both novels illustrated in the examples below is undeniable:

> The roar of the streets has become deafening. The Moderates have no chance there. They met by invitation, their electioneering takes the form of a vigorous house-to-house canvass of all possible supporters. The streets scent danger. Patriots meet and speak openly. Why this sneaking conspiracy? It must be stopped. But how? There is only one means. And so the last, worst happens. (*The Australian Crisis*, p. 134).

> The truculence was unfortunate. The Feverish Party was in power and it was stimulated by that truculence to a most notable Feverishness. Promptly there was a resolution to uproot this Arcadia there and then, stock and branch, and repatriate all the generations of Cambodians, even to the third. Indignant White Australia was putting the resolution into effect when a halt was cried. Cambodia was resentful. Appeal was made to Great Britain. There were points of international law, not to speak of international courtesy, to be considered. (*Beneath an Ardent Sun*, p. 119).

This preoccupation of Fox with racial conflict and with Australian security in the Pacific can be found also in a number of his other works. See particularly *From the Old Dog, being the letters of the Hon., — —, ex-Prime Minister to his Nephew*, Melbourne 1908, especially pp. 93–103 and 155, and *Problems of the Pacific*, London 1912, especially pp. 278–80.

[5] *DT*, 22 October 1905; *Age*, November 1906.

the story in 1912 and 1913 in order to discourage readers from viewing the events related in the book as a futuristic fantasy. He wished to stress that he was dealing 'exclusively with realities'. And the central reality was the possibility of an Asian invasion of Australia under circumstances which prevented Britain from coming to the assistance of the Commonwealth.

In *The Australian Crisis*, Japan secretly landed soldier-settlers on the unpopulated coasts of the Northern Territory. After learning of the Japanese incursions, the Australian government appealed to the British for diplomatic and naval support in bringing about the removal of the alien intruders. The British, caught up in a web of European troubles and tensions, were unable to send a fleet to the Far East for they realized that after the despatch of such a force, the Royal Navy would not be strong enough 'to guarantee the safety of the heart of the Empire against the ambitions of European rivals'. Consequently they urged the Commonwealth to pursue a policy of caution and compromise in treating with the Japanese. The Australians then for the first time understood that their faith in 'the Supremacy of the British Navy which had justified their shocking neglect of the first principles of defence' had been misplaced.[6]

Confusion followed. The nation with one accord undertook a great programme of defence and development. But neither the government nor the parliament were able or willing, in the face of British opposition to take direct steps to eject the Japanese. The people on the other hand demanded action. Demagogues harangued angry mobs. Those leaders who called for moderation were hounded out of public life. Law and order broke down in the city and the country. Western Australia, not wishing to offend the Mother Country, tried to secede from the federation.[7] In these circumstances the initiative in repulsing the invaders fell to a volunteer force, drawn from 'the sturdy sons of the Australian bush' and supported by recruits from Canada and the United States. This 'White Guard' saw in Japan's actions a menace to 'Aryan ideals' in every part of the Pacific.[8] Despite valiant efforts, the White Guard, when it confronted the enemy, had to fall back before the superior numbers and organization of the Japanese. The Commonwealth was thus compelled to tolerate the presence of the Asian trespassers, and to cede nominal control over the occupied area to Great Britain.

All Australians recognized that this was but a temporary respite, that the day of reckoning in the war between the races had only been postponed. In his conclusion, Fox summed up the Australian predicament. He wrote,

> A truce has been cried until 1940 A.D. … Till then the Commonwealth must get ready for its relentless march to the North to save the purity of the race by sweeping the brown invaders back over the coral sea. The alternative is the irretrievable conquest of tropical Australia by the hordes of the Orient.

Placing the issue in a world-wide context he declared that

> In this struggle the still larger issue is bound up whether the White or the Yellow Race shall gain final supremacy. Christian civilization cannot afford the loss of this Continent. FOR

---

[6] Charles H. Kirmess, pp. 72–4.

[7] Kirmess, pp. 124–41.

[8] Kirmess, pp. 144–7.

AUSTRALIA IS THE PRECIOUS FRONT BUCKLE IN THE WHITE GIRDLE OF POWER
AND PROGRESS ENCIRCLING THE GLOBE.[9]

The war clouds gathering over Europe and the Pacific in 1907 and 1908 sharpened the focus of Australian leaders, and, in this atmosphere of crisis they embroidered and embellished their picture of the Asian menace. No politician produced an analysis which was as elaborate or fantastic as that of Fox, but the tone and intent were remarkably similar. Joseph Cook, who had become the most energetic spokesman for the free-traders and who, on Reid's resignation at the end of 1908, became the leader of that party, wrote in his diary in April that the

> Peace of Europe rests on the slenderest foundations. Constant frictions and criticisms must sooner or later end in explosion. … Real problem of world is racial. … Relations with yellow and black is urgent all round the globe. India, Africa, China — Japan and Russia, Japan and America.

Cook thought that it would be possible to 'Only arrange at present a temporary peace. … Problems may be acutely upon us before long.' And he defined Australia's 'Yellow Peril' problem,

> Japanese have proved beyond all doubt the immense potentialities of the Asiatic renaissance for war, industry, civilization. … Japan, leading India and China[10] would be a menace to the world … Hitherto the field of commerce — Now the venue [is] changed to the field of diplomacy. Maybe next to the battlefield.[11]

---

[9] Kirmess, pp. 332–5. Fox developed a plot composed of similar elements in *Beneath an Ardent Sun* but the twist he gave them, writing as an expatriate Australian in the aftermath of World War I, was very different. His identification of the Asian invader is rather more discreet. It was probably his frankness about British failure and Japanese aggression in the first novel which caused him to write under a *nom de plume*. In the later work, he had a little colony of 'let us say, Cambodians', established on an island at the entrance to the Gulf of Carpentaria. When the Commonwealth learnt of this violation of the principle of White Australia, the 'Feverish Party' in power stirred up public opinion and sponsored a resolution favouring the eviction of all the coloured settlers. The hero of the book, Henry Trent, then spoke up for soundness and sense, and 'pricked the government of the day and let out the rank gases of the bombast'. With the support of the Bush, for 'at the bottom the Australian has a good fund of sober earnestness', Trent then became prime minister. When Britain, fearful of Germany's ambitions in Europe, urged care in handling the situation and after one British minister had denounced 'Australian jingoism', the cry went up that Britain was about to betray the Commonwealth and that the White Australia policy was in danger (pp. 119–24). The new prime minister rejected calls for defiance and direct action and set out on a path whose end was to 'secure all that is necessary for the safety and racial purity of Australia … without being offensive to a chivalrous, friendly nation' (p. 166). The prime minister's quiet diplomacy succeeded. The 'Cambodians' were co-operative. The Australian government eased the way to an amicable agreement by offering liberal compensation and providing comfortable ships for the departing migrants (pp. 285–90). The crisis faded away almost as quickly as it had appeared, and Trent was able to retire from politics, marry his loved one and, presumably, to live happily ever after.

[10] Shades of the Okuma speech reported in the *Age,* 25 December 1907.

[11] Diary and Notebooks of Sir Joseph Cook, Notebook, April 1908, pp. 4 and 24–5.

At the other end of the political spectrum. J. C. Watson in supporting the adoption of a compulsory military training resolution at the 1908 Australian Labor Party Conference declared that

> Very desirable as peace undoubtedly was, they had to pay every regard to the facts that faced them today. They had to face the position with respect to a people who were clever and warlike and who were not governed by altruistic motives. There was the prospect, too, of the awakening of the sleeping giant — China.

The conference approved the motion by a vote of twenty-four to seven.[12] In this atmosphere the federal government was at last able to bring to fruition its defence policy and to pass legislation founding an Australian navy and providing for compulsory military service. Moreover, as a result of the Japanese-American tensions, Deakin was inspired, much to the chagrin of the British, to seek a special relationship with the United States and to persuade the greater Anglo-Saxon power in the Pacific to guarantee Australian security.

### The visit of the great white fleet: symbol and incentive

In late December 1907 and early January 1908 Deakin approached the American Consul-General in Melbourne and the American Ambassador in London and intimated that the Commonwealth government would welcome a visit from the American fleet during its proposed world cruise. Subsequently, at the end of January, he requested the British to forward an official invitation to President Roosevelt. Deakin hoped that a visit from the American fleet would help arouse popular support for his naval defence scheme, would indicate, even if only indirectly, Australian dissatisfaction with Britain's neglect of the empire in the Pacific and, finally, would give symbolic expression to a concept of Anglo-Saxon solidarity, based on an identity of interests and enemies in a region of common concern.[13] Writing to Whitelaw Reid, the United States Ambassador to Great Britain, he said,

> We are naturally deeply interested in the significant voyage and anxious to have some opportunity of expressing our sympathy with our kinsmen in their timely demonstration of naval power in what may be loosely termed our Oceanic neighbourhood.

After the Americans agreed to include Sydney and Melbourne on the fleet's Pacific itinerary, this latter motive grew in importance and came to overshadow the others.

Impatient of Colonial Office protocol and annoyed by Admiralty obstruction, Deakin contacted the American representatives in Melbourne and London, informing them of the Commonwealth's intention to invite the American fleet and urging them to use their good offices on behalf of Australia. Deakin called personally on J. P. Bray, the Consul-General, on Christmas Day, in order to solicit his assistance and he appealed to Whitelaw Reid, whom he had met during the 1907 Colonial Conference, on the basis of that acquaintance. He was determined to prevent

---

[12] Official Report of the Fifth Commonwealth Political Labor Conference, Brisbane, 7 to 10 July 1908.
[13] *MP*, 14 and 25 April 1908.

the British from frustrating his purpose.[14] He waited a further three weeks before asking the British government to send the official invitation to Washington. 'It [the visit]', Deakin explained, 'would be a further token of the close alliance of interest and sympathy which already exists between the two countries.'[15] However, by early February public interest in the possibility of such a visit had grown to such an extent[16] that the government felt compelled to make an early announcement, and so the prime minister short-circuited the earlier sea-mail despatch and cabled the same message to London, requesting a prompt reply.[17]

The cable of 12 February set the wheels of the Colonial Office machinery turning. The initial response was tepid to cool. The new permanent undersecretary of state, Sir Francis Hopwood, understood immediately the Australian intention. 'Yes', he commented, 'I suppose this is a demonstration for the delectation of Japan.' The parliamentary under-secretary, Winston Churchill, was more forthright. 'It ought certainly to be discouraged from every point of view.'[18] The Admiralty were embarrassed by the suggestion; they could not hope to match such a demonstration of naval force in Pacific waters. Yet, though they thought it 'inconvenient' and stated that they 'would be glad if it were not entertained by the United States government', they left the decision to the Foreign Office.[19]

British hands were forced by events. On 21 February the American cabinet had dealt with Bray's letter which they considered to be an Australian invitation to send the fleet 'Down Under'. At the conclusion of the meeting, the Secretary of State, Elihu Root, had announced that they would be happy, if, on the world cruise, some of the American battleships 'could be sent by the Australian route'.[20] On the following day Deakin publicly declared that it was possible that the American armada might visit Australia.[21] And the British found themselves confronted by a *fait accompli*. Given this barrage of publicity, the British were left with no choice but to endorse the Commonwealth's invitation and send it on to Washington.

The Colonial and Foreign Offices were irritated and indeed infuriated by Deakin's diplomatic indiscretions. Sir Edward Grey felt that though it was 'undesirable to say anything at the moment which might prompt Mr Deakin to say that it was evident, because of the Japanese alliance, that

---

[14] Letter, Deakin to Bray, 24 December 1907, and letter Deakin to Whitelaw Reid, 7 January 1908, United States National Archives, Record Group 59, States Department Numerical File, 1906–10, Vol. 597, 8258/124–5. Copies also in despatch, Northcote to Elgin, sent 4 March 1908, received 4 April 1908, CO 418/60/106.

[15] Despatch, Northcote to Elgin, sent 28 January 1908, received 2 March 1908, enclosing letter, Deakin to Northcote, 24 January 1908, CO 418/60/16–18.

[16] *Age*, 10, 20, 21, 23 and 31 January 1908; *SMH*, 5 February 1908. On 4 February the Sydney County Council passed a resolution requesting the Australian government to invite the fleet to visit Sydney. The New South Wales premier passed it on to Deakin.

[17] Cablegram, Northcote to Elgin, 12 February 1908, CO 418/60/42.

[18] CO 418/60/42.

[19] Letter, C. I. Thomas, secretary to Board of Admiralty to Hopwood, 22 February 1908, CO 418/65/28–9.

[20] *Washington Post*, 22 February 1908.

[21] *Age*, 24 February 1908.

we did not approve of this having been sent', Deakin might nevertheless be admonished that 'invitations to foreign governments should not be given except through us as circumstances are conceivable in which grave inconveniences might result'.[22] Grey and Elgin shared the conservative paternalism in Imperial matters which marked the Liberal administration. They were aggrieved by any signs of self-assertion on the part of the Dominions and were opposed to all proposals for constitutional reform which threatened the British government's unfettered control over imperial foreign policy. Grey thought that there was 'too much tendency to slobber' over the colonies, that their governments were 'too much given to spit at us', and that 'for Australia it might be put even stronger'.[23] Since Canada's external interests did not conflict with those of Great Britain, the imperial authorities were not so alarmed by a proposal that Ottawa should conduct its negotiations with Washington without the interposition of London as they were by Deakin's diplomatic initiatives. Sheltered by the Monroe Doctrine, Canada was not greatly concerned with the larger issue of imperial defence and foreign policy. Even so, Elgin was disturbed by a Canadian desire to have their own foreign office for the purpose of expediting Canadian-American business. In rebutting the suggestion Elgin argued that 'there might be a risk, possibly in Canada, more probably in Australia, that this might lead the self-governing colonies on to claims which might be inconvenient to the Imperial Foreign Office'. He was certain that, 'if Canada had a foreign office, our friend Deakin would certainly claim the same'.[24] And therein lay the rub.

For the moment though the British had to swallow their objections. By a skilful manoeuvre, Deakin had deprived them of their traditional weapons. They believed that Deakin was 'hopelessly in the wrong', and in terms of historical precedent and customary practice there was no gainsaying this judgement, yet both Elgin and Churchill agreed that on this occasion it was 'useless to explain to Mr Deakin'.[25] The British forwarded the invitation and President Roosevelt, aware of the advantages to be gained from having Dominion allies inside the British Empire should the Japanese troubles erupt into war, accepted with alacrity.[26] The Japanese question was becoming a vexed one for the British. In a paper written in July 1908 on 'The Self-Governing Dominions and Coloured Immigration', C. P. Lucas of the Colonial Office pointed out that 'the growth of democracy and science and education has not diminished but increased antipathies of race and colour'. He summed up Britain's dilemma,

---

[22] Letter, Grey to Elgin, 22 February 1908, CO 418/66/73.

[23] Letter, Grey to Lady Helen Munro Ferguson, 19 April 1908, George Macaulay Trevelyan, *Grey of Fallodon*, London 1937, p. 153.

[24] Letter, Elgin to Grey, 22 February 1908 and 7 March 1908, FO 800/90.

[25] CO 418/60/105.

[26] Letter, J. Bryce, British Ambassador in Washington, to Elihu Root, 1 March 1908, R.G. 59, State Department Numerical File, 1906–10, Vol. 598, 8258/215; D. C. Gordon, 'Roosevelt's "Smart Yankee Trick", *Pacific Review*, XXX (November 1961), 351–8. Roosevelt had been working with Mackenzie King and Laurier to try and make the British government sympathetic towards the Japanese immigration problems being encountered on the Pacific coast by Canada and the United States.

> The danger of it [immigration exclusion based on racial groups especially when it affects Japan] is obvious. We may conceivably have to choose between our self-governing Dominions and the Japanese alliance, … and the matter is now and will always be one which may give cause or pretext for complaint against us by the United States, and for attempts at interference on the part of the United States in our relations with the Dominions.[27]

On 14 March Deakin, while speaking to a well-attended and enthusiastic public meeting on defence, announced the news of Roosevelt's acceptance of the Australian invitation. For Deakin it was a political coup or, as he himself described it, 'a hit—one of those rare hits applauded both by opponents and supporters, and receiving the unanimous endorsement of the public'. He prophesied correctly that 'Should its [the United States] battleships visit our shores their reception will be enthusiastic to the pitch that Cousin Jonathan himself loves to reach.' He ascribed the popularity of such a visit as in part due to 'hospitality and curiosity' but he readily conceded that 'its chief inspiration was racial and political'. Australia associated the presence of the American fleet in the Pacific with the racial disputes on the west coast of North America. Deakin proudly claimed that 'Nowhere in the Empire, and perhaps nowhere outside the Southern States of the Union is the importance of the colour question more keenly realised than in the Commonwealth.' Thus when the ties of kinship were 'invoked in connection with a visit of the imposing American fleet to our ocean, in which the Union Jack has foregone its old supremacy, the significance of the invitation given by our Government assumed its true importance.' The failure of the Hague Peace Conference in 1907 augured ill for the future. Australians wished to see 'an alliance, whether expressed or implied', between the British Empire and the United States. To placate the British readers of the *Morning Post* he added that the visit of the American fleet would 'foster these feelings … without prejudice to any other existing engagement in Europe or Asia.'[28]

Deakin had caught the pulse of his fellow countrymen. Australia's fear of Japan dominated and explained the fervent welcome extended to the Great White Fleet. For Australians the fleet carried its symbolism on the ship hulls. The *Age* on first learning of the invitation had rhapsodised 'we are unfeignedly glad that America has invaded the Pacific. It is a move that cannot help but lessen our danger of Asiatic aggression and strengthen the grounds of our national security.'[29] Captain Creswell rather regretfully confided to Richard Jebb that the American fleet's visit was the direct result of Britain's 'abandonment' of the Far East. 'The grave result is the spectacle of Australians appealing for American aid in the Pacific, Australians looking outside the Empire for protection.' In Creswell's view the most dangerous contingency hovering over Australia was 'a German-Japanese alliance'. It would be 'our death-knell'.[30] Deakin put the matter succinctly and bluntly when he told Jebb in a private letter,

> The visit of the United States fleet is universally popular here, not so much because of our blood affection for the Americans though that is sincere but because of our distrust of the

---

[27] CO, Confidential Print, Dominions, No. 1, CO 886/1.

[28] *MP*, 14 and 25 April 1908.

[29] *Age*, 25 February 1908.

[30] Letter, Creswell to Jebb, 24 March 1908, Jebb Papers, 813/1/42.

Yellow Race in the North Pacific and our recognition of the 'entente cordiale' spreading among all white men who realise the Yellow Peril to Caucasian civilization, creeds and politics.[31]

In the event the visit of the American fleet was a huge success. It was in Senator E. Findley's words a triumph for 'gush, gorge and guzzle'.[32] Australians contracted what one American correspondent called 'Fleetitis'. In Sydney and Melbourne, crowds of from 400,000 to 600,000 turned out to greet the American navy.[33] More than a quarter of Australia's population massed the foreshores and streets of the two cities and celebrated the advent of American naval power into the southwest Pacific. The major buildings and thoroughfares were dressed up for the occasion. Flags, buntings and pictorial representations of Anglo-American history and solidarity decorated the major public offices. For the Sydney visit the government proclaimed two public holidays and many business houses following this lead also closed down. The trams in the city carried nearly one million passengers on 20 August the day that the sixteen battleships steamed into Port Jackson. Parades, illuminations, dinners and festivities of every kind followed each other in frightening succession. The 14,000 sailors were overawed, and indeed some were overcome, by the hospitality. However, scarcely one discordant note marred the scene of friendly fraternization.[34] Some Australians did not know how to reconcile the presence of blacks in the American navy (the Japanese stewards had been sacked before the fleet left Hampton Roads) with the celebration of Anglo-Saxon amity and unity. There was some anxious speculation ahead of time about the number of Negroes in the crew. Stories about blacks either played up their 'fiendish appearance', as in a report of the robbery of an Auckland woman, or their supposed lack of civilized manners and child-like 'coonery' as seen in a Sydney bar.[35] On the whole though, Australians ignored this black complication, refusing to allow it to spoil the spirit of harmony and good fellowship which pervaded the visit. Indeed, in terms of its splendour and spontaneity, in terms of popular participation and emotional enthusiasm, the welcome accorded 'Cousin Jonathan' had no precedent. Even the ceremonies accompanying the inauguration of the Commonwealth lacked the same fervour and fullness. The departure of one governor-general and

---

[31] Letter, Deakin to Jebb, 4 June 1908, Deakin-Jebb correspondence, 339/1/19A(-B).

[32] Cook Notebooks, 1908, p. 31.

[33] *SMH*, 21 August 1908; *Age*, 1 September 1908.

[34] *SMH*, 20 to 28 August; *DT*, 20 to 28 August; *Age*, 29 August to 6 September; *Argus*, 29 August to 6 September; despatch, Northcote to Crewe, sent 8 September 1908, received 12 October 1908, CO 418/61/116–29; F. Matthews, *Back to Hampton Road*, pp. 57–148; letter, Admiral Charles S. Sperry to Roosevelt, 12 September 1908, Container 1/87–8, Sperry Papers, 'The sustained enthusiasm of the cheering crowds in the cities of Auckland, Sydney and Melbourne has not been equalled in our experience, even on the West Coast, and has been fully justified by the cordiality of the press and of all the officials highest to the lowest', letter, Sperry to Edith Sperry, 28 August 1908, 'Decorations of the city were most beautiful and the crowds prodigious. There was certainly 500,000 people on the cliffs and shores', Container 5, Sperry Papers; see also Robert A. Hart, *The Great White Fleet. Its Voyage Around the World, 1907–1909*, Boston 1965, which contains the most authoritative account of the world cruise.

[35] *Age*, 27 August 1908.

the arrival of another on 8 September 1908 were as nothing in comparison.[36] The Americans themselves admitted that nowhere, including the West Coast of America, had they met with such a reception.[37]

The coming of the American fleet had touched a responsive chord in the national psyche. The tumultuous reception was a sign of Australia's sense of cultural as well as strategic isolation. Lost in the Pacific, a Pacific being made ever more uncomfortable by the emergence of great Asian powers to the North, the Australians, aware of the diminution of the British presence, looked expectantly to the Americans. Even more the excess of emotion sprang from a belief that Australians, after having been cut off from their cultural roots, for two or three or four generations, were at last being brought into touch with their Anglo-Saxon cultural inheritance, even if at one remove. They required tangible evidence of that outer world to reassure them. The Americans coming in the full panoply of their naval might satisfied that need in a very dramatic way. The relief at recognition let loose a flood of feeling and gave rise to a plethora of verse and doggerel. They all expressed much the same message. It was perhaps best summed up in the crude, callow words of 'Walk Right In':

> The call of the blood rings true in
>> the world's confusing din;
> Who's friends unless us and you — so
> Walk
>> Right
>>> In![38]

C. E. W. Bean, who later became a noted man of letters and a war historian, sang the same refrain:

> For one staunch mother bore them
> Of one staunch Northern race
> To find the world before them
> And look it in the face.[39]

Others were more specific in identifying what in the world needed to be looked in the face. F. J. Burnell called on Americans to be 'firm allied' with their British kin:

> Not heedless of your high descent,
> The grand old Anglo-Saxon race,
> To check with stern unflinching mace
> The swarming, hungry Orient[40]

---

[36] *Age*, 9 September 1908.
[37] Letter, Sperry to Roosevelt, 12 September 1908, Container 1/87–92, Sperry Papers.
[38] Matthews, *Hampton Road*, p. 91.
[39] *SMH*, 20 August 1908.
[40] *SMH*, 21 August 1908.

The most popular song was 'Big Brother', the work of a Western Australian newspaperman, 'Dryblower' Murphy. It was written during the last week of the Americans' visit, while the fleet was anchored off Albany. It told the story of 'Big Brother' Jonathan's visit to 'the lonely kangaroos' and how with Big Brother's help the Pacific would be kept 'clean and free'. The chorus appealing to the 'thin red line' of kinship plaintively invoked the protection of Uncle Sam.

> We've got a big brother in America
>> Uncle Sam, Uncle Sam!
> The same old blood, the same old speech,
> The same old songs are good enough for each,
> We'll all stand together, boys,
> If the foes want a flutter or a fuss,
> And we're hanging out the sign
> From the Leeuwin to the Line
> This bit o' the world belongs to us![41]

The press was only a little behind the poets in its anxious deference and race patriotism. Of all the newspapers, the *Age* produced the most coherent editorials. On 3 August as the American battleships were on their way to Auckland from Honolulu, a leading article bemoaned Australia's defenceless position and warned against relying on the British navy.

> A war declared tomorrow between Britain and almost any hostile power would infallibly involve us in the direst trouble. The Imperial Australian squadron, poor thing as it is, would be withdrawn immediately from our waters to the main scene of conflict. … Our situation then would be positively helpless, hideously hopeless.[42]

Britain had to be compelled to accept the Commonwealth's government's scheme for naval defence. A week later, reporting the fleet's arrival in Auckland, it began to invent a mythology about the significance of America's naval presence in the South Pacific. The fleet had come to proclaim 'a new dixie's [sic] line. … Draw a line from San Francisco to Hawaii and thence to the Philippines, south of that line America cannot afford to allow any Asiatic domination. This makes our policy in the Pacific a common one.'[43] As the fleet approached the Australian coastline, a leader article argued that

> the common interests of the whole English-speaking race may become so manifest to the statesmen on both sides of the world that there may grow up between them an alliance

---

[41] Matthews, pp. 107–8. On 14 September at a state luncheon in honour of the American visitors presided over by the premier of Western Australia, a 'professional artist' sang 'We've got a big brother in America' and 'the entire company joined in the chorus'. *West Australian*, 15 September 1908.
[42] *Age*, 3 August 1908.
[43] *Age*, 10 August 1908.

stronger than treaties—a sense of the common thread of kinship which may be expressed in our own Australian motto of 'one people, one destiny'.[44]

With the Americans in Melbourne, the *Age* brought its theme to a climax. It not only reproved the British for overlooking the needs of Australian security, but also extended the target of attack from the naval to colonial and diplomatic policy. 'All these great and salient facts form reasons why Australia feels no sort of confidence in Imperial guidance on matters pertaining to Australian interests.'[45] It asserted that 'Trouble must come some day. … We shall indeed be worse than fools if we fail to provide against the common lot.' It was cheering for Australians to know that 'Americans were watching their efforts with more than a friendly interest and ready at a pinch to show that blood is thicker than water.'[46] Resurrecting something of its old radical character, the *Age* drew on arguments from political philosophy in addition to those taken from racial ideology in order to claim that Australian-American relations in comparison with Anglo-American relations were more intimate and complete.

> The meeting of Australia and America is the meeting of the broad and free democracies—each of them grasping in its fullest meaning what is known as the Sovereignty of the People. … We can conceive of nothing in which we cannot share each other's aims and further one another's purposes.[47]

The *Sydney Morning Herald*,[48] the *Daily Telegraph*,[49] the *Sydney Mail*,[50] the South Australian *Register*,[51] the *West Australian*,[52] without self-consciously pointing up the defence lesson and without overtly criticizing the Mother Country, joined in the call of common history and common heritage.

Deakin's political imagination seized on the new feeling in the air and converted it to his own purposes. In his message of greeting, he bade the Americans welcome 'as guests, as the honoured representatives of a mighty nation, and thrice welcome as blood relations.'[53] In Sydney he announced that 'the celebrations of today are instinct with the truth of blood and race (loud cheers)',[54] and in Melbourne he portentously declared 'we [the Australians and Americans] stand together at the opening of a new chapter of Australian history'. In his account as the *Morning Post*'s Australian correspondent he underlined the importance of the

---

[44] *Age*, 17 August 1908.
[45] *Age*, 31 August 1908.
[46] *Age*, 2 September 1908.
[47] *Age*, 5 September 1908.
[48] 21 August 1908.
[49] 20 and 21 August 1908.
[50] 26 August 1908.
[51] 5 September 1908.
[52] 6 September 1908.
[53] *SMH*, 20 August 1908.
[54] *SMH*, 21 August 1908.

sudden development of an overmastering emotion by a keen conception of race unity … It is blood that tells, the vital instinctive force. … The familiar phrase 'Our American cousin' has suddenly become the imperfect expression of a deeply realised relationship whose ultimate consequences cannot be forecast.[55]

Unlike the press and popularisers, most political leaders exercised considerable tact and circumspection in referring to the more enduring benefits which they hoped would accrue from America's visit. Deakin had to forego, at least for the immediate future, any thought of obtaining an American guarantee of Australian security. R. O'Connor, former Vice-President of the Executive Council, High Court judge and friend of Deakin's, was the only notable figure to speak openly of the desirability of an Anglo-Saxon alliance under which the British Empire and the United States would act together to maintain peace in the Pacific.[56] The Australian political leaders, not wishing to embarrass their guests, were reticent on the subject of an American alliance or naval protection.

Admiral Charles S. Sperry understood well his delicate position and was grateful to his Australian hosts for their forbearance. He recognized that Australia, like other countries in the South Pacific, 'considers that we alone stand between the Japanese and a career of adventure'. He added that 'Our cruise is in no way a menace to Japan but it established a curious sort of protectorate—a new Monroe Doctrine.'[57] At least this was symbolically true as far as the Australians were concerned. For the Americans, though, in reality it meant rather less. Writing to Roosevelt, he explained that he felt

> that the visit of the fleet to Australia, while there has not been a trace of an attempt to construe it as promising armed alliance, has awakened a very strong feeling of a community of material interests in the Pacific which is the necessary basis for any friendship.[58]

Both Sperry and Roosevelt[59] did sympathize to some extent with the desire of the Australians for a British-American alliance in the Pacific. However, they had to be careful not to give offence to Japan[60] nor to alarm Congress with reports of entangling alliances. And so Sperry had to tread softly and carry a feather duster. He avoided all references to Asia and Japan in his speeches. He had 'to be very careful [in Sydney] for the Asiatic question causes great excitement' and the Australians were 'keenly alive to the fact that we are a great factor in the development and control

---

[55] *MP*, 14 October 1908.

[56] *Age*, 24 August 1908.

[57] Letter, Sperry to Edith Sperry, 9 September 1908, Sperry Papers, Container 5.

[58] Copy of letter, Sperry to Roosevelt, 12 September 1908, ibid., Container 1/87–92.

[59] Oscar K. Davis, *Released for Publication: Some Inside Political History of Theodore Roosevelt and His Times, 1890–1918*, Boston 1925, pp. 87–8. In commenting on a bizarre interview that William B. Hale had had with Kaiser William II and which his editor, Davis of the *New York Times*, had sent to Roosevelt, the President had told Davis 'It is true the invitation to the fleet to go to New Zealand and Australia was to show England—I cannot say a 'renegade mother country'—that these colonies are white men's country—and that is why the fleet was sent there.'

[60] Letter, Roosevelt to Sperry, 21 March 1908, Sperry Papers.

of the Pacific'.[61] In order to establish an Australian-American axis Sperry, adopting the Chamberlain view of the nature of political alliances, privately urged Deakin to build up trade between the two countries through the chain of islands separating them.

> The gospel I have preached, is that, if we, Great Britain and ourselves [the United States] develop our territories in the Pacific it will consolidate our material interests without which mere blood ties count for little, and I told the prime minister of the Commonwealth, a very clever man, that every dollar they spent in developing trade in their Pacific Islands, on the route to Vancouver and San Francisco was worth ten put into fortifications because the world would recognise the community of our commercial interests and would not dare affront us as long as we hold together.[62]

Though Deakin was not greatly influenced by Sperry's dream of trans-Pacific trade as a substitute for defence, he was encouraged to build on the foundations of Australian-American goodwill which were laid down at the time of the fleet's visit to the Commonwealth. And in thanking the President for making the visit possible, he conveyed the Commonwealth government's wish that Roosevelt might include Australia in the foreign tour which he was proposing to take after he left office in March 1909.[63] Roosevelt gracefully declined[64] and Deakin had to find other ways of achieving his American objective.

The Australian government acted more directly in trying to collect the British benefits coming out of the American visit. They had hoped to shame the British into taking a more active interest in Pacific affairs. As soon as the American fleet had left Melbourne Deakin was sounding out London on the question of a Pacific tour by a British fleet.[65] The Colonial Office found themselves in a cleft stick. They did not want to appear to be competing with the Americans for Australia's favours. The colonial secretary's advisers were unanimous on the point. They feared that it would be seen as a 'counterblast' to the Americans. The British could not afford to send a naval force less imposing than the Americans, and the Admiralty did not have the ships available for such a purpose. A public refusal, however, would be the greatest humiliation of all.

When this Australian request was followed almost immediately by the invitation to President Roosevelt to visit the Commonwealth, the insult seemed complete. The British saw in Australia's approach to Roosevelt the suggestion that it had 'a second string to its bow'. The Australian strategy was deeply resented. 'To play off the United States against us is not only foolish (for U.S. will not fight Japan for Australia), but is intended to be used to induce us to break our Japanese alliance.' This was a frequent misunderstanding of the British. The Australians never sought to have the British renounce the Japanese alliance. Rather they wanted the British to recognize that the alliance was not an adequate protection for imperial interests in the Pacific. Lord Crewe, who had succeeded Elgin as colonial secretary, thought the Australians must have 'lost their heads' and

---

[61] Letter, Sperry to Edith Sperry, 28 August 1908, ibid., Container 5.

[62] Letter, Sperry to Edith Sperry, 9 September 1908, ibid., Container 5.

[63] Telegram, Lord Dudley, governor-general to Crewe, 18 September 1908, CO 418/61/147–54.

[64] Copy of telegram, Bryce to Foreign Office, 11 October 1908, CO 418/66/32.

[65] Telegram, Dudley to Crewe, 14 September 1908, CO 418/61/130–5.

he consulted with Asquith, who on Campbell-Bannerman's death in 1907 had become prime minister, about the best course to pursue. Even though the Presidential invitation was 'objectionable', it could not be blocked. The invitation to the British fleet's visit was difficult to handle. In order not to be embarrassed by an Admiralty refusal, the navy was not directly brought into the matter. Crewe wrote personally to the new Australian governor-general, Lord Dudley, explaining in detail the impossibility of satisfying the Australians and urging him to use his influence 'to induce your Ministers to withdraw the request'. At the same time Crewe replied to the Commonwealth government simply saying that such a visit by a British fleet was 'not expedient' and expressing the hope that Australia would not press its invitation.[66] Though rebuffed initially, the Australian government had through the American fleet's visit made the British government much more sensible of its fears and feelings with respect to Pacific affairs. The British proposal at the 1909 defence conference to create an Imperial Fleet for the Pacific was in part inspired by the success of the Great White Fleet's grand tour to the antipodes.

In Australia, the Commonwealth government, capitalizing on the emotionally-charged atmosphere, brought down legislation to establish a National Guard. In accordance with the defence policy outlined by Deakin in December 1907, the legislation provided for compulsory cadet-training in schools and for compulsory military training over a three-year period for all eighteen-year-olds. The latter were to be required to attend ten regular day parades and an eighteen-day camp each year. When parliament met on 16 September, the governor-general in announcing the government's programme gave priority to two measures, the determining of the site of the federal capital and national defence.[67] The movers and seconders of the address-in-reply, in commending the defence bill, pointed to the example of the American fleet, the weakness of British naval power in the Pacific and the ambitions of Japan.[68] Ewing, the minister for defence, in introducing the bill on 29 September offered a similar justification. He contended that 'It is more difficult here, beset as the Commonwealth is with the greatest dangers and difficulties in regard to the future life and preservation of white occupation, than exist in any part of the British dominions.' Influenced by Charles Pearson's forecast of racial conflict and change, he stated, 'If honourable members take into consideration our environment, they will recognize that civilization in Australia stands in more danger of absolute destruction than it does in any other part of the British Empire.' Egged on by Deakin, he remarked on the changes that had taken place in Britain's naval position in the world.

> We have to face the facts as they present themselves to us, and it is idle to orate about Britain being mistress of the sea and to indulge in mere talk. Facts control the situation, and … we find that within fifty years the British Navy has passed from the stage of absolute control of

[66] Minute on Australian invitation to the American president to visit Australia, telegram Crewe to Dudley (personal), 22 September 1908, and telegram, Crewe to Dudley, 22 September 1908, CO 418/61/135–8.
[67] *CPD*, 1908 session, XLVII, 5, 16 September 1908.
[68] J. M. Chanter and Dr C. C. Salmon, ibid., 26–7, 34–6; Senators C. St Clair Cameron and W. A. Trenwith, ibid., XLVII, 117–18, 17 September 1908. See also Hughes on the strategic argument for compulsory military training, ibid., XLVII, 862–3 and 877, 7 October 1908.

the oceans of the world to one which impels some British statesmen to declare that it is doubtful whether it will be able in a little time to hold its own successfully.

He said that the British Navy had 'something more to do than to look after our shipping and our foreshores'. Its 'main responsibility' was 'the protection of the heart of the Empire'. Australia's responsibility then was to provide for its own defence.[69]

The official leaders of the opposition, Reid for the free-traders and Forrest for the conservative-protectionists, who disliked Deakin's alliance with Labor, played their role and opposed the bill. Echoing articles published in the *Argus* by Colonel Hubert Foster, Director of Military Studies at the University of Sydney,[70] they expressed confidence in the capacity of the British Navy to protect Australia and denounced fears of Japan as 'chimerical'.[71] Though it is possible that both men spoke their true mind on the matter, other opposition spokesmen criticized the bill merely out of a desire to embarrass the government. Joseph Cook, while allowing that there was a threat from the north, denied that the danger was such as to justify a breach of British tradition and interference with the nation's industrial life. Cook declared that Germany was the British Empire's chief antagonist.[72] Cook's diary records must throw some doubt

---

[69] *CPD*, 1906 session, XLVII, 431 and 454–5, 16 September 1908.

[70] *Argus*, 3 and 14 October 1908. Colonel Foster had been seconded by the War Office to train scholars and gentlemen to become officers in the colonial defence force. Foster had made himself an apologist for the British view of Australian defence needs. In response to the government's defence policy he had regurgitated the substance of the CDC and CID reports on the Commonwealth's strategic position. 'Australia', he wrote, 'is by her geographical position, in less danger of attack than any other part of the Empire.' He pointed out that Japan was as far away from Australia as Turkey from the United States. The distance from Sydney to Yokohama was equal to that between London and Delhi. European powers with colonies in the Pacific did not have soldiers or resources to mount an attack. An invasion was impossible. The British navy by adopting the principles of concentration of ships and unity of command ensured the safety of the whole empire. He quoted with approval Mahan's strictures against the clamour for 'local security which is apparent and not real'.

   The Commonwealth government commissioned Creswell to write a reply and his letters to the minister of defence of 16 and 26 October were subsequently printed as a parliamentary paper. The arguments now came trippingly from Creswell's pen. The Australian naval commander recited all the familiar criticisms of the CID papers. The Commonwealth could not rely in time of war on the maintenance of British naval supremacy in Australian waters. Rather the Commonwealth's security was 'a charge on the kindness of an Asiatic power'. Using material taken from *The Times* and the *United Services Magazine*, he showed how Britain, due to German naval competition, was not free to despatch a large naval force to the Far East. He publicly repeated his anxiety with respect to a German-Japanese alliance. Australia faced risks far in excess of the raids by 'four unarmed cruisers and one thousand men', as predicted by the CID. Consequently the government had to shape its policy accordingly. CofA, *Parliamentary Papers*, 1908 session, Vol. II, No. 35, 'The Defence of Australia. By Colonel H. Foster (Director of Military Studies, Sydney University), together with remarks thereon, by Captain W. R. Creswell, Naval Director'.

[71] *CPD*, XLVII, 840–2, 7 October 1908; ibid., 1128–37, 14 October 1908.

[72] Ibid., 116–18, 17 September 1908.

on Cook's emphasis here. Moreover, a year later Cook himself, in his capacity as defence minister, brought down an even more costly and extensive defence and military training programme.

In the upper house, where party passions were less evident, the leader of the opposition, Senator E. D. Millen of New South Wales, in contradistinction to his colleagues in the House, gave an unqualified support to the Asian threat thesis. Millen, who in 1913–14 was to become minister of defence in the Cook administration, gave voice to those fears which Cook had confided to his diary. Speaking of the visit of the American fleet, he declared that

> One of the lessons which it teaches us is that science is annihilating space, and that as progress and development proceed, that isolation which surrounds Australia, and which has been to some extent its protection, is rapidly disappearing—that the time has gone by when Australia could proceed 'forgetful of the world and by the world forgot.' We are daily being brought closer to those great movements which may tend to disturb that of other countries. Australia has undertaken a peculiar mission, and one which has never before been attempted—the mission of establishing a western civilization amidst Oriental surroundings. There is no need to be an alarmist, but if history teaches us anything at all, it teaches that where racial feeling is aroused, friction sooner or later must result. We all hope that Australia will never know anything but peace. At the same time, I am unable to shut my eyes to the fact that 'East is East and west is west, and never the twain shall meet'. It is, therefore, a source of satisfaction to know—should diplomacy prove unequal to the task—that our American kinsmen have evidenced that they intend to take a hand in the development of the Pacific.[73]

Once more, however, the government's defence policy was not put to a vote. Neither its military policy as embodied in the defence bill nor its naval policy as found in the Admiralty-approved scheme which was received in Melbourne on 20 September was put to the test. Before this could happen, Labor, dissatisfied on a wide range of domestic issues, withdrew its support from the Deakin ministry[74] and on 13 November Fisher took office.

### The Labor interlude :the British 'Dreadnought scare' and Australian defence

The two men in the Labor government formally responsible for defence policy were Andrew Fisher, the prime minister and treasurer, and Senator George F. Pearce, the minister for defence. They were men of limited education and ordinary circumstances. Fisher, migrating from Scotland at the age of twenty-three, had established himself as a leader of the miners on the Gympie coalfield and had taken an active part in organizing the nascent labour movement in Queensland. Pearce, a native Australian, who had been variously carpenter, prospector and itinerant worker, had played a prominent role in the formation of a carpenters' union in Western Australia. Their politics, like that of most Labor men, came directly out of their working lives and local community interests. They were ill-prepared in terms of their background for dealing with Australia's relations with the wider world.

---

[73] Ibid., 47, 17 September 1908.
[74] ALP caucus minutes, Vol. II, 60 4, meetings of 21 October, 5, 8 and 12 November 1908.

In the absence of experience and knowledge, they had brought with them into the federal parliament utopian socialist views which tended to attribute wars to the self-serving aims of militarists and capitalists and to see their prevention in the rise of popular self-government and the solidarity of the working classes in all nations. Both men were at first instinctively suspicious of those who called for an extensive or costly defence programme. In the first years of the Commonwealth they had voted for defence reductions, opposed subsidies for the British navy and rejected compulsory military training.

By 1908 the Labor leaders had undergone a change of heart. Pearce, with his racial view of world politics, had been quick to perceive a threat from Asia and had been among the first to sound the alarm following Japan's victory in the Russo-Japanese war.[75] Fisher had been a rather more tardy convert. Down at least to the end of 1905 he had continued to denounce the war 'craze' evoked by the Japanese success at the Battle of Tsushima. In 1906 he could still find no merit in Hughes' compulsory military training proposals and he dissociated himself from them. However, by the time they assumed office, both men had come to accept Deakin's full programme of defence under democracy. Fisher had ultimately succumbed before the logic of the 'Commonwealth Crisis'. In 1908 in response to criticism, he stated that the Labor party's support for the White Australia policy was not motivated primarily by industrial and employment considerations. He said that 'The real danger it involved was the racial one.'[76]

Fisher and Pearce also felt the tug of tribal loyalties. At first they had, like most Labor men, tended to stress the need to protect Australia's rights and freedom of action inside the empire. And as a symbol of Australian independence they had endorsed the idea of an Australian navy. Fisher sympathized with the advice tendered by an old friend shortly after he accepted office in the Watson ministry. G. J. Hall, a former Gympie editor, wrote from London,

> Your only safe way of dealing with the Home Government, is to consider Australian interests *only*, do not go out of your way to favour the old land, for the people here only look upon the colonies as aid for its use, both in trade and war, above all do not consent to an Imperial defence tax.[77]

Though the transformation in international relations from 1904 to 1907 did not cause Labor men to waver in their determination to put Australia first, nevertheless in the atmosphere of heightening tension it did make them more willing to acknowledge the responsibilities imposed by ties of kinship. Answering a conservative imperialist in the House, Fisher declared that

---

[75] Pearce carried his fears to irrational lengths. Perhaps he had drunk too deeply of Fox's 'Commonwealth Crisis'. The spectre of racial conflict and invasion unhinged his judgement. While Minister for Defence he told the Australian Natives Association that 'He knew already of a nation which was not Germany but darker-skinned that was spying out for land with a view to what had been called confiscation' (*SMH*, 1 April 1909). These accusations referred to rumours concerning Japanese showmen who were touring northern Australia. Though, when the Japanese consul-general challenged him, Pearce could not produce evidence to substantiate his insinuations, he never apologized (*SMH*, 3, 4 and 5 April 1909).

[76] *CPD*, XLVII, 131, 17 December 1908.

[77] Letter, Hall to Fisher, 8 May 1904, Fisher Papers, 2919/1/1.

> If we had any fighting ships and Great Britain was in trouble, I should not be at all alarmed about them being removed from our waters. We do not belong to a race of that kind. The ships should be free to go into the thick of the fight. It would not be an Australian sentiment to say that we should keep them in our waters … I wish to guard myself against a jingoistic utterance. I do not think that … Australian warships should be sent to take part in any paltry trouble which might arise. But if there was a contest between Great Britain and a power of the same class, I believe that our ships would undoubtedly find a place alongside the British warships during the trouble.[78]

Neither man had anything distinctive or original to contribute to the analysis of Australia's strategic position or to the broad diplomatic and defence policies which the Commonwealth adopted. Fisher lacked the quick wit and platform eloquence of Deakin and Hughes. He could not match their analytical powers and imaginative flights. Nevertheless his simple honesty in dealing with men and measures won him a trust and respect which no other Australian of his time was able to command. Too often historians have undervalued in a politician the virtues of common sense, common decency and common language. In face of an obvious problem, such as Australian defence after 1907, he took direct and certain action, and his record as prime minister was in this respect outstanding. Pearce similarly lacked intellectual and rhetorical gifts of the first order. Moreover, he lacked also the personal qualities which caused men to give their loyalty to Fisher. However, fired by his racial fears he was dedicated to defence and during the thirteen years he held the portfolio—the longest term of any defence minister in the history of the Commonwealth—he proved himself a most capable administrator.[79]

In November 1908 the Fisher government was not in a strong position to make policy. It had changed roles with the Deakin protectionists and depended upon them for a majority in parliament. Defence however was a field where Labor could expect to secure the co-operation of the Deakinites. Fisher and Pearce were convinced of the need for action.[80] Since parliament had already in the preceding May set aside £250,000 for 'commercial and harbour defences', they were able to take immediate steps to obtain the first ships of an Australian navy. Pearce in January suggested the government 'should order torpedo destroyers and take the responsibility when parliament meets'. He was 'more than convinced' of the 'justice, wisdom and urgency' of taking such a decision. Creswell made a submission to cabinet along the lines of his earlier recommendation urging the acquisition of three torpedo-boat destroyers and in early February the government without any further reference to the Admiralty despatched the order for the

---

[78] *CPD*, XLVII, 1459, 22 October 1908.

[79] Peter Heydon, *Quiet Decision: A Study of George Foster Pearce*, Melbourne 1965.

[80] See letter, R. B. Wise (London) to Fisher, 26 November 1908, containing an interview with Wise reported in the *Australian Star*, 25 November 1908. Wise claimed that Louis Harcourt, a Liberal minister, had informed him that Germany would endeavour to postpone war with Britain until 1916 when the Japanese alliance terminated. Germany was looking for overseas empires and Australia would be the prize. Wise's warning confirmed in large part the Creswell picture of trends in international affairs as they affected the security of Australia and the British Empire and reinforced the advice the government was already receiving and gave substance to the fears which the ministers shared. R. B. Wise Papers.

vessels to England.[81] The Commonwealth government after years of debate and discussion had taken the first positive steps towards the creation of an Australian navy.

While Fisher during the next month was working on a more comprehensive defence programme as part of a general policy statement, the tranquillity of the nation and empire was rudely shattered by a crisis of confidence in Britain's capacity to maintain its naval supremacy. On 16 March Asquith and R. McKenna, the First Lord of the Admiralty, in speaking to the naval estimates had revealed that Germany's battleship building programme threatened British supremacy at sea. To this end they asked the House of Commons to approve an increase of £2,750,000 for 1909–10 which would enable the government to lay down four new Dreadnoughts and in addition they sought the right to commence four further Dreadnoughts should German competition require it. For the first time the British government tacitly confessed that they had abandoned the two-power standard. British naval-building was directed exclusively against Germany. The question before the country was what comprised a safe margin of superiority. Balfour, for the Unionists, denied that the government's programme provided any margin of safety and Conservative press and politicians demanded immediate action to meet a deteriorating situation. Panic spread quickly and the cry 'We want eight, and we won't wait' was taken up by every part of the British Isles.[82] The repercussions of the 'naval scare' were felt throughout the length and breadth of the Empire and New Zealand rushed impulsively to the aid of 'the Empire in danger' and offered to make a gift of a Dreadnought to the Mother Country.

The Australian government however refused to be swept off its feet by an emotional campaign. The revelations of British weakness *vis-à-vis* Germany served more to accentuate Australia's fears of Asia rather than its dependence on Britain. Fisher had told reporters that though 'the full resources of the Commonwealth will be at the command of Great Britain in time of trouble', he could not see the wisdom of making an offer to contribute a Dreadnought to the British navy. New Zealand and Australian circumstances were not the same. Australia, unlike the sister dominion, was committed to building a navy of its own.[83] Fisher making the same point in writing to the Colonial Secretary said that while 'in the event of any emergency, the resources of the Commonwealth would be cheerfully placed at the disposal of the Mother Country', the Australian government's policy was 'to provide for its own defence'.[84] And on 30 March at Gympie in the heart of his Queensland electorate he set forth the Labor policy.

The Gympie speech was a call to action. It presented a policy of national development rather than social reform and at the core of the programme was defence. Fisher stated that the

---

[81] Macandie, *Genesis of the Royal Australian Navy*, pp. 216–21; *SMH*, 23 March 1909.

[82] Great Britain, 5 *Parliamentary Debates* (Commons), II, 930–63, 16 March 1909; see Marder, *From Dreadnought to Scapa Flow*, Vol. I, pp. 164–71 for the best short account of the 'naval scare'.

[83] *SMH*, 23 March 1909.

[84] CofA, *Parliamentary Papers*, 1909 session, Vol. II, No. 1. 'Defence: Correspondence Regarding a Conference between Representatives of His Majesty's Government and the Governments of the Self-Governing Dominions on the Subject of Naval and Military Defence', copy of telegram, Fisher to Lord Dudley, Governor-general, 22 March 1909.

government was profoundly disturbed by the international situation. 'We have no reassurance at all', he said, 'that next year or the year following, the centre of gravity may [not (the whole sense of the speech indicates that 'not' was omitted here)] lie in the near East.' And by this expression he clearly meant the European 'East' near to Australia, not Britain. This geographical reference, though a confusion of two different frameworks of reference, nevertheless represented an advance on Edmund Barton's 1903 description of France as 'our nearest neighbour across the channel'. To meet the threat from the North Labor proposed a three-pronged defence scheme. Firstly, Fisher outlined a plan for compulsory military training which went beyond the Deakin-Ewing bill of the previous spring. Secondly, he promised to establish a munitions industry in Australia which would make the Commonwealth independent of overseas supplies. Finally, the most dramatic and costly element, he committed the government to building an Australian navy composed of four ocean-going destroyers, nineteen river class destroyers and an island patrol boat.[85]

The Labor leaders drew effectively on Creswell's authority in order to justify their naval proposals. Pearce cited Creswell's view that it was 'absolutely imperative for us [the British empire] to maintain our supremacy both in the Home Waters and in the Far East' and that 'in the event of trouble' the British would not be able to come to Australia's assistance 'without leaving their shores at the mercy of rivals across the North Sea'.[86] Yet, even though the government, in arguing its strategic case and in selecting the ships for the local flotilla, had used Creswell's rather than the Admiralty's analyses and recommendations, nevertheless, the policy was plainly its own. Its proposals went far beyond anything Creswell or the naval officers had urged. Fisher's naval building programme was to be completed in three not five years and the total cost of the defence policies announced at Gympie was £2,250,000. Since Labor insisted on paying for defence out of revenue, it was clear that Labor's land tax, the first fruits of the Henry George influence on the Labor party, would be used to finance the preparedness programme.

The Labor government, like its predecessors, had, in adopting a naval policy, to decide how the local force should be co-ordinated with the British navy. Fisher had maintained in his policy speech that 'Australia is an integral portion of the British Empire' and that 'Any naval force must be a portion of the sea-power of the British nation.' But the question was 'under what conditions?'. The Admiralty had been concerned by the Australian government's unilateral decision to purchase torpedo-destroyers. But they put a bold front on the matter and assumed in discussions with the Australian representative in London that the vessel would be 'an integral part' of the Royal Navy.[87]

On 15 April Fisher sent the British government Australia's 'Basis of cooperation and mutual understanding'. Australia would help preserve the 'permanent Naval Supremacy of the Empire' by

---

[85] *SMH*, 31 March 1909.

[86] *SMH*, 23 March 1909; see also Creswell's letters to the Minister for Defence, 16 and 26 October 1908, CofA, *Parliamentary Papers*, 1908 session, Vol. II, No. 35; CofA, *Parliamentary Papers*, 1908 session, Vol. II, No. 37; 'Report for 1907 by the Director of Naval Forces, January 1, 1908', Captain Creswell's Memorandum to the Minister for Defence, 22 February 1909, Macandie, *Genesis of the Royal Australian Navy*, pp. 223–34.

[87] Letter, R. Muirhead Collins to Fisher, 2 April 1909, Fisher Papers, 2919/1/1.

developing its own local defence force. In implementing the new policy, Fisher agreed to continue to contribute to the upkeep of the imperial squadron until the 1903 naval agreement expired. He stated that the Australian navy, in local waters in peacetime, would remain under the sole control of the Commonwealth government and promised that in time of war or emergency it would be placed under the Admiralty's orders though even then the Dominion's ships were not to be permitted to leave Australian waters without the consent of the Commonwealth government. This last curious and complex condition followed from the intervention of the governor-general. Dudley had complained when in the first draft Fisher, contrary to Admiralty wishes, had reserved control over the navy whether in peace or war to the Commonwealth government. Though the final phrasing represented a compromise, it was more one of form than of substance.[88] This then was the Labor government's response to 'the naval scare'.

The Australian press and conservative politicians worked themselves up into a fury of imperial indignation. They demanded that the Commonwealth rally to the cause and, following New Zealand's example, offer a Dreadnought to the Royal Navy in its hour of need. Great public meetings were held under the banner of empire in the Sydney and Melbourne Town Halls.[89] By 7 April the opposition leaders had to a man come out in favour of a Dreadnought gift. Deakin was the last to support the campaign and it may be doubted whether his commitment was a wholehearted one. His decision was at least partly influenced by his desire to bring about a fusion of all the anti-Labor forces in parliament.[90] Neither Hughes' vitriol nor Pearce's Yellow Peril could stay the torrent of emotive criticism.[91] The governor-general himself 'suggested to the Prime

---

[88] Letter, Atlee Hunt on behalf of Fisher to Dudley, 10 April 1909, CP 290/15/6; cable, Dudley to Crewe, Colonial Secretary, 15 April 1909, CO 418/70/250, and copy in letter book of governor-general's correspondence CP 78/8; despatch, Dudley to Crewe, 18 April 1909, CO 418/70/274–7.

[89] SMH, 25 March 1909.

[90] SMH, 8 April 1909.

[91] SMH, 2 April 1909. Pearce in addressing the Australian Natives Association in Melbourne said in defence of Labor's policy that 'He knew already of a nation which was not Germany but was darker-skinned' that was spying out the land with a view to what he had called 'confiscation'. Hughes picked on earlier statements by Cook and Reid in which they had declared that the Empire was not in any danger. 'Extraordinary that those who hitherto denied necessity for action should now be roused to frenzy in the matter' (SMH, 7 April 1909).

Many of the Labor ministers were, however, privately shaken by this outburst of imperial fervour. Perhaps they recalled the politics of imperialism which had been used so tellingly against them during the Boer War. Certainly they saw the danger of a union of the Deakin liberals and the Cook conservatives under the umbrella of imperialism. With these considerations in mind Hughes, with the consent of Pearce and two other Labor ministers, devised a strategy which, while keeping within the letter of Labor policy, would in substance have gone a long way towards meeting the criticisms of their opponents. On 8 April he wired Fisher, 'Confidential—Pearce and I speaking at Richmond tonight. I propose meeting Deakin's criticism re—Dreadnought by repeating your despatch that in case of emergency whole of resources of Commonwealth at disposal of Great Britain. Matter now rests with Great Britain. If she should declare further action than our own naval policy advisable in interests of Empire generally and that we should offer Dreadnought, then we should construe that into a declaration of emergency and forthwith make offer of

Minister that the moral effect of presenting a Dreadnought might be very great as illustrating the solidarity of the Empire' but Fisher remained 'so wedded to his opinion' that Dudley refrained from pressing the point.[92] To the end of the crisis, Fisher held to the view that he had announced when first challenged on the subject. He said,

> It would be pleasing to any man in my position, to ride on the popular wave of feeling and be the first man to make an offer. It would be flattering to any man; but it is because I think it would be an error in the present position of Australian and Imperial policies to do so that the Government has resisted the public appeal.

Such an offer was 'no policy'. He clung to his decision to pursue 'a steady, persistent and determined policy to provide for the adequate defence of Australia, and assist the Mother Country in the time of emergency.'[93]

In defiance of the government the imperialists opened public subscription lists. The premiers of Victoria and New South Wales placed themselves at the head of the movement and promised their support. Australia would, despite its national leaders, prove its imperial loyalty. However, as in so many other instances in Australian history, imperial fervour ran somewhat ahead of national performance. Contribution only trickled in. By the end of August the New South Wales Fund had reached only £86,020 and was far short of the target of £250,000.[94]

Both Deakin and Cook had spoken also in favour of an Australian naval force. Deakin indeed used much the same language as Fisher: 'Australia requires to be able to hold her own while Britain's navy is looking after itself'.[95] Cook said that 'Australia was rich enough, not only to present the Mother Country with a dreadnought but to provide for her own defences as well. And she ought to do both.'[96] Reid was the least enthusiastic. 'Have destroyers if you like', he declared, 'but don't forget that the great Waterloo on which the destiny of Australia will be at stake will happen in distant seas.'[97] They all took issue with Fisher's failure to consult the Admiralty before ordering the destroyers and with his failure to work out mutually agreed terms for Anglo-Australian naval co-operation in peace and war.[98]

Troubled by the uncertain state of imperial defence and by the threatened union of the anti-Labor factions, Fisher was provoked into seeking a solution for his problems in an imperial conference. In the aftermath of the 'naval scare' the issue of defence which Fisher had thought

---

Dreadnoughts to the extent desired. The matter really now rests with Britain.' But the prime minister would have none of it. His simple, stolid virtues stood him in good stead. He was willing to ride out the political storm rather than compromise his judgement. 'Keep to policy outlined at Gympie', he replied. 'Be steady, Cannot entertain Dreadnought proposal.' (Memoirs of Malcolm Shepherd, CRS A1632).

[92] Despatch, Dudley to Crewe, 18 April 1909. CO 418/70/274–7.

[93] *SMH*, 24 March 1909.

[94] *SMH*, 28 August 1909.

[95] *SMH*, 8 April 1909.

[96] *SMH*, 1 and 9 April 1909.

[97] *SMH*, 9 April 1909.

[98] *SMH*, 1 April 1909.

would be most likely to keep the Deakinite protectionists on his side, had in fact been turned against him and exploited to produce an alliance of all opposition parties. An imperial conference offered the best chance of resolving the problem and breaking up the alliance. It is difficult not to believe that Fisher saw his opportunity and took it. This was not like the bleatings of the imperial panjandrums a blind act of faith. Rather, an imperial conference composed of autonomous partners was fully congruent with his view of empire and the rightful place of the dominions within it. Fisher hoped that through such means rational policies which took into account the needs of all parts of the empire could be agreed upon. To this end, following on from a report that the British prime minister was interested in holding such discussions,[99] Fisher on 29 April despatched a cable to the Colonial Office requesting the British government to call a conference 'at the earliest possible suitable date to consider definite lines of co-operation for the naval defence of the Empire.'[100]

The British government had been working on a similar proposal and before the Australian message reached London, a British invitation arrived in Melbourne. The two cables must have crossed in mid-ocean. The widespread excitement and apprehension aroused by the 'Dreadnought' affair, the Canadian Prime Minister's suggestion in Ottawa for consultation and Australian plans for an independent naval force had precipitated the British government into summoning a defence conference for the late summer of 1909.[101] The Labor government promptly accepted the invitation.

## The Imperial defence conference, 1909

When, following the consummation of the anti-Labor union, Deakin on 2 June took office as head of a Fusion government, he reaffirmed Australia's willingness to attend the defence conference. In preparing for the conference, Deakin had to wrestle with two tricky questions; firstly, what to do about the promised gift of a Dreadnought and secondly, whom to send as Australia's representative. Though the public interest had slackened, the obligation incurred by fusion had to be formally discharged and in a carefully worded cable, Deakin on behalf of the Commonwealth government offered the Empire 'an Australian Dreadnought or such addition to its naval strength as may be determined after consultation with the naval and military conference in London.'[102] Deakin had had second thoughts about the good sense of providing a Dreadnought for Britain which would not contribute in any direct way to Australian defence. He thus hoped

---

[99] *SMH*, 19 April 1909.

[100] Letter, M. Shepherd, Prime Minister's Secretary, to the Governor-general's Official Secretary, 29 April 1909, CP 290/15/1. The cable was transmitted to the CO on 1 May 1909.

[101] Cable, Crewe to Dudley, sent 30 April 1909 and received 1 May 1909, ibid.

[102] Cable, Dudley to Crewe, 4 June 1909, CO 418/70/375. Deakin, pursuing his interpretation of constitutional relations, addressed the message to the British Prime Minister 'as President of the Imperial Conference' much to the annoyance of the Colonial Office; also in CofA, *Parliamentary Papers*, 1909 session, Vol. II, Pt 2, No. 64, 'Correspondence and Papers relating to a Conference with Representatives of the Self-Governing Dominions on the Naval and Military Defence of the Empire'.

that, by delaying any decision until the conference, some way could be found to exploit the offer for the purpose of strengthening imperial defences in the Pacific. In a personal cable, the governor-general explained Deakin's position. If the money could be spent on naval vessels for the South Pacific, then the 'Australian government would be relieved of considerable difficulty and would be able to harmonize a patriotic offer with local prejudice'.[103]

Who to send to the conference was an equally perplexing problem. In those early days of the anti-Labor fusion it was impossible for Deakin to hand over the leadership of the government to his erstwhile enemies. Cook, the defence minister, and Forrest, the treasurer, had similar reservations about leaving Australia at that time. Moreover, Deakin did not wish the Commonwealth to be represented by men whose views, at least in the past, had diverged significantly from his own. The choice, in the event, fell on Colonel J. F. G. Foxton, an honorary minister and member for Brisbane. Though new to office, Foxton had an interest in the subject. He owed his selection to Deakin and carried out his instructions faithfully. He kept the prime minister fully and continuously informed of the conference proceedings and so enabled Deakin to keep in close touch with the negotiations being undertaken in Whitehall. Captain Creswell and Colonel Bridges, the Chief of Intelligence, accompanied Foxton as technical advisers.

Naval defence was the major topic before the conference, and the Admiralty placed before the Dominion representatives a revolutionary plan for local naval units and imperial naval co-operation. Though the origin of this novel scheme is still to some degree shrouded in mystery, some of the factors leading up to its adoption seem clear. Despite the outcry over Germany's supposed challenge to the Royal Navy's superiority in capital ships, the British government had been compelled by the tensions in Japanese-American relations, by the problems over Japanese immigration in Canada and by the Australian fears of Japan's intentions and ambitions to reappraise the Anglo-Japanese alliance and to reconsider the adequacy of British naval defences in the Pacific. On 29 June 1909, the Committee of Imperial Defence decided that so long as the Anglo-Japanese alliance was in force, British possessions in the Far East were secure. However, looking towards its termination they agreed that care should be taken to reinforce naval forces in the Far East well before that date since any sudden increase after the expiration of the treaty would be seen as a hostile act. And, of course, even if the building of battle-cruisers for this purpose was begun immediately, they would not be ready for service until 1912 or 1913, only two years or so before the end of the existing treaty.[104]

At the same time, the Admiralty in pondering how best to incorporate Dominion demands for local naval forces into an imperial framework, had come to the conclusion, contrary to their earlier opinion, that each of the Dominions or group of Dominions should obtain 'a distinct fleet unit' comprising an armoured cruiser, three light cruisers, six destroyers, three submarines plus auxiliaries. Through this meant the Dominions would be able to relieve the imperial fleet 'of its responsibility in distant seas'. The imperial squadrons on the Australasian, Cape and North Atlantic Stations would be replaced by an Australian and New Zealand squadron, a South African

---

[103] Cable, Dudley to Crewe, 22 July 1909, CO 418/71/52.
[104] Minutes of 102 Meeting of CID, 29 June 1909, Cab 2/2.

squadron and a Canadian squadron, each of which would be able to take care of coastal and trade defence in its area.[105] Sir John Fisher, the innovative and imaginative First Sea Lord, perhaps influenced by Australian anxieties with respect to Japan and by the Great White Fleet's triumphal progress across the Pacific, linked the two proposals. Returning to an earlier Admiralty concept of autonomous regional fleets, he suggested that the Dominion units along with refurbished British squadrons on the East Indies and China stations should form an Imperial Pacific Fleet which would ultimately achieve the same supremacy in the Far East that the British navy already possessed in the Atlantic and the North Sea. On 3 August the Admiralty surprised the Dominions with this proposal and subsequently it became the central focus for debate and decision at the imperial defence conference.

The essence of the Admiralty plan was 'a remodelling of the squadrons in the Far Eastern waters on the basis of establishing a Pacific Fleet'. The fleet was to be made up of an East Indies, a China, an Australian and possibly a Canadian unit. Each unit was to consist of a battle-cruiser of an improved Dreadnought or 'Indomitable' type, three second class cruisers of the 'Bristol' type, six River class destroyers and three 'C' class submarines. Foxton welcomed the scheme and explained his enthusiasm for it in strictly Australian terms.

> There is always present with us in Australia — and the same remarks apply with equal force to New Zealand — the fact that we are in close proximity to the teeming millions of two great Asiatic powers, and although at present everything is as one could wish from the Australian and New Zealand point of view, we have to look far into the future, and there might be possibilities in that connection which it is necessary for us to make provision for.

It was, perhaps out of deference to the British setting, a temperate exposition of the 'Commonwealth Crisis', but it was clear and to the point. McKenna acknowledged this and in reply asserted that 'It was by these means that the Dominions would be able to cooperate most materially in solving the whole problem of Far Eastern defence.'[106]

Each Dominion reacted differently to the Admiralty's scheme. Because the interests and outlook of the self-governing colonies were so disparate, the British authorities had to negotiate separately with each one. The Canadians, sheltering under the Monroe Doctrine, were concerned neither about Atlantic nor Pacific dangers. Thus they had a low key attitude to the conference. The Canadian representatives rejected the idea of a fleet unit stationed in the Pacific. Rather they thought that, if their parliament could be persuaded to establish a local naval force, it would be made up of light cruisers and destroyers and divided equally between their two ocean littorals. New Zealand accepted the general scheme with some reluctance. Sir Joseph Ward, the Dominion's premier, regretted the concession to national independence. He had not shifted one iota from the 'One Empire, One Flag, One Fleet' position. He considered that contributions to the Royal Navy

---

[105] 'Memorandum by Admiralty for consideration of CID sub-committee, Overseas Defence Committee, July 13, 1909', Cab 17/78; 'Admiralty Memorandum concerning 1909 Imperial Defence Conference for consideration by CID, July 20, 1909', Co, Confidential Print, Dominions No. 16, CO 886/2.

[106] 'Imperial Defence Conference, Minutes of Proceedings', CO, Confidential Print, Dominions, No. 5, CO 886/2, 5 August 1909 meeting, pp. 44–6.

was still the preferable course. Foxton, at Deakin's behest, pressed Ward to join with the Commonwealth in providing an Australasian fleet unit, but to no avail. Ward preferred to have the New Zealand Dreadnought gift used as the flagship for the China Station fleet unit and to continue to pay £100,000 subsidy direct to the Royal Navy.[107]

Australia more than any other Dominion found the Admiralty's scheme tailored to its needs. Foxton had, from the outset, approved 'their general tenor' and Deakin had confirmed his action. Creswell, who had been wedded to a destroyer flotilla, was easily convinced that a naval unit as part of a 'Far Eastern or Pacific Fleet' offered Australia greater security.[108] Looking at the conflicting advice tendered the Commonwealth by the Admiralty from 1906, in which they had argued, on each occasion with equal assurance, that firstly submersibles, then destroyers and finally a fleet unit centred on battle cruisers were the only sensible form for local naval defence to take, it is surprising that the Admiralty's credibility on technical questions was not seriously undermined. The history of the Admiralty's approach to Australian defence does illustrate the frequently political and often accidental nature of 'expert' opinion, no matter how much experience and authority might seem to sustain it. Foxton, in accordance with his instructions, protested at the Admiralty's desire to take automatic control of the Australian navy in time of war and demanded that when the fleet units came together, the senior naval officer, whether British or Australian, should take command. Further, at Deakin's insistence, Foxton pressed for interchangeability for officers and men between the Australian naval force and the Royal Navy in order to give Australian officers a wider experience and the prospects of a career with larger horizons.[109]

As a result of Foxton's meetings with McKenna, Sir John Fisher, W. Graham Greene and Sir C. L. Ottley, the secretary to the Committee of Imperial Defence, it was agreed that Australia should acquire a fleet unit as specified by the Admiralty memorandum. The capital cost of the unit was put at £3,695,000 and the annual cost, including interest on a loan for purchase of the ships, at £750,000. The Commonwealth was to continue to pay the £200,000 subsidy under the Naval

---

[107] Telegram, Deakin to Foxton, 12 August 1909, Deakin Papers, 1540/1/472; Foxton reported on his return 'I urged upon him [Ward] the desirability of New Zealand throwing in its lot with the Commonwealth and joining in the responsibility for a truly Australasian fleet unit but unsuccessfully.' Ward had 'pinned his faith to the Royal Navy, one and indivisible, on which as he put it, New Zealand must continue to rely for immunity from external aggression' (SMH, 5 November 1909). Not all leading New Zealand politicians agreed with Ward. Colonel James Allen, who became defence minister in William Massey's Reform Government of 1912 said on 11 June 1909, 'I am one with the Australians in believing that we have a duty to do in the Pacific... I ask honorable members to think whether there is not something more for us to do — whether the Australians are not upon the right lines' (NZ, *Parliamentary Debates*, Vol. 146, p. 60. See also Herries, who became Minister of Railways and Native Affairs, ibid., p. 161, 14 June 1909). This was the substance of the agreement which the Admiralty reached with New Zealand at the Conference. (CofA, *Parliamentary Papers*, 1909 session, Vol. II, No. 64).

[108] Letter, Foxton to Deakin, 13 August 1909, Deakin Papers, 1540/1/473; cable, Foxton to Deakin, 4 August 1909 and cable, Foxton to Deakin, 11 August 1909, Deakin Papers, 1540/38/460.

[109] Deakin to Foxton, 12 August 1909, Deakin Papers, 1540/1/472.

Agreement until it expired in 1913, at which time it was expected that the new fleet unit would be ready to take over responsibility for the Australian station. Since the Admiralty was being relieved of the financial burden of the Australian station, the British government agreed to pay £250,000 annually towards the upkeep of the Australian unit until the Commonwealth government felt able to bear the full cost. The £250,000 represented roughly the interest on the loan which the Commonwealth had agreed to raise in order to finance the building programme. The Australians won their point with respect to control. Ultimately the Admiralty had to yield to the principle that he who pays the piper calls the tune. The Dominion navy would not come under Admiralty control in peace or war without the Commonwealth government's consent.[110] Even on interchangeability of personnel Foxton made some progress but this was a more intricate problem and was left over for more detailed negotiations.[111] For the Australians, though, the most important outcome of the conference was the British assurance, repeated in the minutes of Foxton's meeting with the Admiralty, that the Dominion's fleet unit was to 'form part of the Eastern Fleet of the Empire to be composed of similar units of the Royal Navy, to be known as the China and East Indies units.'[112] On 26 August the British prime minister, in reporting to parliament on the Conference, publicly confirmed this commitment to reinforce and reconstruct these squadrons as part of a Pacific fleet.[113]

The British decision to join with Australia in creating a Pacific fleet along the lines enunciated in the Admiralty paper was to prove greatly embarrassing and to become the cause of much ill-feeling and many testy exchanges in the years immediately preceding the outbreak of World War I. That the British government did enter into such a compact is incontrovertible. Why they should have assumed such an obligation is, however, more difficult to establish. Under the agreement the British promised that within four years they would, at the cost of more than £5,500,000, provide

---

[110] Cable, Deakin to Foxton, 19 September 1909, Deakin Papers, 1540/38/460. In this cable Deakin on behalf of the Cabinet accepted the principles of the agreement which Foxton had negotiated with the Admiralty. On the relation of the Australian unit to the Royal Navy Deakin wrote, 'Offer of our unit always certain on outbreak of war'. However, Deakin in conformity with Foxton's agreement with the Admiralty understood that this would be an offer to join the Far Eastern Fleet and that the senior officer whether British or Australian would assume command. The question of supreme direction of the Far Eastern Fleet was not explored. Deakin seizing the opportunity to develop imperial institutions sought Australian representation on the 'Imperial Council of Defence' in order that the Australian government might be able to prepare properly for emergencies, 'forewarned is forearmed'.

[111] Cable, Foxton to Deakin, sent 24 September and received 25 September 1909, Deakin Papers, 1540/38/460. Foxton was able to announce that McKenna conceded 'the principle of full interchange — that personnel Australian fleets will be ex officio members of Royal Navy and vice versa but actual exchange must be by arrangement mutually between two Admiralties.' He was unable to make any progress with the 'political' question of Australian representation on the Committee of Imperial Defence. Deakin had to make do with an assurance that 'Australia, as a matter of course would be confidentially informed through the Colonial Secretary of any impending foreign difficulties necessitating precautionary preparation.'

[112] CofA, *Parliamentary Papers*, 1909 session, Vol. II, No. 64.

[113] Great Britain, 5 *Parliamentary Debates* (Commons), IX, 2311, 26 August 1909.

for Pacific naval defence, one battle cruiser of the Indomitable class for the East Indies station — New Zealand was contributing the battle cruiser for the China Station — six light cruisers of the Bristol class, twelve River class destroyers and six 'C' class submarines. Given the financial strain involved in keeping up with Germany's naval building programme it is not easy to explain how the Admiralty and, even more the British government, came to take on such an additional burden.

There were, as already noted, a number of factors such as Japanese-American tensions, Australian anxieties about Asia and a desire to reassert British prestige in the Far East, which had prompted the Admiralty to conceive the notion of a 'Pacific Fleet'. What Sir John Fisher who claimed to have coined the phrase 'Pacific Fleet' had in mind was to see 'eventually Canada, Australia, New Zealand, the Cape (that is, South Africa), and India *running a complete Navy!* We manage the job in Europe. They'll manage it against the Yankees, Japs and Chinese, as occasion requires out there!'[114] In the meantime the Admiralty by its own example had to set the scene for such a development. To this end Fisher could assure Esher that 'the 3 "New Testament" ships with their attendant satellites will be in the Pacific in 1913'. Writing to the naval correspondent of *The Times* in 1910, Fisher again exulted over his dream of restoring British naval hegemony throughout the world. '*The keel is laid* (though no one knows it) of that great Pacific Fleet, which is to be in the Pacific what our Home Fleet is in the Atlantic and North Sea — *the Mistress of that Ocean as our Home Fleet is of the Atlantic*'.[115] It seems indeed probable that 'The Pacific Fleet' was Fisher's bright idea and that it was his eloquent advocacy which in a decisive moment committed the British government. Fisher's enthusiasm for the first time had outrun his judgement. When he retired as First Sea Lord in 1910, the momentum behind the scheme ebbed, the problems surfaced and a heated Anglo-Australian controversy over naval defence in the Pacific ensued.

### The making of an Australian defence force

When the Fusion government came to office in the winter of 1909, defence matters were pressing. Though four years had passed since Deakin's call to vigilance, his 'Be prepared' speech of 1905, nothing substantial had been done. Among the party leaders there had evolved a consensus in favour of both an independent naval force and compulsory military training. Plans had been laid, policies announced and bills introduced into parliament but for one reason or another, the exigencies of domestic politics or the effects of British procrastination, they had never been carried through into legislation. The union of the anti-Labor forces did much to eliminate the jockeying for political advantage and office which had so marred the processes of parliamentary government during the first decade of the Commonwealth. The Fusion ministry had an assured majority and was able to turn its attention more confidently to implementing policy.

Though the Imperial Defence Conference had put the question of sea defence back into the melting pot, land defence was not so affected. Imperial military co-operation was discussed at the

---

[114] Letter, Sir John Fisher to Viscount Esher, 13 September 1909, Marder (ed.), *Fear God and Dread Nought*, Vol. II, p. 266.

[115] Letter, Fisher to Gerald Fiennes, 14 April 1910, ibid., Vol. II, p. 321.

conference. However, since military matters did not involve issues of control and external policy, the decisions arrived at were limited in their extent. Once again the conference had agreed on the desirability of having uniformity in organization, administration, training, discipline, arms, equipment and stores, so that if the Dominion should decide to furnish troops to fight alongside those of the Mother Country in time of war, they would be able to move into place quickly and easily. The conference also expanded on the 1907 decision to set up a so-called Imperial General Staff. Local branches were to be established, Dominion officers attached to the Imperial General Staff and discussions on co-operation and strategy encouraged.

Unlike any other general staff the Imperial General Staff had no decision-making powers. It was simply the shell remaining from War Office schemes seeking an effective integration of imperial forces. The conference offered no guidance as to the nature of the military defence which each Dominion should adopt. That was, as the Dominions had always insisted, left to each government to determine in the light of its own circumstances.[116]

Deakin, perhaps to meet the objections of some of the 'doubters' in his coalition government, had asked Lord Kitchener, the most prestigious military figure in the empire, to visit Australia and advise on the Commonwealth's military requirements.[117] Kitchener accepted but could not reach Australia until December.[118] Neither Deakin nor the Labor opposition[119] nor the press[120] were

---

[116] CofA, *Parliamentary Papers*, Session 1909, No. 64.

[117] Telegram, Dudley to Crewe, 14 June 1909, CO 418/70/386.

[118] Copy, telegram, Kitchener to Deakin, 10 July 1909, and telegram, Kitchener to Deakin, September 1909, Deakin Papers, 1540/38/459. Deakin also wished to gain Kitchener's support for Australia's Pacific-centred strategic analysis. He sought to obtain a powerful friend at court whose authority could be invoked in the continuing debate with the CID and the CDC over Australia's defence requirements. In an undated memorandum on 'Questions relating to Australian Defence on which is needed the Advice of the Highest Authorities' he asked Kitchener whether 'In view of —

1. The change in the relative strengths and disposition of the Naval and Military forces of nations in Eastern Waters since, 1906,

2. The change in the armaments of battleship during the last 5 years,

3. The development of the "Imperial Idea ..."

4. The conclusions of the Imperial Conference on Defence, 1909,' the Commonwealth government should 'in its ... future policy modify the applications of the principles enumerated by the CID in its Memo of May 1906 especially in respect to the following matters

(a) The nature and strength of the PROBABLE form of attack to which Australia is liable.

(b) The nature and strength of the POSSIBLE form of attack to which Australia is liable', Deakin Papers, 1540/38/459. Deakin had already committed himself to a defence policy which was based on an Australian threat perception and which ignored the CID's advice. Nevertheless he recognized that it would be tactically useful to have Kitchener's approval of Australian policy and also to acquire a sympathetic advocate of the Australian viewpoint in London.

[119] *CPD*, LI, 3523, 16 September 1909.

[120] *SMH*, 15 September 1909, 'The demand to be satisfied is definite and imperative' and 'Delay is dangerous and it will not be easily tolerated by public opinion.' See also *Age*, 29 September 1909.

willing to delay further and on 21 September the Minister for Defence, Joseph Cook, introduced a bill to provide for compulsory military training.

Cook admitted that he was new to the job. Yet in speaking on the bill he took the opportunity to give the house a comprehensive survey of the government's defence policy, naval and military, and to set out very fully the strategic reasons underpinning that policy. Australia could not help but notice 'the development of armed forces in the Pacific region and the unequal distribution of these forces'. Comparing naval strengths of the different powers, he noted that while Japan had fifteen battleships and America had one battleship and eleven battle cruisers in the Pacific, Britain was represented, in terms of capital ships, by only four outdated battle cruisers.[121] Moreover, he added, scarcely disguising his reference to the Japanese, that there were 'not far from our shores … two or three million of the best trained troops in the world', troops which belonged to a nation 'whose ideals are in many respects as unlike our own as it is possible for them to be'. Since Britain relied on the Anglo-Japanese treaty to protect imperial interests in the Far East, Australia was 'absolutely dependent' on this alliance, that is, on the good faith of the Japanese. When Andrew Fisher interjected that the treaty would be honoured only 'so long as it suits the parties as is the case with every treaty', Cook put the Australian position more candidly, even if for diplomatic reasons understating it somewhat. 'No nation', he replied, 'depends entirely for its security upon treaties and this is our position at the moment'. He went on to say that 'Australia is the most distant, the richest and at the same time the most vulnerable part of the British Empire. … We are surrounded by nations hungry for room and breathing space.' It was a classical exposition of the Australian crisis. All the elements were present. Japan, a nation alien in race and culture, was the dominant power in the region. British naval power was weak and the Anglo-Japanese alliance upon which the British set so much store was no adequate substitute. Australians would not put their trust in alliances or Japan. The Commonwealth was exposed to danger and was, hopefully, in conjunction with the rest of the empire, intent on taking action to meet the threat.

With respect to naval defence Cook endorsed the agreement reached at the conference by which Australia would take responsibility for one of the units in the empire's projected Pacific Fleet. On military defence, the immediate object of the bill before the house, the government proposed the compulsory training of youths and young men from fourteen to twenty years of age. They were to undergo training for sixteen days each year. Those not substantially of European origin or descent were excluded from the scheme. Presumably the government was not willing to take chances with 'the enemy' within their doors. Fox in 'The Commonwealth Crisis' had remarked on the uncertain loyalty of Aborigines in defending Australia against Asian invaders. The trained men were to remain on an active reserve, through one day annual musters, until they were twenty-six. It was understood that the scheme would be reviewed after Kitchener had reported on Australia's military needs. The cost of this measure for providing a first and second line military force of 66,000 men would rise from £1,407,000 in 1910–11 to £1,742,000 in 1914–15

---

[121] Compare T. A. Brassey (ed.), *The Naval Annual*, pp. 49 and 56–8.

when it would be fully operational.[122] This represented not only a 30 per cent to 50 per cent increase over the Ewing-Deakin scheme of November 1908, and the Fisher-Pearce scheme of March 1909, but also more than a 100 per cent increase over military expenditure for 1908–9.[123] When the cost of the naval policy was added to that of the military, it could be seen that the Commonwealth government was undertaking to raise its defence expenditure by more than 200 per cent. This willingness to accept such a vast increase in defence costs was an earnest of the government's concern for national security.

There was little opposition to the principle of the bill either inside or outside parliament. Two conservatives in the House of Representatives expressed a blind faith in Britain and saw the bill as a vote of no confidence in the Mother Country. There had been a debate in the Labor Caucus over the compulsory principle as it appeared in the government's bill but by a vote of fifteen to nine it was agreed that the party should support the principle. Indeed, the caucus went further and proposed an amendment which would require young men from twenty to twenty-six to spend seven days in camp each year instead of the one day muster proposed by the government.[124] In parliament, King O'Malley, bemoaning the military madness which, as he saw it, had the country in its grip, was the only opposition speaker to deplore the principle of the bill.[125] Hughes applauded the government's action but thought it did not go far enough. Cook's plan would produce 'an army of children'. Hughes wanted the compulsory training to begin with adults and to extend through to the age of twenty-six.[126] With some minor amendments the bill passed both houses on a voice vote and was finally sent to the governor-general in December.[127] After a five-year struggle compulsory military training had become law.[128]

Deakin and Cook waited until the return of Foxton from London before seeking parliamentary sanction for their naval policy. There could be little opposition. For the former subsidy, 'One Empire, One Flag, One Navy', meant the fact that the Admiralty had sponsored the agreement was enough to quell any doubts about its propriety, and for those Protectionists and Labor men, who had led in the campaign for an Australian navy, the promise of a more substantial British presence in the Pacific, of an imperial fleet instead of just a coastal flotilla, more than made up for any vague misgivings about the loss of national identity. In the debate over the defence bill, Fisher and Hughes had expressed the fears that control over the fleet unit would not be vested in the Commonwealth. They lingered lovingly over the unquestioned national

---

[122] *CPD*, LI, 3607–36, 21 September 1909. For a copy of the memorandum distributed to members of parliament, see *SMH*, 22 September 1909. Cook showed enterprise as defence minister. On 1 September, he offered a prize of £5,000 for the inventor and designer of the best aircraft 'suitable for military purposes'. *SMH*, 2 September 1909.

[123] *Official Year Book*, No. 17, 1924, p. 595. See Appendix B.

[124] ALP Federal Caucus Minutes, II, 115–17, meetings of 13 and 14 October 1909.

[125] *CPD*, LII, 4691, 19 October 1909.

[126] *CPD*, LII, 4461, 13 October 1909, see also similar criticisms offered by the executive committee of the Australian National Defence League, *SMH*, 7 October 1909.

[127] *CPD*, LIV, 7109, 7 December 1909.

[128] CofA, Act No. 69 of 1909.

character of the Gympie policy and the rules they had drawn up to regulate Anglo-Australian naval co-operation. However, all they contended for was that the fleet units should not be sent to 'remote seas' without the Commonwealth government's consent.[129]

Cook had caused more confusion around this point than was warranted by the facts. The agreement, which Foxton had secured, reserved to the Commonwealth government the right to dispose the Australian naval force as it saw fit whether in peace or war. Cook, however, had been reported as saying at Lady Best's Melbourne 'salon' that 'There could be but one navy with one discipline and one control.'[130] In parliament in so far as he said anything clearly on this topic, it was not too dissimilar from Fisher's Imperial gesture at the time of the 'naval scare', that is 'When danger threatened the Mother Country Australian resources would be placed at the disposal of the Empire.' And on 24 November the Labor leaders rallied to Cook's resolution approving the new scheme of naval defence and urging 'immediate steps to provide the proposed Australian unit of the Eastern Fleet of the Empire'. The motion was carried thirty-nine to nine in the House and, as one of the Labor dissidents later explained, they voted against the motion, not because they opposed the resolution but simply as a protest against the gagging of the debate.[131]

The Naval Loan Bill which followed hard on the heels of the House's resolution did not receive the same bipartisan support. The Fusion government wished to finance the naval unit from a London loan which would be paid back over sixteen years. The Labor party, consistent with the 1908 Federal Conference decision, opposed such a non-productive loan. Fisher claimed that the financing of defence by loans instead of direct taxation as well as the acceptance of £250,000 subsidy from the British government showed little pride in the Australian nation.[132] More significantly some Labor men took the opportunity to ventilate their suspicion of the new naval policy which had been stifled in the earlier debate on the naval scheme emerging from the London Conference. They questioned whether it would provide an effective protection of Australian interests. They wondered whether it might not be a wily ruse on the part of the British in order to gain further reserves for the defence of their home islands. Senator Pearce was the most vocal, asking whether this new scheme did not amount to a disguised contribution. Citing Percival A. Hislam's *The Admiralty of the Atlantic: An Enquiry into the Development of German Sea Power, Past, Present and Prospective*,[133] he showed that, despite the growth of the Royal Navy in recent years, there were fewer British capital ships in distant waters. To his mind, Hislam had proved conclusively the feeble nature of the Anglo-Japanese alliance. Hislam's warnings about the

---

[129] *CPD*, LII, 4460–3, 13 October 1909.

[130] *Age*, 14 September 1909.

[131] *CPD*, LIV, 6251–9, 24 November 1909.

[132] *CPD*, LIV, 6656–64, 2 December 1909; William Webster (Labor, Gwydir, NSW) asserted that 'They are handing the Commonwealth over for the first time into the hands of the Jew moneylender'. This was an exceptional reference to the international Jewish financial conspiracy and Robert Harper, a Victorian merchant who held Mernda for the Protectionists, denied the charge and repudiated the aspersions on the Jewish people. Ibid., 6774.

[133] London 1908, see especially pp. 29–30, 154, 177–9.

grave dangers of a German-Japanese alliance—that such a conjunction of European and Asian power posed the greatest threat to the Empire—had to be heeded for it was evident that the Admiralty could not spare the number of warships which would be needed to repulse a Japanese attack against Australia.[134] By traversing such familiar territory Pearce did not intend a serious criticism of the scheme as it stood. Rather he wished to warn future Australian and British governments against deviating from its professed aim, namely the protection of British interests in the Pacific. The Naval Loan bill was passed over Labor objections. And before parliament rose, the Admiralty had been asked to arrange for the construction of the flagship of the Australian navy,[135] the battlecruiser *Australia* and in March 1910 the tender was accepted. Deakin, in his last few months in office, had after much travail finally placed on the statute book legislation providing for the establishment of a substantial Australian defence force.

## Deakin's diplomacy and the search for American protection

Deakin's experience with defence and imperial problems had revealed to him the intricate relationship between defence and foreign policy. Since nearly all Australian diplomacy was conducted with or through London, it was felt to be important that the Commonwealth should be well-represented at the centre of the empire. A majority of political leaders had been agreed since Federation on the need to set up a High Commissioner's office in London; Fisher had included it as an aim of the Labor movement in his Gympie speech. But as with defence, for one reason or another, it had been postponed. As with defence, the Fusion government found that the time was ripe for such a measure and in September 1909, a bill for this purpose was introduced. In the debate the major talking point for Labor was that the salary should be sufficient to enable a good man of slender means to hold the post. A few muttered that the appointee should be a 'true Australian', who would be impervious to the 'coquetry' of London clubs.[136] On the whole though Labor exhibited little isolationist feeling and the bill was carried easily in both houses.

In December, Deakin appointed George Reid as Australia's first High Commissioner. Reid's translation to London could be seen as a reward for his acquiescence in the fusion of the Free Trade and Protectionist parties. At the least it was a welcome relief for the Deakin-Cook coalition. Reid was out of step with the new Australia. For the same reason, however, his role in England was greatly circumscribed. Because of his past differences with Deakin and even more because of his hostility to Labor Reid did not have the confidence of the Australian government for most of the period in which he held office, namely from 1910–15. Even during Cook's brief administration there is no evidence that he had an important role in the conduct of Anglo-Australian relations. He contented himself perforce with ceremonial and administrative duties. It would be fair to remark in this connection that, with the exception of the Lyons and Menzies era prior to and during World War II, when S. M. Bruce was High Commissioner, Australian prime

---

[134] *CPD*, LIV, 6945, 4 December 1909.

[135] Cable, Dudley to Crewe, 9 December 1909. CO 418/71/513; see also for destroyer order, Cable, 29 December 1909, CO 418/71/527.

[136] *CPD*, LI, 3546, 8 September 1909.

ministers have guarded jealously their relationship with the British government and the High Commissioner has played little part in the negotiating of high policy matters.

Since 1905 Deakin's interest in imperial relations had quickened. Following the lesson learnt in the struggle to have Britain acquire the New Hebrides and in the negotiations with Japan over immigration and commercial matters, Australian leaders had, after the Battle of Tsushima and the Moroccan incident, come to sense that the empire was heading for a moment of trial and, in preparing for that day, the British government, in order to ensure the security of the United Kingdom, was stripping 'the outer empire', as Whitehall saw it, of effective imperial protection. Spurred on by these considerations, Deakin tried without success at the 1907 Colonial Conference to gain for the self-governing colonies direct access to the policy-making processes so that they could share in the framing of imperial policy. He had hoped thereby to compel the British government in developing its defence and foreign policy to take more seriously the situation of the Pacific Dominions. The American-Japanese war scare of 1907–8 and the Anglo-German naval rivalry of 1909 had intensified and clarified this Australian sense of strategic vulnerability. The naval agreement which emerged from the Imperial Defence Conference offered some comfort and was seen as a step in the right direction. However, even at best, the Pacific Fleet, as envisaged by the Admiralty, would not be built and on station until 1913 and even then it would be no match for the Japanese navy.

Deakin, pondering these problems, finally turned to diplomacy in an attempt to find an alternative or, more probably, additional means of providing against the threat from the north. He had had this object in mind in inviting the American fleet to visit Australia in 1908, and a year later, when the press reported that Americans contemplated a second world cruise he was inspired to try to give some substance to his notion of a Pacific 'entente cordiale'. To this end on 27 September 1909, he wrote to Lord Crewe suggesting 'an Agreement for an extension of the Monroe Doctrine to all the countries around the Pacific Ocean supported by the guarantees of the British Empire, Holland, France and China added to that of the United States'.[137] In effect, Deakin wanted the United States, joined by other friendly powers, to underwrite the existing political and territorial *status quo* in the Pacific.

This 'proposition of the highest international importance', as Deakin described it, came six days after Cook had spoken to the second reading of the Defence bill and undoubtedly the timing of Deakin's diplomatic initiative was in part a consequence of the care and attention which the government had been giving defence matters. Even more immediately Deakin's letter to Crewe followed a question from O'Malley in the House concerning press rumours that the Americans

---

[137] Copy of letter, Deakin to Crewe, 27 September 1909 enclosed with letter, Crewe to Sir Edward Grey, 3 November 1909, FO 800/91. The original cannot be found in the CO records. However, there is an identical draft, dated 27 September 1909 in Deakin's handwriting in the Deakin Papers, ms. 1540. Deakin had written to Crewe direct, bypassing both the Governor-general and the Colonial Office. It is noteworthy that Deakin did not distinguish friends and enemies in terms of race. China, though not a white nation was welcome as an initial signatory to the Agreement. Germany, though a European power, was not.

intended sending their Atlantic fleet on a second tour of the Pacific.[138] Deakin was 'delighted' by the thought but at that stage had not read the reports. Had Deakin in the next day or two checked the newspapers, he would have seen that the *New York American* story, which the Australian press was carrying, mentioned not only a projected fleet visit, but also that 'at the back of it all is a Japanese decision to denounce the existing treaty with the United States in order to formulate new demands on America'.[139] If he were not already aware of the Root-Takahira agreement of November 1908, which was obviously the treaty referred to, then it would not have been difficult to unearth a copy of the text since it was widely published and discussed at the time it was signed.[140] From such elementary research, any shrewd mind which accepted the accuracy of the *New York American's* report would have perceived that that was a propitious moment to seek a diplomatic accord with the United States.

A study of the text of the letter itself does seem to confirm this interpretation. In the first place, the Deakin scheme was directed against Japan or against the possibility of a German-Japanese alliance. He declared that it would 'serve to some extent the present interests of every country affected except perhaps Japan and Germany.' These two countries were not initially to be invited to adhere to the Pacific pact. Deakin could scarcely have expected the United States to enter into such a discriminatory arrangement unless its own understanding with Japan had been broken off. The proposal also did not contemplate a technically difficult alliance treaty, but rather an executive 'Agreement' after the pattern of the Root-Takahira notes. Finally, the Deakin 'Agreement', like the Japanese-American one, was designed pre-eminently to preserve the existing power balance in the Pacific though now under the overarching principle of the Monroe Doctrine.

In England neither the Colonial Office nor the Foreign Office had any sympathy with the proposal. They saw it as another example of Deakin's meddling in things that were better left to those who knew their business. From the time of the New Hebrides affair, through the local navy controversy and the 1907 Imperial Conference to the visit of the American fleet, the British authorities had been troubled by Deakin's enterprise and tenacity. The Asquith government, beset round by grave problems at home and abroad, did not wish to add to these problems by opening up the field of Dominion diplomacy. The Liberals, the so-called Imperialists and Little Englanders alike, were conservative paternalists in their attitude to the Dominions and were quite unwilling to try to understand the Australian point of view until forced to do so. They would not consent, except under the greatest pressure, to reconsider their own defence and alliance systems so as to take into account the needs and concerns of 'Greater Britain beyond the seas'. Lord Crewe in sending on 'this curious letter' to Sir Edward Grey expressed this view succinctly when he told the Foreign Secretary that 'Personally, I rather dread a concrete discussion between Australia and ourselves on these subjects.'[141]

---

[138] *CPD*, LI, 3771–2, 24 September 1909.

[139] *Age*, 18 September 1909.

[140] *Age*, 30 November 1908; *SMH*, 30 November and 4 December 1908.

[141] Letter, Crewe to Grey, 3 November 1909, FO 800/91.

Grey expressed no opinion on the value of the proposal as such either in terms of imperial or Australian interests. Nor, strangely, did he suggest America's likely reaction — there is no evidence that American opinion was ever sounded. Rather he elaborated on the shortcomings which the Foreign Office saw in the scheme as it stood. He was providing the Colonial Office with ammunition that it could throw back at Deakin. The Foreign Office noted that Japan and Germany could not be excluded from the initial negotiations; otherwise an ally would be offended and Germany alienated. The proposal was also seen to be too inflexible since it would prevent Britain—and Grey took an example which touched Deakin nearly—from acquiring the New Hebrides from France without first gaining the consent of the United States and the other signatory nations. Such a procedure would be 'tiresome'.[142]

Crewe repeated these arguments at more length and with some additions of his own when he replied to Deakin on 15 December. He prefaced his comments with a short homily on the nature of the Monroe Doctrine.

> One had to remember, that the so-called principle is really only an assertion, which those who advance it are presumably prepared to back by force. We acquiesce in it generally because it suits us to do so, but I don't know that we should agree to every application which the United States might conceivably choose to make of it. You will remember how nearly we came to blows with them over the Venezuelan boundary question.

After listing the British objections as set out by the Foreign Office, he concluded, 'I certainly do not want to press unduly the obstacles to a project which might be the subject of endless discussion.' If Deakin should 'have a spare moment to develop further the idea of the arrangement', Crewe said that he would be happy to continue the correspondence.[143] The British government's response had been correct but discouraging. Certainly the objections which it put forward were well-founded. On the other hand, the British officials had not indicated whether they would under any circumstances be willing to entertain such a scheme and, if so, what amendments would be required in order to secure their support. Dreading 'concrete discussion', they hoped to shunt the idea off into the limbo of 'endless discussion'.

However, before Deakin could take the discussion a step further, the Fusion government was defeated by Labor in the election of April 1910, and lost office. Though Andrew Fisher did come to espouse similar views about an Anglo-Saxon 'entente' or alliance, he made no attempt to prick the British government into taking action nor did he lay before it any precise project designed to achieve that goal. No other Australian leader down to World War I had the imperial 'boldness' of Deakin or the tenacity to venture into what was for colonials 'the uncharted sea' of international diplomacy. This was Deakin's last term as prime minister and, with his fading from the political scene, the Pacific pact proposal disappeared also to vex the Whitehall mandarins no more.

These were Deakin's years. Since 1905, apart from the brief Labor interregnum in 1908–9, he had presided over Australia's defence and foreign policy. Deakin had had the leading role in alerting Australia to the new international situation which followed from Japan's victory over

---

[142] Letter, Grey to Crewe, 11 November 1909, ibid.
[143] Letter, Crewe to Deakin, 15 December 1909, Deakin Papers, 1540/2/1340

Russia in 1905 and from Germany's naval challenge to Great Britain. From 1907 to 1909 a political and popular consensus had gathered around this new strategic perspective, a perspective which for the first time assumed, as a serious possibility, an invasion of Australia and moreover an invasion which would be launched by an Asian power. As a result, Deakin had with the support of all parties implemented a far-reaching programme of defence and diplomacy. In December 1907, he adopted compulsory military training as government policy and in 1909, under his aegis, compulsory militia-style training for young men aged eighteen to twenty-six years of age became law. Australia was the first English-speaking nation to adopt a law compelling compulsory military service in peacetime. From August 1905 he had pressed the Admiralty to co-operate in establishing a local naval force and in 1909, partly as a result of his solicitations, the Admiralty promised to help create a 'Pacific Fleet' in which the Australian navy would become an autonomous unit.

Turning to diplomacy, Deakin had sought to persuade the United States, as an Anglo-Saxon nation confronted similarly with a self-assertive and expansionist Japan, to take a benevolent interest in Australia's plight. Through the Pacific pact proposal he attempted in essence to have the United States fill the void left in Australia's security structure by Britain's withdrawal from the region. The same conditions which prompted Deakin to take this initiative in 1909, the felt-threat from Asia, the weakness of British power, the need for American support, became ever more distinct with the passage of time and, with the exception perhaps of the nineteen-twenties, have remained at least until very recently the central concerns of Australian foreign policy. At the 1937 Imperial Conference, the then prime minister, Joseph Lyons, put forward a Pacific pact scheme very much like its 1909 precursor. External Affairs minister, Dr H. V. Evatt, at the end of World War II made overtures to the Americans for a similar defence alliance. The 1952 Anzus pact, which was consummated under a somewhat different set of circumstances, has come to be regarded by Australian political leaders of all parties as vital to the Commonwealth's security. Though Deakin's plan was at the time, as he conceded himself, probably 'chimerical', nevertheless it was, in its fanciful way, a major initiative in international affairs and it did represent an attempt to reorganize and reorient imperial foreign policy and the British alliance system to meet Australian anxieties.

In a world in which the Pax Britannica was no more, a world in which new nations in Europe and Asia challenged the existing balance of power, a world in which the great powers were dividing themselves into rival camps, a world in which these same powers were arming to the teeth and in which each diplomatic incident threatened a war of each against all, Australians looking particularly at the Pacific had, not unnaturally, become alarmed at what they saw and had taken steps to provide against the evil hour. And by 1910 they felt they had achieved a reasonable promise of security.

# 7

# Labor Government, Australian Defence and the Imperial Conference of 1911

The 'Commonwealth Crisis' was not an issue in the Federal election of 13 April 1910. The great public debate about defence was over. The politicians and people had realized a consensus of views. Following its electoral victory, the Labor government set about consolidating and expanding Deakin's defence scheme and, facing up to the diplomatic dimension of defence, it began to seek the co-operation of the empire and indeed even to look to an Anglo-American partnership in order to ensure Australia's Pacific security.

## *Labor's defence programme*

In the 1910 campaign both party leaders produced similar policies on defence and external affairs. Deakin in his policy speech at Ballarat on 7 February declared that the 'foundations for Australian defence by land and sea' had been laid down. 'It is not complete', he went on 'but it is fundamental and permanent so far as it goes. It will go much further when our experience is riper.' He then spoke of the two great events in the history of Australian naval defence which had taken place in 1908–9; 'first, the visit of the American fleet, which gave a splendid object-lesson of naval power; … and the Imperial Defence Conference, which gave us a plan of united Imperial action.' And in his peroration he hinted at the problems of a London-centred foreign policy which had inspired his proposal for a Pacific pact and which he was to develop most fully in parliament on the eve of the 1911 Imperial Conference. He told his listeners,

> When we turn to the Pacific, we find that even where we have no jurisdiction we have important interests, and we are entitled to share in the Mother country's sphere of influence. With foreign Powers and coloured populations, a condominium in the New Hebrides, and the Foreign as well as the Colonial Office to deal with, we are moving in a network. But these questions occupy a good deal more time than might be supposed.[1]

Fisher, on 9 February at Maryborough, Queensland, though having less to say on defence, nevertheless declared that defence was one of two fundamental aims of the Labor party. 'Labor was in Parliament for the principle of white labour and defence', and to this he added that 'defence was only effective when money and men were found by the country intending to defend itself.' Labor was willing and determined to pay the cost of defence. Fisher tried to score off Deakin by ridiculing the Fusion offer of a Dreadnought to Britain. But events had made this kind of sally irrelevant. His only real criticisms of Deakin's defence policy were financial. In accord with Labor's view that unproductive costs such as defence should not be a burden on future

---

[1] *SMH*, 8 February 1910.

generations, he maintained that Labor would pay for the whole defence programme out of revenue, and as much as possible of the naval construction programme would be 'made in Australia'. As a matter of national pride, to remove any possible lien or control over the Australian navy, Labor would reject the £250,000 subsidy offered by the Mother Country.[2] There was no substantial defence issue at stake in the election and thus Labor's great success at the polls—it gained a comfortable majority in both houses for the first time in federal history and was the first national party to do so—must be ascribed to other reasons. It is even doubtful whether the nationalism versus imperialism issue which Fisher had vaguely tried to inject into the election played any role in the outcome.

The Labor government which took office on 29 April was much like its predecessor of a year earlier. The ministers most concerned with defence and foreign policy, Fisher, Pearce as defence minister, and Hughes as attorney-general[3] formed a very influential and determined nucleus in cabinet favouring an extended defence policy and for the most part during Labor's three years in office they had their way. Japan's annexation of Korea and interest in Manchuria, new crises in Europe—in Morocco and then in the Balkans,—renewed Japanese-American tensions, Britain's hedging over its Pacific commitment, all these factors in the external situation reinforced the convictions of the defence minded. Indeed, during this first unqualified period of Labor rule in Australian history, defence provided one of the unifying principles in a very creative legislative programme.

In office the Fisher government had to deal immediately with two defence issues. Firstly they had to decide how far they would adopt Lord Kitchener's report on Australian military defence and secondly they had to face up to the administrative and technical consequences of having an Australian navy and to settle on a policy for naval bases, training and discipline. In both cases the decisions that they made went beyond the recommendations of Kitchener and the requirements for the naval unit as set out at the 1909 Imperial Defence Conference. In both cases the Labor government took steps to strengthen further the fundamental capacity of Australia to defend itself.

Kitchener, who, as a result of Deakin's invitation had been travelling around the country and studying Australia's military forces and military needs during the mid-summer of 1909–10, presented his report in February. Kitchener's general conclusion was that 'the present forces are inadequate in numbers, training, organization, and munitions of war, to defend Australia from the dangers that are due to the present conditions that prevail in the country, as well as to its isolated position.' The present condition that he pointed to was the relatively small population and the 'consequent ineffective occupation in many parts of the country'. Coming from Japan he took into account 'the armed strength and power of transportation over sea of any conceivably hostile nation', and his conclusion was that Australia's isolation was no longer a defence asset. Kitchener recommended a substantial extension to the Dominion's military defences—80,000 fighting

---

[2] *SMH*, 10 and 11 February 1910.

[3] Neither E. L. Batchelor who was the External Affairs Minister until his death in October 1911 nor his successor in that portfolio, Josiah Thomas, had an important say on major strategic questions.

troops in place of the 66,000 under the Cook Defence Bill—and in his view the nineteen- and twenty-year old recruits could not properly be reckoned in the total. To obtain the 80,000 he urged that these recruits be required to continue their military training until the twenty-fifth year, including a six-day period each year in camp. Kitchener also suggested the establishment of a military college to provide material for a future staff corps. Cadets, according to his plan, should pay fees of £80 per annum.[4]

These criticisms of the 1909 Defence Act were very similar to those raised in the debates of October 1909, and Hughes and Pearce had little trouble in convincing their colleagues to adopt the essential features of Kitchener's report.[5] Under the Labor government's defence bill, compulsory training was to extend to the twenty-fifth year with one inspection parade in the twenty-sixth year. Convinced by Hughes' argument that the compulsory principle was only justified by the effectiveness of its execution,[6] the government proposed to make the adult soldiers, who were the backbone of Kitchener's scheme, undergo an eight-day camp annually, two more days than the number Kitchener advised. The bill established the military college but rejected the idea of fees, which was unacceptable to a democratic socialist party; it based selection on state examinations and provided for scholarships for all successful candidates. The first recruits were to be drafted in 1912 and the scheme was to be in full operation by 1919–20. Including the men between the ages of eighteen and twenty-six, trained and under training in that year, Pearce predicted that the government would have available a total fighting force of 127,000 men. The government believed that the annual cost would be about £2,00,000 or £200,000 to £250,000 more than either the Fusion defence scheme or Kitchener's estimates.

The arguments which in 1908 and 1909 had brought the Labor party to support a strong defence policy were once again enunciated by Pearce when introducing the bill into the Senate. But now they were brought up to date and presented in a comprehensive form. It was a Labor version of the justification for the Fusion defence policy advanced by Cook the preceding September.

> We have been remarkably fortunate in the past, but what guarantee have we that we are going to be so fortunate in the future? What guarantee can we have? Even our very powerlessness and inoffensiveness offer no guarantee that we shall never be attacked. There could not be a more inoffensive people than the Koreans. But where are they as a nation today? They have been brought under the control of another country, which rules them with a rod of iron. … The fact that it has not been necessary for Australia to defend herself in the past is due to the unassailable supremacy of the British Navy, and to nothing else. It is certainly not due to ourselves. Hitherto the British Navy has been unchallenged and unchallengeable upon the seas. But today the British Navy is challenged seriously. Today the British Navy in the

---

[4] CofA, *Parliamentary Papers*, 1910 session, Vol. II, No. 8, 'Defence of Australia. Memorandum by Field-Marshal Viscount Kitchener of Khartoum'.

[5] ALP caucus minutes, Vol. II, 140, 23 and 24 June 1910, and Cabinet notes of meeting, 8 August 1910, Fisher Papers, 2919/1/2 ANL.

[6] See the speech of Hughes who, as acting prime minister, introduced the bill into the House of Representatives, *CPD*, 1910 session, LIX, 6117, 15 November 1910.

Pacific—our ocean—the ocean, which laves our shores—is the third navy in point of strength. But, it is said, Australia is isolated; that we are so distant from the world's conflicts that we need not fear. We were distant forty or fifty years ago, but we are not now. The sound of war has been even nearer than that to our shores. We cannot prophesy that, in future, we are going to be as exempt from attack as we have been in the past. We also have to bear in mind that we are part of the British Empire; and, whilst the British Empire has been our source of protection in the past, … still our connection with it carries the possibility of our being involved at any time in war with countries which have no immediate designs against ourselves. They may have designs against the Empire, of which we form a part, however and consequently their attacks may be directed against us … we may at any time be involved in a war in the causing of which we have had no voice, and in which we have no desire to take a part. But, nevertheless, by reason of the fact that we are part of the Empire, we may be called upon, willy nilly, to bear the consequences of our Imperial connexion.

Here were the chief elements once again in Australian post-1905 defence thinking. Firstly, the emergence of Japan as the greatest power in East Asia, a Japan which had shown itself to have imperialist and expansionist ambitions. The Japanese decision to annex Korea which was made public during the very week in which Pearce brought down the bill was taken as evidence to substantiate Australia's worst fears. On this issue it would seem that once again the Australian press's general acceptance of Japanese action was a reflection of British attitudes rather than of responsible Australian leaders' opinions or even possibly public opinion.[7] Secondly Pearce not only pressed the point of the British loss of naval supremacy in the Pacific, but accepted that the challenge to Britain in Europe also threatened to involve Australia in war. Since the Boer War this had been probably the most important reason for Labor's reservations about the imperial connection. Pearce's speech contained the residue of this resentment, 'the possibility of our being involved at any time in war with countries which have no immediate designs against ourselves … a war in the causing of which we have had no voice, and in which we have no desire to take a part.' Yet Pearce—and undoubtedly he was speaking for the Labor movement as its views had developed under the pressure of events and politics—accepted, if in a degree reluctantly, this consequence of the imperial connection. Severance of the tie was unthinkable. The emphasis on the lack of a voice in imperial policy was a signpost showing that Labor in office was beginning to follow the course which Deakin had already charted in trying to resolve the dilemma of Australian foreign policy.

---

[7] *SMH*, 26 August 1910. The *SMH* quoted from the London papers, most extensively *The Times* which said that Japanese expansion was 'doubtless an economic and political necessity'. Earlier the *SMH*, 11 August 1910, in its editorial on 'Australia and Japan' predicted the formation of a Japanese-German alliance after the Anglo-Japanese alliance expired in 1915. Such an alliance would leave Japan free in the Pacific. 'It is uncertain how far we could count on the United States for a counter move, and we are brought face to face with the fact that in this possible set of circumstances … we should be left to our own devices, and, with our present resources, should have a very hard, if not impossible task in trying to hold our continent.' But that was in the future. Perhaps more significant was the comment of Australia's first example of the tabloid press, the Sydney *Sun*, which on 26 August saw 'the Korea steal' as evidence of 'real peril' to Australia.

When British power had been adequate to meet all threats to its *imperium* and imperial wars were essentially colonial grass-fires, then the consequences for Dominion acceptance of an imperial foreign policy determined in Britain were limited, but a great war arising out of the German challenge to British naval supremacy was of a new order. Britain's vital security was now directly menaced and therefore the empire's survival might very well turn on the ability and willingness of the Dominions to come to the aid of the Mother Country. The separate geo-political interests of the autonomous nations of the empire made them unhappy about accepting these responsibilities, especially since they had no say in determining the imperial policies which ultimately led to war. Yet even if it were difficult for Australia to defend itself while Britain was pre-occupied in Europe, nevertheless Australian security was ultimately bound up with Britain's survival. What is more, because of sentimental attachment, tribal loyalty would allow no other course. Thus even while building up Australia's own defences, the Labor government acknowledged, as Fisher in March 1909 had stated, that at the time of Britain's emergency, Australian resources would be placed at the empire's disposal. Even so, Australia's defence policy remained exclusively concerned with local security. Australia did not like the awful alternatives opening before it, Labor least of all. But the answer at the end was clear. They came to believe that perhaps it could be made more bearable if the Australian government had a voice in those imperial policies which 'willy nilly' seemed to be drawing Australians into the European imbroglio.

The last part of Pearce's speech was aimed at those socialists who complained that Labor was 'trailing the flag of militarism'. Pearce contended that it was just because Labor in Australia was 'nearing the realization of our industrial, social, and political ideals more than is any other country in the world' that defence was so important. He said that Labor believed in arbitration to settle international disputes. Like so many Western liberals and Labor men of the period Pearce held that the time was coming when the 'ideal of the brotherhood of a man' and 'a better understanding formed amongst the workers of the world' would end all war. But his optimism was not unalloyed. He reminded his critics among the Labor backbenchers that 'We have seen, in many countries, that even the workers themselves have thrown up their hats for war. Some of us have seen a mad mob rushing down the streets of this big city—mad with the war fever.' The nature of power politics placed grave limits on the possibilities of international arbitration. 'Where is the nation that is prepared to arbitrate in the event of an international misunderstanding, either with us or with the British nation?' Pearce asked. 'Is Japan or China prepared to arbitrate with us about our Immigration Restriction Act? And, even if they were prepared to arbitrate on that question, of course, we are not.'[8]

Despite its enlarged scope, the bill met hardly any resistance. Only Senator St Ledger, a Manchester liberal who opposed the principle of compulsion, and W. G. Higgs, the Labor member for Capricornia, whose idealism was not negated by the practicalities—there was, he

---

[8] *CPD*, 1910 session, LVI, 1661–72, 18 August 1910. See also Pearce's speech reported in the *SMH*, 28 November 1910.

pointed out, the saving power of a Socialist party 'even in Japan'—spoke against the measure.[9] For the rest, all spoke of the broad merits of the bill and avowed their fear of Japan, and before the end of the session Labor's Defence Act became law. It came into effect on 1 January 1911.[10]

The Labor government at Pearce's behest also moved quickly on outstanding naval problems. On 24 May 1910 the Cabinet gave formal approval to the principles of the 1909 Naval Agreement. At the same meeting it decided, responding to a memorandum of the minister of defence, to seek the advice of a British expert on:

1. locality of Main Naval Base;
2. secondary bases;
3. Training College (already fixed, Sydney);
4. Gunnery, Torpedo and Signalling Schools;
5. Boy's Training School.[11]

Lord Fisher, the author of the 1909 scheme, who had resigned as First Sea Lord on 10 January was the obvious choice. Lord Fisher, however, declined. 'I'd go as Dictator', he told Viscount Esher, 'but not as Adviser.' Moreover, he seems to have been unhappy with the large appropriations earmarked for compulsory military training. 'They have commenced all wrong and it would involve me in a campaign I intend to keep clear of with the soldiers.' Finally, the thought of being out of touch with Admiralty politics for the time, which such a tour would demand, was not agreeable to him.[12] On Lord Fisher's advice, Admiral Sir Reginald Henderson was given the post. Henderson had been Superintendent of Dockyards at Sheerness and Portsmouth and had commanded the coastguards and reserves. He seemed to have the qualifications necessary for a technical assignment. But on his arrival in Australia the Fisher government entrusted the Admiral with a broader mission, requesting him to report on 'all the measures to be taken, both forthwith and in the future, in the formation of the Fleet'.[13] Henderson took this wider commission literally and, after a thorough examination of Australia's circumstances, he presented on 1 March 1911, a blueprint for a comprehensive scheme of naval defence which was to be realized over a twenty-two year term. The government, impressed by the magnitude of the recommendations, postponed making a decision on the report until after the Imperial Conference of May-June 1911.[14]

---

[9] *CPD*, 1910 Session, LVI, 2266–70, 31 August 1910 and LIX, 6138, 15 November 1910.

[10] CofA, Act No. 37 of 1910.

[11] See Memorandum, 'Strictly Private and Confidential, Naval Defence', Melbourne, 16 May 1910, AWM, Pearce Papers, 5/26/c. See also ALP caucus minutes, Vol. II, 140, 23 June 1910. Caucus apparently approved the government's naval policy without debate.

[12] Marder (ed.), *Fear God and Dread Nought*, Vol. II, p. 327. Letter, Admiral Fisher to Esher, 27 May 1910.

[13] CofA, *Parliamentary Papers*, 1911 session, Vol. II, No. 7, 'Naval Forces. Recommendations by Admiral Sir Reginald Henderson', ordered to be printed, 14 September 1911.

[14] Council of Defence, minutes of meeting, 1 March 1911, CRS, A 2032. There were present Pearce as President, Fisher, Treasurer, Captain Creswell, Major-General Hoad, Major-General Kirkpatrick, and Secretary of the Navy Department, Mr Pethebridge. Senator McGregor, Mr C. Frazer and Admiral Sir Reginald Henderson also attended by invitation. On 31 March Fisher announced after a Cabinet meeting in Melbourne, 'that any decision with regard to the partial or complete adoption of the Henderson naval

Meanwhile in the 1910 session the Labor government had proceeded to give legislative sanction to its criticisms of Deakin's naval policy. Labor's bill, while accepting the general principles of the 1909 agreement, rejected the British offer of a £250,000 subsidy and provided for payment from revenue. Since financial liability entailed political responsibility, Cabinet had decided to reject the £250,000 in order to ensure 'Complete local control'.[15] Following Henderson's advice, the bill also provided for a restructuring of the Naval Board, which had been created under the 1904 Defence Act, so as to bring it more into line with the Admiralty's own organization; in addition to the minister and the civil head of the department, there were now to be three naval members on the board. Both Hughes and Pearce, in presenting the bill to Parliament, stressed that the Australian naval force would become a section of the Pacific Fleet which was to be formed in accordance with the decision of the Imperial Defence Conference and that in time of war it would 'of course be under one command' for the purpose of protecting the British Dominions and interests in the Far East.[16] There was once again in the debate a general agreement that Japan posed the greatest danger to national security; only Senator Thomas Chataway, a Queensland Liberal, thought that Germany was a more serious threat.[17] It was the contention of both Hughes and Pearce that the British Pacific Fleet proposal offered the best chance of a successful defence against an attack from the north.

The more radical nationalists in the Labor ranks were suspicious of the British scheme. Senator Stewart predicted that by the end of the twentieth century the empire would have crumbled away, the United States absorbing Canada, South Africa drifting away, India gone and Australia an independent republic—a prediction which even yet may be completely fulfilled. He feared a possible German-Japanese alliance which would show up the emptiness of British pledges and leave Australia at Japan's mercy. He urged that the keynote of Australian policy should be 'Australia first, Australia last, Australia all the time'.[18] Senator Arthur Rae of New South Wales, in a milder vein, also questioned the wisdom of merging Australia's navy in a British Pacific Fleet.[19] Pearce joined with the indignant Liberals in rebutting the isolationists' argument.

> If we had not the protection of the British Fleet and if, in the event of war, Japan chose to send a single battleship to Sydney or Melbourne … we could not make an effective reply. In the absence of that protection our White Australian legislation could not stand for a day. … The idea is that the Pacific Fleet must be one. It must be one to be of any use. In the case of war, … before a decision could be arrived at … the Japanese Fleet would be able to sail round the Pacific attacking and defeating each unit in detail.[20]

---

scheme would be deferred until the return of himself, Mr. Batchelor and Senator Pearce, from England', *SMH*, 7 April 1911.

[15] Cabinet notes of meeting, 8 August 1910, Fisher Papers, 2919/1/2.

[16] *CPD*, 1910 session, LVIII, 4490, 13 October 1910.

[17] Ibid., 5577–8, 3 November 1910.

[18] Ibid., 3 November 1910.

[19] Ibid., 5590–1

[20] Ibid., 5597–8.

The bill passed both chambers without amendment and royal assent was reported on 25 November. The preceding day the first fruits of the new naval policy, the two destroyers ordered by Fisher in February 1909, the *Yarra* and the *Parramatta* entered Australian waters.[21]

## The development of Labor's foreign policy: preparing for the Imperial conference

By 1911 the Imperial Conference had become the high point for Dominion diplomacy. Deakin, because of his long acquaintance with the imperial problem, was well aware of its importance. Indeed he had for this reason helped raise the status of these meetings of the Dominion and British governments. The Labor leaders, in contrast, were not well equipped to deal with matters of imperial and external policy. Though deeply concerned by the threat to Australian security posed by the international situation, the Fisher government had little in its own experience or the experience of the Labor party upon which it could draw in order to translate the assumptions underpinning their defence policy into an effective imperial and foreign policy. The Labor movement, born out of the economic and social discontent of the 1880s and 1890s had had little to say about such matters. For the most part it had turned its back on such questions, looking with suspicion upon conservative attempts to embroil Australia in imperial commitments and foreign wars. In office then the members of the Fisher government, as Labor leaders, Australians and even, in their own way, imperialists, did not quite know what they should require of an Imperial Conference.

During the first six months in office they had had to deal with two diplomatic issues, the Declaration of London and the Anglo-Japanese commercial treaty. The Declaration of London drawn up by a conference of leading seafaring nations in February 1909, contained a statement of rules for the conduct of naval warfare. The British government had not consulted the Dominions and when Deakin had sought to have Australia's views considered he had been snubbed rather curtly. The Foreign Office had replied, 'that its terms are satisfactory to the naval authorities and that under the circumstances Sir Edward Grey feels that he cannot advise the King to withhold ratification as it would be quite impossible to introduce any amendments at this stage.'[22] The Fusion government's main objection had been that the Declaration of London permitted merchant vessels to be converted to men-of-war immediately after the outbreak of hostilities. The Deakin-Cook government had been concerned that 'there was not a single British battleship in the Pacific within the region of Australian influence' and felt that for this reason the British government should have paid some heed to their complaints.[23] The Labor government's quarrel with the substance of the London code was somewhat different. Their specific objections were

---

[21] *SMH*, 25 November 1910.

[22] Cable, Sir F. A. Campbell, Under-secretary of State for Foreign Affairs to Atlee Hunt, Secretary of External Affairs Department, 15 September 1909, Atlee Hunt Papers, 52.

[23] See the statement by P. McMahon Glynn, Attorney-General in the Fusion government, in *CPD*, 1910 session, LIX, 6864, 25 November 1910.

economic rather than strategic, that is, they were opposed to the inclusion of Australia's major food exports in the list of contraband goods and to the articles permitting the destruction of neutral vessels upon which they might depend in war-time to carry on their commerce. Above all, though, the Labor government deplored the failure of the imperial authorities to consult them beforehand.

The other external issue upon which the Fisher government had to form an opinion during its first few months in office was the Anglo-Japanese commercial treaty of 1894. Though Queensland had adhered to it in 1897, successive Commonwealth governments had refused to accept that the Queensland decision bound the Australian government and, under the terms offered by Japan, had themselves declined to become a party to it. Once more in a despatch of 15 July 1910, the British government had sought Australia's acceptance but Fisher was adamant. 'Owing to the vast discrepancy in rates of pay for labour in the two countries' they refused to entertain the idea of reciprocal trade relations between the two countries.[24]

When at the end of 1910 Hughes, who was acting prime minister while Fisher was representing Australia at South Africa's Union celebrations, found himself called upon to prepare a list of agenda items for the 1911 Imperial Conference, his selection reflected the Labor government's recent experience. The items were approved by Cabinet on 22 November[25] and placed before the House of Representatives on 25 November, the last day of sitting before the Australian delegates left for England. Among the topics which Hughes told Parliament the government intended taking up were 'the importance of promoting fuller development of commercial intercourse with the Empire' and the desirability of favouring British manufactures and shipping and so counteracting the unfair competition from subsidized foreign steamer lines. On the Declaration of London Hughes said that Australia was proposing a resolution expressing regret at the failure of Britain to consult the Dominions and condemning the articles which allowed foodstuff to be seized and neutral vessels destroyed. Apart from the motion reaffirming the 1907 Conference decision on the desirability of British migrants going to British Dominions rather than foreign countries, the other topics which the Australian government announced its intention of bringing before the Imperial Conference were rather trivial.[26]

Obviously the Labor government's major suggestions were inspired by immediate experience and not by any well-considered reflections on the general drift of imperial affairs and imperial relations. The 1908 Brisbane Conference of the ALP had, as the Liberals gleefully hammered home, declared that no Australian government should bring up any subject at an imperial conference unless it had been discussed and dealt with beforehand by parliament. Thus, the Labor government felt a formal duty to parliament and party in the matter. However, as the Imperial Conference was still six months off, the government was not ready to give its mind to the subject and the duty was only performed in a perfunctory manner; the agenda proposals were rushed

---

[24] Cable, governor-general to colonial secretary, 1 August 1910, CP 78/8; CO 532/17.

[25] *SMH*, 23 November 1910.

[26] *CPD*, 1910 session, LIX, 6852–3, 25 November 1910.

together and placed before the House of Representatives without warning on the last day of the 1910 session of parliament.

Though taken by surprise, Deakin rose to the occasion. The role of the Dominions in the empire and the place of Australia in the world were subjects to which he had perforce given considerable attention. Since 1907, when he had represented Australia at the previous Imperial Conference, much had happened. His focus had sharpened and his views had become more deeply defined. Responding to Hughes' trite remarks on what might be expected of the 1911 conference, Deakin gave parliament the benefit of the wisdom which he had accumulated during a quarter of a century of wrestling with the problems of Australia's external relations. It was Deakin's last great speech on imperial and foreign affairs and in retrospect it must be seen as one of the greatest and most prescient ever heard in the Australian parliament.

> I hope that Ministers will not forget to impress upon their colleagues at the Conference that Australia, in spite of herself, is being forced into a foreign policy of her own because foreign interests and risks surround us on every side. A Pacific policy we must have. It cost us a long fight to obtain the very unsatisfactory share in the control of the New Hebrides which we now have. That may ripen into something better. Our first steps in Papua, commenced long ago, were frustrated and partly defeated by official neglect on the other side of the world. Malaysia denotes an enormous, prosperous, fertile, and productive region in the hands of civilised powers, and capable of being transferred from one to another, with consequences which may be of the utmost moment to us. ...[27] They [foreign politics] affect our business more and more. We must be observant, like every other nation, providing buffers to prevent shocks, and placing intervals between us and danger centres. ...

> Let Ministers impress upon the Foreign Office in London that there are Pacific problems in which the Australian interest is inexpressible; which, though they may not be made the subject of public debate, should be perpetually and consistently considered, particularly by the Naval and Military authorities, and those charged with the foreign affairs of the Empire.

Deakin agreed with Labor's agenda topics but felt that something more general and more far-reaching was required to meet the necessities of Australia's case.

> The creation of this Conference was a great stride, and another stride was made when the Conference was required to meet at least once in every four years. But it is not sufficient that this should remain a mere advisory Conference. Its powers require to grow with the needs and the emergencies of the Empire. These needs and emergencies every year make greater demands for Imperial action and often for united action by all Dominions overseas.

---

[27] By Malaysia Deakin meant the whole Malay-speaking archipelago encompassing the Malayan Peninsula, the Philippines and the Dutch East Indies, but the context in which he used the term would seem to indicate that he was thinking primarily of the Dutch East Indies. After the growth of Anglo-German tensions in Europe, Australia saw its main danger from European imperialism not in France's control of New Hebrides but in pressure on the Dutch to hand over their East Indian Empire to Germany. Thought it is true that after 1905 all Australian governments in calculating their Pacific strategy regarded Japan as the main threat to their security, nevertheless this indirect threat from Germany was a recurring, if subsidiary, theme.

> That united action is only to be obtained when, instead of a Conference separated by breaks of four years, continuity and character are given to its policy by providing a means of keeping up the work, following up its suggestions, and giving effect to its resolutions. … By that means, and that only, can we clothe this Conference with the powers that rightly belong to it, making it a thoroughly Imperial body, representative of our race in every part of the world, without trenching on the local Governments of the Dominions or on the sphere of the British Government.

His precise proposal then was

> for a central Imperial body, on which all the self-governing Dominions are represented, and have an effective voice. Its binding decisions being arrived at, not by counting votes, but through the unanimity reached by inquiry, argument and mutual concession, are then ripe for endorsement by the Parliaments which represent their peoples. It is by means of an Imperial Conference, and in no other way, that the peoples overseas can obtain a voice in Imperial affairs, which are their own affairs, as they are affected by interests or actions within or without the Empire.

And by imperial affairs here he meant primarily imperial defence and foreign policy. In urging continuity and consistency Deakin reaffirmed his 1907 policy that Dominion affairs should be taken out of the hands of the Colonial Office and given to an imperial secretariat which should be staffed by and be responsible to all the self-governing members of the empire. Australians, he believed, should represent Australia in this imperial department of state.

Under the existing constitutional arrangements Deakin pointed out that Australian pleas with respect to the Pacific were often disregarded by the British government which did not consider Australia's area of concern with the same urgency as it did the affairs of Europe or even India. Here clearly he must have had in mind the discouraging response of the British government to his Pacific pact proposal; it was this very disinterest at the centre of the empire which was forcing Australia into a foreign policy of its own. Concluding, Deakin hoped that he would be able to congratulate the Labor ministers on their return from the Imperial Conference 'for having assisted in this development of our power and sphere of influence, our authority, and our right to be heard on all questions directly affecting Australia.' He told the government that 'We are entitled to claim this now that we are assuming the responsibilities of our position. … Ministers have before them an immense opportunity.'[28]

Deakin's oratory and bearing had always captivated his audiences. Cook, who even as a political opponent had felt the impact of this ineffable charm, once likened Deakin to 'a beautiful, stately but timid giraffe.'[29] It was a very apt image for it was true that though there was grace of manner and beauty of style, there was also a mildness of temper, something almost approaching self-effacement in his delivery. Such 'timidity' indeed was valuable politically. It made him few enemies and made compromise in policy and politics more easily attainable. Perhaps here lies one of the reasons why Deakin, despite his weak party position during the first decade of the

---

[28] *CPD*, 1910 session, LIX, 6857–60, 25 November 1910.
[29] Notebooks, 1905–6, Joseph Cook papers.

Commonwealth, was able to dominate its politics. At the end of the decade with the fusion of the anti-Labor forces achieved, his great work behind him and darkness beginning to close around him, he felt, for once, the necessity to speak, more firmly and assertively than was his custom. His speech rose above party politics. He spoke as if he knew Labor in their hearts shared his vision. He outlined a scheme for reconciling Dominion autonomy with imperial unity and warned that if the compelling Australian views on defence and foreign policy could not be found an adequate place in the imperial structure then it might well lead Australians, despite themselves, to adopt an independent policy.

Deakin, elegantly tall and slightly stooped, commanded attention. Yet, though the parliamentarians were held, they did not understand. Not one of the subsequent speakers in the debate took up the issues he raised. Higgs who took the primitive Labor line that imperial federation meant the loss of self-government and that the ministers should espouse the Labor platform and nothing else, tried to extricate the debate from the spell of Deakin's eloquence by 'knocking' him in a folksy satire. He introduced a poem which poked gentle fun at 'Alf Deakin'. Two stanzas read:

> Gawd blimey, Alf does like to get his old
> > chin whiskers waggin'!
> A real nice bloke 'e is, but, Lord, 'e's
> > never finished maggin'!
> 'E'd rather stand an' make a speech than
> > sit an' eat his dinner!
> 'E'd rather 'itch up to a star than 'itch
> > up to a winner.
> I never seen him load up like you, or me,
> > or Snowy;
> But, all the same, old Alfie D. gets
> > rolling tight as Chloe
> 'E don't get it at Murphy's pub—the stuff
> > 'e drinks ain't likker;
> Th' dictionary 'olds th' stuff on which
> > old Alf gets shikker.

As another line put it, "'E sorter mesmerises yer with talk of death an' ruin.'[30] This is what Deakin's speech had meant to parliament, rhetorical splendour and little more. Deakin's own supporters seemed to be as lacking in comprehension as the Labor men.[31] The debate went on almost as though Deakin had not spoken. What Deakin had already mastered and perceived the other

---

[30] *CPD*, 1910 session, LIX, p. 6865, 25 November 1910.

[31] The press ignored Deakin's speech. The *SMH* report on 26 November 1910, excised all the guts of Deakin's address.

Australian leaders would have to grope towards through their own experience in successive decades.

Hughes added two more resolutions to the Australian list of agenda items for the conference; Deakin's proposal for an imperial tribunal on which Dominion judges would sit, and a Labor backbench suggestion advocating international arbitration. Indeed Hughes in adopting international arbitration confessed to the haste in which the agenda items had been prepared for submission to parliament. He had forgotten to read the resolutions which the government had already approved. 'The Government are heartily in favour of international arbitration', Hughes said, 'and it is a proposal of first importance that will be discussed with a view to its adoption by all the civilised nations of the earth.'[32] Strangely the Australian government failed to submit this resolution along with the others and so it never came before the Conference.[33]

Though Deakin's prescription for Australia's external policies evoked no immediate response, the Labor government, guided by a sure political instinct, was beginning to feel and think its way towards a position which was not too dissimilar. The acceptance of the international arbitration resolution was primarily a gesture towards the universalist and utopian strand in the Labor movement. Undoubtedly most Labor leaders, at that level of generality, sincerely believed in the ideal. Many argued that just as industrial arbitration was in the process of securing economic peace, so international arbitration might achieve world peace. Fisher himself was a consistent and warm advocate of this thesis.[34] However, such redemptive principles rarely provide a policy for present problems. Indeed they do not even offer a clear pointer as to the direction a government should take in dealing with such problems since they assume that men and nations will act on a basis entirely contrary to that on which they are accustomed to act.

At the same 1908 Labor Party Conference which had adopted compulsory military training, a resolution calling for the settling of international disputes 'by a council of civilised nations' had been defeated.[35] The party leaders had feared that if carried at that time it might be used to oppose the building up of Australia's defence forces. Once their defence measures had been approved, they were willing to affirm the principle of international arbitration. For some it was perhaps lip service intended to quieten the consciences of colleagues troubled by such an enormous increase in defence appropriations. For others it was equally a declaration of faith and hope. The Labor leaders did not reconcile intellectually or practically the dreams with the realities. And who can blame them? Too often in history such resolutions have produced little more than the cloaking of national interest in the armour of self-righteousness. Labor was the only party to give any attention to the general question of peace-keeping but its external like its domestic policy was essentially a pragmatic one, governed by the immediate practical considerations. Thus the Labor leaders while urging arbitration as an ultimate goal, recognized its shortcomings as a policy for Australia in the given situation and began to sketch out an approach

---

[32] *CPD*, 1910 session, LIX, 6871, 25 November 1910.

[33] Copy of cable, governor-general to colonial secretary, 24 December 1910, FO, 800/90.

[34] For one example, see Fisher's address to the Australian Natives Association, *SMH*, 31 January 1911.

[35] Official Report of the Fourth Commonwealth Political Labor Conference, June 1908.

to foreign and imperial relations which by the time of the London conference was very similar to that advocated by Deakin.

During 1910 and the early months of 1911 the education of the Labor leaders proceeded. Perhaps triggered off by rumours about the renegotiating or renouncing of the Anglo-Japanese alliance, a new bout of 'crisis fever' seized the country. Reporters, reflecting this sense of panic and at the same time revealing their own gaucheness, welcomed the new Japanese Consul-General to Sydney by taxing him with questions on the likelihood of 'a Japanese invasion'; it was recorded that in response the tolerant, or was it sinister, Mr Miki Saito 'smiled'.[36] Books, lectures and press editorials contributed to the Australian 'scare'. Seemingly serious studies of Pacific questions, such as General Homer Lea's *The Valour of Ignorance*,[37] which claimed that America with all its ninety million people and great wealth could not prevent Japan from invading and occupying the whole of its west coast, were much quoted.[38] Fisher himself used it in arguing Australia's case at the Imperial Conference. When Canada's prime minister pooh-poohed the idea that 'Japan has some ulterior motive of conquest' in the Pacific, Fisher replied that 'one of your [sic] greatest military writers in the United States has alarmed the world by a book which states that the Japanese were going to run over the United States.'[39] An address by Archibald Colquhoun at the Royal United Service Institute which predicted that the Pacific would be 'the new theatre in which the world drama is to centre' and that Australia, due to Britain's problems in Europe, was to be left to look after itself was widely commented on.[40] The *Sydney Morning Herald* had ten editorials or major articles on these themes during the six months preceding the Conference.[41] These essays developed the strategic propositions which since 1905 had become the orthodox Australian position, namely that Japan's naval power and national ambitions and China's potential might and Asian future when juxtaposed against Britain's withdrawal east of Suez—put Australia's national security at risk. However, since the *Sydney Morning Herald*, like most Australian daily newspapers, was unwilling to face up to the awkward questions for imperial relations posed by such an analysis, they had little that was positive in the way of advice to offer the Labor government.

It is noteworthy that the two constructive ideas which the newspaper did tentatively explore in this context, that is the turning to the United States for succour and the handing over of all British interests in the South Pacific to Australian control, were policy suggestions which Fisher made his own at this time. Perhaps much can be implied from Australia's enthusiastic reception of

---

[36] *SMH*, 20 October 1910.

[37] New York and London, 1909.

[38] *SMH*, 21 November 1910.

[39] Minutes of 111 meeting, CID, 26 May 1911, Cab 2/2.

[40] *SMH*, 26 November 1910 and 28 January and 20 May 1911.

[41] They appeared under the following headings: 'American in the Pacific', 21 November 1910; 'Our Unit in the Navy', 26 November 1910; 'China and Japan', 29 December 1910; 'Control of the Pacific', 4 January 1911; 'Britain and Japan', 27 January 1911; 'The Future of the South Seas', 28 January 1911; 'The Defence of Australia', 18 February 1911; 'Australia and Japan', 10 May 1911; 'France and Morocco', 10 May 1911; 'The Problematic Pacific', 20 May 1911.

the Great White Fleet, but down to 1911 there was little open discussion of the need to seek American protection. It was realized that the adequacy of such an idea would be a reflection on Britain's international standing and a blow to Britain's prestige. By the end of 1910 all such inhibitions were being cast aside. The *Sydney Morning Herald* asserted that Australia would 'look with favour upon the appearance of an American battleship fleet as a permanent fixture in the Pacific ... there is much to be said for such a development of the Pacific fleet of the white nations as will preserve something like a balance of power.'[42] Considering the 'unnatural' Anglo-Japanese alliance, the *Sydney Morning Herald* felt that in case of a Japanese-American conflict Australians would have 'a divided duty.'[43] On the other hand, it was convinced that there was 'Nothing more certain than that the brown and yellow races must come south in course of time,'[44] and that 'the United States stands between her [Japan] and the control of the Pacific.'[45] Increasingly the *Sydney Morning Herald*, pondering the possible termination of the Anglo-Japanese alliance in 1915, began to look towards the United States. It seemed to be the only alternative to falling back on the desperate policy of 'ourselves alone.'[46]

The suggestion to establish Australian hegemony over British policy and territory in the South Pacific was a variant of the old Australian Monroe Doctrine, an old dream dressed out in the urgent and novel uniform of 1910–11. At the time of the appointment of a new British High Commissioner for the Western Pacific, the *Sydney Morning Herald* took the line that the position should become 'a Commonwealth instead of an Imperial one'. But it conceded the difficulty of convincing the British authorities 'that Australian interests in the Pacific have now absorbed and outgrown the Imperial interests.'[47] The acceptance of Australian predominance was urgent, not merely because of Japanese infiltration but also because it was feared that German pressure in the North Sea might bring about 'a possible alteration in the map on this side of the world. Broadly speaking, all the island territory from Timor to Bougainville, with the exception of British New Guinea, is a possible, if not an actual, sphere of German influence.' Britain, for European reasons, might be willing to accept such a change in the Pacific *status quo*. It was therefore necessary for Australia to act. 'The main idea to an Australian community now really for the first time taking large views of its place in the Pacific is that within its sphere the British race shall be supreme in the South Pacific.'[48]

Fisher in South Africa was echoing these themes. In explaining Australia's defence policy he said that

> History would show whether Australia, close as she was to the gates of the great Asiatic empires, had done wrong in insisting on the training of every youth to arms. They had to take

---

[42] *SMH*, 21 November 1910.

[43] *SMH*, 27 January 1911.

[44] *SMH*, 28 January 1911.

[45] *SMH*, 29 April 1911.

[46] *SMH*, 18 and 21 February 1911.

[47] *SMH*, 4 January 1911.

[48] *SMH*, 28 January 1911.

measures for defence and for the inculcation of national sentiment. That was the reason for their navy. If it cost £10,000,000 of money, it would have to be provided and he believed that the people of Australia were prepared to pay the price.

Cook, for the opposition, published a long letter which took a similar view of Australia's strategic predicament.

> We must, whether we like it or not, recognise that we are part of a very wide world, some portions of which are neither so happy nor prosperous as ourselves. Around us are nations more hungry as well as angry to whom the God of Nations has been less benign.

Referring to an article from the English press on the deterioration of Anglo-German relations, he pointed up its significance for Australia. 'The plain answer is that not only should we not avoid the European catastrophe, but in addition the Eastern menace, now happily in the background, would, by the same token, have moved into the forefront.' Citing Mahan, he complained that Australia's second line of defence, the army, was to cost £2,000,000 per annum, while only £750,000 was to be spent annually on the first line, the navy. He called for a greater expenditure on the Australian navy.[49] Notwithstanding the great advances in Australian defence preparedness that Deakin, Cook, Fisher, Hughes and Pearce had already pioneered, the Lord Mayor of Sydney sponsored a great rally on 21 February 1911 to consider 'the defenceless position of Australia.'[50]

It was in this atmosphere that the Labor government was called upon to develop an external policy which could support its strategic analysis and back its defence commitments. Isolationism was never regarded as a viable answer. The Labor leaders recognized the binding nature of the imperial connection; it was a function of British race pride, constitutional liberty and strategic weakness. From the time of the Dreadnought crisis Labor ministers had actively affirmed their loyalty to the empire.[51] Few of Labor's opponents doubted their word. Deakin, writing in the *Morning Post* after Labor's victory in the 1910 election, stated: 'In this respect [systematic co-operation inside the empire] the advent of the Labor Government probably does not make any vital difference. The essentials of Imperialist policy have in Australia … passed out of party controversy into the accepted national policy of the Commonwealth.'[52] Yet within this imperial framework the Fisher government, moved by the same inexorable geo-political factors which had conditioned Deakin's imperial and foreign policy, began to demand a say in the formulation of the empire's Pacific policy and to seek greater co-operation with the other Dominions and even with the United States in order to strengthen regional security.

Fisher's trip to South Africa had broadened his perspective and it was there that the Australian prime minister first publicly advocated the closer union of the British Dominions in

---

[49] *SMH*, 2 January 1911.

[50] *SMH*, 22 February 1911.

[51] For a further example, *Daily Telegraph*, 28 November 1910.

[52] *MP*, 14 May 1910. See also SMH, 30 July 1910, 'Notwithstanding the occupancy of office in the Commonwealth by a Labour Ministry … there never has been a time in the history of Australia when the Imperial sentiment has been stronger that it is today.'

the Pacific and Indian Oceans, for 'all the interests of the Southern seas were alike'.[53] Returning to Australia he went further and argued the case for bringing all British interest in the South Pacific under Australian control and taking his cue from Canadian-American reciprocity discussions and Anglo-American arbitration negotiations he began to espouse the idea of an English-speaking alliance, especially for the maintenance of stability in the Pacific. As far as the disposition of the British interests in the Pacific was concerned, Fisher proposed that the High Commissioner for the Western Pacific should be an Australian not an imperial appointment and that British interests in the South Pacific should come under Australian administration. Fisher promised that at the Imperial Conference he and his colleagues would 'press the question with the argument that Australia is the predominant power in the Pacific.'[54]

In South Africa Fisher also conceived the notion of an American alliance and on his return it blossomed forth. Speaking to an Adelaide audience on 28 December, he said that he 'believed it would be possible, if the English-speaking peoples and the peoples associated under the British flag would cooperate, that they would be able, not only to protect their own interests, but to a considerable extent to protect the peace of the world and almost ensure it.'[55] On 20 February 1911 he extended the idea of a rapprochement to tariffs. 'If any scheme of inter-dominion preference were to be extended without the limits of the empire, the first step would be to do what Canada had done, and enter into reciprocal arrangements with a people akin to ourselves, and aiming in the main at the same standards of comfort and living.'[56] A month later, referring to the proposed Anglo-American arbitration treaty, he repeated the nub of his argument. 'If the United Kingdom, the self-governing dominions, and that other great English-speaking country, the United States of America, were linked up and associated in the interests of peace, progress, and humanitarian development, there was a possibility, notwithstanding the great armaments of other countries, to secure peace in our time.'[57] Granted the prime minister's unlikely assumption, assuredly his prognostications of what would follow were more credible than Neville Chamberlain's when using the same unhappy phrase almost thirty years later. Such an assumption, however, was untenable. Such an arrangement was for the American people unthinkable. They had no need of 'entangling alliances'.

On Fisher's return home, plans for Australian participation in the Imperial Conference were accelerated. On 4 January cabinet chose Fisher, Pearce and Batchelor as the Australian delegates and shortly thereafter they asked that the subject of 'co-operation and the mutual relations of naval and military forces as well as the status of Dominion navies' be discussed while they were in England.[58] By the end of this period of gestation the Labor government had come to share to a

---

[53] *SMH*, 21 November 1910.

[54] *SMH*, 5 January 1911; there is no evidence that it was in the event discussed during Fisher's visit to London.

[55] *SMH*, 29 December 1910.

[56] *SMH*, 20 February 1911.

[57] *SMH*, 31 March 1911.

[58] Cable, Dudley, governor-general to L. Harcourt, colonial secretary, 9 January 1911, FO, 800/90.

considerable degree Deakin's attitude to imperial and external relations. As a result of their negotiations with respect to the Declaration of London, their fears of colonial transfers in the Pacific and their concern over the rumoured renewal of the Anglo-Japanese alliance, they submitted a further resolution on 8 May; 'This conference affirms the desirability of Dominions being informed and consulted in negotiations with foreign Powers as to matters affecting any of them or the Empire generally.' The resolution also recommended the setting up of a foreign relations advisory committee of Dominion representatives which would be presided over by the British foreign secretary and which would meet not less than once a month.[59] The Labor government had come to see that the methods by which imperial policy was determined were not adequate to meet the needs and aspirations of Australia. For this reason Fisher looked upon the Imperial Conference 'as the most important step taken during the present century, from the Government's point of view.'[60]

---

[59] Copy of cable, governor-general to colonial secretary, 8 May 1911, FO, 800/90. It is possible that this was in origin at least the work of Atlee Hunt. Fisher was on the high seas when the cable was sent. It is uncertain whether he knew about it until he arrived in London. Letter, Atlee Hunt to Sir George Reid, Atlee Hunt Papers, Australian National Library. It is possible that Australian thinking on imperial problems was stimulated by the evangelism of the Round Table, a 'ginger' group inspired by Lord Milner and his South African 'kindergarten'. The aim of the London-based group was to promote the discussion of imperial affairs so as to influence the British and Dominion governments to move towards 'consolidated action' or some form of Imperial Federation. Corresponding groups were set up in each of the self-governing colonies. They tried to recruit influential figures in each country. It was intended that the Round Table should act as an undercover lobby in promoting the restructuring and reunification of the empire, though, as with the Victorian 'Imperial Federation League' there was little agreement among the members as to what in specific terms this objective meant. By September 1910 John Dove, who had been sent from London to establish branches in Sydney and Melbourne, had made substantial progress towards this end. Lionel Curtis' *Memoranda on Canada and the British Commonwealth*, the so-called 'Green Memorandum', was given to the Dominion members as a starting point for their discussions and the central theme of that document was the relationship between Dominion and Mother Country in the making of foreign policy. Curtis denied that the Dominions could have self-government while their foreign policy was still made in Whitehall, without their knowledge and without their consent. He argued that such an anomaly could not endure; the empire could not continue 'half-slave and half-free'. Either the Dominions would have to separate completely from Britain and take responsibility for their own foreign relations, or they would in some way have to join in a unified imperial government and thereby gain a voice in the framing a policy for the whole empire. Walter Nimocks, *Milner's Young Men; The 'Kindergarten' in Edwardian Imperial Affairs*, London 1970, pp. 159–62, 174; see also John Edward Kendle, *The Colonial and Imperial Conference, 1887–1911. A Study in Imperial Organization*, London 1967, pp. 137–47. Certainly Deakin's speech of 25 November 1910 and the Labor leaders' concerns as they approached the Imperial Conference did focus on the issue of foreign policy. But, even if the Commonwealth statesmen did take part in the Round Table's clandestine meetings the arguments which they presented emerged authentically out of Australian experience, and the proposals which they made were not of the Round Table mould but responded to what had much earlier been identified as Australia's distinctive circumstances.

[60] *SMH*, 31 March 1911.

## The Imperial conference of 1911

The Imperial Conference represented to Australia 'the most important step taken during the present century' because it was hoped that, by means of the conference, Australia would at last obtain a voice in the shaping of imperial foreign policy, especially those aspects of policy which bore directly on the Commonwealth's security and interest in the Pacific.

As the conference drew near these considerations were uppermost in the minds of the Australian representatives yet they received little support or understanding from the rest of the empire. New Zealand thought that the Australian solution of consultation between equal and independent governments did not go far enough. Influenced by the centralizing doctrines of the Royal Colonial Institute and Lionel Curtis' Round Table propaganda,[61] the New Zealand government had sent forward a resolution proposing the creation of an Imperial Council which would be clothed with executive power to deal with all the external interests of the different British communities. Newfoundland was too small and South Africa too new to have any pronounced views. Canada, sheltering under the umbrella of the American Monroe Doctrine, did not share the strategic anxieties of the Dominions in the South pacific. Quite the contrary. Fearful of increased responsibilities, Canada opposed closer and more continuous consultation. Indeed, so content was Canada with the *status quo* that it failed to forward any items at all for the conference agenda.

The response of the British government was much more complex. Though it was embarrassed by the Australian and New Zealand demands and was reluctant to share the responsibility for the making of imperial policy, still it recognized that the Dominions' grievances could not be altogether ignored. British power could no longer provide complete and permanent defence for every part of the empire. The Dominions were being called upon to help with their own defences. It was natural therefore that they should want a say in policies which directly affected them. Similarly, since imperial policy committed the Dominions to war and peace it was not unnatural that they should wish to have a right to be at least consulted on these matters. Finally, it was recognized that resistance to Dominion pleas might sour imperial relations, and at a time when the British government desired to marshal all imperial resources to meet the challenge from Germany, this would be most undesirable. Already by February 1911 Churchill, as Chancellor of the Exchequer, was looking to Australia and New Zealand to lighten Britain's burden of naval defence in the North Sea. He suggested that 'an arrangement should be made with New Zealand and, if possible, with Australia which will secure us one or both of the Colonial ships in the North Sea in the period, 1914–1916.'[62] Influenced by these considerations the British government, during the period January to May 1911, slowly moved from antagonism to conciliation in responding to the Australian request.

---

[61] See J. E. Kendle, 'The Round Table Movement, New Zealand, and the Conference of 1911', *Journal of Commonwealth Political Studies*, III (July 1965), 104–17; see also Keith Sinclair, *Imperial Federation: A Study of New Zealand Policy and Opinion, 1886–1914* (Commonwealth Papers, No. 11), London 1955, p. 43.
[62] Randolph S. Churchill, *Winston Churchill*, 2 vols, London 1967, Vol. II, 'Young Statesman, 1901–14', p. 518–19.

The British government and its defence advisers did not, for the most part, appreciate Australian fears. In response to a Commonwealth government query as to the probable scale of any attack against the Dominion, the Overseas Defence Committee concluded that circumstances had not substantially changed since its report of 1906 and reaffirmed its finding 'that it is not reasonably probable that any military attack on Australia more formidable than a raid by a small landing force will be undertaken.' When its report was discussed at the Committee of Imperial Defence meeting of 26 January 1911, Chief of the Imperial General Staff, Sir William Nicholson, did express some doubt as to whether the report should go to the Commonwealth government 'in its present form' as it would be 'likely to discourage them in the measures they were now taking to develop their military force.' He thought that the conclusions as to scale of attack were 'based upon a naval situation that no longer existed'. He said that 'The British fleet was no longer supreme in all waters.' In the Western Atlantic the Admiralty had conceded that 'in certain eventualities we might not be able to assert our supremacy over the United States fleet for an indefinite period after the outbreak'; and Nicholson believed the Pacific situation to be similar, for, if the empire were at war with Japan, fear of a hostile Germany would compel Britain to keep its fleet in home waters. R. B. Haldane, secretary for war, defending the report said that in fact there had been no material change in Australia's strategic situation since 1906 but he agreed that a termination of the Anglo-Japanese alliance would have 'far reaching effects' and that the Commonwealth government should be advised to proceed with its defence programme 'to meet a situation which might arise in a few years' time.' Grey thought that such a negative attitude to the alliance should not be countenanced lest it be taken as indicating a preference. Rather, in place of a statement of hypothetical consequences which might follow from the abandoning of the alliance, the foreign secretary favoured the insertion of a paragraph which would attribute Australia's comparative immunity' from overseas dangers to the Anglo-Japanese alliance and would point out that with the passing of the alliance 'a new strategic situation would arise in the Pacific which would profoundly modify the circumstances of Australia.' The British prime minister concurred. The report was to be a weapon in the British government's campaign to have the Anglo-Japanese alliance renewed before its time.[63]

The move to renew the Anglo-Japanese alliance was already well under way by the time the Australian defence report came before the CID and here again there is evidence of a lack of understanding of Australia's position and a conservative resistance to the idea of consultation. The early renewal of the alliance—it did not as it stood expire until 1915—was urged for two main reasons. Firstly, it was desired, parallel with the negotiation of an arbitration treaty with the United States, to insert a clause which would prevent the alliance being invoked against a country with which either party had an arbitration agreement. Thus it was hoped that American apprehension about the Anglo-Japanese alliance might be allayed. This would seem to be

[63] Minutes of 108 meeting, CID, 26 January 1911, Cab 2/2. For the Australian request and the British reply see copy, cable, Dudley to Crewe, 15 September 1909, enclosing letter, Deakin to Dudley, 15 September 1909, and despatch, Harcourt to Dudley, 7 July 1911 enclosing Memorandum No. 438 M. of the Overseas Defence Committee, CP 290/15/2.

manifestly the most important reason. Secondly, the British government troubled by a steep rise in naval expenditure hoped to avert the necessity of a substantial naval build-up in the Pacific. Such an expansion of naval power could not take place suddenly and therefore, if the alliance were not soon renewed, Britain would have to increase its Pacific navy in a year or so or abandon any pretence of protecting British interests in that region. These discussions were carried on without any reference to the 1909 imperial defence agreements and commitments. It was as though the whole matter was being opened up *de novo*.[64]

The secretary of the Committee of Imperial Defence, in forwarding to the Foreign Office the report on defence questions to be submitted to the Imperial Conference, had said, while urging the desirability of renewing the alliance, that if the Dominion representatives raised objections they should to told 'that it would devolve upon them to assist us materially in providing the increase of naval force necessitated by the new international situation.' Sir Charles Ottley, giving vent to the feelings of nearly all British ministers and governments since the emergence of the crisis situation in Europe and the Pacific, wrote 'Frankly I dread any sort of *discussion* with our brethren in Australasia on these delicate and secret topics.' But he allowed that their views could not be ignored. 'The last thing [the British] want is a howl from Australia or Canada, if and when the British government decide to renew the alliance.' Therefore he concluded that it would be wise to consult them on the question in a secret session of the Imperial Conference.[65] The British government's first response was to reject this advice. Asquith commented that he could not 'conceive a more inopportune topic to bring before the Imperial Conference'[66] and the Foreign Office replied to Ottley that the government believed the maintenance of the alliance to be

> of such vital Imperial interest that its prolongation or otherwise should not be dependent on the views of the Dominions, and it is therefore one solely and exclusively for the Imperial Government to decide, without any reference whatever to the Colonies ... the decision in which the Prime Minister concurs, is that H.M.'s Government will not bring the matter before the Conference or discuss it there if it can be avoided.[67]

This decision did not last. Three factors changed the British government's mind, the 'howl'[68] for consultation, the Dominion demand for absolute control over their naval forces and the intensifying of the naval competition with Germany.[69] At the end of January Sir Edward Grey,

[64] Minutes of 111 meeting, CID, 26 May 1911, Cab 2/2. Grey said that 'the reason why we have sounded the Japanese Government now as to prolonging it [the Anglo-Japanese alliance] is this Arbitration Treaty with the United States', and urged support for an extension of the alliance 'in the interests of strategy, in the interests of naval expenditure and in the interests of stability.'
[65] Letter, Sir Charles Ottley to Sir Arthur Nicolson, permanent under-secretary of state for foreign affairs, 15 January 1911, Cab 17/74. Also cited in I. H. Nish, 'Australia and the Anglo-Japanese Alliance, 1901–1911', *Australian Journal of Politics and History*, IX (November 1963), p. 208.
[66] Minute by Asquith, 17 January 1911, cited in Nish, 'Australia and the Anglo-Japanese Alliance', p. 209.
[67] Letter, Nicolson to Ottley, 18 January 1911, Cab 17/74.
[68] Minutes of 109 meeting, CID, 24 March 1911, Cab 2/2.
[69] Cabinet letter to the King, 1 March 1911, Vol. 6, Asquith Papers. Asquith reported to the King that Cabinet after 'carefully and anxiously' reviewing naval estimates had agreed upon a record appropriation of

who always showed more flexibility than Asquith, wrote that he was willing to discuss the Japanese alliance 'privately when the Dominion Premiers are over this year.'[70] He suspected that the Australians would require 'a good deal of education' on the matter. However, he felt that if the Australians realized that 'the logical conclusion of denouncing the Japanese Alliance would be that Australia and New Zealand should undertake the burden of naval supremacy in the China Seas' then they would be reasonable. By mid-May 1911, when the Colonial Office was considering the Australian 'foreign relations advisory committee' resolution, it had already been decided that Grey should give the Dominion premiers an explanation of British foreign policy, including the place of the Japanese alliance within it, at a secret meeting of the CID.[71] The British government had decided to extend the precedent of 1909 and to invite the Dominion premiers to discuss in the privacy of the CID not merely imperial defence but also imperial foreign policy.

At the meeting of the CID on 26 May in the first week of the conference, Grey delivered to the assembled representatives of the Dominion governments a comprehensive and considered statement of British foreign policy. It was an impressive event. As Lloyd George pointed out later, the British Cabinet itself had never been treated to such an analysis.[72] Grey explained this unprecedented act by pointing to the consequences of the growing strength of separate fleets and forces in the Dominions.

> It is not possible to have separate fleets in a united Empire without having a common Foreign Policy which shall determine the action of the different Forces maintained in different parts of the Empire. If the action of the Forces in different parts of the Empire is determined by divergent views of Foreign Policy, it is obvious that there cannot be union, and that the Empire would not consent to share an unlimited liability the risks of which it cannot gauge, because this liability would be imposed upon it by different parts of the Empire having different policies. Therefore, the first point I want to make is this, that the creation of separate Fleets has made it essential that the Foreign Policy of the Empire should be a common policy. If it is to be a common policy, it is obviously one on which the Dominions must be taken into consultation, which they must know, which they must understand, and which they must approve; and it is the hope and belief that the Foreign Policy of this country does command the assent and the approval, and is so reasonable that it must command the assent and approval of the Dominions, that we wish to have a consultation, and I wish to explain, as fully as I can, the present situation of Foreign Affairs.

The argument was directed primarily at Australia. After describing the rise of the German 'Napoleonic' policy in Europe, the threat to British naval supremacy and what that would mean to

---

£44,400,000 with the hope that with stabilization of the naval situation there would be a reduction in 1913–14 of £3,000,000. So concerned was Cabinet with the situation that a committee was set up to see if the Mediterranean, China and Pacific squadrons could be further pared down.

[70] Letter, Grey to Earl Grey, governor-general of Canada, 27 January 1911, G. M. Trevelyan, *Grey of Fallodon*, London 1937, pp. 203–4.

[71] Note by 'L. H.', Louis Harcourt, on Australian resolutions, 13 May 1911, FO, 800/90.

[72] D. Lloyd George, *War Memoirs*, 2 vols, London 1933, Vol. I, pp. 46–7.

the Dominions, especially Australia and New Zealand, Grey turned to the pressing question of the Anglo-Japanese alliance, and gave it more attention than any other topic. To assuage United States' fears, the British government proposed an immediate ten-year renewal of the alliance; it was necessary for reasons of strategy, naval expenditure and world stability. Japan's good faith was praised. Provided the migration question was omitted, and Grey pointed out that Japan 'has never mentioned it in connection with the alliance at all', then he could not see any objection to extending the alliance. He hoped 'a decision' could be reached by the Committee.

The Australian prime minister with little hesitation approved the British proposal provided only that it did not entrench upon the Dominions' authority over their immigration policies. Fisher thought the renewal of the alliance would be 'a great satisfaction to the people of Australia, because we are undoubtedly somewhat apprehensive of the immediate future'. Indeed Fisher and Pearce wished to know what naval preparation would be made if the alliance was not renewed again in 1921. The First Lord gave them cold comfort. Laurier 'ribbed' them for their excessive anxieties, citing in contrast Canada's success in resolving the Japanese emigration question through a gentleman's agreement. For their different reasons, all could agree to sanction the negotiating of a ten-year extension to the Japanese alliance.[73]

Fisher was elated by this unprecedented act of the British government. The *Morning Post* quoted him as saying that as a result of the CID meeting

> All the barriers of reserve have been broken down and mutual confidence has been established for all time. A community of interests of the highest immediate importance and vast possibilities has been created. I will go back equipped with knowledge that will qualify the federation I represent for co-operation with the mother country of a more effective kind than has ever been possible before. By the revelation of the British policy Australia has been admitted into the very innermost confidences of the Imperial government.
>
> Hitherto the conferences have been consultative and advisory gatherings, and the British government has remained the sole consulting authority; today the Dominions are part of the Empire in all things, and no development however sudden should now be beyond our understanding.[74]

So overwhelmed was Fisher by the compliment paid to the Dominions and by the victory for the principle of Dominion consultation that, as the colonial secretary had foreseen,[75] he readily agreed not to press the Australian resolution on a foreign relations advisory committee in the conference.[76]

---

[73] Minutes of 111 meeting, CID, 26 May 1911, Cab 2/2.

[74] *MP*, 31 May 1911.

[75] Note by L. H., 13 May 1911, on telegram, Dudley to Harcourt, 8 May 1911, 'and it may be expected that in view of his [Grey's] explanation, the proposal for such an Advisory Committee will not be pressed', FO, 800/90. Since the agenda had been prepared before the telegram's arrival this item had not been included on the official programme.

[76] Fisher's failure to press this resolution might have also been due to the Labor party's hostility to it. In the Hughes Papers there are a transcript of a cable from Fisher to Hughes, 16 May 1911 and a draft reply from

However, the problem of codifying and institutionalizing this advance in consultation remained. Indeed the role of the Dominions in the making of imperial policy was the central issue of the conference. It was a puzzling question. In the first two days of the conference Fisher, along with the other representatives, had rejected the New Zealand proposal for an imperial parliament to control imperial affairs including 'determining peace or war', 'Imperial Defence', 'foreign policy', and 'International treaties'.[77] Sir Joseph Ward in a very confused and confusing speech had advocated the creation of an executive body which would be subject to an imperial parliament. In the proposed imperial parliament, which would have power to tax the whole empire for imperial purposes, Britain would have a clear majority of delegates. Fisher no less than Laurier was unwilling to lose the autonomous self-governing powers of the Dominions and to submerge the Dominions' interests in and under those of Great Britain. Imperial federation was as much anathema to the Australians as to the Canadians.[78]

The reasons for the opposition of the Dominion leaders were, however, very different. Canada, free from any threat to her own security, did not wish to assume a positive responsibility for imperial problems and, with it, onerous obligation for others' troubles. Australia, on the other hand, felt itself subject to a threat from Asia which Great Britain did not share nor really understand and it saw in the integrating of the decision-making process under the New Zealand plan the sacrifice of Australia's defence needs to those of the Mother Country. Therefore, though both opposed Sir Joseph Ward's resolution, Laurier argued against any closer association with the making of imperial policy while Fisher urged more intimate and continuous inter-government consultation.

> I am not going to say that there are not possibilities of having an Advisory Council of some kind associated with the Imperial government, who would be able to be in close touch with them at all times, especially in times of crisis and emergency, so that certain communications might be made by them to representatives on the spot directly responsible to the governments

---

Hughes which seems to suggest this. Fisher in his message referred to a cable from Hughes of the same date which stated that 'Cabinet Council unanimously of opinion that not advisable to submit resolution Conference.' Fisher found this 'surprising considering that full Cabinet Council affirmed and forwarded to Conference in connection with Declaration of London resolution that in such matters Dominions should be advised and consulted'. He assured Hughes the proposal did not affect the independence of Australia. The cabinet could not however be dissuaded and Hughes replied that he had consulted all the ministers and they agreed it was 'inadvisable' to proceed with the resolution. The only explanation offered was that it was 'a distinct innovation, to which we can't agree' (Hughes Papers 950/5/76). Even if Fisher were influenced to withdraw Australia's resolution, he enthusiastically endorsed a more limited suggestion for consultation proposed by Sir Edward Grey.

[77] Great Britain, *Parliamentary Papers*, 1911 session, Vol. LIV, Cd. 5745, 'Imperial Conference, 1911. Dominion No. 17. Minutes of the Proceedings of the Imperial Conference, 1911', p. 56.

[78] Ibid., p. 68.

of the Dominions, and we should be informed. On those lines I think something might be done.[79]

Fisher had the opportunity of making his case out when, at his insistence, the Australian resolution on the Declaration of London came before the conference on the third day. By this time the Australian representatives had decided that their specific objections to the Declaration were not important enough to cause them to stand in the way of ratification and when Asquith, as president of the conference, insisted on it being put to a vote, they abstained. Fisher focused attention on the principle involved. In his opening remarks on the resolution the Australian prime minister stressed that his government attached 'great importance' to that part expressing regret at the lack of consultation.

> Hitherto the Dominions have not, as far as my knowledge goes, been consulted prior to negotiations being entered into by the Mother Country with other countries, as regards treaties or anything that led up to a treaty or a declaration of this kind. I hold strongly the view … that that is a weak link in the chain of our common interests. Since we are now a family of nations, has not the time arrived for the overseas Dominions to be informed, and whenever possible consulted, as to the best means of promoting the interests of all concerned, when the Mother Country has decided to open negotiations with foreign powers in regard to matters which involve the interests of the Dominions? We do not desire in any way to restrict the final arbitrary powers of the Mother Country; that is not our desire at all, but we do think and we shall press upon you … that it would be advisable for you wherever possible, at any rate in important matters which concern us, … to take us into your confidence prior to committing us.[80]

The British government did not suffer the Australian criticisms gladly. The colonial secretary had stated in the House of Commons on 15 February that 'It has not been the custom to invite criticism on these matters, though His Majesty's Government is always prepared to receive it.'[81] On 29 May the Colonial Office, at Harcourt's instance, sent to the Foreign Office a memorandum praising Laurier's *laissez-faire* attitude and pointing up the awkward implication of the Australian suggestions. However, the strength of Australian feeling could not be ignored and the inherent logic of their position could not be denied, and so the Colonial Office suggested that Dominion representatives be associated with the interdepartmental committees which were usually appointed before diplomatic negotiations began.[82] Sir Edward Grey, in answering Fisher at the Imperial Conference, said he understood their position and cautiously conceded a right of consultation to the Dominions which he thought might take place best, as the Colonial Office suggested, when the interdepartmental committee was formed. He urged that there could still be some cases where time or matter would make consultation undesirable. Laurier stuck to his last

[79] Ibid., p. 69.
[80] Ibid., pp. 97–8.
[81] Great Britain, 5 *Parliamentary Debates* (Commons), XXI, 1034–5, 15 February 1911.
[82] Memorandum, H. Just to William G. Tyrrell, private secretary to Sir Edward Grey, 29 May 1911, FO, 800/90.

and poured cold water on the idea. 'In my humble judgment if you undertake to be consulted and to lay down a wish that your advice should be pursued as to the manner in which the war is to be carried on, it implies, of necessity, that you should take part in that war.' Canada, he went on, has taken the position 'that we do not think we are bound to take part in every war.'[83]

Fisher, unmoved by Laurier's admonitions, eagerly accepted Grey's offer and on the following day substituted in place of the expression of regret at not being consulted a new resolution,

> That this Conference, after hearing the Secretary of State for Foreign Affairs, cordially concurs in the proposal of the Imperial Government, viz:
>
> (a) that the Dominions shall be afforded an opportunity of consultation when framing the instruction to be given to British Delegates at future meetings of the Hague Conference, and that Conventions affecting the Dominions provisionally assented to at that Conference shall be circulated among the Dominion Governments for their consideration before any such Convention is signed; and
>
> (b) that a similar procedure, where time and opportunity and the subject matter permit, shall as far as possible be used when preparing instructions for the negotiation of other international agreements affecting the Dominions.[84]

Fisher, grasping at what seemed to him a real breakthrough, accepted the qualification which left the British government's freedom of action essentially unimpaired. However, the inclusion of the qualifications ensured unanimity and the resolution was passed finally without opposition.

The two remaining constitutional issues at the conference which touched on the general question of consultation were the move for the establishment of a standing committee of the conference and the resolution to provide for the holding of the next conference in one of the Dominions. The colonial secretary proposed a standing committee to try and head off the New Zealand move to give the Dominions greater authority over the Dominion section of the Colonial Office and perhaps to meet the Australian desire for a foreign relations committee. But, in contrast to the Australian proposal, Harcourt's standing committee was to be responsible to the colonial secretary and not the foreign secretary. It was to be made up of high commissioners or other Dominion representatives and was to be restricted to dealing with matters arising out of the previous Imperial Conference and 'any cognate matters which may be properly referred to it'.[85] Only Fisher and Ward supported the idea. Fisher felt that the Committee of Imperial Defence revelations had made it all the more necessary to establish some subsidiary body to facilitate closer communications. But Laurier was content with the present system. Others felt that it would derogate from the status of the Imperial Conference and in face of such criticisms the British dropped their proposal.[86]

---

[83] Cd. 5745, pp. 114–17.
[84] Ibid., pp. 130–1.
[85] Ibid., p. 77.
[86] Ibid., pp. 173–93.

From the time that he first gave thought to Australian-Imperial relations Fisher had seen that the British ministers lacked any appreciation of the strategic views of the Pacific Dominions. After his visit to South Africa he had come to believe that travel could be an important educational influence and so on the last day of the Imperial Conference he introduced a resolution urging reciprocal visits between British and Dominion Ministers, and suggesting that consideration be given to holding the next conference in one of the Dominions. Asquith demurred about the possibility of holding the conference outside London where all the resources of the imperial departments were at the disposal of the members. Fisher refused to withdraw his motion but added 'or a subsidiary conference' as a compromise gesture, and in the amended form the resolution was agreed to. The Australians had little immediate success with any of their other agenda items. The principle of encouraging British migration to the Dominions was again approved. But the resolutions supporting closer co-operation in commercial matters and special protection for British goods and ships were replaced by a motion to set up a Royal Commission to inquire into the resources of the empire. The Imperial Court of Appeal was left in the hands of the British government.

Fisher when he had first arrived in London had said that 'by far the most important matter to be dealt with was Imperial Defence.'[87] If he had in mind a further British or Dominion naval commitment to defence in the Pacific he must have been disappointed in the event. The most notable achievement during the conference in the defence field was the delineation of the areas of responsibility of the Australian and Canadian naval units and the determining of the precise relations that were to exist between these units and the Admiralty. On the initiative of Australia a committee had been set up in London to prepare a statement on the matter. The Admiralty still fighting a rearguard battle on behalf of the unitary 'blue sea' school doctrine, wished to persuade the Dominions to agree that in time of war their naval forces would automatically come under the control of the Royal Navy unless the Dominion governments specifically withheld them.[88] But Pearce for Australia and Laurier for Canada would not tolerate any proposal which abridged their full technical control. At the meeting of the Committee of Imperial Defence on 30 May Asquith, arguing for unity in time of war, stated that if the United Kingdom were at war, then the whole empire would be at war. He declared that though it was true Canada could not be invaded, nevertheless it had a large commerce worth defending. Turning to the Australians, he contended that it was 'wholly unthinkable' that their interests would be neglected. However, he allowed that the British must accept naval co-operation 'upon the terms which you are prepared to give it'. In the end the only infringement of their authority which the Dominions would permit was that once their ships in time of war had been placed under Admiralty control they would leave them there until the end of hostilities.[89] In the final agreement it was decided that 'The naval services and forces of the Dominions of Canada and Australia will be exclusively under the control of their

---

[87] *SMH*, 17 May 1911.
[88] Minutes of 109 meeting, CID, 24 March 1911, Cab 2/2.
[89] Minutes of 113 meeting, CID, 30 May 1911, ibid.

respective Governments.'[90] Under the agreement the area covered by the Australian station was considerably reduced in comparison with that given to the Australian Imperial Squadron under the 1903 agreement. In the north the limits were drawn back to Papua and in the east to Norfolk Island. All foreign and other British territories were put outside the limits of the Australian station. It is difficult to know whether this was due to Admiralty jealousy or Australian parochialism; the weight of evidence would seem to point to the former explanation.[91]

By the end of the 1911 Imperial Conference the Labor government had come a long way. Its response to a threatening Pacific and world situation had grown in substance with time and experience. It needed little education on the broad requirements of defence. Its military training scheme went far beyond that envisaged by its predecessors. It invited Admiral Henderson to advise it on the completion and extension of Australian naval defence. It almost doubled expenditure on defence from £1,535,405 in 1909–1910 to £3,006,026 in 1910–1911,[92] an increase from seven shillings and three pence per head in 1909–10, to twelve shillings and eight pence per head in 1910–11, and it accepted the necessity of assuming an even more onerous burden in the future.

But defence was not enough. Australia could not hope to survive merely by strengthening its own defences even in such a marked manner. As Deakin had warned, diplomacy, too, was important. The rest of the empire, especially the British government which had the initiative in and responsibility for foreign policy, had to be compelled to take heed of the hard facts of Australia's position in the Pacific. Australia had to have a voice in the councils of the empire. Slowly the Fisher government had come to recognize this and at the end of the Imperial Conference Fisher claimed that a measure of success had been secured. For the Australian prime minister the great achievement of the conference was to be found in the fact that the Dominions had been brought 'into the inner counsels of the nations' and been given an opportunity to 'discuss the affairs of the Empire as they affect each and all of us'. He was uncertain as to what this portended for the future but he was optimistic.[93]

Certainly Asquith had said that authority over foreign relations could not be shared,[94] and the British representatives had managed to hedge around the resolution on consultation with qualifications that virtually left them still with a free hand. Yet the principle had been conceded. The Dominions had been treated to a survey of imperial foreign policy which had not even been vouchsafed to the British Cabinet. Their approval of the renewal of the Anglo-Japanese alliance and the Declaration of London had been sought. Perhaps Fisher claimed too much for the changes which had been wrought. Certainly, he was too sanguine about the future; Australia was

---

[90] CofA, *Parliamentary Papers*, 1911 session, Vol. II, No. 12 'Memorandum of Conference Between the British Admiralty and the Representatives of the Dominions of Canada and Australia', June 1911.

[91] See Schedule to Naval Agreement of 1903 and Schedule B to 'Memorandum of Conference Between the British Admiralty and the Representatives of the Dominions of Canada and Australia', June 1911, ibid.

[92] CofA, *Official Year Book*, No. 17, 1924, p. 595.

[93] *The Times*, 21 June 1911.

[94] Cd. 5745, p. 71.

never consulted about the Agadir crisis which occurred just two months after the conference had disbanded.

It could be argued that Fisher should have pressed more vigorously the case for consultation and for an advisory committee on foreign policy. It might be suggested that he was corrupted by the aristocratic hospitality or overawed by the imperial splendour which marked the coronation. Yet there is little to support either proposition. He did his duty by the British labour movement, accompanying Keir Hardie to the Welsh coalfields where he wished the striking miners of Ton-y-pandy success in their struggle.[95] Similarly when Oxford University offered Fisher the honorary degree of LLD, he declined on the ground of, as he flippantly put it, 'youth and other disabilities'.[96] Fisher lacked the self-assurance and creative drive of Deakin. On questions of 'high policy' he felt a little out of his depth and was therefore more apt to take the line of 'sweet reasonableness'. Moreover, Australia had little to offer the British government in return for a say in the making of imperial policy and, even more important, the Dominions themselves could not agree either on the desirability of such a reform or the best means of achieving it.

Fisher did not define very precisely the advance which had been made at the conference—he was not noted for the clarity of his exposition—but the changes themselves were elusive and to a degree uncertain and so this was not surprising. When all was said and done, what was remarkable was the tenacity with which the Australians had pursued their object and the important precedents for consultation and co-operation which, primarily because of their efforts, had emerged from the conference.

---

[95] *South Wales News*, 11 July 1912 and *SMH*, 12 July 1912.
[96] *SMH*, 21 June 1911.

# 8

# The Breakdown in Imperial Co-operation, 1911–13

The Australian representatives returned from the Imperial Conference of 1911 in a distinctly hopeful mood.[1] The success of the conference, the seeming willingness of the British government to consult the Dominions on foreign policy and the renewal of the Anglo-Japanese alliance when added to the 1909 assurances of a restoration of British naval power in the Pacific did much to allay Australian fears for their safety. However, within almost twelve months this promise of imperial co-operation and Pacific security, so hardly won, was in ruins and as a result the Australian government undertook an expanded naval building programme, began to look more directly to the other Pacific Dominions for assistance and, rebuking the British authorities for failing to honour their obligations, pressed for another conference to reconsider the question of imperial defence.

## *The calm before storm*

The fruits of the 1911 conference were generally welcomed in Australia. The announcement of the renewal of the Anglo-Japanese alliance met with scarcely a ripple of opposition. The press gave their unanimous approval.[2] The *Sydney Morning Herald* editorial was not unrepresentative.

> It is a proof that now she [Japan] has resolved for ten years at least to abandon all ideas of extension of territory. It may be that in the intervening period she will be able to prepare for further adventures. But the next ten years will give Australians time to test the value of their own resolves to become capable of self-defence.[3]

Though accepted by many as some kind of assurance of Japan's good behaviour in the immediate future, the relief which was widely felt was qualified by apprehension as to what might happen when the treaty expired.

The attitude of the government and parliament was similar. Perhaps the political leaders were rather more sceptical. Fisher, who had given his consent to the extension of the alliance at the Committee of Imperial Defence meeting on 26 May had failed either to consult or inform the acting prime minister or the Australian cabinet. They learnt of the extension of the Japanese treaty through the press.[4] Hughes was peeved at having been ignored.[5] It is highly unlikely that Fisher's

---

[1] *SMH*, 9 August 1911.

[2] D. C. S. Sisson, *Attitudes to Japan and Defence, 1890–1923*, p. 67.

[3] *SMH*, 17 July 1911.

[4] *SMH*, 19 July 1911. On being questioned Hughes said 'No, we were not consulted.' He conceded it might have been mentioned to Fisher but he maintained that 'the Government as a Government had not received any communication on the subject.'

[5] *SMH*, 25 July 1911.

weak apology on his return to Australia would have soothed the little man's ruffled feelings. At the ministerial luncheon given by his colleague on his return to Melbourne, Fisher said 'someone had to take the responsibility. I accepted with my colleagues the responsibility of saying that we approved of an extension of that treaty.'[6] Fisher had approved because he saw the treaty having a restraining influence over Japan. He considered that the conditions of renewal were 'more favourable' in that a mechanism which seemed certain to offer a means of excluding the United States from the provisions of the treaty had been inserted.[7] Hughes's view, though necessarily expressed after the event, was identical: 'This gives us breathing time, and, in spite of everything, makes distinctly for the maintenance of peace.'[8]

The defence minister was more forthright in voicing his reservations. Pearce had returned from the Imperial Conference through Russia and Japan and in the journal that he kept he recorded his impression that though militarism did not obtrude itself nevertheless 'government ironworks, coalmines, wireless stations, docks and shipyards, forts, barracks and naval stations all proclaim Japan's readiness for war and the deadly earnestness with which she makes that readiness.'[9] In speaking at a Pleasant Sunday Afternoon under the auspices of the Brunswick Political Labour Council, he said that

> Until he had visited Europe he had been of the opinion that Australia was an appanage of England. He now saw that Australia's future would be more largely affected by the nations to the north than by any group of European powers. Europe was a month's journey from the Commonwealth, but it took only eight days to go from Japan to Australia. It was imperative that Australians should arm themselves to be in readiness for any emergency.[10]

He was against Australians being lulled into a false sense of security by the renewal of the Japanese alliance.

A number of backbenchers were still more outspoken. Colonel Granville Ryrie, the Liberal member for the blue ribbon seat of North Sydney, thought that Japan might prove a 'menace' and repeated Cook's old dictum that 'treaties are easily broken … if there is a desire to break them.' Sir Robert Best, a Victorian conservative, warned that though Australia would have an opportunity in the next ten years to develop its defence, nevertheless Japan would be able 'to develop, at an infinitely greater rate, her powers of offence and defence.'[11] Yet, even taking these anxious voices into account, it is clear that the renewal of the alliance did ease a little the fears which had been

---

[6] *Argus*, 15 August 1911.

[7] Ibid.

[8] *Argus*, 18 July 1911.

[9] Account of G. F. Pearce's trip from England to Australia, June-August 1911, AWM, Pearce Papers, 4/7. Pearce's brief tour did not alter the views of Japan which he had held, at least from 1905, in any material way.

[10] *Argus*, 23 October 1911. Pearce also used the first-hand evidence of the 'Yellow Peril', gained through his visit to Japan, to silence the militant Labor critics of the government defence policies. See his speech to the Australian Miners Association at Broken Hill, *SMH*, 13 January 1912.

[11] *CPD*, 1911 session, LX, 142 and 389, 6 and 13 September 1911.

building up prior to the conference. While approving the treaty of alliance, the Labor government, holding to the Australian policy adopted immediately after Federation, was still unwilling to give any ground on a commercial agreement and when the British government, following the renewal of the alliance, signed a new commercial treaty, the Australian government once again refused to become a party to it.[12]

Just at this time when Britain's position in the Far East was apparently being stabilized, a new diplomatic crisis which had repercussions for Australia emerged in Europe. Using the pretext of an insurrection against the Sultan of Morocco, France had in May despatched a military force to restore order there. Germany, seeing in France's action a desire for annexation, was intent on exacting compensation and on 1 July had sent a gunboat to Agadir on Morocco's Atlantic coast to demonstrate its concern. Unwilling to have France bullied into submission, the British government by the end of July was seriously considering war preparations. Though the Moroccan crisis had dominated British diplomacy since the end of May, the Dominions, curiously enough in the light of the promises made at the Imperial Conference, were neither consulted nor informed about British policy. It could be that the British ministers at first did not think the incident worthy of Dominion consideration, and then, when it reached an explosive stage in the middle of July and immediate decisions were called for, they found that the Dominion premiers who were on their way home from the conference were out of reach. On the other hand, there is no evidence that the British considered consulting the Dominions and the more plausible explanation is that they had no intention of letting the carefully qualified resolution interfere with their freedom of action.

But the Australian government did have a particular and general interest in the outcome of the Moroccan affair. When it was rumoured that compensation was to be found for Germany in the Pacific, the *Sydney Morning Herald*, speaking for many Australians, said that the presence of Germany to any greater extent in the Pacific would be absolutely intolerable to the Commonwealth. 'It would mean an ever-threatening menace right at our door.' Since Australians had 'to rely more and more on ourselves for defence in the Pacific' they had 'the right to reserve to ourselves the Australasian seas.' The *Sydney Morning Herald* suggested that Australia and New Zealand should, through a joint note, make their opposition to such a proposal unmistakably clear.[13] After a cabled exchange with the New Zealand prime minister, Hughes on 9 August announced that he had 'emphatically protested' to the British government against any such solution to the Franco-German crisis.[14] The Germans denied the rumour and the issue quickly died away.

Australia had an interest too in the general question of peace and war for the Commonwealth could not stand apart from an Anglo-German conflict in Europe. This was a point of particular sensitivity for the Labor government since, in the latter part of July, Fisher's loyalty to the empire

---

[12] Copy of cable, Lord Denman, governor-general to Lewis Harcourt, colonial secretary, 14 September 1911, letter books of governor-general, CP 78/8.

[13] *SMH*, 4 August 1911.

[14] *SMH*, 10 August 1911.

had been brought under question as a result of the report of an interview which was published in the *Review of Reviews*. W. T. Stead, the journal's editor, who was an eccentric crusader on behalf of pacifist and other humanitarian causes,[15] had had breakfast with the Commonwealth prime minister in London on the eve of his departure for Australia. In the published account of their conversation, Fisher was quoted as saying

> Don't talk of Empire. We are not an Empire. We are a very loose association of five nations, each independent, and each willing, for the time, to remain in fraternal and cooperative union with Great Britain and each other, but only on condition that if at any time, for any cause, we decide to terminate that connection, no one can say us nay.

Further, Stead had Fisher assert that if Britain went to war, and the Commonwealth government considered its cause unjust and its enemy in the right, then Australia might well 'haul down the Union Jack and hoist our own flag and start on our own.'[16] While Fisher was on the high seas, news of this sensational interview reached Australia and caused a great stir.[17] The anti-Labor forces seized their opportunity. Self-appointed guardians of the imperial religion arose to berate the apostate. Hughes replied as best he could, urging that judgement be suspended until Fisher could speak for himself. He denied vehemently that Australia would not assist Britain in time of war.

> I have no doubt at all in my own mind—because I know Mr. Fisher's views very well—that in what he said he was merely emphasising the other side of the idea [of imperialism]. ... I have no doubt that in his view we ought to be consulted, that we ought to have a voice in those matters in which we may all be involved. I feel very sure that it will be found, upon inquiry, that Mr. Fisher's views are quite other than those which the fragments cabled out from London would have us believe.[18]

And when Fisher was able to explain, Hughes's opinion was vindicated. Fisher after being apprised of the article, dubbed it a 'grotesque misrepresentation'. He claimed that he had simply repeated to Stead his established formulae: 'my objective was peace among the nations of the world, that my policy is one of effective defence and my aim unity among the British nations.' He denied ever having used the expression 'haul down the flag'; this had never been in his mind. Rather '"Keep the flag flying" is my ambition', he added. There was no suggestion that Australia should break away from the empire.[19] All who knew Fisher's record had to accept his account of the interview.[20] Perhaps Fisher's lack of verbal dexterity and lucidity contributed to the confusion, but the essence of the matter was that Stead had used the Australian prime minister for his own purposes. Hughes, in complimenting Fisher on clearing up the question, expressed Labor sentiment when he wrote 'Next let me join you in damning that blighter Stead. May he perish

---

[15] Frederic Whyte, *The Life of W. T. Stead*, 2 vols, London 1925, Vol. II, pp. 122–6, 287–90.

[16] *The Review of Reviews*, July 1911, p. 25.

[17] *SMH*, 22 July 1911.

[18] *SMH*, 25 July 1911.

[19] *SMH*, 29 July 1911.

[20] Deakin, who had been the only one among the Liberal leaders to refrain from comment, was happy to accept the explanation, *MP*, 2 September 1911.

miserably and in the end be compelled to interview himself—at breakfast with Old Nick'.[21] When then, in the first week of September, talk of war breaking out over the Moroccan issue once again claimed press headlines, Fisher declared that 'the people of Australia consider that the rights and liberties upheld by the British government and British traditions are too sacred for us to allow the Old Land to be attacked with impunity'.[22] Certainly Fisher's imperialism, as that of the Labor party, in general, had a different emphasis from that of Deakin, Cook and their supporters. Labor spoke less of 'the instinct of blood', 'race patriotism' and 'pride in world power' and more of the shared ideals and the inheritance of liberty. But despite this difference in accent, they could all agree that autonomy inside a united empire was the settled policy of the country.

It was not altogether a misfortune for the Australian government's peace of mind that it was kept in the dark over Morocco. Had the Labor ministers learnt of the divisions between the Admiralty and the War Office, the casual approach at critical moments to the threat of war and the lack of integrated contingency plans[23] they might not in the succeeding year have been able to approach their own defence planning in so relatively relaxed a manner. As it was, the Agadir crisis had subsided by October—Germany receiving colonial compensation in Africa—and the Australian government, from this more stable vantage point, felt able to relegate defence questions for the first time in five years to a subsidiary place in the legislative programme.

The Henderson report on naval defence, which had been submitted in February, was presented to parliament in September. Henderson had recommended a very ambitious twenty-two-year naval construction programme. In Henderson the Australian government had found an unusual Admiralty product, a naval expert who appreciated Australia's national aspirations and Pacific concerns. Though in his report Henderson had, after the orthodox manner, declared the primary objective of an Australian navy to be 'the immediate support of the rest of the Empire's Naval Forces in their determination to retain the Command of the Seas', nevertheless he had in his conclusions taken into account 'the whole Naval situation in the South Pacific', giving consideration to 'the positions of New Zealand, Fiji, and other portions of the Empire in the Pacific'. He recognized that imperial obligations in other parts of the world might require the Pacific Dominions to fend for themselves.

The report was a substantial piece of work; sixty-eight printed pages in length. In it Henderson recommended that Australia, over a period of twenty-two years, should acquire a fleet of eight armoured cruisers, ten protected or light cruisers, eighteen destroyers, twelve submarines, three depot ships and one fleet repair ship. It would, on completion, be comprised of fifty-two vessels and fifteen thousand men. The process of building up the fleet was divided into four stages. During the initial stage, 1911–18, the fleet unit agreed to at the 1909 Defence Conference was to be completed and the bases necessary for its reception, including one at Cockburn Sound in Western Australia, were to be constructed. In addition, Henderson suggested that in this first period a depot vessel should be laid down by 1914, three more submarines by 1916 and three

---

[21] Letter, Hughes to Fisher, 31 July 1911, Fisher Papers, 2919/1/3 Stead went down with the *Titanic* in 1912.

[22] *CPD*, 1911 session, LX, 131, 6 September 1911; see also *SMH*, 11 September 1911.

[23] Marder, *From Dreadnought to Scapa Flow*, Vol. I, pp. 242–5.

more destroyers each in 1917 and 1918. There were to be three more stages, each of five years' duration. In 1918–23, two armoured cruisers, three protected cruisers, six destroyers, six submarines and two depot ships were to be built; in 1923–8 three armoured cruisers, two protected cruisers, and one fleet repair ship; and in the final period, 1928–33, two armoured cruisers and two protected cruisers. The total cost of construction was estimated to be £23,290,000. Henderson argued that in terms of cost borne by British taxpayers and in consideration of the Australian commerce to be protected it was not unreasonable to ask for an appropriation of £3,000,000 annually, that is about twice the 1910–11 level, in order to provide and maintain this fleet. Ultimately the fleet was to be divided equally into eastern and western units, which would be stationed respectively at the two main naval bases, Sydney and Fremantle.[24]

It was obvious that Henderson accepted the Australian axiom that the Japanese alliance could not be relied upon for the continuing protection of British interests in the Pacific. The more cynical could perhaps argue that he was exploiting Australian fears of Japan in order to gain a more substantial reinforcement from the Dominion towards the general British naval supremacy. But, whatever the reason, Henderson's recommendations were drawn up before the renewal of the Anglo-Japanese alliance and when the Australian government came to examine them in the more tranquil atmosphere following the Imperial Conference, the Labor leaders seemed in no hurry to adopt them in full. The Henderson scheme went far beyond the proposals of the 1909 Defence Conference; it was a much more costly and long-range plan. The government had good reason to respond cautiously.

Speaking for the government in the Senate on 9 November, Pearce declared:

> We had a report from Admiral Henderson as to what, in his opinion, were the best lines on which to base the Commonwealth naval policy. In their naval policy, the Government are endeavouring to follow these lines, as far as the recommendations made cover the immediate future. In his report, Admiral Henderson saw fit to refer to a period of time covering twenty-one years, which he divided into three [sic] periods of seven [sic] years each. So far the Government are directing their attention to the first period of seven years.[25]

Indeed Pearce's error in describing the Henderson stages of development, citing three seven-year periods instead of one seven and three five-year groupings, suggests that he had not really looked beyond the first stage. At the end of 1911 the Labor government was content to rest on their 1910 achievements and to wait and see how the external situation developed.

## *The seeds of doubt and disillusion*

Though the Moroccan incident had ended quietly and peacefully, it had not left European diplomacy unscathed. For the Germans the outcome was seen as a diplomatic rebuff and a blow to their self-esteem while for the British the crisis had revealed serious weaknesses in their

---

[24] CofA, *Parliamentary Papers*, 1911 session, Vol. II, No. 7, 'Naval Forces Recommendations by Admiral Sir Reginald Henderson', ordered to be printed 14 September 1911.
[25] *CPD*, 1911 session, LXII, 2378–9, 9 November 1911.

defence preparations. The result was a renewal of the naval arms race and a heightening of Anglo-German tension. The slack in Anglo-German relations was taken up and the British government concentrated its diplomacy and defence planning even more single-mindedly on meeting the German challenge. For the Australians this meant the abandonment of the hopes and plans for imperial protection which they had carefully nurtured and developed since 1909. By mid-1912 the Australians were coming to realize that they had expected too much from imperial co-operation.

The British Cabinet at the critical moment in July 1911 had discovered to their astonishment that the army and navy were ill-prepared either for mobilization or co-ordinated action. They learnt that, in the absence of the First Sea Lord, the Admiralty were quite unable to offer the government a war plan: 'It was locked up in his brain.'[26] Under threat then of resignation from Haldane, the War Secretary, Asquith in October replaced McKenna at the Admiralty with Winston Churchill. Churchill found the task of reform no easy one and it was soon complicated and ultimately overshadowed by a new round in the naval building competition with Germany.

From September German naval authorities had been urging the Kaiser's government to make good their diplomatic defeat at Agadir by adopting a supplementary naval bill which would provide for the addition of three new battleships to the High Seas Fleet. Churchill, supported by the British government, tried to head off the German admirals, first by holding out the possibility of a naval building holiday, then by assurances of non-aggressive intent and offers of colonial compensation, and finally through a declaration freezing the capital ship ratio between Britain and Germany at 16 : 10. Negotiations, however, broke down when Germany insisted on the unconditional neutrality of Britain in a continental war. The British refused to give the Germans a free hand to upset the balance of power in Europe, and so in May 1912 the Reichstag passed a supplementary naval appropriation of ten million pounds.

Churchill had now to find the extra squadron for the Home waters as well as four new Dreadnoughts in order to maintain what he had asserted to be the necessary margin of safety. However, when brought face to face with the politically troublesome question of ways and means, the First Lord concluded that subordinate responsibilities would have to be disregarded to ensure superiority for the empire at the decisive point of the struggle, that is in the North Sea. In the estimate-speech of March 1912, he had indicated that the additional active squadron would be constituted by withdrawing pre-Dreadnought battle-cruisers from Malta and creating a new naval unit at Gibraltar. The new squadron could either come to the aid of the Home Fleet or, if free to do so, be deployed to protect British interests in the Mediterranean. In announcing British determination to respond to the expanded German naval programme Churchill on 15 May made it clear that in his view the 'true division' of labour in imperial naval defence was to be found in the Mother Country maintaining naval supremacy at the heart of the empire while the daughter-states guarded and patrolled the British possessions in the rest of the world.[27]

---

[26] Marder, *From Dreadnought to Scapa Flow*, Vol. I, p. 244.

[27] *The Times*, 16 May 1912. As early as January 1912, Churchill was exercised over the problem of Dominion navies and the 1909 commitments to build up naval forces in the Pacific. Writing to the colonial secretary

But the policy of withdrawal of British power from the far-flung empire—the ending of Pax Britannica—was not universally acceptable. Many Conservatives inside and outside the Westminster parliament refused to acknowledge that Britain was faced by mutually exclusive alternatives. Especially were they unwilling to abandon the Mediterranean, the gateway to Egypt and India. Their criticisms, supported by the powerful voice of Kitchener, caused the Liberal government to pause and temporize. At a meeting of the British Cabinet on 5 July the recommendation of the Committee of Imperial Defence that, providing a reasonable margin of superior strength was kept ready and available in Home waters, 'we ought to maintain, available for Mediterranean purposes and based on a Malta post, a battle fleet equal to a one power Mediterranean standard, excluding France' was adopted.[28] The financial burden of this policy went far beyond anything that had previously been contemplated, for a one-power standard against Austria entailed the building of three battleships over and above the supplementary programme with which Churchill had threatened Germany in March.

The ever-resourceful Churchill, seizing upon the opportune visit of Canada's new Conservative prime minister, Robert Borden, to the Mother Country, turned to the North American Dominion to seek a way out of his dilemma. Ignoring the 1909 agreements, Churchill urged that the most useful contribution which Canada could make to imperial naval defence would be the provision of the three battleships for the Mediterranean. Churchill, though admitting to the financial difficulties faced by the British government, stressed mostly the specious argument that if Canada rather than Britain contributed these Dreadnoughts then the Germans would be unable to use them as a pretext for stepping up again their own naval building programme. The Canadians had arrived on the day of the cabinet decision, 5 July, and Borden

---

he sought an opportunity to talk over the colonial naval question. 'I do not think anyone can doubt', he told Harcourt, 'that the arrangements made in 1909 with Australia were not very satisfactory so far as British Naval interests were concerned'. He continued, 'The whole principle of local Navies is, of course, thoroughly vicious, and no responsible sailor can be found who has a word to say in favour of it.' In trying to meet the pressing demands on Admiralty resources Churchill, while allowing that Australia could not be moved from its settled policy, indicated that it was his intention to approach the New Zealand government in order to persuade that Dominion to agree to let the Admiralty retain the battle cruiser *New Zealand* in the North Sea and to approach the new Conservative government in Canada to see whether it would consent 'to do something effective for the British navy'. (Letter, Churchill to Harcourt, 29 January 1912, Harcourt Papers, Box 468.) When Harcourt replied that he doubted whether Canadian opinion would tolerate such a proposal and that such a change in policy would have to be brought before cabinet, Churchill at first drew back, arguing that if the Germans failed to proceed with their building plans the Admiralty might be able to make do without calling on the Dominions. (Letters, Harcourt to Churchill, February 1912 and Churchill to Harcourt, 11 February 1912, Harcourt Papers, Box 468.) But by April, even before the German decision was known, Churchill returned to the matter, warning Harcourt that he was going to raise the question of the *New Zealand* in cabinet and asking Harcourt to seek the Dominion government's agreement (Letter, Churchill to Harcourt, 2 April 1912, Harcourt Papers, Box 468).

[28] Minutes of 117 meeting, CID, 4 July 1912, Cab 2/2 and cabinet letter, Asquith to George V giving summary of cabinet proceedings, 5 July 1912, Asquith Papers.

recorded that Churchill that very afternoon 'discussed the naval situation for an hour. Very serious?'[29] It was arranged that Borden should attend the next meeting of the Committee of Imperial Defence on 11 July when Churchill was to put forward his precise proposals.[30] The Canadians were convinced and returned home with the aim of persuading the Dominion parliament to appropriate the required funds.[31]

The 1909 naval defence agreements were now in ruins. For the British government they were now nothing more than scraps of paper. Churchill in May had said that, although it might still be possible by partial mobilization to send a squadron to the aid of colonies or Dominions across the sea, they had to face 'real and great facts', 'facts as hard as Kruppcemented steel'. He went on to amplify the point, 'pending a decision in the critical theatres, there is no doubt that the general mobility of our fleet is reduced. It cannot move safely and freely to every part of the world to the same extent as in former years.' Defence of the rest of the empire had to be left to the Dominions. Just as the concentration of British sea power in Home Waters had been the noteworthy development of the last ten years, so he expected that 'the growth of effective naval forces in the great Dominions overseas' would be the hallmark of the next few years.[32]

This new departure in British defence strategy was not part of a well-thought-out imperial plan. It was simply an attempt to make a virtue out of necessity and an attempt to anticipate Dominion criticism. When the possibility of exploiting Canada for immediate British purposes offered itself, Churchill actively discouraged the idea of developing a Canadian navy to help protect the outposts of empire. Instead he sought subsidies which would increase strength at the centre and add directly to Britain's own security. Grey in the House of Commons on 10 July explained further the double standard which Britain applied in imperial defence.

> You must keep up a sufficient margin of naval strength in home waters whatever your foreign policy is. If you do not, your foreign policy will become impossible, because in every diplomatic situation that arises, if you are inferior in strength in home waters to a neighbouring fleet or fleets, in every diplomatic question you will have to give way. … When you get further afield into other parts of the world it is a very different matter; then foreign policy and naval strategy do and must depend upon each other to a large extent. Take the question of the Far East Of course, the … relation between the Japanese Alliance and naval strategy is a most intimate one.[33]

Grey was saying that while the imperial government would not leave the security of the British Isles *vis-a-vis* Europe to the uncertainties of diplomacy and alliance systems, in the Far East such

---

[29] Diary of Sir Robert Laird Borden, 5 July 1912, Borden diaries in the possession of Mr Henry Borden of Ottawa, deposited with the Borden Papers in the Canadian National Archives.

[30] Minutes of 118 meeting, CID, 11 July 1912, Cab 2/2.

[31] Borden after consulting his colleagues saw Churchill on 16 July 1912. 'Interview quite satisfactory. He is quite willing to play the game. Will give us assurance in writing as to the necessity. Will come over and bring with him P.M. Also Fleet'. Borden Diary, 16 July 1912.

[32] *The Times*, 16 May 1912.

[33] Great Britain, 5 *Parliamentary Debates* (Commons), XL, 1991–2, 10 July 1912.

risks were natural and necessary. In other words, risks could be taken with interests that were subsidiary and therefore expendable. Churchill had always regarded the empire as an appanage of British prestige, an appendage to British power. The other members of the Liberal government under stress could not dissent from such a conclusion. And so in a crisis situation British necessity without one word of consultation had overridden and nullified a clear imperial compact.

The Australian government only slowly awoke to the significance of this revolution in imperial defence planning. Perhaps at first it was impossible for them to believe that the Mother Country could treat them in this way. Both Fisher and Pearce approved Churchill's speech of 15 May, seeing in it a warm endorsement by the Admiralty of the principle of independent Dominion navies.[34] They were oblivious to its full implications. In answer to a question in the House on the adequacy of Australia's defence policy to protect Australia, Fisher replied 'we may rest assured that it [the British government] will not take any action that will weaken its prestige or power in any sea in which it is necessary to maintain its strength.'[35] Yet the situation in Europe troubled the Australian government and by the end of the year they were well aware of what the British were doing and had launched a three-pronged counter-attack to meet the new situation. Taking Churchill seriously, the Australian government sought closer co-operation with New Zealand and Canada in the Pacific. They rebuked the British government and sought a new defence conference. In the meantime they adopted the Henderson scheme in its entirety and took steps to increase substantially the size of Australia's own navy.

Surveying the problem of defence in the Pacific, Fisher, like Deakin before him, had become convinced of the desirability of establishing the most intimate co-operation between the two South Pacific Dominions. His South African tour had brought forth the first expression of the idea; and his experience at the Imperial Conference had revitalized it. On his return he had told parliament that he had 'never been able personally to discover any limit to reciprocity between Australia and New Zealand. New Zealand is really a country that ought to be associated, as its destiny undoubtedly is linked up, with Australia.' He hoped that it was not too late for each Dominion to consider whether a closer relationship would not be advantageous to both.[36] At the Hobart conference of the ALP the prime minister carried this idea forward sponsoring a resolution supporting closer union with New Zealand. Fisher said that 'the fate of one would be the fate of the other, if they ever happened to come into conflict with greater peoples and those more powerful than themselves.' It behoved the Labor party to take the lead in the matter. The resolution was carried unanimously.[37]

With the coming to power in New Zealand in August 1912 of the Reform party, the prospects for such a rapprochement suddenly brightened. The Reform government, under William Massey as prime minister and Colonel James Allen as defence minister, looked more favourably on the

---

[34] *Argus*, 18 May 1912.

[35] *CPD*, 1912 session, LXV, 1790, 7 August 1912.

[36] *CPD*, 1911 session, LX, 131, 6 September 1911.

[37] Official Report of the Fifth Commonwealth Conference of the ALP, 8 to 12 January 1912.

Australian development of an independent naval unit than had Sir Joseph Ward and his Liberal colleagues; they were critical of the British government for failing to honour its commitments under the 1909 defence agreement. After the Reform party's victory, Fisher, in explaining to the United Commercial Travellers' Association that 'Australia had a position more vulnerable against a foe than any other parts of the British Empire', evinced again his desire for closer trade and defence associations with New Zealand.[38]

In September the New Zealand defence minister indicated his sympathy with these suggestions. Fisher welcomed the New Zealand show of interest[39] and during the next three months with the encouragement of the Commander-in-Chief of the imperial Australian Squadron, Sir George King-Hall, the Australian government entered into conversations with New Zealand on the question of Pacific defence. King-Hall, acting independently of the Admiralty, reinforced Australian fears, pointing out that the position of Canada with the Monroe Doctrine 'at its back door' was 'quite dissimilar'; he warned against the danger of a future alliance of Germany and Japan. A Far Eastern fleet of which the Australian navy should comprise one division was, he thought, the answer.[40] On 1 October Fisher indicated to Lord Denman, the governor-general, that the Commonwealth ministers wished to consult with the admiral and two weeks later Denman so informed King-Hall.[41] At the Lord Mayor's dinner on 10 November in Melbourne, King-Hall aired his views in public: 'Both the Commonwealth and the Dominion of New Zealand would be forced by circumstances to enter the orbit of world politics, which affected the Empire.' He said that he would like to see New Zealand join forces with the Commonwealth 'forming in time a formidable Pacific division of the Imperial Fleet.' Fisher responded with enthusiasm.

> Australia stood as a great white population situated in the South Pacific, far removed from the mother country … and lying between Australia and the other white nations of the world were great nations, great in themselves, but with ideals which were not British ideals.

He said that the safety of Australia lay in naval defence and, from private and semi-official correspondence, he expected New Zealand to co-operate closely in providing such defences in their area of common concern. He hoped that Canada, too, would join in the creation of an imperial fleet for the Pacific.[42]

Three days later the New Zealand defence minister wrote that he would like to discuss the defence question with the Australian government before going to England in the New Year[43] and

---

[38] *Argus*, 19 August 1912.

[39] *CPD*, 1912 session, LXVI, 3405, 25 September 1912.

[40] Despatch, King-Hall to governor-general, Lord Denman, 13 September 1912, CP 78/64.

[41] Ibid.

[42] *SMH*, 11 November 1912. King-Hall's views had been to some degree shaped by a semi-official note on 'Suggestions as to the Establishment of a New Zealand Navy as a Branch of a Royal Australasian Navy to be provided and maintained by the Commonwealth of Australia and the Dominion of New Zealand' which the Naval Secretary, H. Manisty, had drawn up specifically for the Admiral. Pearce on 18 November approved Manisty's action, noting that his scheme was 'very practical', MP 1049/1, Box 5, File 14/0161.

[43] Letter, J. Allen to G. F. Pearce, 14 November 1912, AWM, Pearce Papers, 5/19.

at the end of December he broke his journey to London at Melbourne for this purpose. He attended a meeting of the Council of Defence on 23 December 1912 along with Pearce, Fisher and their chief naval and military advisers. The minutes rather non-committally recorded that the prime minister and defence minister explained the future proposals of the Commonwealth 'and an informal discussion ensued'.[44] However, the substance would seem to have been greater than the record suggests. Plans were laid for raising a joint division of 18,000 men in case either country were attacked.[45] Moreover, in the light of Allen's subsequent statements in England, it would appear that agreement was also reached on the urgency of Pacific naval defence, on the failure of the British government to honour its obligations and on the need for Canadian participation.

Australia-New Zealand co-operation did not meet with the Admiralty's approval. Churchill reprimanded King-Hall for interfering in high policy.[46] Though he had earlier espoused the cause of Dominion navies, Churchill, after Canada had become the make-weight in his revised scheme of home defence, dropped the idea of independent fleet units and turned a further somersault in imperial policy in order to try and reconcile the needs of British strategy with the requirements of domestic politics. On 10 November he had asserted that 'what has made this year memorable in the history of the navy has been the spontaneous and simultaneous movement of the great Dominions of the Crown towards an effective participation in Imperial naval defence.' Then he went on to explain what effective participation meant: 'The Prime Minister of the Commonwealth, at such a banquet as this at Melbourne, is explaining the arrangements under which the Royal Australian Navy will pass under the general control of the Imperial Admiralty in times of war.'[47] But Fisher disappointed him. The Australian government, despite British importuning, was unwilling to make a public statement on this aspect of naval defence at that time.[48]

---

[44] Minutes of 9 meeting of the Council of Defence, I, 87, 23 December 1912, CRS, A2032(9).

[45] C. E. W. Bean, *The Official History of Australia in the War of 1914–18*, 12 vols, 'The Story of Anzac', Sydney 1940, Vol. I, pp. 27–8.

[46] Letter, W. S. Churchill to Lord Denman, 13 December 1912, Denman Papers, 769/42. See copy of cable, Churchill to King-Hall, 7 November 1912, 'Joining up of Dominion and Commonwealth Forces raises many difficult questions which should not be prejudged on the spot without full consultation with Admiralty. Withdrawal of New Zealand cruiser would be extremely inconvenient. You should temporise tactfully and urge reference to Admiralty before final decision', and also copy of cable, Churchill to King-Hall, 5 December 1912, Adm. 116/1270, 'You should not attempt to influence NZ Government to join Commonwealth naval forces. You have received no instructions from Admiralty to intervene in such matters. I am not at present convinced of the advantage of such a policy.' When, in anticipation of Allen's visit to London, the Colonial Office prepared a memorandum setting out a basis for Australian-New Zealand agreement on 'Joint Naval Defence' the Admiralty stood aloof and the question was never broached with the New Zealand defence minister (Letter, Harcourt to Churchill, January 1913, ibid.).

[47] *The Times*, 11 November 1912.

[48] *SMH*, 11 November 1912. For Churchill's request, see letter, King-Hall to Pearce, 8 November 1913, AWM, Pearce Papers, 5/22, and for King-Hall's explanation of Fisher's failure to comply with the request

## *A sense of betrayal*

Indeed, by November the Australian government had become suspicious of British intentions; the seducing of the Canadian government and the betrayal of the 1909 agreement was stirring resentment. Even before Borden brought down his bill to provide the three battleships for the Mediterranean, the facts of the situation were known. British and Canadian press comment on Churchill's memorandum on imperial requirements in naval defence provided the clues. The first precise statement from the Australian side of a sense of betrayal came from Senator Pearce in a letter of 3 December to the Australian naval representative in London. Discussing the failure of the Imperial Conference experiment Pearce wrote

> We had the Imperial naval conference in 1909 which drew up a scheme for the co-operation of the Imperial government and Dominions in matters of defence. The proposals were not rejected at the 1911 Conference, although they were extant; yet what has happened? Australia is the only one of the parties to the 1909 Conference that has carried out its share of the scheme then arrived at. None of the other governments have stated that they will not carry out their share; they have merely ignored it, and in my mind this action or want of action on the part of these governments is the greatest blow yet dealt to Imperial cooperation. … It seems to me that it would have been better for the 1911 Conference to have frankly and clearly advised that the 1909 Conference resolutions should not be given effect to.[49]

This feeling explains partly Australia's rejection of the British suggestion to send a permanent representative to the Committee for Imperial Defence and fully explains Australia's pressing requests for a further full or subsidiary conference.

At no stage in its reappraisal of imperial naval strategy nor during the negotiations with the Canadian government did the British government consult the other Dominions. Borden himself, however, had raised again and again the consultation issue. Unlike Laurier, he was a staunch recentralizing imperialist. Borden had regarded his electoral victory as a vindication of the imperial connection[50] and with the encouragement of the Round Table men in England and Canada,[51] had come to take a Deakin-type view of Dominion responsibilities in the empire and of

---

see letter, King-Hall to Churchill, 26 November 1912, 'The fact is that Mr. Fisher is *most cautious*, and a great stickler for constitutional forms, not only from a temperament disposed that way, but also he has always to remember the Caucus, (I believe at times that he chafes at the controlling power behind the Throne). He also remembers that he is the prime minister of the Commonwealth. … Both Mr. Fisher and Mr. Pearce … have often told me that the statesmen of the Old Country seem ignorant of the state of affairs and feeling out here. … Mr. Fisher and others are most anxious that you should come out to Australia … but I hope that if this is out of the question, it will be possible to have a naval conference at Vancouver under your auspices.' (Adm. 116/1270).

[49] Letter, Pearce to R. Muirhead Collins, 3 December 1912, AWM, Pearce Papers, 7/106.

[50] Letter, Borden to Walter Long, 24 October 1911, Borden Papers, OC 46.

[51] Letter, Milner to Borden, 24 September 1911, Borden Papers, OC 46 and letter, Lionel Curtis to Borden, 19 December 1911, letter, Curtis to Borden, 17 March 1912, and letter, Borden to Lord Curzon, 3 April 1912, Borden Papers, OC 130. See also Viscount Esher, *The Committee of Imperial Defence: Its Functions*

the proper role of the Dominion in the making of the imperial policies which defined those responsibilities.

When he arrived in England Borden made it clear that he considered the question of Dominion representation in imperial councils to be as important as naval supremacy; indeed he saw Canadian participation in policy-making as the natural corollary to naval contributions. In his first public address, the Canadian prime minister told the members of the Royal Colonial Institute, 'and I would like you to remember that those who are or who become responsible for the Empire's defence must, in the very nature of things, have some voice in that policy which shapes the issues of peace and of war. ... Canada does not propose to be an adjunct.'[52] When Churchill pleaded for naval assistance, the Canadians demanded in return recognition of the right to have a say in the making of high policy,[53] and the British in their need accepted the principle that, as Asquith put it,

> side by side with this growing participation in the active burdens of the Empire, on the part of our Dominions there rests with us undoubtedly the duty of making such response as we can to their obviously reasonable appeal that they should be entitled to be heard in the determination of the policy and in the direction of Imperial affairs.[54]

But the British government was to be no more hurried by Borden than it had been by Fisher into surrendering its control over foreign policy. 'Wait and see', Asquith added in the same speech, 'Arrangements ... cannot be made in a day. They must be the result of mature deliberation and thought; they will probably have to develop from time to time.' In 1912 the most the British government would do was to offer, as it had in 1911, permanent representation on the Committee for Imperial Defence and a vague promise to give such representatives full and free access to the prime minister and foreign secretary for information on all questions of imperial policy.[55] Borden probably claimed too much when, in introducing his naval bill, he asserted that, 'pending a final solution of the question of the voice and influence ... in London', the British government had agreed that in addition to the seat on the Committee for Imperial Defence, which had been accepted, 'No important step in foreign policy would be undertaken without consultation with ... a representative of Canada.'[56]

The British government could not ignore the other Dominions in such a development though it waited until Borden was publicly committed to his £7 million naval contribution bill before

---

*and Potentialities*, London 1912. In this paper which was delivered at the United Services Institute 20 March 1912, Esher urged 'that there should be no concealment of policy or intentions between the Prime Minister of this country and the Prime Ministers of the Dominions and that no new departures in Foreign Policy involving Imperial interests should be taken without the approval of the Dominions.' A copy is to be found in the Borden Papers, OC 36.

[52] *The Times*, 11 July 1912.

[53] Minutes of 118 meeting, CID, 11 July 1912, Cab 2/2.

[54] Great Britain, 5 *Parliamentary Debates* (Commons), XLI, 872, 22 July 1912.

[55] Minutes of 119 meeting, CID, 1 August 1912, Cab 2/2.

[56] Canada, *Parliamentary Debates* (Commons) CVII, 692, 5 December 1912.

approaching the other overseas governments. Intimations were reaching Australia in September of the proposals that were afoot and from the beginning Fisher was opposed to the idea of participation in policy-making through a representative permanently stationed for the purpose in London. He maintained that such a representative in London would get out of touch with Australian opinion and become 'a dead channel'.[57] This reasoning does not altogether ring true and one wonders whether Fisher's opposition was due more to his inability to bypass Reid, the Australian High Commissioner, in making such an appointment or whether his suspicions of British policy were already such that an indirect and second-hand influence was unacceptable. Certainly by 10 December when the British government forwarded the official invitation to send a representative to sit on the Committee for Imperial Defence,[58] it was this latter motive which, more important than any other, caused the Australian government to reject it out of hand.[59] The introduction of the Canadian bill on 5 December when added to Churchill's defence of Canadian policy confirmed Australia's worst fears. Churchill's memorandum showed clearly that the Asquith government was committed to a policy of concentrating British naval forces and, where possible, Dominion naval forces in the North Sea and adjacent waters. Though Churchill allowed that naval supremacy was 'of two kinds, general and local', it was the general naval supremacy of Great Britain in the decisive theatre which was 'the primary safeguard of the security and interests of the great Dominions of the Crown'.[60]

On 19 December the Australian government, because of the coming election, replied that it was impractical for any Commonwealth minister to visit England in 1913. As an alternative the Fisher government urged that

---

[57] *Argus*, 30 September 1912; *CPD*, LXVI, 3583, 27 September 1912.

[58] Telegram, colonial secretary, L. Harcourt, to governor-general, Lord Denman, 10 December 1912, Great Britain, *Parliamentary Papers*, 1914 session, Vol. LX, Cd. 7347, 'Correspondence Relating to the Representation of the Self-Governing Dominions and the Committee of Imperial Defence and to a Proposal for a Naval Conference', pp. 5–6.

[59] Copy of letter, Pearce to R. Muirhead Collins, 3 December 1912 in Papers of Richard Jebb, Institute of Commonwealth Studies. Pearce, in discussing the proposal for permanent Dominion representation in the CID, said that there was 'Danger lest Imperial Conferences and Defence Conferences should become theoretical' and he cited what had happened to the agreements arrived at during the 1909 Defence Conference as an example of what he meant; see also letter, Arthur W. Jose, Australian correspondent to *The Times* to A. Fisher, 8 December 1912, Fisher Papers, 291/3/1. 'I do not think that the British politician has even yet realised how independent is the actual colonial standpoint. He always imagines that the great majority of Canadians or Australians are still willing to accept the guidance of himself and his fellows at home. ... And so, where he talks about "consultation" he pictures to himself a good little boy admitted for the first time to hear his father discuss politics and sitting there ready to say "Yes, papa" and "No, papa" in the proper place.'

[60] CofA, *Parliamentary Papers*, 1912 session, Vol. II, No. 66, 'Naval Defence of the Empire (Memorandum prepared by the Board of the Admiralty at the request of the Prime Minister of Canada)', ordered to be printed 9 December 1912.

in view of the great importance of the Dominions adopting a common policy, and having a complete understanding on question of co-operation for naval defence ... a subsidiary conference should be convened in Australia in either January or February, 1913. If this not practicable, Ministers would be prepared to attend a conference in New Zealand, South Africa or Vancouver, Canada.[61]

In explanation of their request Fisher said that they recognized

the need for further and fuller cooperation for the maintenance of Imperial rights in these distant seas, and especially for the defence of the North and South Pacific Oceans. ... Our discussions with the New Zealand government have not matured, but they should be considerably advanced if the proposed conference is held.

Australia was deeply concerned by the effect of the British change of plans on Pacific naval defence and it looked primarily to the Dominions to fill the gap left in the 1909 Pacific defence arrangements as a result of Britain's failure to play its part. Whatever happened to the proposal, 'the present system', as Fisher put it, 'cannot continue, and I welcome any attempt to coordinate the present scattered naval forces of the Empire overseas.'[62]

The British rejected the Australian suggestions. The proposed date and place were 'owing to situation of public affairs' in the United Kingdom, out of the question. Rather gratuitously the Colonial Office telegram went on to add that 'it is doubtful whether they [the other Dominions] would desire a general conference at present.'[63] The blunt and unsympathetic answer released the pent-up resentment of the Australians. Pearce, shortly afterwards, for the first time publicly criticized the British government for failing to carry out its part of the Pacific naval defence bargain of 1909.

The Australian agreement is the only one that has been carried out. If co-operation is to be ensured, therefore, it becomes necessary for Canada and New Zealand either to carry out its schemes of the 1909 conference or propose some other to take their places.

We have not been given any hint either by the British Government or the Admiralty that they have changed their minds in regard to the wisdom of the agreement with Australia.[64]

Australia thought it would be mutually beneficial if Canada and New Zealand would join with them for the protection of their common interests in the Pacific. Andrew Fisher, at the end of his patience, declared that the responsibility for the failure to hold a conference rested entirely with

---

[61] Cable, governor-general, Lord Denman to colonial secretary, Louis Harcourt, 19 December 1912, Cd. 7347, p. 6.

[62] SMH, 14 January 1913.

[63] Telegram, colonial secretary to governor-general, 10 January 1913, Cd. 7347, p. 7. Churchill on January 6 urged the holding of 'a further conference with the Dominions on Naval Defence' (Scribbled note, Churchill to Asquith, Adm. 116/1270).

[64] SMH, 22 January 1913.

'the home Government' and he concluded 'But whatever they do … we are going on with our work.'[65]

The fear that Australia would be left to fend for itself in the Pacific was revived. The press was once again full of pessimistic analyses and dire warnings. Britain, pressed by European rivals, found a Pacific fleet beyond its capability. The other Pacific Dominions were divided in their attitude. The Mother Country was unwilling to help in finding an imperial solution to Australia's strategic problems. Once more, the Australian government turned back on itself in order to acquire through the extension of its own naval power a more tangible reassurance and, early in 1913, the Cabinet asked the Naval Board to prepare estimates for the next three financial years, that is 1913–14, 1914–15, and 1915–16. Basing their proposals on the Henderson report the Board asked for an expenditure of £3,000,000 in each of the three years or £9,000,000 over the whole period. More than half of this sum was to be spent on building bases and on new construction over and above the 1909 fleet unit. The £3,145,000 allotted to new construction was to provide one battle cruiser, three destroyers, two submarines, one supply ship and a naval aircraft.[66] The report was handed to Pearce on the very day that Cabinet met to frame its policy for the May elections and the programme was approved. Fisher, in his policy-speech, announced that the Henderson recommendations had been generally adopted as a guide to policy, and that, if returned, Labor intended to carry out a construction programme identical with that of the Navy Board's. He promised also that they would do their best to reach 'a proper understanding' with the other Dominions and Great Britain 'on the question of the protection of British interests in the Pacific.'[67]

Despite the Australian outcry and despite the fact that Allen, in England, was praising Australia's efforts and calling for greater attention to Pacific defence,[68] Churchill was not to be deflected from his course. He used his naval estimates speech on 26 March 1913 to try and bolster Borden's position in the Canadian Parliament's debate over the three Dreadnoughts.

> The people of these islands cannot be expected to go on indefinitely bearing the whole burden of Imperial naval defence. We have done, and are now doing, our duty, and more than our duty to the Empire as a whole … it therefore behoves the Overseas Dominions to make exertions for their own and for the common security, whether by what are called local navies, or by *what … is more effectual, by additions to the Imperial navy* [emphasis added by author] to preserve, restore or increase the world-wide mobility of the Imperial Fleet.

---

[65] *SMH*, 25 January 1913.

[66] Minutes, H. W. Manisty, permanent secretary to minister for defence, 4 March 1913, AWM, Pearce Papers, 5/34.

[67] *SMH*, 1 April 1913.

[68] Minutes of 122 meeting, CID, 6 February 1913, Cab 2/3. Colonel Allen told the meeting that he had come to London to discuss naval defence with the Admiralty and that the new New Zealand government did not think that its predecessor's policy of contributions could be 'a permanent policy'. He disclosed that he had talked with the Australians 'who were anxious for New Zealand to join with Australia on these matters' and expressed his sympathy with this approach.

As a sop to Dominion opinion, he announced also his intention of creating a trouble-shooting imperial squadron based on Gibraltar which would be available for service in any part of the world. It would be made up of the colonial contributions, the battle cruisers, *New Zealand* and *Malaya*, and the three Canadian battleships. The squadron would be but twenty-three days' steam away from Vancouver, twenty-eight days from Sydney and thirty-two from New Zealand, and 'the Channel in a very much shorter time'.[69]

The New Zealand and Australian Ministers were not deceived by this sleight of hand—twenty-eight and thirty-two days, indeed—and they were shocked by the general tenor of Churchill's remarks, especially his assertion, in contrast to his speech of the previous May, of the superior efficiency of contributions. Sir George Reid said that Australia did not regard the Gibraltar squadron 'as a sufficient guard for a world-wide Empire'.[70] Allen echoed Reid on this. Churchill's assurance that the Gibraltar squadron could reach the outlying parts of the Empire before any other European powers did not hold any comfort for, as Allen put it, 'we do not fear a European force. That is the crux of the matter'.[71] At the Committee of Imperial Defence meetings of 11 and 23 April 1913 Allen, in explaining Australasian disquiet over the Admiralty's failure to carry out the 1909 agreement, stated that they feared 'a situation might arise in which the Japanese alliance had come to an end while the challenge to the U. K. from Germany still prevented the Admiralty from strengthening the British forces in the Pacific adequately.' Moreover, the Pacific Dominions did not feel happy that their security should rest solely on the maintenance of that alliance. He assured the meeting that in both Australia and New Zealand the movement for local naval forces proceeded primarily from strategical considerations rather than from a desire for national self-esteem.[72]

Fisher wisely kept his own counsel on this matter. Since he was in no position to challenge the Admiralty's policy, a more or less discreet silence was a reasonable response. Inwardly, however, he continued to be troubled by the belief that they were heading toward a Pacific crisis. This belief was strengthened by the renewed Japanese-American tensions over California's discriminatory legislation which came to a peak in April.[73] However, he refused to castigate the Home government. Such a course was clearly unprofitable. Since British policy rested on the substantial pillars of economic, political and strategic necessity, complaining letters were not likely to alter anything. They had to accept that an imperial conference was not feasible in the immediate

---

[69] Great Britain, 5 *Parliamentary Debates* (Commons), L, 1760–2, 26 March 1913.

[70] *SMH*, 29 March 1913.

[71] Ibid.

[72] Minutes of 123 and 124 meeting, CID, Cab 2/3.

[73] *SMH*, 7 April 1913, see editorials on 'Japan and America', 'The whole incident provides food for Australian thought. It is a thing which might conceivably happen to us at any time'; also *SMH*, 11 April 1913, 'The Fleets of Great Britain'; *SMH*, 17 April 1913, 'Japan and America'; *SMH*, 22 April 1913, 'Japan and America'.

future. The Labor government sought rather to enlist the co-operation of the other Pacific Dominions,[74] and to develop further its own defence capability.

The Labor government had come a long way since 1910 and it had carried the party with it. At the 1908 and the 1912 Commonwealth Conferences of the ALP there was evidence of dissent and dissatisfaction and of a desire to find a more positive and peaceful answer to world problems than military training and arms expenditure. In 1912 a resolution was passed urging the government to try and secure international peace by bringing together the workers of the world. Even so, the conference allowed that such an initiative must not be inconsistent with Australian defence needs.[75] Discontent was also voiced in caucus and on 22 August 1912 Senator Arthur Rae of New South Wales moved 'That in the opinion of this party the expenditure on defence is excessive and should be reduced next financial year by at least £1 million.' But consideration of the motion was adjourned and never resumed.[76] The views and policies of the government prevailed in conference and caucus.

When in March 1913 the landing of the first British settlers at Farm Cove was symbolically re-enacted in the laying of the foundation stone of the national capital, Canberra, in the hinterland, on the uncivilized banks of the Molonglo River, two Labor ministers put into words, each in his own idiosyncratic way, the essential sentiments of the people whom they represented and whom they led. What they had to say on this historic occasion was, in its curious blend of romance, realism and ruthlessness, peculiarly Australian. King O'Malley, the American-born Minister for Home Affairs, concluded his address, 'I believe, according to the Divine plans and specifications, God commanded the English-speaking people to secure control of, and constitutionally govern, the earth in the interests of civilisation.' The race patriotism of Australians was undeniable but dressed up in the rodomontade of 'he who never says anything in just the ordinary way that ordinary men say things', the speech drew laughter as well as cheers. Not so the harsher words of W. M. Hughes who, recalling that they were there to mould the destinies of the nation, declared,

> Mr. O'Malley has added another assurance, which I presume he got from the fountain head—that the Deity has fashioned us out for the purpose from the beginning. We were destined to have our own way from the beginning and America—two nations that have always had their way, for they killed everybody to get it. I declare to you that in no other way shall we be able to come to our own except by preparing to hold that which we have now. … The people are incapable of nourishing abstract ideals. They must have a symbol. Here we have a symbol of nationality. … The first historic event in the history of the Commonwealth we are engaged in today without the slightest trace of that race we have banished from the face of the earth. We must not be too proud lest we should, too, in time disappear. We must take steps to safeguard that foothold we now have.[77]

---

[74] See Fisher's speech reported in *SMH*, 30 April 1913.

[75] Official report of the Fifth Commonwealth Conference of the ALP, January 1912.

[76] Minutes of the meetings of the Federal ALP Caucus, III, 62, 22 August 1912.

[77] *SMH*, 13 March 1913.

# 9

# Anglo-Australian Conflict over Pacific Naval Defence, 1913–14

In January 1913, following Deakin's retirement, Joseph Cook became leader of the Liberal party and on 20 June after winning a very narrow majority in the House of Representatives in the May election, he brought the Liberals to office. During the ensuing year the critical situation in Australian-Imperial relations which had been brewing for some time came to a head and the Liberal government, taking the bull by the horns, laid bare the conflict of views and interests over Pacific defence and imperial strategy which divided the Mother Country and the Commonwealth.

When the issue had first emerged under Labor, Cook had had little to say on the subject. As a trusting conservative imperialist of the old school, he found it difficult to believe that the British government would renege on the 1909 agreement, an agreement which had been the brain-child of the Admiralty itself.[1] In the election campaign of April and May he ignored the topic. In contrast to Fisher, the Liberal leader had not offered a new naval-building programme or any other substantial addition to the defence of Australia; rather in his election speeches he had concentrated on the centralizing tendencies of Labor and a promise to introduce a comprehensive contributory insurance scheme which would provide sickness, accident, maternity, widow and unemployment benefits.[2] Once in office, however, he was compelled to take heed of the decline of the Pax Britannica and the change in British policy towards Dominion and Pacific naval defence.

Though in public Cook said nothing of the breakdown in Anglo-Australian co-operation over Pacific defence, there is, in his rather scrappy note books, some evidence to suggest that he was privately exercised over the question. Of course, Cook had a very keen interest in the success of the 1909 defence arrangement for he had, as defence minister in the Fusion government, been responsible for its acceptance by parliament, and, in presenting his case for an Australian naval unit, he had shown a keen perception of the danger which a militarist and expansionist. Japan represented to Australia. In 1910 he had confided to his diary that 'National security must be considered above everything else. The nation which depends for its defence upon other powers is lost.'[3] By early 1913 the implications of the failure to develop a British fleet in the Pacific had come home to him. 'Our influence in South Pacific not extending. Monroe Doctrine not in sight.'[4] After assuming the reins of office, circumstances forced the Liberal government to take a stand and

---

[1] *CPD*, 1912 session, LXIX, 7274, 20 December 1912.
[2] *SMH*, 4 April 1913.
[3] Cook Diary, 1910, Cook Papers.
[4] Cook Diary, 2 January 1913, ibid.

seek a clarification of imperial policy. At the end of June the 1903 naval agreement expired. The greater part of the Australian fleet unit was completed and the Commonwealth government, under the 1911 arrangements, took over control of the Australian station. So far, so good. But whither was all this leading?

In a series of articles on Japan and the white race in the Pacific, the *Sydney Morning Herald* pointed to the one-sided nature of Churchill's defence strategy by turning it on its head.[5] Supposing, as the leader put it, Australia had the only fleet for the defence of the empire, Britain would be sure to object if, when the situation clouded over in the East, the whole fleet with the exception of an obsolete cruiser or two were withdrawn to Hong Kong with vague promises of further help in case of an emergency.[6] Again, a fortnight later it said

> Australians have some reason to complain of the uncertainty of Mr. Churchill's views as to the best means of defending the outlying portions of the Empire. … The need of a fleet in the Pacific is greater than ever and so is the importance to Australia of possessing a navy of their own which they may see in their own waters.[7]

While preparing the budget Cook became aware that it was necessary to know where Australia stood in imperial strategic planning in order intelligently to work out defence policy and estimates; and so on 15 August the Australian government sent a reasonably clear but temperate inquiry to the Colonial Office:

> Government of Commonwealth of Australia are considering naval defence situation, especially arrangements come to at Imperial Conference in London, August 19, 1909 by which Australian Fleet unit will form part of Eastern Fleet of the Empire with similar units of the Royal Navy to be known as China and East Indies units respectively. Completion of Australian Fleet unit as then agreed to is near at hand, but it does not appear to my Ministers that China and East Indies units are in course of being provided. Government of Commonwealth of Australia anxious … to know exactly intentions of His Majesty's Government in this respect. If any new circumstances have arisen which it is considered should necessitate an alteration in this agreement to provide units, my Ministers would be glad to be informed, and, if thought

---

[5] *SMH*, 14, 21 and 28 June 1913.

[6] *SMH*, 28 June 1913.

[7] *SMH*, 15 July 1913. The *Sydney Morning Herald's* alarmist articles influenced policy makers. In the Defence Department an article in the *SMH*, 31 May 1913 which claimed that Japanese interests had established control over the Admiralty islands caused considerable disquiet. In a letter of June 12 to the secretary of the department, H. W. Manisty, the Naval secretary, urged that since 'The position of the Admiralty Islands would render them most important to Japan in the case of an attack on Australia … every endeavour should be made to obtain full information' and Creswell supported Manisty. Following on from this a cable was sent to the Colonial Office on June 20, requesting any information the British government might have on the matter. Though a vaguely reassuring response was received on July, the Australian government remained suspicious and apprehensive, and on August 22, after being informed by the British ambassador in Tokyo that Japan was acquiring ambitions for trade and immigration in the South Sea islands, their worst fears seemed to be confirmed (MP 1049/1, Box 2B, File/0286).

necessary, will arrange for representation at a conference, should His Majesty's Government consider such a course necessary.[8]

Since they had not officially been informed to the contrary, the Cook government refused to accept that the new British naval policy for the North Sea and the Mediterranean in itself necessarily meant the abandonment of the Pacific plans of 1909, and so they sought a direct answer to the question. Similarly, because of their strong emotional attachment to the Mother Country and their sentimental view of British political traditions, they found it almost impossible to credit that Britain, even under the direst circumstances, would not honour its pledged word; it was unthinkable that Britain would not treat her loyal Dominions fairly. Thus, they confronted the British government more directly than Labor had done with the seeming contradictions in its policy and when they discovered that Labor had been right, that the 1909 agreement was but a scrap of paper, they reacted with more feeling and with greater indignation than their predecessors.

The Admiralty took two months to furnish the Colonial Office with a reply. The Australians, pressed by their need to bring down a budget, sent a further telegram urging haste but without any perceptible result,[9] and when finally the reply did come, it proved to be highly unsatisfactory. The Admiralty, while accepting 'the general policy' laid down at the 1909 and 1911 Imperial Conferences, argued that

> The development of the general naval situation … since the Conference of 1911 has been such as to cause Their Lordships [Lords Commissioner of the Admiralty] in the interests of the Empire unwillingly to defer carrying the arrangements into effect in the precise form contemplated, and the exact time when and the extent to which it may be possible to make further progress in carrying out these arrangements in detail must depend upon the course of future events.

The passing of the new German Fleet Law in 1912 had so increased German naval strength in the North Sea that 'it became imperative for the Board of Admiralty to review the proposed distribution of the naval forces of the Empire strictly from the point of view of securing the preponderance of strength over our most probable adversary in all parts of the world', namely, Germany in the North Sea.

In carrying out the redistribution the Admiralty denied that it had violated the principles upon which the 1909 scheme had been predicated; rather they claimed that, as a result, the protection afforded the Dominions in the Pacific had been 'substantially increased'. Dealing with the first point the Admiralty contended that the precise composition of the Far Eastern units was 'primarily based not on strategic requirements' but on what was thought desirable for forming a nucleus for the Royal Australian Navy; the other units were to conform simply 'for the sake of homogeneity'. Consequently, they hoped the Australian government would accept that the new

---

[8] [8]Telegram, Denman to Harcourt, sent 15 August, received 16 August 1913, Cd. 7347, p. 11.
[9] Telegram, governor-general to colonial secretary, 12 September 1913, CP 290/15/2.

disposition adequately safeguarded British interests in the Pacific and therefore 'broadly fulfilled the purposes which the arrangements decided upon in 1909 were intended to serve'.

The distribution of battle cruisers and light cruisers projected by the 1909 agreement bore no relation to the dangers which 'actually require to be encountered in different quarters of the world'. A 'Table Showing the Naval Strength of Nations other than British in Eastern Seas—China, Pacific, East Indies and Australia', which was attached to the despatch, was meant to illustrate this point, Japan 'being excluded in view of the existing alliance'. There were 'no enemy ships in the Pacific which would not be adequately dealt with by vessels of a somewhat less powerful type' and so the *New Zealand* and the other battle cruiser of the Indefatigable class, which it had been intended to send to the East Indies station, were to be kept in the European zone where the great challenge to British naval supremacy lay and where they would meet ships of equal calibre.

*Table* 1 The British view, 1913, 'Showing the naval strength of nations other than British in eastern seas—China, Pacific, East Indies and Australia'

| Country | Battle ships | Battle cruisers | Coast defence vessels | Cruisers | Light cruisers | Torpedo vessels, gunboats and sloops | Torpedo boat destroyers | Torpedo boats | Submarines | Mine-layers | Special* vessels |
|---|---|---|---|---|---|---|---|---|---|---|---|
| Austria-Hungary | | | | | 1 | | | | | | |
| France | | | | 2 | | 5 | 3 | 9 | | | 6 |
| Germany | | | | 2 | 3 | 6 | 2 | | | | 5 |
| Holland | | | 1 | 4 | 1 | 2 | 6 | 9 | | 3 | |
| Italy | | | | 1 | | | | | | | |
| Portugal | | | | | 1 | 2 | | | | | |
| Russia | | | | 1 | 1 | 20 | | | 12 | 3 | 36 |
| USA | 1 | | 3 | 10 | 13 | 13 | 16 | 1 | 12 | | 16 |
| Chile | 1 | | 1 | 2 | 4 | 2 | 7 | 12 | | | 7 |
| China | | | | | 9 | 17 | | 18 | | | 21 |
| Colombia | | | | | | 3 | | | | | 2 |
| Ecuador | | | | | | 1 | | 1 | | | 1 |
| Mexico | | | | | | 1 | | | | | |
| Nicaragua | | | | | | 1 | | | | | |
| Persia | | | | | | 2 | | | | | |
| Peru | | | | 1 | 3 | 1 | 1 | | 2 | | 3 |
| Salvador | | | | | | | | | | | 2 |
| Sarawak | | | | | | 1 | | | | | 2 |
| Siam | | | | | 1 | 2 | 2 | 3 | | | 9 |
| Turkey | | | | | | 5 | | | | | |

*including river gunboats, transports, fleet auxiliaries, training ships and small craft of little or no fighting value. [10]

---

[10] CP 290/15, Item, 'Naval Defence of Pacific'. Japan by the end of 1913 had twenty battle ships and battle cruisers at least half of which were of post-Dreadnought construction. This latter group included the *Kongo*,

On the other hand, the British asserted that both squadrons 'had been reconstituted with careful reference to the strength of any possible enemy force which they might have to meet'. Instead of two battle cruisers of the Indefatigable class, the Admiralty had sent out two battle ships of the Swiftsure class and two cruisers, the *Minotaur* and the *Hampshire*. The result, they claimed, was to strengthen both squadrons 'substantially'.[11] The Admiralty felt confident that the naval defence of Australia and the Royal Australian Navy would 'in no way suffer by the course which events have taken'.[12]

Though Cook was unhappy with the Admiralty's attitude, it took him three months to translate this disquiet into a considered statement. For Cook the issue which had been raised was a difficult one. As a staunch champion of imperial co-operation in naval defence and a great admirer of the Admiralty's wisdom and judgement, he could not easily bring himself to question directly the soundness of their advice. In his reply of 28 February 1914 he tried to avoid a head-on clash. 'Doubtless' he wrote 'the considerations submitted would be given in a conference the great weight due to the experience, knowledge and consequent authority of those who adduce them.' However, as the minister of defence who had taken responsibility for an Australian unit on the basis of what had seemed to him to be clearly a mutual engagement and as one who was keenly aware of Japan's power and Australia's vulnerability, he could not help but draw attention to what he politely called 'some relevant considerations'. The aim of the 1909 conference, as Australia saw it, had been one 'of laying down and consistently developing a basis of Naval Defence, at once Imperial and local' and 'the primary object' sought in the agreements was 'the permanent protection of British interests in the Pacific'. While the Australian ministers recognized that changing conditions might call for adjustments, they could not accept that any new disposition should affect the primary object. They believed 'that the immunity of the Commonwealth should not be left to depend upon the continuance of such a delicate security as an alliance, however desirable and honourable, with a great and friendly power.' They could not see why the intensified

---

a battle cruiser superior to the Indefatigable class in displacement, armour, gun-power and speed (*The Naval Annual*, 1913, pp. 85–6, 257–9).

[11] Since it was the great new ships with their superior guns, stronger armour and greater speed which in the post-Dreadnought age were supposed to win the battles, the combined tonnage of capital ships, even when it was double that originally proposed, meant little. The Admiralty had simply put obsolete units out to grass. All were inferior in every respect to the Indefatigables. The latter laid down in 1909 were of 18,750 tons, were armed with eight 12-inch and sixteen 4-inch guns and were capable of 25 knots. The replacements were all pre-Dreadnought vessels. The *Swiftsure* and *Triumph* had been built in 1903, the *Hampshire* and *Minotaur* in 1906. The two battleships were only 11,800 tons each. They were armed with four 10-inch and fourteen 7.5-inch guns and could make only 19.6 knots. The *Minotaur* was 14,600 tons, had four 9.2-inch guns and ten 7.5-inch guns. The *Hampshire*, of 10,850 tons, had four 7.5-inch and six 6-inch guns. Their best speed was 23.5 knots. (*The Naval Annual*, pp. 216–20.)

[12] Cable and despatch, Harcourt to Denman, 17 October 1913, CP 290/15/2. The cable which reached Cook on 20 October was a summary of the despatch which did not arrive until 17 November. Since it was the despatch to which Cook replied, the substance of the Admiralty position presented here has been taken from the more extended treatment in that document.

threat from Germany could not be met 'by a special provision for Home waters that would not fundamentally alter the composition of the Eastern Fleet, the strength and disposition of which are of vital interests to the Commonwealth.'

Now that the challenge had come, Cook spelled out what might be called the Australian view of strategic defence inside the empire:

> In nothing is the British Empire more unique than in the fact that its component parts, while bound by allegiance and affection to maintain the interests and integrity of the whole, have special international relations and dangers which necessitate local provision for defence that strategic dispositions of the Fleet for protection of the interests of the Empire as a whole may not at all time adequately meet. A disposition of the Naval Forces of the Empire, 'strictly from the point of view of securing a preponderance of strength over our most probable adversary in all parts of the world' [quoting the Admiralty] may, indeed at times must, subordinate the special defence requirements of a distant Dominion to those of the Imperial centre or of the Empire as a whole.

But this was to be the exceptional case. He proceeded:

> Our common aim should be to adopt and consistently develop a scheme of Naval Defence which, as far as possible, meets the special, as well as the common danger, and which does not admit of the adequacy of a Dominion's defence being from time to time affected by the changing requirements of Imperial interests elsewhere. This is a consideration essentially different from those set forth in the Despatch from Mr. Harcourt of the 17th October, 1913, and to which, possibly, the Lords Commissioners of the Admiralty may not have given due weight.

Cook was willing to allow that

> general naval supremacy, 'the power to defeat in battle and drive from the seas the strongest hostile navy or combination of hostile navies, wherever they may he found' is a safeguard and end to be sought alike by the United Kingdom and the great Dominions of the Crown.

However, he put it to them

> that local superiority also, if not always an essential condition of general supremacy, may be of such vital importance to a particular Dominion that provision made for it should not be altered to remove any avoidable defects in provisions for the protection of British interests elsewhere. Both should be aims of a sound Imperial system, and, it is submitted, may without undue sacrifices be attained.

Finally, in calling for a new conference to re-examine Pacific naval defence, Cook struck a further glancing blow at the Admiralty's procedure. 'Indeed', he declared, 'the statement that an agreement come to at one conference should not be materially altered except by the parties at another, might well be accepted as of general application.'[13]

---

[13] Letter, Cook to Denman, 28 February 1914, CP 290/15/2, enclosed in despatch, Denman to Harcourt, 3 March 1914, CO 532/66. This despatch was received at the Colonial Office on 11 April 1914. Neither the Admiralty's despatch of 17 October nor Cook's reply found its way into Cd. 7347 which purported to contain the essential correspondence on the Pacific naval defence question. Cook agreed with the Colonial

Cook had charged the British with upsetting an agreed plan for developing naval defence in the Pacific and also had indirectly rebuked them for failing to consult with the Australians about this change in policy. But the main thrust of his criticisms focused on a conflict in strategic analysis. In a polycentred empire there might be as many views on the nature of external threat as there were self-governing members. This was clear with respect to Australia's fears of Japan. In contrast to the United Kingdom, Australia felt itself in danger from Japan and 'local superiority' in the Pacific was, therefore, as vitally important to the Commonwealth as 'general superiority' was to Britain or the empire. Cook's interpretation of imperial strategy challenged British assumptions. These Anglo-Australian exchanges over Pacific naval defence gave expression to fundamental differences concerning the principle of imperial defence. They represented at bottom a conflict of views and interests. Australia would not, as a general rule, allow its Pacific interests to be treated as dispensable or given a second priority in order to meet a challenge in the North Sea; Britain, on the other hand, insisted on leaving the care of British interests in the Far East to its ally, Japan, so that a maximum defence effort could be concentrated around the Home islands. Cook, the imperialist, insisted that permanent protection should be accorded for British interests in the Pacific as well as in the Home waters, that both 'local' and 'general' superiority could be provided for and that the Australian and British and the more broadly imperial interests could be reconciled.

A new conference came to be regarded as the panacea for the imperial dilemma. Before the Admiralty's cable of 17 October had arrived, Sir John Forrest, the Liberal treasurer, in bringing down his defence estimates, explained the lack of any provision for expanding the navy; the British government had failed to fulfil its part of the 1909 Pacific fleet plan and the Australian government in its correspondence with London had asked for a new conference 'with the view of deciding upon a further increase of construction in conjunction with the Mother Country and other portions of the Empire.'[14] Cook, in reply to a question in the House, confirmed Forrest's statement that a conference had been sought. Perhaps the time-lag in extracting a reply from the Admiralty had led the government to see the necessity of a conference and then to believe that the conditional suggestion in the August cable amounted to a definite proposal. Whatever the explanation, the assertions of the responsible ministers drew a rather starchy query from the Colonial Office. After reading the parliamentary debates, the colonial secretary wrote to say that he was 'unable to trace such a request. … No such request appears to have been contained in your telegram of August 16.'[15] Doubtless, the administrators had to keep the record straight but the unsympathetic and unimaginative, what one might call the 'clerkly' nature of their response, was not unusual. Though they pretended there was a significant ambiguity in the record, the inquiry had not merited more than a sea-mail despatch.

---

Office suggestion to exclude them: 'It would be too disquieting to public opinion' (cable, Denman to Harcourt, 9 February 1914, CP 290/15/2).

[14] *CPD*, 1913 session, LXXI, 1787, 2 October 1913.

[15] Ibid., LXXI, 1918, 10 October 1913.

After being told that indeed the Australian government had meant the reference in the cable of 16 August,[16] the British government on 13 March 1914 said they would gladly meet with Australian ministers to discuss Pacific defence. They would also invite New Zealand to join in the discussions. By this time the near approach of a sitting of parliament made it impossible for Cook, with his narrow majority, to send a minister to London that year. However, Australian interest in the summoning of such a conference was reaffirmed, and in the hope of winning Canada and even South Africa to their cause, Cook urged that all self-governing Dominions should be represented. The Colonial Office heaved a sigh of relief; now they could shelve the matter for a while. And on 1 April, they told the Australian government what was obvious—namely that the question of a defence conference would have to be postponed.[17]

## The climactic phase

Yet before the Australian reply to the Admiralty reached England and while diplomacy over the holding of a conference was still proceeding, a further incident took place which brought the conflict of views and interests out into the open and caused this issue in Anglo-Australian relations to reach a climactic point. The rejection of Borden's navy bill by the Canadian upper house severely embarrassed the British government. After promising relief to the British taxpayer in the previous year, Churchill now found himself compelled to accelerate two Dreadnoughts in the new programme and to ask for a record appropriation of £51,580,000. In his speech introducing the Admiralty's estimates, Churchill, as part of a plan to obtain Dominion assistance for protecting 'the heart of the Empire' against Germany's naval challenge, felt called upon for the first time to question the efficacy of Dominion navies and Dominion capital ships which were retained in local waters. He praised the wisdom of New Zealand in placing its contribution to naval defence under Admiralty control. He denied that the British government had failed to live up to its obligations or had placed the security of Australia and New Zealand in jeopardy. He argued very forcefully that the safety of Australia depended on British naval power and the allies that this power could purchase.

> No European state could invade or conquer Australia or New Zealand unless the British Navy had been destroyed. The same naval power of Great Britain in European waters also protects New Zealand and Australia from any present danger from Japan. While Japan is allied to Great Britain and while Great Britain possesses a sufficient margin of naval superiority, Japan is safe from attack by sea from the great fleets of Europe. In no other way in the years that lie immediately before us can Japan protect herself from danger of European interference.

He believed that 'the reasons which had led Japan to contract and renew the alliance will grow stronger with time', that the increasing European interests in China and their increasing naval power beyond the level which Japan could afford would make the latter increasingly dependent upon Great Britain. Churchill, the hard-headed realist in action, was perfectly aware of

---

[16] Despatch, Harcourt to Denman, 21 November 1913, Cd. 7347, p. 11.
[17] Ibid.

the rules governing diplomatic relations and went straight to the heart of the strategic issue. The Anglo-Japanese alliance was based on more than the plighted word; rather, it was premised on 'strong continuing bonds of interests'. It could be relied upon. Therefore he concluded, echoing the Admiralty's letter of 15 October, that there was no good reason for keeping the new battle cruisers in the Pacific where they would not meet their match. Further, to prove the British government's sincerity, he maintained that in fact the Admiralty had stationed more than double the force of the Australian unit in the Pacific and Indian Oceans.[18]

Churchill's speech was a *tour de force*—a two and a half hour exposition of British naval problems and policies. Though the discussion of the Dominions' role in imperial defence was only of subsidiary importance in the context of the whole speech, nevertheless, it was extensive and explicit and, in this respect, had no precedent. In the Commonwealth it was seen quite properly as a challenge to Australia's strategic view of local security as well as a unilateral effort to overthrow the 1909 agreement and it provoked a most explosive and critical reaction. The crisis over Pacific naval defence entered a new stage.

The Australian leaders publicly and unanimously rejected Churchill's assertions. Senator E. D. Millen, the minister of defence, immediately after the first reports reached Australia, denied that Churchill's proposals either for an imperial flying squadron based on Gibraltar or for the despatch of Dominion capital ships to British waters would find acceptance in the Commonwealth; the 1909 and 1911 policy might be disregarded, but a return to contributions was impossible.[19] He promised in due time to present a more considered reply. Cook was even more trenchant in his initial comment. He said that they were told

> that the Pacific was being made safe and secure not by the might and majesty of the British fleet but by the Japanese treaty. That raised for Australia very serious questions … when asked to rely upon the Japanese treaty alone for the peace of the Pacific, a very serious situation was created. They were under treaty obligations with a nation whose people they might not admit to their shores. They had their white Australia policy and they must at all costs defend it.

He was reported as hoping that

> the time was not distant when just as they had welded and standardised their land preparations in the south seas, so they would their naval preparations. … Time was ripe for such a development. They not only wanted to develop their sea-forces in relation to Imperial interests but they wanted so to combine as to make it possible to concentrate at any point where the Dominions happened to have the greatest menace. Forces should be so available that they might never need depend absolutely on treaty obligations of foreign powers.[20]

Fisher too, on behalf of Labor made the point that Churchill's suggested changes in Australian policy were unacceptable. Reiterating the policy which he had developed in office and which Cook had subsequently adopted, he looked forward to greater Dominion co-operation in the

---

[18] Great Britain, 5 *Parliamentary Debates* (Commons), LIX, 1931–5, 17 March 1914.
[19] *SMH*, 19 March 1914.
[20] *SMH*, 26 March 1914; *Argus*, 2 April 1914.

Pacific.[21] And the time did seem ripe for such co-operation. Though Churchill had cited the profound wisdom of New Zealand contributions as a worthy model which others might well follow, his example was peculiarly inept and showed up the desperate opportunism and naive arrogance which informed his attitude. The New Zealanders had already expressed their disquiet with British policy and their interest in developing co-operation between Dominion fleets in the Pacific. Now the New Zealand prime minister reproved Churchill for his presumption. He said at Greymouth on 22 March that 'he did not believe for one moment that the Anglo-Japanese Alliance had secured the safety of either Australia or New Zealand and it was just as well for Mr. Churchill to know it.' He was going to ask parliament to authorize the government to build cruisers for their own defence. He looked forward to the time when a British navy in the Pacific would by itself be able to cope with any other foreign power.[22]

The Australian press and informed public opinion were with few exceptions equally antagonistic. The *Sydney Morning Herald* praised Massey and agreed that the Anglo-Japanese alliance did not secure Australian safety.[23] Only the most conservative and deferential imperialist paper, the *Argus*, attempted an apologia for Churchill. While recognizing that Australian public opinion would not tolerate a policy of contributions, the *Argus* accepted that neither of the two great powers in the Pacific, the United States and Japan, posed a threat to Australia and therefore they believed that super battle ships and cruisers would do more good for the empire in 'Home Waters'.[24] The *Argus* leader, so out of keeping with the general tenor of Australian thinking, drew a most lucid and compelling reply from Frederic W. Eggleston, a leading spirit in and the Commonwealth correspondent for the Round Table movement. Eggleston was both a devoted imperialist and an intelligent and self-respecting Australian,[25] and it is highly probable that his views, conveyed by Creswell to Cook, had helped frame the despatch of 3 March which contained the most complete rebuttal of the Admiralty's position on Pacific defence.[26]

---

[21] *SMH*, 21 March 1914.

[22] *SMH*, 23 March 1914.

[23] *SMH*, 23 March 1914.

[24] *Argus*, 28 March 1914.

[25] Frederic W. Eggleston, *Reflections of an Australian Liberal*, Melbourne 1954.

[26] Eggleston wrote the only account of Australian-Imperial relations for this period which has given any inkling of the Australian search for security in the Pacific and the ensuing conflicts with the Mother Country over world strategy and defence policy. See J. Holland Rose (ed.), *The Cambridge History of the British Empire*, 8 vols, Cambridge 1929–36, Vol. VII, 'Australia and New Zealand', chapter XVIII. Both Creswell and Eggleston were members of the Melbourne-Adelaide branch of the Round Table, and during 1913 they had been debating the Henderson scheme and defence against Japan. In October Eggleston had presented to the group a paper on imperial naval defence in the Pacific (Sir William Harrison Moore papers, University of Melbourne, Round Table Box, 1913 Folder and 'Australian Defence' by Eggleston, 7 July 1912, Australian Defence Box, Folder 'Eggleston Miscellaneous notes and correspondence'). The despatch reveals the hand of Eggleston not only in its argument but also in the logic and precision with which it was presented. However, these views were shared widely among Deakin's young men who made up the core of the Australian Round Table movement. J. G. Latham, an influential figure in the group had given vent to the

In his answer to the *Argus*, Eggleston declared that Churchill had wrongly assessed the security afforded by the Anglo-Japanese treaty. He met Churchill's tough calculations with an even more rigorous analysis. He went along with Churchill's view that the binding force of a treaty between nations depended 'almost entirely upon the continued interest of the contracting parties in its maintenance.' Britain needed protection for its Pacific interests, a protection which pre-occupation with Germany in Europe prevented it from providing itself. Thus, the treaty conferred clear benefits on Great Britain. But the same could not be said for Japan. Churchill had claimed that British naval supremacy in Europe safeguarded Japan against European predators. This Eggleston refuted. In Europe 'an equilibrium of armaments' had been established and as a result, no nation could safely detach a part of its fleet to attack Japan. The balance of power in Europe, not British naval supremacy, gave Japan an immunity from attack from that quarter. The United States was Japan's only possible rival for control of the Pacific and the British government had made it clear that the treaty could not be invoked against the United States. The Anglo-Japanese alliance, therefore, differed in what it offered to the two parties and to Japan it offered little. It was not buttressed by an exchange of equal interests and was consequently a fragile reed. A further weakness was that, unlike the Anglo-French entente, it had not emerged out of a settlement of outstanding disputes. The White Australia Policy was still an issue in Japanese-Australian relations. Until an agreement was reached, Australia's migration policy would continue to be a cause of dispute between Japan and the British Empire. Eggleston believed that a truly imperial defence policy must provide equal and complete security for all parts of the empire. 'A policy which disregards the Pacific, or leaves it to Japan, cannot be regarded as a truly Imperial policy.' If Churchill's attitude reflected that of the British government, then the sooner the full Henderson programme was built, the better it would be for Australian national security.[27]

Eggleston's articles opened up a brief exchange with Archibald Hurd, a British advocate of the Blue Water doctrine, an exchange which was, because of its reasonableness and lucidity, a high-point in the Anglo-Australian debate. Hurd asserted that the Japanese alliance was 'at present more essential' to the Japanese than the British but 'it accords with both our needs.' He conceded, however, that it would not be a permanent factor guaranteeing British interests in the Pacific and the only solution he could offer was imperial unity so that British forces would be used most effectively. Even so, the British navy could never be supreme in all seas and the first consideration would still have to be the general supremacy. Eggleston's criticisms were devastating. He claimed that Hurd did not allow for the special circumstances justifying the Australian position. Hurd had not answered Eggleston's careful balance of power analysis. The most effective strategic disposition and unity of control were not necessarily complementary and compatible. Everything depended on the resources available and the nature of control. Hurd's 'whole point' was that when

---

Australian crisis syndrome as early as September 1908. See his 'Australia and the Pacific', *Trident*, 1 September 1908, pp. 90–2. For the fully developed views of the Naval Board on this question in 1913 see MP 1049/1, Box, File 15/054.

[27] *Argus*, 31 March 1914.

strains emerged in the Pacific, a large part of the British fleet would be moved from the Atlantic to meet them. In reply Eggleston asked what would happen in the most likely eventuality, namely when there were tensions in the Atlantic and the Pacific at the one time. He seized on Hurd's admission that the Pacific would become the future 'storm-centre' of world policy and urged that it was necessary now to prepare for the day.[28]

Two days later Millen with government approval issued his detailed comments on Churchill's speech in the form of a special memorandum. Millen took Churchill to task for his unilateral abrogation of the 1909 agreement. He pointed out that the battle cruisers which had been regarded by the Admiralty as the *sine qua non* of a local naval unit were now being described as superfluous for Dominion needs. The implication of Churchill's speech was that 'a definite inter-Imperial co-operative policy for Pacific naval development' was to be replaced 'by an unco-ordinated, ephemeral scheme possessing neither permanence nor clear purpose and function.' Ineffective, isolated units were to be substituted for 'a powerful joint Imperial Fleet in the Pacific'. Millen disputed the grounds which Churchill had advanced in defence of these changes. Firstly, he pointed out that strategic concerns had not been the sole and exclusive basis for the 1909 scheme. Other considerations such as the stimulation of 'a … healthy naval sentiment and national and imperial consciousness in Australia' had been taken into account. Secondly, and more importantly, he did not believe that the conclusions drawn by Churchill from the existence of the Anglo-Japanese alliance were correct. The Anglo-Japanese alliance was a factor in 1909 and 1911 when the original scheme had been established and confirmed. What had changed? He could not, of course, disparage the value of the alliance too directly in an open document yet he maintained that 'the pages of history are strewn with the wreckage of fruitless alliances' and Australia's efforts were directed to providing protection for British interests in the South Seas 'for all times'. Australia 'will not be deflected from her course by pronouncements of the First Lord of the Admiralty for she regards the task she has undertaken as vital to the cause of Imperial defence and Imperial union and an essential safeguard for her own protection.' Once again the final shaft was directed at Churchill's arbitrary methods, at the failure to consult before announcing such 'a vital departure' from a policy agreed upon between the Dominions and the imperial government.[29]

Millen thus traversed much of the ground already covered in Cook's letter of 28 February but, provoked by Churchill, his criticisms were more sharply worded and he had made the disagreement public. In Australia there was almost unanimous support for Millen's outspoken denunciation of the Admiralty's tergiversations. Fisher was 'more than delighted' by the government's pronouncement.[30] Pearce, in submitting a statement on defence to the retiring governor-general—a statement requested by Denman—centred his criticisms of Admiralty policy, like Millen's, on the strategic elements. He wrote:

---

[28] *Argus*, 11 April 1914.

[29] CofA, *Parliamentary Papers*, 1914 session, Vol. II, No. 1 'Naval Defence Memorandum by the Minister of Defence, 13 April 1914. Together with the first Lord of the Admiralty as Reported in Australia'.

[30] *CPD*, 1914 session, LXIII, 54, 16 April 1914.

> We insist that there ought to be a British Fleet for the Pacific; without it British diplomacy is nullified in one of the great oceans of the world and we are compelled to allow our policy to be dictated by our ally.
>
> … A British-Japanese alliance is better for Australia than a German-Japanese alliance would be.
>
> But the alliance is temporary, it suits both Japan and us at present, it may suit neither in a few years.

To acquire self sufficiency in naval defence in the Pacific would take a number of years. Naval units and naval bases could not be built up overnight. Subsidies were demeaning. 'Are the Dominions', he asked, 'never to hope to build, are they never to command or man their own ships or the Empire's ships in their home waters?'[31] On the government side there was equal agreement. Two staunchly conservative back-benchers, Sir Albert Gould and Colonel Ryrie, defended Millen's action.[32] Only two Liberal backbenchers, one of whom was Bruce Smith, the President of the British Empire League, dissented.[33] The press likewise approved.[34] Even the most subservient Blue Water school paper, the *Argus*, found Churchill guilty of failing to observe due process, to consult or inform Australia about the changed international situation.[35] It was the opinion of all that a further Imperial Conference should be held as soon as possible.

Though the outburst in the antipodes would seem to have given a new urgency to the Anglo-Australian dispute, nevertheless, the leisured and formal, if certain, procedures of the British bureaucracy were not accelerated or streamlined to meet the case. Cook's letter of 28 February with 'reflections on the changes in Admiralty policy' did not reach London until 1 April, well after Churchill's naval estimates speech, and five days later, on the very day that the Australian parliament ordered the printing of Millen's memorandum, the Colonial Office sent it forward to the Admiralty.[36] On 19 May the Admiralty made reply. Since the British government was not officially informed of Millen's statement until 1 June[37] this new development was completely ignored in framing their answer. Though the newspapers had reported the Australian furore fairly fully, the Colonial Office and the Admiralty took no cognizance of such unofficial sources.

In their suggested reply the Admiralty, hiding behind their mystique, said that it was not possible in correspondence to reveal fully the basis of their view on naval defence in relation to the Dominions. They saw 'a danger of despatches assuming a controversial character'. Yet, like Cook, they permitted themselves an extended comment which amounted to a substantial rejection of the Australian position. They conceded that the aim of the 1909 scheme was 'the

---

[31] Letter, Pearce to Denman, 4 May 1914, Denman Papers, 769/84–91.

[32] *CPD*, 1914 session, LXXIII, 553–4, 28 April 1914; ibid., LXXIV, 1589, 28 May 1914.

[33] Ibid., LXXIII, 54, 16 April 1914; ibid., LXIII, 233, 23 April 1914.

[34] *Daily Telegraph*, 13 and 15 April 1914; *SMH*, 13 and 22 April 1914; *Hobart Mercury*, 15 April 1914.

[35] *Argus*, 18 April 1914.

[36] Letter, H. Lambert, principal clerk, CO, to W. Graham Greene, secretary to the Admiralty, 16 April 1914, CO, 532/66.

[37] Despatch, Denman to Harcourt, sent 30 April 1914, received 1 June 1914, ibid. It contained six copies of the Memorandum.

permanent protection of British interests in the Pacific', and asserted that the reconstituted Eastern squadron amply fulfilled that aim. They denied that their failure to supply the Indefatigable affected the strategic situation 'considered in relation to Japan'. On this head they referred the Australian government to Churchill's speech of 17 March. The Admiralty repeated their view that the 1909 agreement was not based purely on strategical grounds. Rather, the answer hinted that the Admiralty had been obliged to propose a scheme which would pander to Dominion desires for local units. The detailed provisions for the other Pacific units were merely suggested from consideration 'of uniformity and general commerce'. The Admiralty said

> My Lords do not concur in the view now urged that their precise composition was based on strategical grounds, or was the subject of any definite compact, nor did they in fact so regard it even at the time they hoped to conform very closely to the disposition then foreshadowed.

It said that it would welcome an early opportunity of discussing the question with the Dominions concerned.[38] The Admiralty's answer, even at the time of writing, was, in some respects, already behind the argument. Millen had already refuted Churchill on the value of the Japanese alliance and had stressed 'the other than strategical' considerations as further reasons why the Admiralty should not gratuitously renege on their commitments.

The Admiralty's determination to bluster on despite the weakness of their case sent the cautious clerks in the Colonial Office scurrying for cover. Minute was mounted on minute as they sought to find a position behind which they could take a firm stand. C. T. Davis, a first-class clerk, began the dissection on 28 May. 'This letter requires very careful consideration before action is taken on it', he wrote. Then he turned to the issues of the case. Firstly, he noted that the Commonwealth government's complaint that they had not been consulted was 'well-founded' and the Admiralty had not answered the charge. Secondly, the Admiralty could not easily sustain its assertion that there was no compact. The papers of the 1909 Conference, the telegram and despatch of 17 October 1913 to Australia contained a tacit admission of an agreement; the word indeed had been used. Thus, the Colonial Office 'could not possibly' communicate this passage to the Commonwealth government. Thirdly, on the question of strategic and other grounds in the drawing up of the scheme, Davis argued that the other considerations would, in contrast to the Admiralty's own contention, 'make it more difficult to vary the arrangements on the ground that the strategic position has altered'. Millen had taken this position in April. On the further point raised by Australia, that the 1909 understandings were intended to make permanent provision for the defence of the Pacific, irrespective of conditions elsewhere, Davis concluded that they had, indeed, been made on the basis that 'the Pacific problem was separate or, at any rate, should be treated separately from the general problem of Imperial defence'. Another official believed that the whole problem could have been avoided by explaining the British position before any changes occurred and the colonial secretary concurred. The permanent head of the department, Sir John Anderson, looking to a line of action, ruled out the pursuit of a controversy with the Admiralty

---

[38] Letter, Greene to Sir John Anderson, under-secretary to the Colonial Office, 19 May 1914, CO, 532/68, received in the Colonial Office on 21 May 1914.

'who made a mistake in entering into the Agreement of '09 as a permanency and not reserving the right to vary it for paramount consideration of Imperial defence.' He was for telling the Admiralty that the points they had raised would be dealt with at a future conference which it was hoped could meet 'at not very distant date'. Lord Emmott, who had visited Australia in early 1914, was of the same opinion: 'Nothing but another conference and a new agreement can settle the matter.' He wrote that Australian feelings were very strong on the question and at the subsequent conference the Admiralty must understand that they would have to take this into account. Harcourt gave his consent to the adoption of Anderson's policy and a letter to this effect was sent to the Admiralty on 10 June. Along with a copy of Millen's defence statement they enclosed a suggested draft reply to the Australian despatch, saying simply that the issue could only be resolved by a conference and hoping that one could be held soon. As a palliative to the incensed Australians the Colonial Office offered to consult other Dominions to see whether they would also care to attend.[39]

The Admiralty were not so easily put off. Churchill was piqued by the implied rebuke. 'I don't quite understand why you do not forward to Australia the full and careful answer which we have drafted.' He was aware of public criticism but the Admiralty had clean hands. The First Lord claimed that, for the last two years, he had wanted a conference but the Colonial Office had killed the idea. He thought the Admiralty case 'a good one and I don't quite know how it can be answered'. The Australians were heading towards 'serious disappointment'. He urged a conference between the heads of the two departments 'with a view to avoiding a result which may easily be made grounds of reproach against us both.'[40]

Harcourt would not be brow-beaten and in exchange explained to Churchill in terms of Davis's criticism, why the Colonial Office could not send on the Admiralty letter. That is, he said that the letter did not meet the Australian complaint of failure to consult them, it denied the existence of a compact 'which I think can hardly be maintained' and which, in the light of Millen's charge of 'non-fulfillment of obligations' was 'highly controversial', and it showed a misunderstanding of the Australian position by stating that they based their case only on strategic factors whereas Millen clearly recognized other considerations as being equally important. In explaining their inability to call a conference earlier, Harcourt said that the Colonial Office's opposition to a general naval conference had been primarily due to 'the position of Canada'. They did not wish to embarrass the Borden government in its attempt to squeeze the three Mediterranean ships out of the Canadian parliament. Harcourt asked for Admiralty consent to the despatching of the Colonial Office's alternative draft reply to Australia.[41]

Once again the Admiralty procrastinated. Harcourt's private secretary had to send a 'hurry up' note on 14 July. This nudge was enough and the Admiralty wrote that they would have preferred 'a reasoned reply' to Cook's letter and Millen's memorandum but, 'if Mr. Harcourt considers that no notice should be taken of the Australian complaint otherwise than by the draft despatch', then the Admiralty would not press their objection. However, this was not to be taken to mean that

[39] Copy of letter, Anderson to Greene, 10 June 1914, ibid.
[40] Letter, Churchill to Harcourt, 20 June 1914, CO 532/66.
[41] Letter, Harcourt to Churchill, 23 June 1914, ibid.

they gave their consent to the course adopted.[42] This put the cat in among the pigeons once more and out of a minute examination of language and argument the Colonial Office's case was built up. What was required, as Lambert put it, was 'really for the Admty [sic] to climb down from a wholly indefensible position'. That could not be obtained by Colonial Office memoranda and letters. Nevertheless, even if the Admiralty could not be convinced, it was still necessary to give a full answer to the Admiralty 'to clear ourselves'. On 28 July the last word was said. The Colonial Office repeated to the Admiralty the points they had made in the letters of 10 June and 25 June and concluded 'Mr. Harcourt feels therefore that from the materials supplied to him, it would be impossible to produce an adequate answer to the complaints of the Commonwealth Government'.[43]

The final draft of the despatch was intended to be conciliatory; it was hoped that it would 'do something to mollify the wrath of Australia'.[44] The despatch asserted that the correspondence between Australia and Britain had revealed 'a certain divergence of views' between the Admiralty and the Commonwealth government over the interpretation of the 1909 arrangements. It continued that there was clearly a need for further personal consultation at a conference on naval defence which they expected would be held at a not very distant date. The Colonial Office said that, in deference to Australian wishes, they were circulating the other Dominions for their views.[45] The reply was sent off to Australia on 28 July 1914. But by this time the train of events leading from Sarajevo had come to overshadow all else. On that very day, Austria-Hungary had declared war on Serbia, and within a week the British Empire was at war with Germany. As a result of the European conflagration, the conference on naval defence was abandoned. In the face of this immediate threat to the empire's survival, Australia's defence efforts were turned towards rallying support for the Mother Country. Though Australia's peculiar anxieties were not in any way allayed by Japan's entry into the war on Britain's side, the Commonwealth's leaders recognized that specific decisions for building security in the Pacific would have to be postponed until after the peace, and that, indeed, their capacity to carry out such decisions would probably depend upon Britain achieving victory over the Central Powers.

### Divergent views and interests: the Australian—Imperial dilemma

From 1905 to 1914 Australia's attitude to the world and the empire had undergone a revolution. From a belief in their essential security, an expectation of British rule in the Pacific, a trust in the all-saving power of the British navy, Australians had come to fear for their safety, to take a pessimistic view of their future and to doubt the ability and willingness of the British fleet to come to their rescue. The rise of Japan in the Pacific, the withdrawal of British naval forces to meet the challenge from Germany in the North Sea, the exclusive concentration of the imperial

---

[42] Letter, Greene to Anderson, 17 July 1914, CO 532/68.

[43] Letter, Anderson to Greene, 28 July 1914, ibid.

[44] Minute by Sir John Anderson, 24 July 1914, ibid.

[45] Despatch, Harcourt to Governor-General, Sir Ronald Munro Ferguson, 28 July 1914, CP 290/15/2. The despatches to the other Dominions were all sent on 28 July, see CO 532/68.

government on the defence of the British Isles had produced in Australia an entirely new picture of their external situation. The Australians well knew that the defeat of Britain in Europe would have adverse consequences for the Commonwealth. They were agreed that if the Mother Country were in peril, they would go to its assistance; but they were unwilling to base their own policies on such contingencies. What they were primarily concerned with was the defence of Australia, and it was in the light of this concern that they ordered their naval, military and diplomatic efforts. They would not accept as a general operating principle that they should be left defenceless in the Pacific so that Britain could be more certainly secure in Europe. And so Australia introduced compulsory military training and established a navy, specifically for its own defence. As the *Hobart Mercury* put it, at the time of the Millen memorandum, there was in Australia 'a very large number of people … who pay little attention to the German menace but are seriously disturbed because of what is called the "Yellow Peril" '. This 'deep-rooted opinion that, some day or another, danger will threaten from the Far East' was 'chiefly responsible for the popularity of the scheme for establishing an Australian navy.'[46]

The Australian government attempted to impress Whitehall and Westminster with its deep interest in Pacific security and, to its surprise, the Admiralty in 1909 had proposed the formation of a Pacific fleet which was designed to provide permanent and full protection for British commerce and colonies in the region. The Commonwealth government had snapped up the offer with alacrity and had proceeded, with almost unanimous support, to build the Australian fleet unit. When, after 1912, it became apparent that neither Britain nor Canada, for their different reasons, had any intentions of contributing to this scheme of general defence for the Pacific, the Commonwealth leaders began to agitate against what they considered to be a dereliction in duty. The old strategic arguments, sharpened and refined by a sense of resentful disappointment and by a renewed sense of impending crisis, were again advanced in support of the Australian case. And certainly the level of the debate was equal to that found in any European foreign office.

F. W. Eggleston presented the most extensive and cogent defence of the Commonwealth's position in a paper which he had read to the Australian Round Table group sometime in October 1913. It was an earlier version of the statement which appeared in the *Argus* after Churchill's appropriation speech and the substance of his paper subsequently appeared in the *Round Table* journal. In his paper, Eggleston firmly denied the British arguments that substantial naval forces in the Pacific were wasteful and useless. Eggleston asserted that, from the Australian perspective, the Japanese preponderance in the Far East was unquestionable and it was impossible to predict how that preponderance might be used 'in two, ten or twenty years time'. He repudiated the notion that the Anglo-Japanese alliance could be relied upon to preserve British interests from attack in the Pacific. The specific advantages which Britain and Japan derived from the maintenance of the treaty were too unequal for that. Since Britain's naval power was necessarily concentrated in European waters, it needed Japan to protect its interests in the Far East and it had little to offer Japan in exchange, even in order to deter the Japanese from seizing British possessions or, at the least, from making demands for special concessions. Japan had no territories

---

[46] *Hobart Mercury*, 15 April 1914.

or commerce to protect in Europe. Japan could rely on the balance of terror in Europe to free it from fear of attack in the Pacific. Thus, it had no reason to feel obliged on this account to Great Britain. 'If a question arose between the Empire and Japan in the Pacific', Eggleston wrote 'the Empire would be helpless', and the truth of this claim was to become clear during World War I.

However, Eggleston believed the proposition to be equally true in peacetime. He saw Australia's determination 'to develop a pure Western civilisation unhampered by racial difficulties' as one of the possible points of conflict. In such a situation the empire, threatened by a realignment of Japan's diplomatic and naval influence, would have to submit to Japan's demands. Eggleston was sceptical about the Admiralty's preferred alternative to a Pacific fleet, namely the diversion of a substantial naval force in time of need to the threatened outpost of empire. He doubted its viability. Since Britain had only a minimal margin of safety over the German fleet in the North Sea, he argued that unless Anglo-German relations improved—an unlikely prospect— then the whole British fleet must remain captive to the enduring German threat. It would be impossible to take the risk of despatching a substantial force on a month's journey to the Pacific.

On every count such an *ad hoc* policy was unsatisfactory. 'The action of armaments is not merely *ex post facto*. They are used in peace to give support to policy. A fleet in the Atlantic is of little weight in assisting the settlement of grave issues in the Pacific.' Concentration of naval power in the Atlantic was no solution for what Eggleston described as 'the "two ocean" dilemma which now confronts the Empire'. There was 'a divergence of interests between Great Britain and the Dominions' in the Pacific. It 'should not be slurred over in the supposed interests of unity… It is useless to believe that the statesmen or populace in England understand the point of view or realise the dangers of the Dominions.' He believed that the answer to the problem of Pacific naval defence, both for Australia and the empire, was to be found in the return to the 1909 idea of a Pacific Fleet, a fleet to which all British Dominions in the Pacific would contribute units. Such a fleet should be controlled by an authority 'which whilst not divorced from the British naval authority would be in direct touch with the governments of the Dominions and carrying out a policy agreed to by all.' A new imperial conference was urgently required to consider implementing this policy.[47]

Beyond a doubt, Eggleston's analysis of the Pacific problem was much sounder than that offered by Churchill and the Admiralty. Some have questioned the reasonableness of Australian fears of Japan. The Australian government had not attempted to collect information about Japanese policy and behaviour in a consistent manner; Pearce's brief visit to Japan in 1911 had only confirmed his prejudices. But Australians had followed closely Japan's emergence as a great power. Japan's triumph over Russia in 1905, its annexation of Korea, its naval armaments programmes, its conflicts with the United States over the treatment of its nationals in California

---

[47] 'Naval Policy and the Pacific Question', *Round Table*, IV (June 1914), 391–462. The article was written by G. M. Grigg of the London *Round Table* staff. Grigg acknowledged that the final form had been influenced by an 'excellent memorandum on my draft Pacific article' by Harrison Moore (Letter, Grigg to Harrison Moore and Eggleston, 10 June 1914, Defence Box, Harrison Moore Papers). It would seem highly likely that both Grigg's draft and Moore's criticism owed much to Eggleston's writings on the subject.

in 1907 and 1913 were well reported in the press and referred to frequently in parliamentary debates and private discussions on defence questions. One did not need a foreign office to unveil the self evident. Japan in Asia, like Germany in Europe, was indisputably the 'coming power', searching for its place in the sun, and Britain was no more detached in facing up to the German problem in Europe than Australia was in dealing with Japan in the Pacific. Australia's policy toward Japan was one of precautionary prudence; it was indistinguishable in this respect from that pursued by Britain against Germany. Perhaps in his prescriptions for imperial policy as opposed to his analysis of the issues, Eggleston was too much influenced by sentiment; perhaps by avoiding the question of whether imperial resources were sufficient to support two great navies, he weakened his argument. But whatever the limitations, he spoke for a consensus of concerned, informed Australians. He put forward a view which nearly all Australian political leaders—each in his own individual and often muddled fashion—shared.

Debating points were not, though, of much practical use in meeting immediate defence needs. The British government was not able or willing to revive the 1909 plan. Canada's internal divisions over naval policy made assistance from that direction highly uncertain. New Zealand had only begun to move towards the establishment of its own naval force and its contribution, simply by the nature of its size, could only be small. Churchill had told the Dominions that if British power were shattered in the North Sea, 'the only course for the five millions of white men in the Pacific would be to seek the protection of the United States.'[48] There were a number of Australians who felt that British weakness in the Pacific already made this course desirable. Deakin had urged such a policy in 1909. In 1914, in deciding to send Deakin as Australia's representative to the San Francisco Exhibition, there was some suggestion that he might become 'a permanent High Commissioner for Australia in the United States.'[49] There were a few too, like King O'Malley, who placed much reliance on Theodore Roosevelt's express statement in his *Autobiography*, 'that America should be ready to stand at the back of Australia in any emergency.'[50] But this was a will o' the wisp. Under Woodrow Wilson the United States gave no sign of wishing to accept such a responsibility and the Australian government, facing up to American indifference, left the question of permanent representation over until a more propitious time.

Cook's Liberal government, like Fisher's Labor ministry before them, were compelled to fall back finally on what they could do for themselves in order to augment national security. After presenting to the Senate, in response to inquiries, a statement of the strength of British and foreign naval forces in the Pacific which showed up the great discrepancy between Japanese and

---

[48] Great Britain, 5 *Parliamentary Debates* (Commons), Vol. LIX, 1933, 17 March 1914.

[49] Letter, Atlee Hunt to P. McMahon Glynn, Minister for External Affairs, 16 March 1914, Atlee Hunt Papers, 52; see also letter, Richard Jebb to Alfred Deakin, 8 April 1914 in the Deakin-Jebb Correspondence, 339/1/71A.

[50] *SMH*, 14 April 1914; *CPD*, LXXIII, 390, 28 April 1914; Theodore Roosevelt, *Theodore Roosevelt, an Autobiography*, New York 1914, p. 88.

British forces,[51] the Cook government entered into negotiations with New Zealand for a joint Australasian fleet and sought authorization for an additional naval construction programme. As a minimum four-year programme Senator Millen announced on 25 June 1914 that the government would build two more light cruisers of the Brisbane class and two improved submarines at a cost of £1,700,000; the material for the first cruiser was to be obtained immediately.[52] This was not as great a step forward as Fisher had promised the previous year, but it was only a 'minimum' programme and it did match, if not in exact terms, the plans laid down by Henderson. Australia, nevertheless, had by 1914 achieved much in defence. Since 1909 the Australian naval unit had been substantially completed, part of it being built at Cockatoo Island yards in Sydney Harbour, and the naval bases at Western Port, Victoria and Cockburn Sound, Western Australia were being planned.[53] Similarly, as a result of the compulsory training scheme, the Australian army had grown in numbers, from approximately 20,000 in 1905 to 46,000 in 1914 and by 1920 it was estimated that the numbers, through training of successive years, would approach 130,000. Much attention had also been given to fortifications and armaments. Ammunition factories had been established and the Royal Military College at Duntroon had received its first intake of Australian and New Zealand cadet officers. Even an elementary flying school had been set up at Point Cook, with two instructors and 5 aeroplanes; Australia was the only Dominion to experiment with aviation for defence before World War I.[54] Generals Kitchener and Hamilton and even Hutton's former protégées had, after the event, come around to approving the Australian policy. Brudenell White, who became Chief of the Australian General Staff in 1920, writing to Hutton in 1913, could exclaim 'What has been done in the country in a military sense, is really quite wonderful. The Labour Party certainly deserves great credit for it.'[55] Australian defence expenditure had risen from just over £1,000,000 in 1908–9 to £4,300,000 in 1913–14 and the proportion of a much enlarged Federal budget allocated to defence had doubled in the same period, from 15.5 per cent in 1908–9 to 31 per cent in 1913–14. By 1913–14 Great Britain was spending £1.13.9 *per capita* on defence in comparison with Australia's £0.19.5. But Britain, because of its determination to maintain its naval superiority, led the world in defence expenditure. Australia spent absolutely and

---

[51] *CPD*, LXXIII, 674, 7 May 1914; ibid., LXIII, 838, 13 May 1914; ibid., LXXIV, 2184, 17 June 1914; CofA, *Parliamentary Papers*, 1914 session, Vol. II, No. 33, 'Navies-Relative Strength in the Pacific'. See Table 2.

[52] *SMH*, 27 May 1914; *CPD*, 1914 session, LXXIV, 2521–3, 25 June 1914.

[53] CofA, *Parliamentary Papers*, 1914 session, Vol. II, No. 4, 'Naval Defence. Reports by Sir Maurice Fitzmaurice on Flinders Naval Base (Port Western) and Other Matters'.

[54] CofA, *Parliamentary Papers*, 1914 session, Vol. II, No. 14, 'Report on an Inspection of the Military Forces of the Commonwealth of Australia by General Sir Ian Hamilton'. CofA, *Official Year Book*, No. II, 1918. See also for the origins of the Australian Flying Corps, CRS, A289, 1849/718 and A2023, A38-3-221.

[55] Letter, Brudenell White to Hutton, 4 March 1913, Hutton Papers, BM, add. ms. 50089, Vol. XII, p. 114. Compare his support for the voluntary principle in 1908. 'The Defence Bill was laid on the table of the House of Representatives today… One can only hope that it will not pass. If it does, farewell to any effective military forces in Australia', letter, Brudenell White to Hutton, 29 September 1908, ibid., p. 64.

*per capita* more on defence than European countries of similar population and wealth, such as Sweden and Holland, and much more than any other Dominion.[56]

In World War I Australian statesmen were not by any means innocents abroad, colonial 'Dads and Daves', forced into a strange and alien world of power politics. Australians, by the time of World War I, had their own sophisticated perspective on international diplomacy and had been through a baptism of fire in an effort to reorder imperial diplomacy and internal defence to serve the national interests. Throughout the war years, the promise of the 1909 and 1911 conferences beckoned them on. Could they persuade the other Dominions to co-operate, at the end of the war, in creating a Pacific fleet? Could they obtain a voice in imperial defence and foreign policy as it affected the Pacific? Could they achieve a peace which would safeguard their position in the Pacific? These were the questions which nagged at the Commonwealth leaders. Even while Australian troops were fighting on European battlefields, Commonwealth thinking and planning was still focused, to a marked degree, on securing imperial co-operation in Pacific defence and diplomacy.

*Table* 2 The Australian view, 1914, 'Navies—relative strength in the Pacific. Return showing strength of navies of the various powers now stationed in the Pacific'[57]

| Station | Classification | Number | Displacement Tons | Guns | | Number of ships so armed |
|---|---|---|---|---|---|---|
| | | | | Number | Calibre | |
| | **Great Britain** | | | | | |
| China | Battleship | 1 | 11,800 | 4 | 10" | 1 |
| | | | | 14 | 7.5" | |
| | Cruisers | 2 | 14,600 | 4 | 9.2" | 1 |
| | | | | 10 | 7.5" | |
| | | | 10.800 | 4 | 7.5" | 1 |
| | | | | 6 | 6" | |
| | Light Cruisers | 2 | 4,800 | 2 | 6" | 1 |
| | | | | 10 | 4" | |
| | | | 5,200 | 8 | 6" | |
| | Destroyers | 8 | | | | |
| | Submarines | 2 | | | | |
| East Indies | Battleship | 1 | 11,800 | 4 | 10" | 1 |
| | | | | 14 | 7.5" | |

---

[56] CofA, *Official Year Book*, 1924, No. 17, pp. 595–6.
[57] CofA, *Parliamentary Papers*, 1914 session, Vol. II, No. 33.

| | | | | | |
|---|---|---|---|---|---|
| | Light Cruisers | 3 | 5,200 | 8 | 6" | 1 |
| | | | 4,300 | 2 | 6" | }1 |
| | | | | 8 | 4.7" | |
| | | | 2,000 | 8 | 9.2" | 1 |
| New Zealand | Light Cruisers | 3 | 2,300 | 8 | 4.7" each | 3 |
| Australian Navy | Dreadnought Cruiser | 1 | 19,200 | 8 | 12" | }1 |
| | | | | 16 | 4" | |
| | Light Cruisers | 4 | 5,600 | 8 | 6" | 2 |
| | | | 5,800 | 11 | 6" | 1 |
| | | | 2,200 | 8 | 4" | 1 |
| | Destroyers | 3 | | | | |
| | Submarines | 2 | | | | |

**Japan**

| | | | | | |
|---|---|---|---|---|---|
| Dreadnought Battleships | 4 | 20,000 approx. | 12 | 12" | }2 |
| | | | 10 | 6" | |
| Dreadnought Cruiser | 1 | 27,500 | 8 | 14" | }1 |
| | | | 16 | 6" | |
| Pre-Dreadnought Battleships | 10 | 13,000 to 16,000 | 4 | 12" | }2 |
| | | | 4 | 10" | |
| | | | 12 | 6" | |
| | | | 4 | 12" | }3 |
| | | | 14 | 6" | |
| | | | 4 | 10" | }2 |
| | | | 10 | 6" | |
| | | | 4 | 12" | }1 |
| | | | 6 | 8" | |
| | | | 4 | 12" | }1 |
| | | | 10 | 6" | |
| | | | 4 | 12" | }1 |
| | | | 12 | 6" | |
| Cruisers | 15 | 6,600 to 14,600 | 4 | 12" | }2 |
| | | | 12 | 6" | |
| | | | 4 | 12" | }2 |
| | | | 8 | 8" | |

| | | | | | |
|---|---|---|---|---|---|
| | | | 1 | 10" | 1 |
| | | | 2 | 8" | |
| | | | 14 | 6" | |
| | | | 4 | 8" | 5 |
| | | | 14 | 6" | |
| | | | 4 | 8" | 2 |
| | | | 12 | 6" | |
| | | | 2 | 8" | 1 |
| | | | 8 | 6" | |
| | | | 10 | 6" | 1 |
| | | | 12 | 6" | 1 |
| Light Cruisers | 18 | 1,500 to 5,500 | 2 | 12" | Total guns in the 18 Cruisers |
| | | | 4 | 8" | |
| | | | 56 | 6" | |
| Destroyers | 51 | | | | |
| Submarines | 13 | | | | |
| **France** | | | | | |
| Cruisers | 2 | 7,400 | 2 | 7.6" | 1 |
| | | | 8 | 6.5" | |
| | | 9,000 | 8 | 6.5" | 1 |
| Destroyers | 3 | | | | |
| **Germany** | | | | | |
| Cruisers | 2 | 11,400 | 8 | 8" | 2 |
| | | | 6 | 6" | |
| Light Cruisers | 3 | 3,400 | 10 | 4" | 3 |
| Destroyers | 2 | | | | |
| **Russia** | | | | | |
| Cruisers | 2 | 6,000 | 12 | 6" | 1 |
| | | 3,000 | 8 | 4.7" | 1 |
| Destroyers | 20 | | | | |
| Submarines | 8 | | | | |
| **Italy** | | | | | |
| Cruiser | 1 | 4,500 | 6 | 6" | 1 |

**Austria**

| | | | | | |
|---|---|---|---|---|---|
| Cruiser | 1 | 4,000 | 8 | 6" | 1 |

**United States – East Asiatic Fleet**

| | | | | | |
|---|---|---|---|---|---|
| Cruisers | 3 | 8,000 | 4 | 8" | } 1 |
| | | | 10 | 5" | |
| | | 3,000 | 11 | 5" | 2 |
| Destroyers | 5 | | | | |
| Submarines | 6 | | | | |

**United States – Pacific Fleet**

| | | | | | |
|---|---|---|---|---|---|
| Battleship | 1 | 10,200 | 4 | 13" | } 1 |
| | | | 8 | 8" | |
| Cruisers | 9 | 13,600 | 4 | 8" | } 6 |
| | | | 14 | 6" | |
| Light Cruisers | 10 | 1,700 | 2 | 8" | Total |
| | | to | 12 | 6" | guns in |
| | | 3,200 | 69 | 5" | the 10 Cruisers |
| Destroyers | 9 | | | | |
| Submarines | 8 | | | | |

**Portugal – (Nil)**
**Holland**

| | | | | | |
|---|---|---|---|---|---|
| Cruisers | 5 | 6,400 | 4 | 11" | } 1 |
| | | | 4 | 6" | |
| | | 5,000 | 2 | 9.4" | } 3 |
| | | | 4 | 6" | |
| | | 5,000 | 2 | 4.7" | 1 |
| Destroyer | 8 | | | | |

**China**

| | | | | | |
|---|---|---|---|---|---|
| Light Cruisers | 9 | 1,600 | 77 | 4" | Total |
| | | to | | to | guns in |
| | | 4,300 | | 8" | the 9 Cruisers |

**Chile**

| | | | | | |
|---|---|---|---|---|---|
| Battleship | 1 | 6,900 | 8 | 9.4" | |
| | | | 8 | 4.7" | |

| | | | | | |
|---|---|---|---|---|---|
| Cruisers | 2 | 8,500 | 4 | 8" | |
| | | | 10 | 6" | |
| | | 7,000 | 2 | 8" | |
| | | | 12 | 6" | |
| Light Cruisers | 4 | 2,000 | 4 | 8" | } Total guns in the 4 Cruisers |
| | | to | 22 | 6" | |
| | | 4,500 | 12 | 4.7" | |
| Destroyers | 9 | | | | |

**Peru**

| | | | | | |
|---|---|---|---|---|---|
| Cruiser | 1 | 6,600 | 2 | 7.6" | |
| | | | 6 | 6.5" | |
| Light Cruisers | 3 | 1,790 | 4 | 6" | |
| | | to | 4 | 4" | |
| | | 3,200 | | | |
| Destroyers | 1 | | | | |
| Submarines | 2 | | | | |

Were Australian expectations reasonable? Among commentators there were two schools of thought crystallized most succinctly by Viscount Esher and H. G. Wells. On the one hand, there were those who felt that the threats to the security of the British empire would at last produce a federal unity of all the self-governing parts. 'No British statesmen could have federated the British Empire. That object is going to be accomplished by the menace of the German Fleet.' So asserted Viscount Esher, in calling for a truly imperial control of defence and foreign policy.[58] On the other side was H. G. Wells who, profiting from the imperial experience of 1912–14, answered in reply to the question 'Will the Empire live?' that 'our extraordinary Empire has no common enemy to weld it together from without.' Indeed, he remarked that the differing threats to the various parts of the empire would bring about its downfall.[59] And in this exchange Wells would seem to have had the better of it.

Cook, in early 1914, was preoccupied with the question, 'How to satisfy Imperial requirements with local ones?' He considered that that was 'the art and the problem of highest statesmanship'.[60] This was the dream of an imperialist, a mirage concocted out of cultural dependence; and it was, until recent times, the continuing dream of the majority of Australians. The question was not, however, one essentially of individual wisdom and perspicacity, it was rather one of implacable geopolitics. British and Australian strategic interests, generated by their

---

[58] Viscount Esher, *The Committee of Imperial Defence: Its Nature and Potentialities, Lecture Delivered at the United Services Institute*, 20 *March* 1912, London 1912.

[59] H. G. Wells, *An Englishman Looks at the World*, London 1914, p. 16.

[60] Cook Diary, Cook Papers.

respective geographical settings, were too divergent and their common resources were too limited to provide full and permanent security for both under a united policy. The process of sorting out what had to be done was painful. The Australian leaders, especially the conservatives, were often irrationally impatient in testing times with what they considered Britain's betrayal of the empire; the pull of the empire, of British race patriotism, was not easily overcome. Events conspired with emotions to keep the full impact of this dichotomy from the nation well into the middle of the twentieth century; the accidents of history played into the hands of the wishful thinkers. Australian leaders before World War I had begun the task of coming to grips intellectually with the problem. They made considerable progress in defining the issues and they converted their tentative conclusions into the rudiments of a distinctive Australian defence and foreign policy, a policy which was directed towards attaining security in the Pacific. The succeeding generation failed to learn from the experience of these early years and much of the story of Australia's relations with the empire and the world in the period between the wars consisted of a rather second-rate replay of the debates and disputes of the era of the 'Commonwealth Crisis'.

# Appendixes

## *A note on statistical tables*

The cult of quantification has in recent years led some historians to believe that at last they have found the path to certainty in the social sciences. And indeed it must be admitted that where statistics do exist they can generally be expected to provide a more accurate picture of that in the past which is susceptible to measurement than the personal impressions of travellers, statesmen, journalists or other contemporary commentators upon which historians have so often rested their conclusions.

However, too often a table or a graph is accepted as having an unquestionable authenticity and objectivity. Numbers, like ideas, since they are self-sufficient abstractions, too easily become the refuge of scholars fleeing the world of people. But statistics are neither self-selecting nor self-interpreting. The problems of evaluation and use are no different for statistics than for any other form of historical evidence. A historian has to examine each statistic in just the same way that he would examine each particular documentary or literary source; that is, he must ask who compiled the data, what basis was employed in arriving at the figures cited, what purpose the compilation was intended to serve, how the specific statistic can be correlated with other statistics bearing on the same matter.

In drawing up these appendixes it has been necessary to face up to such questions. In the first place the meaning to be given to the figures for militia and volunteer forces is not self-evident. Without undertaking detailed research into the process by which these statistics were arrived at—a diversion of effort which the purpose of the book would hardly justify—it is impossible to evaluate them. There are *prima facie* grounds for suspecting that the political and military authorities, at least down to 1910, tolerated a degree of padding on the rolls of active military strength in order to enhance their own importance or to reassure the electorate of their security. In the second place—and this has raised a more urgent issue—there are frequently to be found conflicting sets of statistics, either from different official sources in a particular year or in the subsequent tabulation of defence forces or defence expenditure covering a period of years.

These problems are most marked for the colonial period. The six colonies presented their statistics each in a somewhat different way, and some of the colonies changed the methods of compilation one or more times from 1870–1900. T. A. Coghlan's *A Statistical Account of the Seven Colonies of Australasia 1888–1902*, upon which historians have so often relied for their colonial statistics, was not helpful. Its tables of defence expenditure do not follow fixed principles. The Coghlan figures rarely coincide with those given in the Statistical Registers and Blue Books of the different colonies and even where there is close correspondence, it is clear that the items included in these figures have often and inexplicably changed from year to year. For example, in the NSW figures for 1894–5 Coghlan includes the cost of the Australian auxiliary squadron in his total whereas in the 1896–7 figures this item of expenditure is excluded. Similarly in the 1889 Victorian return he has included the cost of construction and maintenance of defence works and warships

(£173,994) whereas for all other years these costs are excluded. In this case the different basis of selection has produced a remarkable bulge in defence expenditure for 1889, £346,623 compared to £175,358 in 1888 and £149,381 in 1890–1. There are also egregious clerical errors. In Coghlan's 1888 table he gives Queensland's defence expenditure out of revenue as £29,336 which is in fact the amount paid out of the loan account, the amount expended from revenue being £71,430.

In all cases figures compiled by the appropriate authorities in accordance with clear and consistent principles have been preferred and those tables prepared for special military or political purposes have been disregarded. Where the basis for annual returns has altered from one year to another, and there are subsequent consolidated tables available, those tables have generally been followed. In the absence of such tables the annual parliamentary statistical reports have been accepted as the most reliable source. Though the appendixes are crude and subject to marginal error, they would seem to show graphically some general trends. In the Commonwealth period it is significant that the steady decline in defence expenditure and defence forces is arrested in 1905–6, the financial year following the Japanese triumph over Russia at the battle of Tsushima, and that from this point there is a steady rise in both the size of the defence allocation and the strength of the armed forces.

## Appendix I  Australian Colonies: Defence Forces, 1870–1900[1]

| YEAR | NSW[2] | | VICTORIA[3] | | QUEENSLAND[4] | | SOUTH AUSTRALIA[5] | |
|---|---|---|---|---|---|---|---|---|
| | Permanent forces | Militia and volunteers | Permanent forces | Militia and volunteers | Permanent forces | Militia and volunteers | Permanent forces | Militia and volunteers |
| 1870 | 22 | 3225 | 156 | 3832 | | 477 | 3 | |
| 1871 | 261 | 3430 | 206 | 4084 | | 507 | 3 | |
| 1872 | 288 | 4113 | 223 | 4002 | | 406 | 3 | |
| 1873 | 143 | 4462 | 339 | 4089 | | 422 | 3 | |
| 1874 | 146 | 4195 | 340 | 4080 | | 515 | 3 | |
| 1875 | 114 | 3701 | 206 | 4295 | | 767 | 3 | |
| 1876 | 223 | 3050 | 321 | 3608 | | 1210 | 3 | |
| 1877 | 358 | 2695 | 376 | 3681 | | 1244 | 12 | |
| 1878 | 352 | 2718 | 467 | 3209 | | 1373 | 22 | |
| 1879 | 353 | 2388 | 404 | 3443 | 1 | 1142 | 19 | |
| 1880 | 319 | 1945 | 327 | 3415 | 15 | 1168 | 19 | |
| 1881 | 300 | 2111 | 199 | 3374 | 15 | 1175 | 19 | |
| 1882 | 325 | 2024 | 357 | 3050 | 16 | 518 | 18 | |
| 1883 | 322 | 2130 | 321 | 2712 | 19 | 996 | 23 | |
| 1884 | 330 | 2551 | 258 | 2549 | 15 | 1191 | 105 | 2123 |
| 1885 | 509 | 8056 | 390 | 5512 | 8 | 2253 | 135 | 3195 |
| 1886 | 406 | 6723 | 407 | 3973 | 84 | 2611 | 132 | 2324 |
| 1887 | 397 | 5655 | 449 | 4198 | 95 | 3094 | 131 | 2912 |
| 1888 | 492 | 4684 | 527 | 5077 | 105 | 2976 | 135 | 2756 |
| 1889 | 581 | 4789 | 539 | 6233 | 130 | 3809 | 132 | 2647 |

[1] These figures include all military and naval, permanent militia and volunteer forces, and exclude cadets and rifle companies.

[2] New South Wales statistics are taken from the *Statistical Register of New South Wales* 1870–82, and 1888–94, and *New South Wales Statistical Register*, 1878–87 and 1894–1900.

[3] Victorian statistics are taken from Victoria, *Votes and Proceedings*, 1871–1900/1, *Statistics of the Colony of Victoria* for 1870 to 1874, and the *Statistical Register of Victoria*, pt. 3, *Blue Book* for 1876–9, 1880–1900, supplemented with the 'Report of the Council of Defence' for 1890–1900.

[4] Queensland statistics are taken from Queensland, *Votes and Proceedings*, 1871/2–1887 sessions, Queensland *Journal* (Legislative Council) 1888–1901 sessions, *Statistics of the Colony of Queensland*, pt. 7. There are no published statistics for marine forces before 1890.

[5] South Australian defence force statistics are taken from South Australia, *Proceedings and Papers*, 1870–1901, *Statistical Register of South Australia*, and for permanent forces 1870 84 the *Blue Book*. There are no published statistics for non-permanent forces available for 1873–1883.

| YEAR | TASMANIA[6] | | WEST AUSTRALIA[7] | | TOTAL AUSTRALIAN COLONIES | | |
|---|---|---|---|---|---|---|---|
| | Perma-nent forces | Militia and volunteers | Perma-nent forces | Militia and volunteers | Perma-nent forces | Militia and volunteers | |
| | | | | | | | TOTAL |
| 1870 | | | | | 181 | 7534 | 7715 |
| 1871 | | | | | 469 | 8021 | 8490 |
| 1872 | | | | | 514 | 8521 | 9035 |
| 1873 | | | | | 485 | 8973 | 9458 |
| 1874 | | | | | 489 | 8790 | 9279 |
| 1875 | | | | | 323 | 9123 | 9446 |
| 1876 | | | | | 547 | 7868 | 8415 |
| 1877 | | | | | 746 | 7620 | 8366 |
| 1878 | 6 | 753 | | 550 | 847 | 8603 | 9450 |
| 1879 | 6 | 714 | | 593 | 783 | 8280 | 9063 |
| 1880 | 9 | 675 | | 580 | 689 | 7783 | 8472 |
| 1881 | 8 | 614 | | 630 | 541 | 7904 | 8445 |
| 1882 | 8 | 588 | 1 | 575 | 725 | 6755 | 7490 |
| 1883 | 8 | 601 | 1 | 535 | 694 | 6974 | 7668 |
| 1884 | 9 | 487 | 2 | 547 | 719 | 9448 | 10,167 |
| 1885 | 12 | 974 | 2 | 578 | 1056 | 20,568 | 21,621 |
| 1886 | 25 | 633 | 2 | 588 | 1056 | 16,852 | 17,908 |
| 1887 | 34 | 745 | 2 | 640 | 1108 | 17,244 | 18,352 |
| 1888 | 34 | 705 | 2 | 517 | 1295 | 16,715 | 18,010 |
| 1889 | 32 | 1916 | 2 | 601 | 1416 | 19,995 | 21,411 |

[6] Tasmanian defence force statistics are taken from Tasmania, *Journals and Papers*, 1870–1900 and *Statistics of the Colony of Tasmania*. Prior to 1878 there appears to have been no forces of any consequence in Tasmania. Sir W. G. Drummond Jervois on 5 February 1878 in his Memorandum on the Defences of Tasmania (Tasmania, *Legislative Journals*, 1878/9, Vol. 27, No. 37, p. 7), commented that there was 'no recognised volunteer force in Tasmania' but noted a move afoot to enrol one. Tasmania had no naval forces.
[7] Western Australian statistics are taken from Western Australia, *Blue Book*, 1875, 1878–95, and *Western Australia: Statistical Register*, 1896–1900. Western Australia had no naval forces.

| YEAR | NSW[8] | | VICTORIA[9] | | QUEENSLAND[10] | | SOUTH AUSTRALIA[11] | |
|------|---------------|---------------|---------------|---------------|---------------|---------------|---------------|---------------|
|      | Perma-nent forces | Militia and volun-teers | Perma-nent forces | Militia and volun-teers | Perma-nent forces | Militia and volun-teers | Perma-nent forces | Militia and volun-teers |
| 1890 | 541 | 4872 | 561 | 5912 | 154 | 3755 | 130 | 2292 |
| 1891 | 666 | 5219 | 639[8] | 7287 | 156 | 4217 | 121 | 2447 |
| 1892 | 628 | 5054 | 635[12] | 6218 | 171 | 4415 | 147 | 2492 |
| 1893 | 537 | 4783 | 621[8] | 5762 | 164 | 3069 | 60 | 2232 |
| 1894 | 638 | 4789 | 621[8] | 5384 | 141 | 2881 | 39 | 2136 |
| 1895 | 631 | 4917 | 515[8] | 4784 | 148 | 2712 | 41 | 1867 |
| 1896 | 625 | 5364 | 556[8] | 4874[13] | 183 | 2875 | 51 | 894 |
| 1897 | 595 | 7130 | 537[8] | 4802[9] | 168 | 2907 | 50 | 1402 |
| 1898 | 741 | 6998 | 531[8] | 5159[9] | 247 | 3739 | 53 | 1433 |
| 1899 | 125 | 8421 | 550[8] | 5348[9] | 307 | 3483 | 49 | 1504 |
| 1900 | 730 | 9157 | 553[8] | 5958[9] | 343 | 4482 | 64 | 3164 |

[8] New South Wales statistics are taken from the *Statistical Register of New South Wales* 1870–82, and 1888–94, and *New South Wales Statistical Register*, 1878–87 and 1894–1900.

[9] Victorian statistics are taken from Victoria, *Votes and Proceedings*, 1871–1900/1, *Statistics of the Colony of Victoria* for 1870 to 1874, and the *Statistical Register of Victoria*, pt. 3, *Blue Book* for 1876-9, 1880–1900, supplemented with the 'Report of the Council of Defence' for 1890–1900.

[10] Queensland statistics are taken from Queensland, *Votes and Proceedings*, 1871/2–1887 sessions, Queensland *Journal* (Legislative Council) 1888–1901 sessions, *Statistics of the Colony of Queensland*, pt. 7. There are no published statistics for marine forces before 1890.

[11] South Australian defence force statistics are taken from South Australia, *Proceedings and Papers*, 1870–1901, *Statistical Register of South Australia*, and for permanent forces 1870 84 the *Blue Book*. There are no published statistics for non-permanent forces available for 1873–1883.

[12] Establishment figures only are given for permanent forces; and in 1891, 1892 and 1900 for volunteer and militia forces.

[13] Establishment figures only are available for permanent and volunteer naval forces 1895–1900.

| YEAR | TASMANIA[14] | | WEST AUSTRALIA[15] | | TOTAL AUSTRALIAN COLONIES | | |
|---|---|---|---|---|---|---|---|
| | Perma-nent forces | Militia and volunteers | Perma-nent forces | Militia and volunteers | Perma-nent forces | Militia and volunteers | |
| | | | | | | | TOTAL |
| 1890 | 33 | 2009 | 2 | 688 | 1421 | 19,528 | 21,139 |
| 1891 | 37 | 1811 | 2 | 657 | 1621 | 21,638 | 23,259 |
| 1892 | 22 | 1758 | 2 | 610 | 1605 | 20,547 | 22,152 |
| 1893 | 18 | 1614 | 35 | 738 | 1435 | 18,198 | 19,633 |
| 1894 | 14 | 1397 | 36 | 740 | 1489 | 17,327 | 18,816 |
| 1895 | 13 | 1221 | 35 | 630 | 1383 | 16,131 | 17,514 |
| 1896 | 13 | 1388 | 35 | 615 | 1463 | 16,010 | 17,473 |
| 1897 | 13 | 1594 | 66 | 699 | 1429 | 18,534 | 19,963 |
| 1898 | 17 | 1928 | 43 | 681 | 1632 | 19,938 | 21,570 |
| 1899 | 22 | 1832 | 45[16] | 929 | 1098 | 21,517 | 22,615 |
| 1900 | 27 | 2484 | 47[17] | 2174 | 1764 | 27,419 | 29,183 |

[14] Tasmanian defence force statistics are taken from Tasmania, *Journals and Papers*, 1870–1900 and *Statistics of the Colony of Tasmania*. Prior to 1878 there appears to have been no forces of any consequence in Tasmania. Sir W. G. Drummond Jervois on 5 February 1878 in his Memorandum on the Defences of Tasmania (Tasmania, *Legislative Journals*, 1878/9, Vol. 27, No. 37, p. 7), commented that there was 'no recognised volunteer force in Tasmania' but noted a move afoot to enrol one. Tasmania had no naval forces.
[15] Western Australian statistics are taken from Western Australia, *Blue Book*, 1875, 1878–95, and *Western Australia: Statistical Register*, 1896–1900. Western Australia had no naval forces.
[16] This does not include 231 Permanent Forces serving in South Africa.
[17] This does not include 475 Permanent Forces serving in South Africa.

## Appendix II Australian Colonies: Defence Expenditure, 1870–1900[1]

| YEAR | NSW[2] | | VICTORIA[3] | | QUEENSLAND[4] | | SOUTH AUSTRALIA[5] | |
|------|--------|--|-------------|--|---------------|--|--------------------|--|
| | Defence expend. | % of total col. expend | Defence expend. | % of total col. expend | Defence expend. | % of total col. expend | Defence expend. | % of total col. expend |
| 1870 | 31,362 | 1.19 | 63,157 | 1.84 | 453 | 0.06 | 5,926 | 0.80 |
| 1871 | 65,913 | 2.41 | 49,145 | 2.80 | 414 | 0.05 | 927 | 0.12 |
| 1872 | 61,859 | 2.51 | 62,814 | 1.72 | 296 | 0.03 | 682 | 0.09 |
| 1873 | 71,092 | 3.05 | 62,930 | 1.80 | 1,057 | 0.11 | 738 | 0.09 |
| 1874 | 66,870 | 2.04 | 70,070 | 1.68 | 759 | 0.06 | 833 | 0.08 |
| 1875 | 66,962 | 1.97 | 53,507 | 1.24 | 262[6] | 0.02 | 823 | 0.07 |
| 1876 | 55,717 | 1.23 | 108,210 | 2.37 | 675 | 0.05 | 1,015 | 0.07 |
| 1877 | 94,362 | 2.10 | 119,055 | 2.73 | 6,105 | 0.41 | 10,530 | 0.73 |
| 1878 | 109,270 | 2.15 | 138,391 | 2.99 | 12,742 | 0.79 | 14,517 | 0.90 |
| 1879 | 125,579 | 2.19 | 119,083 | 2.46 | 28,096 | 1.66 | 24,910 | 1.35 |
| 1880 | 116,158 | 2.11 | 124,429 | 2.55 | 9,267 | 0.55 | 18,994 | 0.99 |
| 1881 | 125,884 | 2.17 | 99,604 | 1.95 | 14,433 | 0.81 | 23,452 | 1.18 |
| 1882 | 151,921 | 2.39 | 106,311 | 2.07 | 17,087 | 0.77 | 21,937 | 1.03 |

[1] These figures include defence expenditure paid from revenue and loans and include contributions to the Australasian Auxiliary Squadron beginning 1891, and to the defence of Thursday Island and Albany, but exclude all British military expenditure, the cost of sending colonial troops to the Boer War and the Naval Contingent to China.

[2] New South Wales statistics are taken primarily from the *Statistical Register of New South Wales*, 1870–7 and 1889–1900 and the *New South Wales Statistical Register*, 1878–87. The financial year ended 31 December from 1870 to 1894, and then changed to terminate on the 30 June; hence the first financial year after 31 December 1894 ended on 30 June 1895.

[3] Victorian statistics are drawn mainly from Victoria, *Votes and Proceedings* (Legislative Assembly), 1871–1902; *Statistics of the Colony of Victoria* for 1870–4, and *Statistical Register of Victoria*, pt. 1, *Blue Book* for 1876–1901. The figures from 1870–5 include £13,333 and from 1876–85 include £49,976 as the average loan expenditure, based on the 1865–74/75 and 1875/6–1884/5 totals in 'Victoria: Expenditure on Defences, 1852–1899/1900', in *Statistical Register of Victoria* for 1899, pt 1, p. 28. The financial year ended on 30 June.

[4] Queensland statistics are taken from Queensland, *Votes and Proceedings* (Legislative Assembly), 1870–1902, 'Expenditure for Volunteer Force since Separation', 1877 session, Vol. I, p. 1271 for period 1870–7, 'The Public Accounts of the Colony of Queensland' for 1878–84, and 'Tables Relating to the Treasurer's Financial Statements' for 1885–1901. The financial year ended on 31 December during the years 1870–4, and on 30 June during the years 1876–1901.

[5] South Australian statistics are taken from South Australia, *Proceedings and Papers, Statistical Register of South Australia*, 1877–1900. The financial year ended on 31 December.

[6] This figure does not include the cost of the military contingent to South Africa, namely, £179,702, and of Naval Contingent to China, namely, £36,006.

| YEAR | TASMANIA[7] | | WEST AUSTRALIA[8] | | TOTAL AUSTRALIAN COLONIES | |
| --- | --- | --- | --- | --- | --- | --- |
| | Defence expend. | % of total col. expend | Defence expend. | % of total col. expend | Defence expend. | % of total col. expend |
| 1870 | 665 | 0.24 | | | 101,563 | 1.16 |
| 1871 | 1,330 | 0.46 | | | 117,729 | 1.83 |
| 1872 | 610 | 0.21 | | | 126,261 | 1.56 |
| 1873 | 531[12] | 0.17 | | | 136,348 | 1.69 |
| 1874 | 518[12] | 0.16 | | | 139,050 | 1.36 |
| 1875 | 531[12] | 0.14 | 559 | 0.33 | 122,644 | 1.13 |
| 1876 | 600[12] | 0.18 | | | 166,217 | 1.36 |
| 1877 | 606[12] | 0.17 | | | 230,658 | 1.87 |
| 1878 | 4,608 | 1.22 | 997 | 0.50 | 280,525 | 2.07 |
| 1879 | 4,976 | 1.03 | 1,350 | 0.69 | 303,994 | 2.05 |
| 1880 | 4,024 | 0.97 | 3,318 | 1.62 | 276,190 | 1.89 |
| 1881 | 5,721 | 1.23 | 2,032 | 1.03 | 271,126 | 1.77 |
| 1882 | 14,863 | 2.96 | 2,125 | 1.03 | 314,244 | 1.89 |

[7] From 1872–7 the only Tasmanian defence expenditure identified as such was listed under the heading 'Powder Magazines and Batteries'. The source for Tasmanian statistics is Tasmania, *Journal and Printed Papers*, 1871–1901, *Statistics of the Colony of Tasmania*. The financial year ended on 29 February of the following year. Tasmanian statistics include Loan Account expenditure from 1882–1900; Total Loan expenditure up to 1882 was £28,844, but not until 1882 were the Loan Account statistics included in the *Statistics of the Colony of Tasmania*; it is probable that the total expenditure up to 1882 covered the period 1878–81, when defence expenditure increased substantially following the Jervois report.

[8] Western Australian statistics are taken from Western Australia, *Blue Book* for 1875, 1878–95, and *Western Australian Statistical Register* for 1896–1900. Financial year ended on 31 December.

| YEAR | NSW | | VICTORIA | | QUEENSLAND | | SOUTH AUSTRALIA | |
|---|---|---|---|---|---|---|---|---|
| | Defence expend. | % of total col. expend | Defence expend. | % of total col. expend | Defence expend. | % of total col. expend | Defence expend. | % of total col. expend |
| 1883 | 176,400 | 2.26 | 121,060 | 2.14 | 22,294 | 0.99 | 27,557 | 1.24 |
| 1884 | 180,677 | 2.15 | 130,137 | 2.28 | 36,040[9] | 1.31 | 28,330 | 1.20 |
| 1885 | 228,519 | 2.67 | 157,553 | 2.57 | 96,204[10] | 3.35 | 56,590 | 2.33 |
| 1886 | 361,222 | 3.98 | 319,003 | 4.90 | 93,772 | 2.93 | 40,996 | 1.72 |
| 1887 | 338,649 | 3.72 | 311.006 | 4.74 | 84,999 | 2.54 | 41,013 | 1.89 |
| 1888 | 301,468 | 3.48 | 323,119 | 4.43 | 100,776[11] | 2.99 | 41,122 | 1.89 |
| 1889 | 279,189 | 4.90 | 353,167 | 4.46 | 77,358 | 2.15 | 46,225 | 2.04 |
| 1890 | 317,434 | 3.37 | 365,321 | 3.79 | 74,839 | 2.00 | 52,170 | 2.17 |
| 1891 | 433,336 | 4.19 | 328,324 | 3.60 | 93,392 | 2.54 | 51,160 | 1.97 |
| 1892 | 326,756 | 3.15 | 292,752 | 3.45 | 111,323 | 2.75 | 63,247 | 1.96 |
| 1893 | 271,891 | 2.68 | 238,644 | 2.99 | 116,453 | 2.93 | 46,555 | 1.35 |
| 1894 | 321,337 | 3.44 | 216,208 | 2.98 | 84,011 | 2.15 | 36,561 | 1.03 |
| 1895 | [12] | | 203,989 | 3.02 | 65,087 | 1.53 | 20,686 | 0.82 |
| 1896 | 243,267 | 2.46 | 169,814 | 2.60 | 99,594 | 2.00 | 24,124 | 0.54 |
| 1897 | 224,116 | 2.36 | 181,960 | 2.77 | 81,653 | 1.85 | 37,928 | 1.04 |
| 1898 | 264,427 | 2.79 | 184,697 | 2.76 | 86,753 | 1.92 | 32,286 | 0.84 |
| 1899 | 298,651 | 3.07 | 197,933 | 2.68 | 107,745 | 2.23 | 31,527 | 0.80 |
| 1900 | 280,058[13] | 2.71 | 196,695 | 2.70 | 139,028 | 2.62 | 46,497 | 1.30 |
| 1901 | 245,867[14] | | 250,594 | | 123,093 | | | |

[9] This figure is for the half year ended 30 June 1875. The financial year ended on 31 December until 1874; after that date it ended 30 June 1875, so that the first full financial year after 31 December 1874 ended on 30 June 1876.

[10] This figure includes £40,708 for the purchase of two gunboats.

[11] T. A. Coghlan, *A Statistical Account of the Seven Colonies of Australasia* puts Queensland's defence expenditure paid out of revenue in 1888 at £29,336.

[12] For the half year ending 30 June 1895 no statistics are available. Until 31 December 1894 the NSW financial year ended with the calendar year. Thereafter it ended on 30 June. Thus the first complete financial year after 31 December 1894 was 1 July 1895 to 30 June 1896.

[13] This figure does not include the cost of the military contingent to South Africa, namely, £158,748.

[14] This figure includes the purchase of two gunboats, £19,192.

| YEAR | TASMANIA[15] | | WEST AUSTRALIA | | TOTAL AUSTRALIAN COLONIES | |
|---|---|---|---|---|---|---|
| | Defence expend. | % of total col. expend | Defence expend. | % of total col. expend | Defence expend. | % of total col. expend |
| 1883 | 21,674 | 4.06 | 2,238 | 0.93 | 371,223 | 1.99 |
| 1884 | 22,961 | 3.97 | 2,657 | 0.91 | 400,802 | 1.99 |
| 1885 | 28,905 | 4.92 | 3,605 | 1.17 | 571,376 | 2.73 |
| 1886 | 22,923 | 3.92 | 3,373 | 0.85 | 841,289 | 3.80 |
| 1887 | 23,306 | 3.48 | 4,212 | 0.92 | 802,187 | 3.60 |
| 1888 | 28,293 | 3.99 | 3,308 | 0.86 | 798,086 | 3.53 |
| 1889 | 23,319 | 3.42 | 3,697 | 0.96 | 782,955 | 3.26 |
| 1890 | 22,036 | 3.05 | 4,013 | 1.00 | 835,813 | 3.18 |
| 1891 | 21,338 | 2.51 | 2,618 | 0.60 | 930,168 | 3.44 |
| 1892 | 26,067 | 2.83 | 7,417 | 1.35 | 827,562 | 3.11 |
| 1893 | 18,684 | 2.23 | 12,020 | 1.91 | 704,247 | 2.73 |
| 1894 | 18,344 | 2.32 | 9,621 | 1.47 | 686,082 | 2.87 |
| 1895 | 13,642 | 1.82 | 13,373 | 1.43 | 316,777 | [16] |
| 1896 | 13,656 | 1.82 | 12,792 | 0.70 | 563,247 | 2.24 |
| 1897 | 14,759 | 1.88 | 18,497 | 0.65 | 558,913 | 2.15 |
| 1898 | 18,307 | 2.21 | 23,859 | 0.73 | 610,329 | 2.29 |
| 1899 | 20,320 | 2.33 | 22,789 | 0.79 | 678,965 | 2.48 |
| 1900 | 21,993 | 2.38 | 16,929[17] | 0.52 | 701,200 | 2.44 |
| 1901 | | | | | | |

[15] From 1872–7 the only Tasmanian defence expenditure identified as such was listed under the heading 'Powder Magazines and Batteries'. The source for Tasmanian statistics is Tasmania, *Journal and Printed Papers*, 1871–1901, *Statistics of the Colony of Tasmania*. The financial year ended on 29 February of the following year. Tasmanian statistics include Loan Account expenditure from 1882–1900; Total Loan expenditure up to 1882 was £28,844, but not until 1882 were the Loan Account statistics included in the *Statistics of the Colony of Tasmania*; it is probable that the total expenditure up to 1882 covered the period 1878–81, when defence expenditure increased substantially following the Jervois report.

[16] Since no New South Wales total is available for the year 1895 (see fn. 13) no total figure is possible.

[17] This figures does not include £30,954 which was spent in connection with the three contingents sent to South Africa.

## Appendix III Commonwealth of Australia: Defence Forces, 1901–14[1]

| | Military forces[2] | | | Naval forces[3] | | | Total | | |
|---|---|---|---|---|---|---|---|---|---|
| | Perma-nent | Militia and volunt. | Total | Perma-nent | Militia and volunt. | Total | Perma-nent | Militia and volunt. | Grand total |
| 1901 | 1,457 | 27,466 | 28,923 | 239 | 1,659 | 1,898 | 1,696 | 29,125 | 30,821 |
| 1902 | 1,428 | 24,176 | 25,604 | 219 | 1,477 | 1,696 | 1,647 | 25,653 | 27,081 |
| 1903 | 1,253 | 21,353 | 22,606 | 181 | 1,282 | 1,463 | 1,434 | 22,635 | 24,069 |
| 1904 | 1,292 | 18,464 | 19,756 | 162 | 890 | 1,052 | 1,454 | 19,354 | 20,808 |
| 1905 | 1,208 | 18,459 | 19,667 | 164 | 831 | 994 | 1,382 | 19,290 | 20,661 |
| 1906 | 1,230 | 19,191 | 20,421 | 185 | 921 | 1,006 | 1,415 | 20,112 | 21,427 |
| 1907 | 1,329 | 20,582 | 21,911 | 196 | 982 | 1,178 | 1,525 | 21,564 | 23,089 |
| 1908 | 1,379 | 21,252 | 22,631 | 208 | 997 | 1,205 | 1,587 | 22,249 | 23,836 |
| 1909 | 1,448 | 21,913 | 23,361 | 242 | 989 | 1,231 | 1,690 | 22,902 | 24,592 |
| 1910 | 1,522 | 21,987 | 23,509 | 240 | 1,001 | 1,241 | 1,762 | 22,988 | 24,750 |
| 1911 | 2,003 | 22,196 | 24,199 | 400 | 1,243 | 1,643 | 2,403 | 23,439 | 25,842 |
| 1912 | 2,235 | 21,461 | 23,696 | 1,026 | 3,983 | 5,009 | 3,261 | 25,444 | 28,705 |
| 1913 | 2,774 | 31,763 | 34,537 | 2,236 | 881 | 3,117 | 5,010 | 32,644 | 37,654 |
| 1914 | 2,989 | 42,656 | 45,645 | 3,627 | 1,910 | 5,537 | 6,616 | 44,566 | 51,182 |

[1] These figures exclude rifle companies, cadets, unattached and reserve officers and chaplains.

[2] These statistics for the military forces are drawn from the CofA, *Parliamentary Papers*, 1901–2 session, Vol. II, 'Defences Forces of the Commonwealth'; ibid., 1903 session, Vol. II, No. 37, 'Naval and Military Forces of the Commonwealth'; ibid., 1903 session, Vol. II, No. 37, 'Annual Report upon the Military Forces … of Australia'; ibid., 1904 session, Vol. II, No. 25, 'Military Forces'; ibid., 1906 session, Vol. II, Report of the Military Board for 1905; ibid., 1907–8 session, Vol. II, Report of the Military Board for 1906; Commonwealth of Australia *Yearbooks*, Nos 1–8, 1908–15.

[3] These statistics for the naval forces are drawn from the CofA, *Parliamentary Papers*, 1903 session, Vol. II, No. 27, 'Naval and Military Forces of the Commonwealth'; ibid., 1904 session, Vol. II, No. 46, 'Defence Department Memorandum …'; ibid., 1906 session, Vol. II, No. 46, 'Report of the Director of Naval Forces'; ibid., 1907–8 session, Vol. II, No. 6, 'Report of the Director of Naval Forces' and No. 193, 'Defence Department: Memorandum …'; Commonwealth of Australia, *Yearbooks*, Nos 1–8, 1908–15.

## Appendix IV Commonwealth of Australia: Defence Expenditure, 1901–2 to 1913–14

| Year | Naval | | Military | |
|---|---|---|---|---|
| | Under ordinary votes and appropriations | Total naval (a) | Under ordinary votes and appropriations | Total military |
| 1901–2 | 178,819 | 178,819 | 777,620 | 780,260 |
| 1902–3 | 149,701 | 149,701 | 595,115 | 600,652 |
| 1903–4 | 240,005 | 240,091 | 502,517 | 615,673 |
| 1904–5 | 200,394 | 206,036 | 533,945 | 728,562 |
| 1905–6 | 250,273 | 252,016 | 548,439 | 718,329 |
| 1906–7 | 255,120 | 256,066 | 585,516 | 779,729 |
| 1907–8 | 259,247 | 510,205 | 634,579 | 824,539 |
| 1908–9 | 263,207 | 267,262 | 686,365 | 783,330 |
| 1909–10 | 269,051 | 329,739 | 928,393 | 1,205,666 |
| 1910–11 | 303,493 | 1,465,034 | 1,092,305 | 1,540,992 |
| 1911–12 | 461,546 | 1,634,466 | 1,667,103 | 2,443,382 |
| 1912–13 | 806,881 | 1,660,616 | 1,802,734 | 2,680,466 |
| 1913–14 | 1,006,424 | 1,987,101 | 1,941,285 | 2,756,404 |

| Year | Air | | Total defence expenditure | Defence expenditure as % of total Commonwealth expenditure |
|---|---|---|---|---|
| | Under ordinary votes and appropriations | Total air | | |
| 1901–2 | — | — | 959,079 | 24.39% |
| 1902–3 | — | — | 750,353 | 19.23% |
| 1903–4 | — | — | 855,764 | 20.12% |
| 1904–5 | — | — | 934,598 | 21.62% |
| 1905–6 | — | — | 970,345 | 21.58% |
| 1906–7 | — | — | 1,035,795 | 20.77% |
| 1907–8 | — | — | 1,334,744 | 21.66% |
| 1908–9 | — | — | 1,050,592 | 16.36% |
| 1909–10 | — | — | 1,535,405 | 20.47% |
| 1910–11 | — | — | 3,006,026 | 22.84% |
| 1911–12 | — | 4,000 | 4,081,848 | 27.72% |
| 1912–13 | 3,072 | 5,223 | 4,346,305 | 27.53% |
| 1913–14 | 3,012 | 8,795 | 4,752,300 | 30.74% |

*Source* : Commonwealth of Australia, *Year Book*, Australia 1924, No. 17, p. 595.
*Note* : All defence expenditure figures are expressed in A£.

## Appendix V Commonwealth of Australia: Trade with Major British and Foreign Countries, 1901–14 (import and export figures)

| COUNTRY | 1901 | | 1902 | |
|---|---|---|---|---|
| | £ Imports | £ Exports | £ Imports | £ Exports |
| United Kingdom | 25,237,032 | 25,194,923 | 23,848,562 | 20,224,491 |
| British possessions | | | | |
| Canada | 330,974 | 37,543 | 346,559 | 33,622 |
| Ceylon | 499,216 | 2,734,198 | 502,942 | 2,596,535 |
| India | 1,201,703 | 545,992 | 821,370 | 1,285,697 |
| New Zealand | 1,814,533 | 1,458,064 | 2,749,957 | 1,396,387 |
| British Pacific Islands | 154,617 | 275,940 | 214,745 | 266,768 |
| South African Union | 6,857 | 6,323,995 | 9,882 | 6,022,715 |
| Other Brit. possessions | 751,256 | 622,782 | 739,441 | 596,135 |
| Total, Brit. possessions | 4,759,156 | 11,998,514 | 5,384,896 | 12,197,859 |
| Total, Brit. countries | 29,996,188 | 37,193,437 | 29,233,458 | 32,422,350 |
| Belgium | 567,802 | 1,505,635 | 352,730 | 1,435,263 |
| China | 159,489 | 128,976 | 226,207 | 107,071 |
| France | 463,449 | 2,309,247 | 525,937 | 2,603,336 |
| Germany | 2,799,991 | 2,552,458 | 2,658,060 | 2,543,360 |
| Japan | 288,216 | 123,355 | 354,327 | 414,913 |
| Netherlands East Indies | 938,231 | 204,315 | 761,295 | 191,768 |
| Pacific Islands | 108,096 | 1,087,084 | 160,536 | 488,868 |
| Russia | 62,984 | 3,211 | 25,701 | 4,268 |
| USA | 5,854,150 | 3,373,876 | 4,989,812 | 2,714,424 |
| Other foreign countries | 1,195,252 | 1,203,915 | 1,390,175 | 989,601 |
| Tot. foreign countries | 12,437,660 | 12,492,072 | 11,444,780 | 11,492,872 |
| Total trade | 42,433,848 | 49,685,509 | 40,678,238 | 43,915,222 |

| COUNTRY | 1903 | | 1904 | |
|---|---|---|---|---|
| | £ Imports | £ Exports | £ Imports | £ Exports |
| United Kingdom | 19,855,340 | 19,962,503 | 19,855,340 | 19,962,503 |
| British possessions | | | | |
|    Canada | 352,939 | 24,837 | 352,939 | 24,837 |
|    Ceylon | 526,755 | 3,973,799 | 526,755 | 3,973,799 |
|    India | 984,463 | 5,607,841 | 984,463 | 5,607,841 |
|    New Zealand | 2,301,792 | 1,748,441 | 2,301,792 | 1,748,441 |
| British Pacific Islands | 299,988 | 300,838 | 299,988 | 300,838 |
| South African Union | 4,055 | 3,348,151 | 4,055 | 3,348,151 |
| Other Brit. possessions | 510,888 | 566,531 | 510,888 | 566,531 |
|   Total, Brit. possessions | 4,980,880 | 15,570,438 | 4,980,880 | 15,570,438 |
|   Total, Brit. countries | 24,836,220 | 35,532,941 | 24,836,220 | 35,532,941 |
| Belgium | 341,275 | 1,809,760 | 341,275 | 1,809,760 |
| China | 244,172 | 98,906 | 244,172 | 98,906 |
| France | 490,341 | 3,216,526 | 490,341 | 3,216,526 |
| Germany | 2,358,553 | 3,134,638 | 2,358,553 | 3,134,638 |
| Japan | 330,121 | 115,992 | 330,121 | 115,992 |
| Netherlands East Indies | 807,810 | 112,642 | 807,810 | 112,642 |
| Pacific Islands | 118,663 | 479,676 | 118,663 | 479,676 |
| Russia | 10,029 | 928 | 10,029 | 928 |
| USA | 6,368,532 | 2,625,399 | 6,368,532 | 2,625,399 |
| Other foreign countries | 1,905,755 | 1,123,433 | 1,905,755 | 1,123,433 |
|   Tot. foreign countries | 12,975,251 | 12,717,171 | 12,975,251 | 12,717,171 |
|   Total trade | 37,811,471 | 48,250,112 | 37,811,471 | 48,250,112 |

| COUNTRY | 1905 | | 1906 | |
|---|---|---|---|---|
| | £ Imports | £ Exports | £ Imports | £ Exports |
| United Kingdom | 23,074,717 | 26,702,390 | 26,575,833 | 32,854,049 |
| British possessions | | | | |
| Canada | 230,981 | 43,288 | 303,751 | 732,688 |
| Ceylon | 693,616 | 3,893,436 | 643,906 | 3,648,645 |
| India | 1,349,424 | 2,943,035 | 1,761,035 | 3,525,109 |
| New Zealand | 2,333,516 | 1,595,368 | 3,156,489 | 2,391,767 |
| British Pacific Islands | 186,445 | 337,917 | 283,855 | 405,249 |
| South African Union | 13,218 | 2,638,860 | 16,797 | 1,860,415 |
| Other Brit. possessions | 576,950 | 1,066,515 | 585,437 | 1,287,039 |
| Total, Brit. possessions | 5,384,150 | 12,519,319 | 6,751,270 | 13,850,912 |
| Total, Brit. countries | 28,458,867 | 39,221,709 | 33,327,103 | 46,704,961 |
| Belgium | 551,984 | 3,212,869 | 909,620 | 4,804,268 |
| China | 69,349 | 453,783 | 58,338 | 222,790 |
| France | 510,950 | 5,762,904 | 462,622 | 5,553,055 |
| Germany | 2,643,412 | 3,888,170 | 3,204,844 | 3,725,974 |
| Japan | 371,761 | 581,157 | 424,583 | 1,210,138 |
| Netherlands East Indies | 276,309 | 187,241 | 512,102 | 239,819 |
| Pacific Islands | 130,266 | 535,412 | 187,040 | 386,439 |
| Russia | 13,355 | 10,339 | 2,073 | 115,608 |
| USA | 4,486,604 | 1,049,773 | 4,633,553 | 4,338,701 |
| Other foreign countries | 842,874 | 1,937,678 | 1,023,034 | 2,436,010 |
| Tot. foreign countries | 9,887,864 | 17,619,326 | 11,417,809 | 23,032,802 |
| Total trade | 38,346,731 | 56,841,035 | 44,744,912 | 69,737,763 |

| COUNTRY | 1907 | | 1908 | |
|---|---|---|---|---|
| | £ Imports | £ Exports | £ Imports | £ Exports |
| United Kingdom | 31,906,447 | 33,975,579 | 31,906,447 | 33,975,579 |
| British possessions | | | | |
| Canada | 386,170 | 124,698 | 386,170 | 124,698 |
| Ceylon | 725,444 | 3,962,420 | 725,444 | 3,962,420 |
| India | 2,003,521 | 2,499,961 | 2,003,521 | 2,499,961 |
| New Zealand | 2,585,264 | 2,565,021 | 2,585,264 | 2,565,021 |
| British Pacific Islands | 331,304 | 420,142 | 331,304 | 420,142 |
| South African Union | 22,249 | 2,080,837 | 22,249 | 2,080,837 |
| Other Brit. possessions | 646,803 | 1,469,594 | 646,803 | 1,469,594 |
| Total, Brit. possessions | 6,701,430 | 13,122,673 | 6,701,430 | 13,122,673 |
| Total, Brit. countries | 38,607,877 | 47,098,252 | 38,607,877 | 47,098,252 |
| Belgium | 1,000,377 | 5,716,069 | 1,000,377 | 5,716,069 |
| China | 81,278 | 416,441 | 81,278 | 416,441 |
| France | 486,550 | 8,148,980 | 486,550 | 8,148,980 |
| Germany | 3,551,255 | 5,140,380 | 3,551,255 | 5,140,380 |
| Japan | 541,286 | 706,279 | 541,286 | 706,279 |
| Netherlands East Indies | 272,425 | 302,799 | 272,425 | 302,799 |
| Pacific Islands | 221,287 | 440,591 | 221,287 | 440,591 |
| Russia | 10,540 | 120,763 | 10,540 | 120,763 |
| USA | 5,869,099 | 2,405,401 | 5,869,099 | 2,405,401 |
| Other foreign countries | 1,167,059 | 2,328,292 | 1,167,059 | 2,328,292 |
| Tot. foreign countries | 13,201,156 | 25,725,995 | 13,201,156 | 25,725,995 |
| Total trade | 51,809,033 | 72,824,247 | 51,809,033 | 72,824,247 |

| COUNTRY | 1909 | | 1910 | |
|---|---|---|---|---|
| | £ Imports | £ Exports | £ Imports | £ Exports |
| United Kingdom | 31,171,828 | 30,917,133 | 36,646,441 | 37,698,312 |
| British possessions | | | | |
| Canada | 508,415 | 80,242 | 649,507 | 100,398 |
| Ceylon | 740,271 | 1,216,754 | 769,985 | 631,225 |
| India | 1,891,293 | 2,031,182 | 2,668,862 | 1,535,372 |
| New Zealand | 2,195,313 | 2,341,625 | 2,203,806 | 2,342,753 |
| British Pacific Islands | 603,539 | 455,250 | 570,654 | 581,257 |
| South African Union | 120,680 | 2,023,931 | 69,472 | 1,826,032 |
| Other Brit. possessions | 825,583 | 1,075,142 | 933,363 | 1,306,449 |
| Total, Brit. possessions | 6,885,094 | 9,224,126 | 7,865,649 | 8,323,486 |
| Total, Brit. countries | 38,056,922 | 40,141,259 | 44,512,090 | 46,021,798 |
| Belgium | 968,481 | 4,753,514 | 1,242,867 | 5,949,060 |
| China | 44,103 | 151,668 | 79,270 | 114,051 |
| France | 409,949 | 6,480,782 | 501,584 | 8,551,579 |
| Germany | 3,331,141 | 6,394,634 | 3,778,666 | 7,340,455 |
| Japan | 601,534 | 1,882,692 | 718,462 | 657,057 |
| Netherlands East Indies | 1,079,648 | 349,767 | 581,398 | 397,353 |
| Pacific Islands | 196,647 | 500,018 | 239,116 | 570,444 |
| Russia | 37,066 | 609 | 85,672 | 1,793 |
| USA | 5,003,130 | 2,599,063 | 6,494,829 | 1,599,102 |
| Other foreign countries | 1,443,275 | 2,064,830 | 1,780,397 | 3,288,458 |
| Tot. foreign countries | 13,114,974 | 25,177,577 | 15,502,261 | 28,469,352 |
| Total trade | 51,171,896 | 65,318,836 | 60,014,351 | 74,491,150 |

| COUNTRY | 1913 | | 1914 | |
|---|---|---|---|---|
| | £ Imports | £ Exports | £ Imports | £ Exports |
| United Kingdom | 47,615,561 | 34,804,548 | 37,896,655 | 38,546,018 |
| British possessions | | | | |
| Canada | 1,158,833 | 169,193 | 1,487,592 | 388,562 |
| Ceylon | 968,500 | 1,123,890 | 977,368 | 435,440 |
| India | 2,964,246 | 1,355,383 | 2,748,173 | 1,425,377 |
| New Zealand | 2,513,934 | 2,356,990 | 2,095,723 | 2,808,860 |
| British Pacific Islands | 940,761 | 611,684 | 823,474 | 773,270 |
| South African Union | 127,263 | 1,941,164 | 116,748 | 2,022,839 |
| Other Brit. possessions | 1,230,267 | 1,898,959 | 1,182,067 | 1,438,362 |
| Total, Brit. possessions | 9,903,804 | 9,457,263 | 9,431,145 | 9,292,710 |
| Total, Brit. countries | 57,519,365 | 44,261,811 | 47,327,800 | 47,838,728 |
| Belgium | 2,258,839 | 7,465,742 | 524,396 | 804,956 |
| China | 89,746 | 194,649 | 126,434 | 130,098 |
| France | 625,397 | 9,684,362 | 237,627 | 1,279,513 |
| Germany | 4,956,834 | 6,873,441 | 1,296,917 | 478,396 |
| Japan | 918,681 | 1,429,310 | 1,392,317 | 1,966,944 |
| Netherlands East Indies | 919,509 | 818,671 | 1,019,364 | 434,749 |
| Pacific Islands | 264,250 | 718,732 | 270,008 | 569,357 |
| Russia | 60,518 | 99,891 | 22,737 | 270,368 |
| USA | 9,522,704 | 2,631,058 | 9,585,617 | 4,947,446 |
| Other foreign countries | 2,613,810 | 4,394,102 | 2,628,620 | 1,872,021 |
| Tot. foreign countries | 22,230,288 | 34,309,958 | 17,104,037 | 12,753,848 |
| Total trade | 79,749,653 | 78,571,769 | 64,431,837 | 60,592,576 |

*Source:* Commonwealth Bureau of Census and Statistics: Official Statistics, Commonwealth of Australia Overseas Trade Bulletin No. 18, 'Australian Statistics of Overseas Imports and Exports and Customs and Excise Revenue, for the year 1920–21'.

# Select Bibliography

*Primary sources*

## 1. Official

(1) Unpublished archival records

**New South Wales** (Mitchell Library, Sydney)
Treasury Papers 95/5907.

**Australia** (Australian Archives Office, Canberra).
    CP 78 Records of the Governor-General's Office.
        Especially:
        78/6 Register of Correspondence received from the Colonial Office, 1900–3, 1905–11.
        78/8 Governor-General's Letter Books, Outward Despatches to the Colonial Secretary, 1900–11.
        78/9 Governor-General's Letter Books, 'Secret and Confidential' Despatches, 1900–11.
        78/22 General Correspondence, 1912–27.
        78/64 Press Cuttings of Lord Dudley's Speeches, 1908–12.
    CP 103 Prime Minister's Department Records—Imperial Affairs.
        Especially:
        103/10 Naval Defence, Imperial Defence, Lord Kitchener' Visit 1909–10.
        103/12 Records of Imperial Conferences, 1897–1933.
    CP 290 Prime Minister's Department. Papers extracted from Governor-General's Records, 1903–26.
        Especially:
        290/15 Pacific Naval Defence.
        CRS A1632 Memoirs of Malcolm Shepherd.
        CRS A2 Prime Minister's Files of Papers, 1900–21.
        CRS A2032 Council of Defence Minutes, 1905–15.
        CRS A2585 Naval Board Minutes, 1905–14.
        CRS A289 Department of Air.
        —— (Australian Archives Office, Melbourne)
    MP 729/1–2 Defence Department Records, 'Secret Series', Classified General Correspondence, 1901–36.
    MP 1049/1 Navy Department Records, 'Secret and Confidential Files, 1911–1922'.

**Great Britain** (Public Record Office, London).
    Adm 116/1270.
    Cab 1/5.
    Cab 2/1–3 CID Minutes (1902–23).
    Cab 5/1 CID Secret, 12 February 1906 (Australian General Scheme of Defence).
    Cab 7 CDC Minutes, 1879–1916.
    Cab 8 CDC Memoranda, 1885–1914.
    Cab 9 CDC Remarks, 1887–1903.

Cab 11/1, 22–6, 119, 121, 125–6 and 133.

Cab 16/5 and 36.

Cab 17/9, 56, 67 and 74–9.

Cab 18/7–9. 1897 Conference of Colonial Premiers.

Cab 18/11A–11B. 1907 Colonial Conference; Proceedings and Papers.

Cab 18/12A. 1909 Imperial Defence Conference: Proceedings.

CO 418. Original Correspondence, 1889–1922 containing most of the communications between the Australian Governor-General and the Colonial Secretary, the minutes by the Colonial Office officials and other departments of state and the draft replies.

CO 532. Dominions Original Correspondence, 1907–25, containing some important correspondence which originates in Australia and which affects both Australia and other Pacific Dominions.

CO 808/66. Proceedings of the First Session of the Federal Council of Australia, 1886.

CO 881. Confidential Prints (Australian Series), especially:

No. 115 Correspondence relating to the Naval Defence of the Australian Colonies and the Defence of King George's Sound and Fremantle.

No. 187 Correspondence concerning Convention with France re New Hebrides, 1907.

No. 193 Report by Sir C. Lucas on Visit to Australia, New Zealand and Fiji, October 1909.

No. 199 Affairs in the New Hebrides, 1908–13.

No. 207 German Trading Rights in the British Solomon Islands, March 1912.

No. 218 Western Pacific Islands, 1911.

CO 885. Miscellaneous Series, especially:

No. 111 Minutes and Proceedings of the 1897 Colonial Conference.

No. 144 Report of the 1902 Colonial Conference.

No. 160 Notes on the Colonial Questions Referred to in Lord Lansdowne's Recent Conversations with M. Cambon, August 1903.

CO 886. Dominions Series, especially:

No. 7 Imperial Conference; Further Correspondence, 1908–9.

No. 12 Memorandum of Alfred Deakin's Meeting with Representatives of the Admiralty, 24 April 1907.

No. 13 Conference on Naval and Military Defence—Correspondence, 22 March to 18 June 1909.

No. 14 Proposed Formation of an Imperial General Staff.

Nos 15–17 Imperial Defence Conference, 1909; Minutes, Papers and Sub-Conferences.

FO 800/90–1. Papers of Sir Edward Grey.

PRO 30/56/1. Papers of Lord Northcote.

**United States** (National Archives, Washington, DC)

Record Group 59, State Department Numerical File, 1906–10, Vol. 597.

## (2) Published records

**Australian Colonies**

New South Wales. Parliamentary Debates, 1st series, 1891–1900.

New South Wales. *Votes and Proceedings of the Legislative Assembly*, 1870–1 session, Vol. II, No. 12-A, 'Inter-colonial Conference. Report and Minutes of the Proceedings of the Intercolonial Conference held in Melbourne in the Months of June and July, 1870'.

——, 1876–7 session, Vol. III, No. 353-A, 'Defences. Preliminary Report by Sir W. Jervois …'.

——, 1880–1 session, Vol. I, No. 143, 'Intercolonial Conference. Minutes of Proceedings of the Intercolonial Conference held at Sydney, January 1881'.

——, 1883–4 session, Vol. IX, 'Intercolonial Convention, 1883. Report of the Proceedings of the Intercolonial Convention held in Sydney in November and December 1883'.

Queensland. *Journals of the Legislative Council*, 1877 session, Vol. XXV, Pt I, 'Defences. Preliminary Report by His Excellency Colonel Sir W. F. Drummond Jervois …'.

——, 1901 session, Vol. IV, A. 56, 'Admission of Japanese into Queensland (Further Correspondence relating to)'.

South Australia. *Parliamentary Papers*, 1877 session, Vol. IV, 'Memorandum on South Australian Defences, December 12, 1877'.

Victoria. *Votes and Proceedings of the Legislative Assembly*, 1877–8 session, Vol. II, No. 46, 'Preliminary Report on the Defences of Victoria, July 20, 1877'.

——, 1889 session, Vol. II, No. 57, 'Inspection of Colonial Forces by an Imperial General Officer'.

**Commonwealth of Australia**

*Parliamentary Debates*, 1901–14, Vols I-LXXIV.

*Parliamentary Papers*, 1901–2 session, Vol. II A. 7, 'Further Report of the Federal Military Committee Assembled at Melbourne, Victoria, 12 June, 1901'.

——, 1901–2 session, Vol. II, A. 12, 'Naval Defence of the Commonwealth of Australia. (1) Copy of Minute by the Right Honorable the Prime Minister … asking … the Admiral Commanding on the Australian Naval Station a Statement of his Opinion on the Subject of the Naval Defence of the Commonwealth of Australia. (2) Copy of a letter from His Excellency Rear Admiral Beaumont in reply to a request to assist in instituting a system of Naval Defence for the Commonwealth of Australia'.

——, 1901–2 session, Vol. II, A. 36, 'Military Forces of the Commonwealth. Defence of Australia by Major-General Hutton, Commandant'.

——, 1901–2 session, Vol. II, No. 27, 'Report of the Conference of Naval Officers Assembled at Melbourne, Victoria, to consider the Question of Naval Defence of Australia'.

——, 1901–2 session, Vol. II, No. 31, 'Defence Forces and Defences (Memorandum by Colonial Defence Committee)'.

——, 1901–2 session, Vol. II, No. 52, 'Report by Captain Creswell on the Best Method of Employing Australian Seamen in the Defence of Commerce and Ports'.

——, 1903 session, Vol. II, No. 2, 'Papers Relating to a Conference between the Secretary of State for the Colonies and the Prime Minister of the Self-Governing Colonies, June to August, 1902'.

——, 1903 session, Vol. II, No. 37, 'Annual Report upon the Military Forces of the Commonwealth of Australia, January 1902–30 April, 1903, by Major-General Sir Edward Hutton, K.C.M.G., C.B., Commanding'.

——, 1904 session, Vol. II, No. 25, 'Military Forces of the Commonwealth of Australia. Second Annual Report of Major-General Sir Edward Hutton, K.C.M.G., C.B., Commanding'.

——, 1904 session, Vol. II, No. 58, 'Defence Forces of the Commonwealth. (Memorandum by a Committee in regard to the Administration of Military and Naval Forces together with Memoranda thereon by Senator the Hon. A. Dawson, and Major-General Sir E. T. H. Hutton, K.C.M.G., C.B.)'.

——, 1905 session, Vol. II, No. 31, 'Hon. Alfred Deakin—Statement re present Condition of Defence of Commonwealth; communicated to *The Herald* on 12 June 1905—Return to Order'.

——, 1905 session, Vol. II, No. 60, 'Despatch from Secretary of State as to previous Colonial Conferences, and suggesting formation of an Imperial Council in place of a Conference, together with a permanent advisory Commission on matters of joint concern, and reply thereto from Prime Minister of Commonwealth'.

——, 1905 session, Vol. II, No. 61, 'Immigration Restriction Act, 1901. Correspondence Respecting Proposals to modify the Administration of the Act in Regard to Visits of Asiatic Merchants, Travellers, etc.'.

——, 1906 session, Vol. II, No. 44, 'Naval Defence. Report by the Director of the Naval Forces for the Year 1905'.

——, 1906 session, Vol. II, No. 62, 'Report of the Committee of Imperial Defence, upon a General Scheme of Defence for Australia'.

——, 1906 session, Vol. II, No. 66, 'Defence of Australia. Reports by Captain Creswell, Naval Director (a) In reply to Questions asked by Minister of Defence as to the Formation of an Australian Navy; (b) Upon Australian Defence; (c) Re Submersibles and Submarines'.

——, 1906, session, Vol. II, No. 81, 'Instructions of the Minister for Defence to Captain W. R. Creswell, Director of the Naval Forces, relative to his Visit to England to Inquire into the latest Naval Developments'.

——, 1906 session, Vol. II, No. 82, 'Report of the Director of the Naval Forces (Captain W. R. Creswell) on his Visit to England in 1906 to inquire into the latest Naval Developments'.

——, 1906 session, Vol. II, No. 86, 'Report of Committee of Naval Officers of the Commonwealth assembled at Melbourne, Victoria to consider the Memorandum of the Committee of Imperial Defence and report as regards the Naval Development of Australia'.

——, 1906 session, Vol. II, No. 87, 'General Scheme of Defence for Australia. Report of a Committee of Officers, appointed by the Minister of State for Defence to consider and report upon the Original Scheme of Defence for Australia as submitted by the Committee of Imperial Defence'.

——, 1906 session, Vol. II, No. 98, 'Naval Agreement with Australia and New Zealand. (Correspondence between the Governments of the United Kingdom and the Commonwealth—Dated 28th August, 1905 to 23rd May, 1906)'.

——, 1907 session, Vol. II, No. 15, 'New Hebrides—Correspondence Relating to the Convention with France, dated 20th October, 1906'.

——, 1907 session, Vol. II, No. 129, 'Report on the Swiss Military System, compiled in the Department of the Chief of Intelligence, 1907'.

——, 1907–8 session, Vol. II, No. 143, 'Naval Defence of Australia (Correspondence in reference thereto, between the Commonwealth Government and the Admiralty)'.

——, 1907–8 session, Vol. II, No. 170, 'Colonial Office. Copy of Despatch from the Prime Minister of the Commonwealth Dated 19th November, 1907 Relating to the Organization of the Colonial Office'.

——, 1908 session, Vol. II, No. 6, 'Naval Defence. Further Correspondence between the Commonwealth Government and the Admiralty in regard to the Naval Defence of Australia'.

——, 1908 session, Vol. II, No. 35, 'The Defence of Australia. By Colonel H. Foster (Director of Military Studies, Sydney University), together with remarks thereon, by Captain W. R. Creswell, Naval Director'.

——, 1908 session, Vol. II, No. 37, 'Naval Defence. Report for 1907 by the Director of the Naval Forces'.

——, 1909 session, Vol. II, No. 1, 'Defence: Correspondence Regarding a Conference between Representatives of His Majesty's Governments of the Self-Governing Dominions on the subject of Naval and Military Defence'.

——, 1909 session, Vol. II, Pt II, No. 64, 'Correspondence and Papers relating to a Conference with Representatives of the Self-Governing Dominions on the Naval and Military Defence of the Empire'.

——, 1910 session, Vol. II, No. 8, 'Defence of Australia. Memorandum by Field-Marshal Viscount Kitchener of Khartoum, …'.

——, 1911 session, Vol. II, No. 7, 'Naval Forces. Recommendations by Admiral Sir Reginald Henderson'.

——, 1911 session, Vol. II, No. 12, 'Memorandum of Conference Between the British Admiralty and the Representatives of the Dominions of Canada and Commonwealth of Australia'.

——, 1912 session, Vol. II, No. 66, 'Naval Defence of the Empire: (Memorandum prepared by the Board of Admiralty at the request of the Prime Minister of Canada)'.

——, 1914 session, Vol. II, No. 1, 'Naval Defence. Memorandum by the Minister for Defence, dated 13 April 1914; together with speech of the First Lord of the Admiralty as Reported in Australia'.

——, 1914 session, Vol. II, No. 33, 'Navies-Relative Strength in the Pacific'.

——, 1914 session, Vol. II, No. 4, 'Naval Defence. Reports by Sir Maurice Fitzmaurice on Flinders Naval Base (Port Western) and Other Matters'.

——, 1914 session, Vol. II, No. 14, 'Report on an Inspection of the Military Forces of the Commonwealth of Australia by General Sir Ian Hamilton … General Officer Commanding-in-Chief, Mediterranean, And Inspector-General of the Overseas Forces'.

*Official Year Books*, Nos 1–17, 1907–24.

*Official Report of the National Australasian Convention Debates*, Sydney, 2 March to 9 April 1891. George Stephen Chapman. Acting Government Printer, Sydney 1891.

*Official Report of the National Australasian Convention Debates*, March 22—May 5, 1897. Government Printer, Adelaide 1897.

*Official Record of the Debates of the Australasian Federal Convention*, Second Session. Sydney, 2 to 24 September, 1897. Government Printing Office, Sydney 1897.

*Official Record of the Australasian Federal Convention*, Third Session, Melbourne, 20 January to 17 March 1898. 2 vols. Government Printing Office, Melbourne 1898.

## Great Britain

*Parliamentary Debates*, 3rd to 5th series, 1885–1914.

*Parliamentary Papers*, 1876 session, Vol. LIV, C. 1566, 'Correspondence respecting New Guinea'.

——, 1883 session, Vol. XLVII, C. 3617, 'Further Correspondence respecting New Guinea (in continuation of C. 1566, July 1876)'.

——, 1886 session, Vol. LXXIII, C. 4656, 'Declarations between the Governments of Great Britain and the German Empire relating to the Demarcation of the British and German spheres of Influence in the Western Pacific and to Reciprocal Freedom of Trade and Commerce in the British and German Possessions and Protectorates in these Regions. Signed at Berlin, April 6 and 10, 1886'.

——, 1887 session, Vol. LVI, C. 5091, 'Colonial Conference, 1887. Proceedings of the Colonial Conference'.

——, 1890 session, Vol. XLIX, C. 6188, 'Correspondence relating to the Inspection of the Military Forces of the Australasian Colonies, by Major-General J. Bevan Edwards, C.B.'.

——, 1900 session, Vol. LVI, Cd. 18, 'Correspondence relating to the despatch of Colonial Military Contingents to South Africa, November, 1899'.

——, 1907 session, Vol. LIV, Cd. 3337, 'Despatches of the Secretary of State for the Colonies with Enclosures respecting the Agenda of the Colonial Conference, 1907'.

——, 1907 session, Vol. LV, Cd. 3523, 'Colonial Conference 1907. Minutes of the Proceedings of the Colonial Conference, 1907'.

——, 1911 session, Vol. LIV, Cd. 5745, 'Imperial Conference, 1911. Dominions no. 7. Minutes of the Proceedings of the Imperial Conference, 1911'.

——, 1914 session, Vol. LX, Cd. 7347, 'Correspondence relating to the Representation of the Self-Governing Dominions on the Committee of Imperial Defence and to a Proposed Naval Conference'.

## Canada

*Parliamentary Debates*, 1911–14.

## New Zealand

*Parliamentary Debates*, 1909–14.

## 2. Non-official

(1) Unpublished materials

*Collections of Private Papers*

**Australia**
Australian Labor Party. Federal Parliamentary Caucus Minutes, 1901–23. Australian National University Library.
Barton, Sir Edmund, ANL, ms. 51.
Batchelor, E. L. ANL, ms. 574.
Cook, Sir Joseph. In possession of Mr Justice Cook, Sydney, NSW
——. ANL, ms. 762.
Deakin, Alfred. ANL, ms. 1540.
Denman, Thomas, 3rd Baron. ANL ms. 769.
Fisher, Andrew. ANL, ms. 2979.
Forrest, Sir John. Battye Library, University of Western Australia.
Higgins, Henry Bournes. ANL, ms. 1057.
Hughes, William Morris. ANL, ms. 950.
Hunt, Atlee. ANL, ms. 52 and 1100.
Jebb, Richard. ANL, ms. 813.
Deakin-Jebb Correspondence. ANL, ms. 339.
Jose, A. W. Mitchell Library.
Moore, Sir William Harrison. University of Melbourne Archives.
O'Malley, King. ANL, ms. 460.
Pearce, Sir George Foster. ANL, ms. 213, 1827, 1927.
——. Australian War Memorial.
Tennyson, Hallam, 2nd Baron. ANL, ms. 479.
Watson, J. C. ANL, ms. 451.
Wise, R. B. ANL.

**Others**
Arnold-Foster, H. O., BM.
Asquith, Herbert Henry, 1st Earl of Oxford and Asquith. Bodleian Library, Oxford University, UK.
Balfour, Arthur J., 1st Earl of. BM.
Borden, Sir Robert. National Archives, Ottawa, Canada.
Chamberlain, Joseph. University of Birmingham Library, Birmingham, UK.
Harcourt, Sir Louis. Bodleian Library, Oxford.
Hutton, Sir Edward T. H. BM.
Jebb, Richard. Institute of Commonwealth Studies, Russell Square, London, UK.
Sperry, Charles S. Library of Congress, Washington DC, USA.

(2) Published materials

**Newspapers**

| | |
|---|---|
| *Advertiser* (Adelaide) | *Morning Post* |
| *Age* (1901–14) | *Register* (Adelaide) |

| | |
|---|---|
| *Argus* (1901–14) | *South Wales News* |
| *Australasian* | *Sun* (Sydney) |
| *Brisbane Courier* | *Sydney Morning Herald* (1901–14) |
| *Daily Mail* | *The Times* (London) |
| *Daily Telegraph* | *Washington Post* |
| *Herald* (Melbourne) | *West Australian* |
| *Hobart Mercury* | |

**Periodicals**

*Brassey's Year Book*, 1901–14
*Bulletin*, 1901–14
*Call*, 1906–10
*Journal and Proceedings of the United Services Institution of New South Wales*, 1889–1912.
*Lone Hand*, 1907–14
*National Review*
*Proceedings of the Royal Colonial Institute*
*Review of Reviews*
*Round Table*, 1911–14.

**Books and articles**

Clarke, Sir George S. *Imperial Defence*, Imperial Press, London 1897.

Clarke, Sir George S. (Lord Sydenham of Combe), *My Working Life*, n.p., London 1927.

——. *Studies of an Imperialist*, Chapman and Hall, London 1928.

Coghlan, T. A. *A Statistical Account of the Seven Colonies of Australasia*, Charles Potter, Government Printer, Sydney 1890–1904.

Cooke, C. Kinloch. *Australian Defence and New Guinea: Compiled from the Papers of the Late Major-General Sir Peter Scratchley*, Macmillan, London 1887.

Craig, George Cathcart. *The Federal Defence of Australasia*, George Robertson and Co., Sydney 1897.

Creswell, William Rooke. *Close to the Wind: The Early Memoirs (1866–79) of Admiral Sir William Creswell*. Paul Thompson (ed.), Heinemann, London 1965.

Cutlack, Frederic M. 'Australia and Imperial Defence', *National Review*, LX (1912), 994–1002.

Davis, Oscar K. *Released for Publication: Some Inside Political History of Theodore Roosevelt and His Times, 1890–1918*. Houghton, Mifflin, Boston 1925.

Deakin, Alfred. *The Federal Story: The Inner History of the Federal Cause 1880–1900*, edited and introduced by J. A. La Nauze. Melbourne University Press, Melbourne 1963.

Dilke, Sir Charles. *Greater Britain*, 2 vols, Macmillan, London 1868.

Edwards, General Sir Bevan. 'Australasian Defence', *Proceedings of the Royal Colonial Institute*, XXII (1890–1), 195–224.

Eggleston, Frederic W. *Reflections of an Australian Liberal*, Cheshire, Melbourne 1954.

Esher, Viscount. *The Committee of Imperial Defence; Its Function and Potentialities*, John Murray, London 1912.

Foster, Colonel Hubert. *The Defence of the Empire in Australia*, Rankine, Dobbie and Co., Melbourne 1908.

——. *War and the Empire: The Principles of Imperial Defence*, Williams and Norgate, London 1914.

Fox, Frank. *Beneath an Ardent Sun*, Hodder and Stoughton, London 1923.

——. *From the Old Dog, being the letters of the Hon. ——, ex-Prime Minister to his Nephew*. Thomas C. Lothian, Melbourne 1908.

——. *Problems of the Pacific*, Williams and Norgate, London 1912.

Garran, R. R. *Prosper the Commonwealth*, Angus and Robertson, Sydney 1958.

Gooch, G. P. and Temperley, Harold (eds). *British Documents on the Origins of the War, 1898–1914*, 11 vols, HMSO, London 1925–38.

Hislam, Percival A. *The Admiralty of the Atlantic: An Enquiry into the Development of German Sea Power, Past, Present and Prospective*, Longmans, Green and Co., London 1908.

Hutton, E. T. H. 'A Co-operative System for the Defence of the Empire', *Proceedings of the Royal Colonial Institute*, XXIX (1897–8), 222–58.

Hutton, Sir E. T. H. *The Defence and Defensive Power of Australia*, Angus and Robertson, Melbourne 1902.

Jebb, Richard. *The Britannic Question*, Longmans, Green, London 1913.

——. *The Imperial Conference: A History and Study*, 2 vols, Longmans, Green, London 1911.

——. *Studies in Colonial Nationalism*, E. A. Arnold, London 1905.

Keith, Arthur Berriedale. *The Theory of State Succession with special reference to English and Colonial Law*, Waterlow and Sons, London 1907.

Kemp, P. K. (ed.). *The Papers of Admiral Sir John Fisher*, 2 vols, printed for the Navy Record Society, London 1960.

Kirmess, Charles H. *The Australian Crisis*, George Robertson, Melbourne 1909.

Latham, J. G. 'Australia and the Pacific', *Trident*, I (September 1908), 90–2.

Lea, Homer. *The Valour of Ignorance*, Harper Bros., New York and London 1909.

——. *The Day of the Saxon*, Harper Bros., New York 1911.

Legge, J. G., 'The Organisation of a Reserve for the Land Defences of Australia', *Journal and Proceedings of the United Services Institution of New South Wales*, XVII (27 June 1905), 87–99.

Lloyd George, D. *War Memoirs*, 2 vols, Ivor, Nicholson and Watson, London 1933.

Maloney, W. R. H. *Flashlights on Japan and the East*, n.p., Melbourne 1905.

*Manifesto of the Social Democratic Party in the German Empire*. Melbourne Fabian Society, Melbourne 1895.

Marder, Arthur J. (ed.). *Fear God and Dread Nought. The Correspondence of Admiral of the Fleet, Lord Fisher of Kilverstone*, 2 vols, Jonathan Cape, London 1956.

Matheson, A. P. 'Australia and Naval Defence', *Proceedings of the Royal Colonial Institute*, XXXIX (March 1903), 194–246.

Matthews, Franklin. *Back to Hampton Road. Cruise of the United States Atlantic Fleet from San Francisco to Hampton Road, July 7, 1908–February 22, 1909*. B. W. Haebsch, New York 1909.

'Naval Policy and the Pacific Question', *Round Table*, IV (June 1914), 391–462.

*Official Minutes and Proceedings, Commonwealth Labour Conference*, Sydney, December 1–4, 1902.

*Official Report of the Commonwealth Political Labour Conference*, Melbourne, July, 1905.

*Official Report of the Fourth Commonwealth Political Labor Conference*, Brisbane, July 7–10, 1908.

*Official Report of the Fifth Commonwealth Conference of the A.L.P.*, January 8–12, 1912.

Parkes, Sir Henry. *Fifty-Years in the Making of Australian History*, 2 vols, Longmans and Co., London 1892.

——. *The Federal Government of Australasia: Speeches Delivered on Various Occasions (November 1889 – May 1890)*, Turner and Henderson, Sydney 1890.

Pearson, Charles H. *National Life and Character. A Forecast*, Macmillan, London 1894.

Pratten, H. E. *Asiatic Impressions*, Ferguson, Sydney 1908.

Pulsford, E. *The British Empire and the Relations of Asia and Australasia*, Sydney, n.p., 1905.

Quick, Sir John and Garran, Sir Robert Randolph. *The Annotated Constitution of the Australian Commonwealth*, Angus and Robertson, Sydney 1901.

Roosevelt, Theodore. *Theodore Roosevelt, an Autobiography*. Macmillan, New York 1914.

Salmon, C. Carty. *An Australian Navy: A Necessary Part of Imperial Defence*, Imperial Federation League, Melbourne 1905.

Seeley, J. R. The Expansion of England: Two Courses of Lectures, Macmillan, London 1883.

Wells, H. G. *An Englishman Looks at the World*, Cassell, London 1914.

## Secondary sources

### 1. Books

Bolton, G. C. *Alexander Forrest: His Life and Times*, Melbourne University Press, Melbourne 1958.

Braisted, William Reynolds. *The United States Navy in the Pacific*, 1897–1909, University of Texas Press, Austin 1958.

——. *The United States Navy in the Pacific*, 1909–1922, University of Texas Press, Austin 1971.

Brogden, S. *The Sudan Contingent*, Hawthorn Press, Melbourne 1943.

Churchill, Randolph S. *Winston Churchill*, 2 vols, Heinemann, London 1967.

Clarke, I. F. *Voices Prophesying War, 1763–1984*, Oxford University Press, London 1966.

Daniels, Roger. *The Politics of Prejudice: The Anti-Japanese Movement in California and the Struggle for Japanese Exclusion*. University of California Press, Berkeley 1962.

Eggleston, Frederic. 'Australia and the Empire, 1885–1921', in J. Holland Rose (ed.). *The Cambridge History of the British Empire*, 8 vols, Cambridge University Press, Cambridge 1929–36, Vol. VII, 'Australia and New Zealand'.

Esthus, Raymond A. *Theodore Roosevelt and Japan*, University of Washington Press, Seattle 1966.

Feakes, Henry J. *White Ensign—Southern Cross. A Story of the King's Ship's of Australasia's Navy*, Ure Smith, Sydney 1951.

Fitzhardinge, L. F. *William Morris Hughes: A Political Biography*, Vol. I, 'That Fiery Particle, 1862–1914', Angus and Robertson, Sydney 1964.

Garvin, J. L. and Amery, J. *Life of Joseph Chamberlain*, 5 vols, Macmillan, London 1932–68.

Gollin, Alfred. *Balfour's Burden. Arthur Balfour and Imperial Preference*, Bland, London 1965.

Gordon, Donald C. *The Dominion Partnership in Imperial Defence, 1870–1914*, The Johns Hopkins Press, Baltimore 1965.

Hall, Henry L. *Australia and England: A Study in Imperial Relations*, Longmans, Green & Co., London 1934.

Hamer, W. S. *The British Army: Civil-Military Relations, 1885–1905*, The Clarendon Press, Oxford 1970.

Hancock, W. K. *Australia*, Ernest Benn, London 1940.

Hart, Robert A. *The Great White Fleet; Its Voyage Around the World, 1907–1909*, Little, Brown & Co., Boston 1965.

Heydon, Peter. *Quiet Decision: a Study of George Foster Pearce*, Melbourne University Press, Melbourne 1965.

Hyam, Ronald. *Elgin and Churchill at the Colonial Office, 1905–1908: The Watershed of the Empire*, Macmillan, London 1968.

Johnson, F. A. *Defence by Committee*, Oxford University Press, London 1960.

Kendle, John Edward. *The Colonial and Imperial Conferences, 1887–1911: A Study in Imperial Organization*, Longmans, London 1967.

Kohn, Hans. *The Idea of Nationalism: A Study in Its Origin and Background*, Macmillan, New York 1944.

Kristianson, G. L. *The Politics of Patriotism: The Pressure Group Activities of the R.S.L.*, Australian National University Press, Canberra 1966.

Kubicek, R. V. *The Administration of Imperialism: Joseph Chamberlain at the Colonial Office*, Duke University Press, Durham, N.C. 1969.

La Nauze, J. A. *Alfred Deakin: A Biography*, 2 vols, Melbourne University Press, Melbourne 1965.

——. *The Making of the Federal Constitution*, Melbourne University Press, Melbourne 1971.

Lucas, Sir C. P. (ed.). *Lord Durham's Report on the Affairs of British North America*, 3 vols, The Clarendon Press, Oxford 1912.

Macandie, G. L. *The Genesis of the Royal Australian Navy*, Government Printing Office, Sydney 1949.

Mander-Jones, Phyllis (ed.). *Manuscripts in the British Isles Relating to Australia, New Zealand and the Pacific*, Australian National University Press, Canberra 1972.

Marder, Arthur J. *From the Dreadnought to Scapa Flow*, 4 vols, Oxford University Press, London 1961.

Monger, George W. *The End of Isolation: British Foreign Policy, 1900–1907*, Thomas Nelson and Sons, London 1963.

Morrell, W. P. *Britain in the Pacific Islands*, The Clarendon Press, Oxford 1960.

Nimocks, Walter. *Milner's Young Men: The 'Kindergarten' in Edwardian Imperial Affairs*, Duke University Press, Durham, N. C. 1968.

Nish, Ian H. *The Anglo-Japanese Alliance: The Diplomacy of Two Island Empires, 1894–1907*, The Athlone Press, London 1966.

——. *Alliance in Decline: A Study in Anglo-Japanese Relations, 1908–23*. The Athlone Press, London 1972.

d'Ombrain, Nicholas. *War Machinery and High Policy: Defence Administration in Peace Time Britain 1902–1904*. Oxford University Press, London 1973.

Oppenheim, L. F. *International Law—A Treatise*, 2 vols, Longmans, Green & Co., London 1905–6.

Palmer, Nettie. *Henry Bournes Higgins: A Memoir*, George G. Harrap and Company Ltd., London 1931.

Preston, Richard A. *Canada and 'Imperial Defence': A Study of the Origins of the British Commonwealth's Defence Organization, 1867–1919*, Duke University Press, Durham, N.C. 1967.

Price, Richard. *An Imperial War and the British Working Class: Working Class Attitudes and Reactions to the Boer War, 1899–1902*, Routledge, London 1972.

Reynolds, John. *Edmund Barton*, Angus and Robertson, Sydney 1948.

Robbins, Keith. *Sir Edward Grey: A Biography of Lord Grey of Fallodon*, Cassell, London 1971.

Sawer, Geoffrey. *Australian Federal Politics and Law, 1901–1929*, Melbourne University Press, Melbourne 1956.

Semmel, Bernard. *Imperialism and Social Reform: English Social-Imperial Thought, 1895–1914*, George Allen and Unwin, London 1960.

Serle, Geoffrey. *The Rush to be Rich: A History of the Colony of Victoria, 1883–1889*, Melbourne University Press, Melbourne 1971.

——. 'The Victorian Government's Campaign for Federation, 1883–1889' in A. W. Martin (ed.). *Essay in Australian Federation*, Melbourne University Press, Melbourne 1969.

Sinclair, Keith. *Imperial Federation: A Study of New Zealand Policy and Opinion, 1880–1914* (Commonwealth Papers, No. 11), Institute of Commonwealth Studies, London 1955.

Trevelyan, George Macaulay. *Grey of Fallodon, Being the Life of Sir Edward Grey, Afterwards Viscount Grey of Fallodon*. Longmans, Green & Co., London 1937.

Ward, John M. *British Policy in the South Pacific, 1786–1893*, Australasian Pub. Co., Sydney 1948.

Ward, Russel. *The Australian Legend*, Melbourne University Press, Melbourne 1958.

Whyte, Frederic. *The Life of W. T. Stead*, 2 vols, Jonathan Cape, London 1925.

Willard, Myra. *History of the White Australia Policy*, Melbourne University Press, Melbourne 1923.

Williamson, Samuel R. *The Politics of Grand Strategy: Britain and France Prepare for War, 1904–1914*, Harvard University Press, Cambridge 1969.

Yarwood, A. T. *Asian Migration to Australia: The Background to Exclusion, 1896–1923*, Melbourne University Press, Melbourne 1964.

## *2. Articles*

Blackton, C. S. 'Australian Nationality and Nationalism: The Imperial Federationist Interlude, 1885–1907', *Historical Studies*, VII (November 1955), 1–16.

Campbell, John P. 'Taft, Roosevelt and the Arbitration Treaties of 1911', *Journal of American History*, LIII (September 1966), 279–98.

Drus, Ethel. 'The Colonial Office and the Annexation of Fiji', *Transactions of the Royal Historical Society*, 4 series, XXXII (1950), 87–110.

Gordon, D. C. 'The Admiralty and Dominion Navies, 1902–14', *Journal of Modern History*, XXXIII (December 1961), 407–22.

——. 'Roosevelt's Smart Yankee Trick', *Pacific Historical Review*, XXI (November 1961), 351–8.

Grimshaw, C. 'Australian Nationalism and the Imperial Connection, 1900–1914', *Australian Journal of Politics and History*, III (May 1958), 140–62.

Hancock, I. R. 'The 1911 Imperial Conference', *Historical Studies*, XII (October 1966), 356–72.

Haydon, A. P. 'South Australia's First War', *Historical Studies*, XI (April 1964), 222–33.

Hooper, Meredith. 'The Naval Defence Agreement, 1887', *The Australian Journal of Politics and History*, XIV (April 1968), 52–74.

Iklé, Frank W. 'Japanese-German Peace Negotiations During World War I', *American Historical Review*, LXXI (October 1965), 62–76.

Jacobs, M. G. 'Bismarck and the Annexation of New Guinea', *Historical Studies*, V (November 1951), 14–26.

——. 'The Colonial Office and New Guinea, 1874–1884', *Historical Studies*, V (May 1952), 106–18.

Kendle, John E. 'The Round Table Movement: Lionel Curtis and the Formation of the New Zealand Groups in 1910', *The New Zealand Journal of History*, I (April 1967), 33–50.

——. 'The Round Table Movement, New Zealand, and the Conference of 1911', *Journal of Commonwealth Political Studies* III (July 1965), 104–17.

Knox, B. A. 'Colonial Influence on Imperial Policy, 1858–1866; Victoria and the Colonial Naval Defence Act, 1865', *Historical Studies*, XI (November 1963), 61–79.

MacCallum, Duncan. 'Defence in the Eighteen Fifties', *Royal Australian Historical Society, Journal and Proceedings*, XLIV (1958), 71–115.

——. 'The Early Volunteer Corps—The Origins of the Modern Australian Army', *Arts: The Proceedings of the Sydney University Arts Association*, I (September 1960), 143–66.

Mackintosh, John P. 'The Role of the Committee of Imperial Defence Before 1914', *English Historical Review*, LXXVII (July 1962), 490–503.

MacKirdy, K. A. 'The Fear of American Intervention as a Factor in British Expansion: Western Australia and Natal', *Pacific Historical Review*, XXXV (May 1966), 123–140.

——. 'The First Australian Department of External Affairs, 1901–16', *Canadian Journal of Economics and Political Science*, XXV (November 1959), 502–7.

McMinn, W. G. 'Sir Henry Parkes as a Federalist', *Historical Studies*, XII (October 1966), 405–16.

Meaney, Neville. 'Australia's Foreign Policy: History and Myth', *Australian Outlook*, XXIII (August 1969), 173–81.

——. '"A Proposition of the Highest International Importance": Alfred Deakin's Pacific Agreement Proposal and its Significance for Australian Imperial Relations', *Journal of Commonwealth Political Studies*, V (November 1967), 200–14.

Miller, J. D. B. 'The Utopia of Imperial Federation', *Political Studies*, IV (June 1956), 195–7.

Nish, Ian. 'Australia and the Anglo-Japanese Alliance, 1902–11', *Australian Journal of Politics and History*, IX (November 1963), 200–12.

Penny, Barbara R. 'The Age of Empire: Australian Episode', *Historical Studies*, XI (November 1963), 32–42.

——. 'Australia's Reactions to the Boer War—A Study in Colonial Imperialism', *Journal of British Studies*, VII (November 1967), 97–130.

Perry, Warren. 'Military Reforms of General Sir Edward Hutton in New South Wales, 1893–96', *The Australian Quarterly*, XXVIII (December 1956), 65–75.

——. 'The Military Life of Major-General Sir John Charles Hoad', *Victorian Historical Magazine*, XXIX (August 1959), 169–204.

Potter, David M. 'The Historian's Use of Nationalism and Vice Versa', *American Historical Review*, LXVII (July 1962), 924–50.

Quigley, Carroll. 'The Round Table Groups in Canada, 1908–38', *Canadian Historical Review*, XLIII (September 1962), 204–24.

Shields, R. A. 'Australian Opinion and Defence of the Empire: A Study in Imperial Relations, 1880–1890', *The Australian Journal of Politics and History*, X (April 1964), 41–53.

Tate, Merze. 'The Australasian Monroe Doctrine', *Political Science Quarterly*, LXXVI (June 1961), 264–84.

Thompson, Roger C. 'James Service: Father of Australian Foreign Policy?', *Historical Studies*, XVI (October 1974), 258–76.

Trainor, Luke. 'British Imperial Defence Policy and the Australian Colonies', *Historical Studies*, XIV (April 1970), 204–18.

Ward, John M. 'Commonwealth Historiography in Canada and Australia', *Lock Haven Review*, Series I, No. 5 (1963).

Wilde, R. H. 'Joseph Chamberlain's Proposal for an Imperial Council in March, 1900', *Canadian Historical Review*, XXXVII (September 1956), 225–41.

——. 'The Boxer Affair and Australian Responsibility for Imperial Defence', *Pacific Historical Review*, XXVI (February 1957), 51–65.

## 3. *Theses*

Atkinson, Leon D. *Australia's Defence Policy: A Study of Empire and Nation, 1897–1910*. (PhD thesis, Australian National University, 1964)

Liik, George. External Threats as a Factor in Australian Politics, 1870–1900: The Background to Australian Defence. (PhD thesis, University of Sydney, 1971)

Melhuish, Kathleen J. Australian and British Imperial Policy: Colonial Autonomy and the Imperial Idea, 1885–1902. (PhD thesis, University of Sydney, 1965)

Grimshaw, H. C. Some Aspects of Australian Attitudes to the Imperial Connection, 1900–1919. (MA thesis, University of Queensland, 1958)

Sissons, D. C. S. *Attitudes to Japan and Defence, 1890–1923*. (MA thesis, University of Melbourne, 1956)

Thompson, Roger C. *Australian Imperialism and the New Hebrides, 1862–1922*. (PhD thesis, Australian National University, 1970)

# Index

www.ingramcontent.com/pod-product-compliance
Lightning Source LLC
Chambersburg PA
CBHW080129270326
41926CB00021B/4410